STRANGER RAPE:
RAPISTS, MASCULINITY, AND PENAL GOVERNANCE

Stranger Rape is an in-depth study of the lives of fourteen men who raped women unknown to them. Using information derived from institutional files, treatment program observations, and extensive personal interviews, Kevin Denys Bonnycastle documents and analyses the men's experiences from boyhood to adulthood and eventual incarceration.

The book attempts to provide an understanding of how the men's identities were formed, and what led them to commit sexual violence and rape. Bonnycastle challenges certain feminist theories and argues that stranger rapists do not necessarily fit existing stereotypes. For the men in this book rape is inextricably linked to the lived contradictions between ideals of masculine power in relation to women and other men, and to their own experiences of pain and powerlessness that were part and parcel of their everyday lives. Bonnycastle argues that in these circumstances rape is a scripted and ritualized response to horrific experiences and memories associated with abuse, neglect, degradation, and failure rather than a demonstration of male power and control. She draws on concepts of hegemonic and embodied masculinity, marginalization, and the contradictory character of manhood to locate and explain the resort to sexual violence and rape. A significant finding is that rapists are active subjects who deploy sexual violence as a gendering practice in a context where no other model of manhood is an option for them.

Deeply disturbing yet ultimately enlightening, the book is a major achievement: it recognizes the particular and complex situations of rapists and rape, thereby restoring awareness and agency to the former in the hope that critical thinking about their lives and about their experiences in penal contexts and programs may eventually lead to what one respondent calls a "road to redemption."

KEVIN DENYS BONNYCASTLE (1956–2011) was an assistant professor in the Department of Sociology and Criminology at Saint Mary's University.

Stranger Rape

Rapists, Masculinity,
and Penal Governance

KEVIN DENYS BONNYCASTLE

UNIVERSITY OF TORONTO PRESS

Toronto Buffalo London

© University of Toronto Press 2012
Toronto Buffalo London
www.utppublishing.com
Printed in Canada

ISBN 978-1-4426-4536-3 (cloth)
ISBN 978-1-4426-1346-1 (paper)

Printed on acid-free, 100% post-consumer recycled paper with vegetable-based inks.

Library and Archives Canada Cataloguing in Publication

Bonnycastle, Kevin Denys, 1956–2011
Stranger rape : rapists, masculinity, and penal governance / Kevin Denys Bonnycastle.

Includes bibliographical references and index.
ISBN 978-1-4426-4536-3 (bound). – ISBN 978-1-4426-1346-1 (pbk.)

1. Rapists – Biography – Case studies.   2. Stangers – Case studies.
3. Masculinity – Case studies.   4. Male prisoners – Case studies.   I. Title.

HV6558.B65 2012   364.15'32   C2012-903744-3

This book has been published with the help of a grant from the Canadian Federation for the Humanities and Social Sciences, through the Aid to Scholarly Publications Program, using funds provided by the Social Sciences and Humanities Research Council of Canada.

University of Toronto Press acknowledges the financial assistance to its publishing program of the Canada Council for the Arts and the Ontario Arts Council.

 Canada Council   Conseil des Arts
for the Arts   du Canada

 ONTARIO ARTS COUNCIL
CONSEIL DES ARTS DE L'ONTARIO

University of Toronto Press acknowledges the financial support for its publishing activities of the Government of Canada through the Canada Book Fund.

On behalf of Dr Bonnycastle, Hugh McNeil, the executor of her estate, dedicates this book as follows:

To my parents, Pat and Dale Bonnycastle, for instilling a love of study and objective thinking; and to all the prisoners who during my research trusted me with their histories with the hope that greater understanding of their situation might lead to increased public awareness and improved public policies in dealing with these human conditions.

Contents

Foreword

JOHN L. MCMULLAN

It is with sadness and pleasure that I write this foreword to Dr Kevin Bonnycastle's important book, *Stranger Rape: Rapists, Masculinity, and Penal Governance*. Sadness, because she passed away on 4 June 2011, before the manuscript was accepted for publication. Pleasure, because I know that I helped fulfil one of her dreams. Bonnycastle entrusted me with her manuscript in February 2011 after she was struck down with cancer for what was to be the third and final time. I was happy to assist, both because her work skilfully asks and answers new and difficult questions about rape and rapists, and also because she teased that I needed another project to stay sharp in the twilight years of my career. How could I refuse? Besides, she may have been right! In the last months of her life we talked about her health, but mostly we discussed her manuscript, which she had worked on fitfully for several years and which she wanted the University of Toronto Press to publish. Now, her work will finally see the light of day and garner the attention it so rightly deserves.

Not a great deal is known about Bonnycastle or her research in academic circles. She was born in New Westminster, British Columbia, on 13 July 1956, and was raised in Surrey, British Columbia, the eldest child of Pat and Dale Bonnycastle. Growing up, she was very athletic, and this athleticism won her a scholarship to study as an undergraduate at Simon Fraser University. She graduated with a BA in criminology in 1992, completed an MA at the Centre of Criminology at the University of Toronto in 1994, and received her PhD from the School of Criminology at Simon Fraser University in 2004. While a PhD candidate, she did additional research consulting on several projects dealing with violence, women, and victimization and health conditions among male prisoners in federal prisons. She taught courses on battered women and the law, as well as on the sociology of deviance and crime. In 2004, she took a full-time academic position at Saint Mary's University, which she held until her death in 2011. While at Saint Mary's, she taught courses on prisons, punishment, and the Canadian criminal justice system, and developed new research interests and projects related to neoliberalism, crime, and media.

Bonnycastle was an intensely private person who did not usually allow people to get to know her very well. She moved easily between different social worlds, but often kept them separate from academia. Her colleagues experienced her as a somewhat mysterious person whose life did not quite fit academic moulds. Bonnycastle had a touch of the pioneer in her when it came to how and where to live, and favoured log homes close to nature and away from the hustle and bustle of urban life. This was sometimes the topic of teasing among her fellow graduate students at Simon Fraser, but more often it was acknowledged as a wise lifestyle choice for a person fond of nature and solitude. She had a "big-ass truck" to get her through the icy winters in Nova Scotia, two dogs who acted as maîtres d'hôtel for visitors, and an uncanny ability to garden both vegetables "for the body" and flowers "for the soul." Her neighbours in Avondale, Nova Scotia, where she last lived, describe her home as "an oasis of colour where she played artist with nature."[1] She despised pretension, eschewed sentimentality, and possessed an enormous capacity for laughter. Right to the end of her life, her sense of humour was her companion.

Bonnycastle was no believer in the cubic-foot-of-publications approach to scholarship. Her published articles are not numerous and are few and far between. Her approach to writing seems to have been what Paul McCartney had in mind with "The Long and Winding Road": a slow process of discovery, persistence, and return that was at times both exhilarating and frustrating. No doubt her poor health limited her ability to disseminate her findings widely and frequently. Some of her papers were solicited and published following ordinary conversations with friends and colleagues on topics that caught her attention. Others were published long after they were written, and then only because colleagues begged her to submit them to academic journals. Still others are drafts on CDs awaiting their fate. An unspoken assumption behind her approach to academic work seems to have been "everything in its time," as she thought about things carefully and honestly, did not worry too much about rules or deadlines, and did not measure quality by quantity.

The results have been passionate scholarship that draws equally from her experiences living in society and from conscious intellectual pursuits. Not surprisingly, Bonnycastle respected those who went into "the field" to work. That meant something quite specific for her: "You don't stay in your office – you go to someone else's turf, and in prisons you don't dictate the rules, you learn to listen." She once told me that "it makes no sense to study attitudes, beliefs, or motivations divorced from contexts, and you have to understand contexts." She was especially critical of psychology and psychiatry experts who study life at a distance, reduce reality to thinking problems, and ignore the immediacy of class, race, and gender in forming people and their motivations. Bonnycastle, however, was no ivory tower intellectual; she combined advocacy work with scholarly reflection. She moved uncomfortably within contemporary academic institutions, detested "administrivia" of all sorts (her most recent CV was dated 2004), and defended those she believed were being victimized by either or both. She wrote legal petitions on behalf of abused inmates and prepared prisoner-based reports aimed at creating safer environments in federal prisons. Dr Michael Jackson, who included two of her habeas corpus petitions in a report to the Solicitor General regarding the Correctional Service of Canada's non-compliance with its own administrative segregation standards, was so impressed with her legal acumen that he offered to hire her to do other petitions despite the fact that she was not a lawyer. Bonnycastle was not sanguine about the imaginative abilities of the prison systems power elite to reform penal conditions in a positive, humane manner for prison populations. Writing about needle-sharing, drug use, and HCV/HIV seroprevalence in one Canadian federal prison, she observed, "Denying prisoners access to health initiatives commensurate with outside communities adds another layer of punishment to prison sentences, increasing the health risks and needs of an already politically, socially, and economically marginalized and stigmatized population."[2] However, she was not biased or ideological. She arrived at her conclusions through sound scholarship and always evinced an open and thoughtful approach to research and debate. She was much more interested in understanding and meaning than in being right or politically correct, and as this book will attest, she appreciated the complex, contingent, and contradictory nature of social relations and institutional practices.

Bonnycastle also wrote creatively about other criminological topics, such as media crime, and rape and sexual assault legislation, in a manner that was decidedly more theoretical than practical. In her article

"Not the Usual Suspects: The Obfuscation of Political Economy and Race in CSI,"[3] she argues that CSI narratives about crime, criminals, and victims deracialize crime in America, obfuscate the true relationships between different types of crime and their political economic contexts, and reduce the complex causes of crime to neoliberal subjecthood that emphasizes choice and individual responsibility. She concludes that CSI shapes and bolsters the legitimacy of existing conservative crime control policies and practices. In her article "Rape Uncodified: Reconsidering Bill C-49 Amendments to Canadian Sexual Assault Laws,"[4] she argues that the existing liberal legal discourse of consent built into sexual assault legislation is fatally flawed because it is profoundly gendered. In her view, sexual assault laws engender and sustain an active masculine sexuality and a reactive and passive feminine sexuality. She concludes that the measure of sexual violence in this legislation is not whether women desire sex, but whether they accede to it.

In addition to her academic work, Bonnycastle once tried her hand at fiction writing and wrote a Harlequin romance novel with Catherine Shields, the daughter of Pulitzer Prize-winner Carol Shields, when they were in residence together at Simon Fraser University. Written mostly for the amusement of its authors, the novel was rejected as being too sly for its intended readership. Catherine recalls: "Neither of us could bring ourselves to do the recommended homework of actually reading any of the books. We laughed so much together."[5] That experience seems to have ended any prospects of a literary career for Bonnycastle, but it does reveal the playful side of her personality. Her friend of seventeen years, Larry Buhagiar, recalls that she used to move the true crime books from the criminology section of the SFU bookstore to other sections in the hope that a science major might find one and change academic careers.[6] For Bonnycastle, the serious and the solemn had a short shelf life, at least in her conversations with colleagues and friends. Humour, on the other hand, was her last fortress of sanity and a necessary condition for understanding people and society. In our last conversation, she joked that she hoped to postpone her "expiry date" by accessing experimental clinical trials and drugs that she had found out about from her family.

Of course, Bonnycastle had a serious side as well, especially when it came to academic work. She was deeply concerned about violence, sexism, racism, social inequality, and the state of penal practices. She travelled where many criminologists and feminists feared to tread. She spent years in the company of sex offenders, and observed their treatments, reviewed their case files, and interviewed them face-to-face in an effort to understand their gendering relationships and practices and how and why these factors contributed to stranger rape. Again Buhagiar recalls, "Kevin was always willing to listen and entertain the thoughts of others," including those that many people might consider "the worst of the worst."[7] She could be fiercely persuasive about things that mattered to her, as the reviewers of this manuscript implied on more than one occasion. She enjoyed debate and her critiques were tough. My most abiding memory of her is from a conversation we had about this book: she gestured vividly, smiled enthusiastically, and coaxed me to see the world her way.

It behoves me then to say something about the content of the book and the process leading up to its eventual publication. From 2006 to 2008, Bonnycastle was on medical disability leave from Saint Mary's while undergoing her first series of cancer treatments. In August 2009, she submitted her manuscript to the University of Toronto Press for consideration. In the summer of 2010, she had a short health relapse but still worked on the book through the fall. She finished the revisions on the methods chapter by September, but the last chapter confounded her. When I saw her that December, she was tired, but she vowed to finish the revisions over the holidays and resubmit the manuscript to the press in early 2011. Her health, however, intervened. The cancer had returned and spread, and she was hospitalized for several weeks in January. In February, I learned that the manuscript had not been sent to the press. She had revised it to her satisfaction but was too ill to oversee the resubmission process. I offered to liaise on her behalf with the publisher, and with her approval, I submitted the revised manuscript in mid-February. The press sent it back to two of the original reviewers for further comment. By the time the second assessments were back to me, she had been hospitalized again. Kevin never learned that the evaluators recommended publication subject to her reply to their final set of suggestions.

Shortly after her death I met with the executor of her estate, who indicated that he wanted to see the manuscript published. He told me that "this is what Kevin wanted," and assured me that her family felt the same way. I responded to the final set of revisions on Bonnycastle's behalf in June. I received a positive reply from the press's publications committee in July and the manuscript review committee in August. I signed a contract between the "Estate of Kevin Bonnycastle," myself as the "Editor of the Work," and the University of Toronto Press in September. We secured funding for the book from the Canadian

Federation for the Humanities and Social Sciences in October. As editor, I attended to three categories of revisions. First, I made the revisions agreed to in my June response to the reviewers: I changed the title, discussed "limiting factors" in the methods chapter, reminded the reader of the situational context of the data and the limits of making generalizations from it, and added future research directions in the last chapter. Second, I attended to matters of language, style, and redundancy, which the reviewers identified as in need of improvement. I clarified content, eliminated repetition, and connected sections of the manuscript thematically to further explicate the relations between the theory, life histories, and critique of penal governance. Finally, I updated and revised the back matter of the manuscript, which was in poor shape. I imagine that Bonnycastle left this to the end and just did not get around to it. I renumbered the notes by chapter and improved the citations and references, which in some cases had conflicting or missing information. In most cases I was successful in correcting the problems, but in a small number of cases I had to guess. In these instances, I almost always found appropriate sources, but I am not sure that the sources I found were necessarily the ones Bonnycastle used. What I can say, however, is that my role as editor was confined to matters of form. The substance of this book is the result of many years of hard work Bonnycastle undertook in difficult research and writing circumstances. I have only admiration for this ambitious book and the remarkable person who wrote it.

This is not, however, an easy book to read. The violent content in chapters 4 and 5 is especially challenging. Many of the offenders and their victims suffered awful violence and I imagine that readers will respond with some degree of disgust and anger as they become acquainted with the life histories of the men, their families, and the women they raped, beat, and killed. Yet at the same time, *Stranger Rape* demonstrates a measure of sympathy for the offenders that grows on the reader as it evolves. Bonnycastle is moving, sensitive, and methodical in her depiction of the narratives of the men and the analyses of the contexts of their offences. This is a book where passionate distance as a researcher and writer is required. It took courage to conduct this research, and talent to produce a book that restores subjectivity to men who experienced and did awful things, while sustaining a level of empathy that they were often denied in their own lives. This book will most certainly stimulate dialogue and debate; it is unique and provocative to read, disrupts existing portrayals of sex offenders, and challenges the centrality of men's power in explaining stranger rape.

Of course, *Stranger Rape* is best appreciated as exploratory and heuristic, and Bonnycastle does not claim that her small compliance sample represents all stranger rapists. The fourteen men whose lives are at the centre of this book come disproportionally from marginalized cultures or communities. They suffered extreme economic, educational, and racial disadvantages. Cycles of constant and intense violence characterized their boyhoods and followed them into adulthood. While psychologists, social workers, and psychoanalysts might want to evoke a pathology model of their behaviour, Bonnycastle prefers to pathologize hegemonic masculinity and demonstrate how it is implicated in stranger rape. According to her, the fourteen rapists in her study are active subjects who deploy sexual violence as a gendering practice in a context where no other model of manhood is an option for them. To establish a masculine gender identity, they manage the lived contradictions between ideals of masculine power in relation to other men, women, and their own everyday experiences of pain and powerlessness. Before entering the treatment program, they were structurally excluded from education and meaningful employment opportunities and thus embodied masculinity in a manner that overemphasized physical body-based gender performances (e.g., fighting, manual labour), and refused to express feelings for others, including the men they beat up and the women they attacked. Bonnycastle argues that because gender is never fully accomplished but is enacted and re-enacted through scripts and ritualized acts, violence was a never-ending performance for these men. For most of them, it was an existential response to painful experiences and memories associated with abuse, neglect, degradation, and failure, rather than a demonstration of male power and control. However, sexual violence was not a solution to their troubled and troubling condition, and was neither an expression of power or control nor an act of pleasure. Sexual violence did little to ameliorate the men's pain or powerlessness, and only affected them temporarily. Bonnycastle argues that pain and powerlessness are entwined in a dialectical relationship and that both appeared repeatedly in her interviews with her subjects and in her analysis of their life histories. It is difficult not to agree with her when she says that these men had choices, but few options.

The astute reader will note that there is a tragedy about these men's lives that mirrors the tragedy they caused for others. There is, moreover, something inevitable about their eventual incarceration and troubling about their involvement in the penal program aftermath. Ultimately, Bonnycastle argues that there is a fundamental contradiction between penal reform programs, which encourage emotional literacy and communication, and the everyday prison environment, which punishes men severely for discussing or expressing their feelings. On the one hand, Bonnycastle appreciates both the benefits of treatment regimes and the effects they had on the men she observed and interviewed, although she says that penal authorities made them less effective by their emphasis on individual responsibility and risk management. On the other hand, she notes that prisoners control prisons, and that prisoners who implement personal changes in accordance with treatment objectives, however well intentioned, commit to serial victimhood. Bonnycastle likens the wisdom of penal governance, in the form of cognitive behaviour models and risk-driven prevention practices that are designed to encourage prisoners to talk, to the neoliberal discourse of choice and self-help. She says that bad choices and faulty thinking are not the most important factors when it comes to rehabilitating sex offenders. If penal governance programs are going to change men by providing alternatives to current models of masculinity and manhood, they must think outside of the psychology box. For Bonnycastle, genuine reforms must start at the intersections of body, personality, community, culture, and social structure, and allow offenders to understand the wider contexts of cultural identity and social location that created them and shaped their behaviours.

Stranger Rape makes important contributions to theory, methods, the study of violence and gender, and penal governance. It offers an intelligent analysis of the lives of fourteen men who raped women they did not know, and provides a cogent understanding of how and why violence formed their identities, and with what harmful consequences. It addresses the limits of some feminist approaches and argues that stranger rapists do not fit existing images of predatory monsters or misogynist everymen. It deploys the concepts of hegemonic masculinity, embodied masculinity, marginalization, and the contradictory nature of manhood to locate and explain the resort to sexual violence and rape. Its major achievement is to recognize men as rapists in their particularity and complexity, and to give them voice in the hope that critical thinking about their lives may eventually lead to what one respondent called his "road to redemption."

In conclusion, it is a pleasant duty for me to thank the people directly responsible for facilitating the production of this important book. Virgil Duff and Doug Hildebrand, editors at the University of Toronto Press, believed this book should exist and helped carry it out. For that I am most grateful to them. Three anonymous reviewers did a wonderful job in improving the quality of the manuscript in a manner that was challenging and helpful – something that Bonnycastle very much appreciated – and I thank them for their assistance. Carolyn Yates was a careful copy editor and Mary Newberry provided the index. Their wise counsel greatly improved the quality of the final manuscript. The fourteen subjects of this book should not be overlooked. They generously shared their time and experiences in a manner that was disturbing, moving, and engaging, and which I hope adds to both the understanding of violence in society and its elimination. They believed in Bonnycastle's research, and on her behalf, I thank them for their willingness to put their private lives into public discourse. My final thanks is to Kevin herself. In trusting me to see this book through to publication, she gave me a fond memory at a time in my career when most of my memories were becoming increasingly faint.

Acknowledgments

Dr McMullan acknowledges the assistance of Lindia Smith and Melissa Kervin, who helped with the typing of the manuscript and the revisions to the in-text references, endnotes, tables, and bibliography; the dean of arts at Saint Mary's University, who provided funding for the revisions to the manuscript; the estate of Dr Kevin Bonnycastle, which aided in the preparation of the index for the book; and the Canadian Federation for the Humanities and Social Sciences, which provided a grant for publication through the Aid of Scholarly Publications Program using funds provided by the Social Sciences and Humanities Research Council of Canada.

Hugh MacNeil, executor of the estate of Kevin Bonnycastle, is very grateful to Dr John L. McMullan for believing in this book and assisting in its publication.

STRANGER RAPE:
RAPISTS, MASCULINITY, AND PENAL GOVERNANCE

1 The Subject of Stranger Rape and Stranger Rapists

I cannot repeat this too often
Anyone is of one's period ...
And each of us in our own way [is] bound to
express what the world in which we are living is doing.

Gertrude Stein (1935, 176–7)

Seeking the truth ...
we find it in the discourse with which we seek it.

Richard Tithecott (1997, 106)

This book centres on the narratives of fourteen men who Canadian prison authorities designate high-risk sex offenders.[1] Each man is a stranger rapist who either raped or raped and killed one or more adult women on one or more occasions. Three of these men have sentence expiry dates that guarantee their release to the street. The other eleven are serving life sentences and will spend the rest of their days in prison or under community supervision. Each man agreed to put his life history on public display in my study. Their stories help me convey perspectives, context, and lived experiences that are otherwise absent in expert and popular culture accounts about rapists, and allow me to highlight issues of gender, power, masculinity, and penal governance in regard to rape.

My study began with field observation in a high-risk sex offender program that I attended at a federal maximum-security treatment centre operated by the Correctional Service of Canada (CSC). The CSC is responsible for approximately 13,000 male and female convicts sentenced to prison terms of two or more years. Canadian penal staff and treatment experts, however, seldom use the term *rapist*, and never use the term *stranger rapist*. Instead, every prisoner convicted of an offence that prison authorities deem sexually motivated is a *sex offender* (Duguid 2000, 167). The penal site where I collected my data is one of four maximum-security treatment prisons in Canada. I spent every working day for seven months at that facility, and observed group treatment, conducted interviews, reviewed institutional files, ate prison food, and spoke with treatment staff and prisoners.

Following American treatment regimes (Burdon and Gallagher 2002), each of the four institutions in Canada delivers generic sex offender programs to prisoner-participants. The working assumption is that a single motivation – power and control – unites all sex offenders. Not surprisingly, this belief results in mixing together of prisoners convicted for old and current sexual offences against women, youth and children, and occasionally men. Victims include strangers, acquaintances, family members, friends, and women or girls raped by their pimps. Convictions vary and include acts such as abduction, anal intercourse with underage persons, assault causing bodily harm, attempted murder, bestiality, gross indecency, incest, sexual touching, indecent assault, kidnapping, manslaughter, murder, necrophilia, rape, sexual assault, sexual assault with a weapon, aggravated sexual assault, sexual exploitation, sexual interference, and unlawful confinement. Canadian penal staff have sometimes even ordered convicts whose original sexual assault charges were withdrawn by the courts to undergo sex offender assessments and complete sex offender programs (*Leach v. Warden of Fenbrook Institution 2004*). However, I observed an exceptional group. Two innovative penal treatment group facilitators convinced prison authorities to run a sex offender group comprised of only men who had committed stranger rape. The facilitators believed that their strategy would enhance trust, openness, and support within the group. Most group members, as we shall see, affirmed that belief.

The Stranger Rapist as the Most Credible Perpetrator of Rape

Each man in my study committed a statistically rare form of sexual assault: each attacked a woman who was a relative stranger[2] to him. Eight of the women were killed or died before, during, or after the attacks. Five others suffered grievous bodily harm. According to official crime statistics, male strangers commit between 18 per cent (Brennan and

Taylor-Butts 2008) to 30 per cent (Levinson 2002) of all sexual assaults reported to police. By contrast, national victimization surveys, which create estimates for crimes unreported to police, reveal even lower rates for stranger-based sexual assault. Of all Canadian adult women who reported sexual assault in a nation-wide *Violence Against Women Survey*, only 7 per cent reported a "sexual attack" by a male stranger and 15 per cent reported "unwanted sexual touching" by a male stranger (Johnson 1996). In the United States, the *National Violence Against Women Survey* found that only 14 per cent of "rapes" against adult women involved unknown assailants (Hopkins and Koss 2005, 694).

Sexual assault-related killings are more rare, but bear in mind that this type of crime category is difficult to estimate because no standardized definition exists. Moreover, North American and United Kingdom justice departments classify sexually related killings as homicides rather than as sex crimes (Chan and Heide 2009, 31). The only available estimate for Canada is that 4 per cent of all homicides occur in the context of a sexual assault (Roberts and Grossman 1993). In the United Kingdom and United States, respectively, 3 per cent of 4,860 murders in 2003 and 1 per cent of 14,121 murders in 2004 were classified as sexually motivated (Chan and Heide 2009, 31). In reality, few sexual assault victims receive injuries severe enough to cause death. Victimization data corroborates that approximately 80 per cent of sexual assaults are classified as unwanted sexual touching, such as grabbing, kissing, and fondling. According to police-based statistics, 68 per cent of sexual assault victims in Canada in 2003 received no injuries, 15.5 per cent received minor injuries, and no victims died from their injuries. Of all sexual assault charges laid by Canadian police that year, only 2 per cent were classified as *aggravating* (involving bodily harm), and less than 2 per cent involved weapons (Brennan and Taylor-Butts 2008). Although few sexual assaults are fatal, the media practice of over-reporting and sensationalizing violent and lethal rape cases skews popular and judicial perceptions about "real rape" and makes it more difficult to secure convictions for rape charges that involve acquainted individuals (Estrich 1987; Mason and Monckton-Smith 2008, 702).

However rare, violent stranger rape is the type of rape that women fear most, and the one they are most likely to report to police (Levinson 2002; Scully 1990; Stanko 2000). In turn, stranger rapists receive significantly harsher punishments than men charged with violence against women they know. This disparity can be only partially explained by the presence or absence of aggravating and mitigating factors. For example, stranger rapists are more likely to use weapons, inflict more trauma, use physical coercion, assault more than once, demand oral sex, and attack in public. Acquaintance rapists are more likely to beat or choke their victims, keep them under coercion for a longer time, drug them, and attack in private (Levinson 2002; Stermac, Dumont, and Kelemba 1995). However, some research finds that spousal rapists can also inflict as much physical trauma as stranger rapists (Bennice and Resick 2003), and women victims also report trauma and anger in the aftermath of acquaintance and marital rape (Rumney 2003).

To account for cultural and legal representations of the stranger rapist as the real rapist, feminist scholars focus on the public/private divide. Feminist historians, for example, note that English common law from the thirteenth century onwards supported a patriarchal model that eschewed judicial intervention into the private family realm, which gave legal support to a prevailing discourse that "a man's home is his castle" and that women and children were not legal persons but chattels. Husbands and fathers were thus viewed as the wronged party to be compensated following rape convictions. Until the late twentieth century, at least in Anglo-European countries, it was legally impossible for a husband to rape his wife (e.g., Cohen 1994; Schwendinger and Schwendinger 1982).

Historical discourses about familial privacy and women-as-male-property still shape legal decision-making in prosecuting and punishing men accused of rape. For example, an analysis of contemporary sexual assault decisions in the United Kingdom reveals that judges still view marital rape as a lesser crime than stranger rape. Male judges routinely mitigate the criminality of marital rapists – including men charged with raping their ex-wives – by representing them as somehow misguided by pain and suffering and thus outside the category of real rapists. By contrast, the same judges vilify stranger rapists as compelled by uncontrollable sexuality and criminal tendencies (de Carvalho Figueiredo 2001).

Then and now, women who know their assailants are made to bear more responsibility for rape. This is due, in part, to culturally prevalent patriarchal values that at once normalize men's aggressive pursuit of multiple sex partners and blame women for allowing sex to occur (Anderson and Doherty 2008; Bourke 2007, 24–8; Ellison and Munro 2009, 295; Wilcox, Jordan, and Pritchard 2003). The fact that average sentences remain higher for stranger rape than non-stranger rape convictions indicates that contemporary judges still view a prior relationship between the rape victim and her assailant as a mitigating rather than an aggravating factor. Judges insinuate that some forms of rape more closely resemble sex, and should not be punished as severely as other forms (Rumney 2003; Hopkins and Koss, 2005). Chamallas (2005) adds that the prototype rapist within Western societies is not only a male stranger, but a Black or racialized male, while the prototype victim is a white middle-class woman. Indeed, nineteenth century American laws codified discriminatory sentencing by legislating harsher penalties for Black men versus white men who raped white women. Although contemporary sentencing law is written in race-neutral language, African American men convicted of rape remain more likely than their white counterparts to receive the death penalty (Bourke 2007, 107–10). Rapes committed outside these prototypes – for example, rapes of Black women by both white and Black men – often go unreported and receive less punishment. This, in turn, provides incentives for perpetrators to attack women who fall outside the prototypical victim category. For some scholars, "prototype theory" helps explain the higher probability of racialized versus non-racialized assailants being convicted for rape, as well as Black women's historical vulnerability to rape and other racialized and marginalized women's overrepresentation among rape victims (Bourke 2007; Carbado and Gulati 2003; Wyatt 1992).

The men in my study – six of whom are racialized men – represent the most credible perpetrator of rape. They are the rape-myth rapists: the dangerous male strangers that women are taught to fear and that men are taught to disdain and protect women and children from (cf. Chunn 2004). My participants embody the monster images conjured in media stories, the effects of which shape women's consciousness and conduct within the public sphere. In essence, my sample is culturally rather than statistically representative of "the rapist," and accounts for 39 incidents of stranger rape in total (Bourke 2007; Cowburn and Dominelli 2001; Greer 2003; Tatar 1995; Tithecott 1997). If discourse produces the things of which it speaks then my focus on these anomalous forms of sexual assault may dramatize and stabilize prevailing representations of the "real rapist." On the other hand, if discourse is also "a hindrance, a stumbling block, a point of resistance and a starting point for an opposing strategy," then there may be another way to speak about stranger rape (Foucault 1990, 101). This book explores cultural and clinical portrayals of the high-risk sex offender as irrational and irredeemable predators who are fundamentally different from ordinary men, and asks if there is another subjecthood associated with stranger rapists.

Starting from Where You Are

My original research plan was to write a sex offender treatment group ethnography and analyse how gender and power work on and through women who had perpetrated serious physical and sexual harm on their children (see Ashe and Cahn 1994). However, sitting in the company of men convicted for stranger rape, I soon realized that no feminist researcher has ever tried to investigate the male stranger rapist using the same contextually sensitive approach that I would have adopted in my interviews with assaultive mothers. I also realized that I had access to a rare sample of men with whom I was developing an enduring rapport. Not surprisingly, my research interest gradually shifted toward life history studies that could explore the interplay between gender(ing) embodied subjectivity and stranger rape from the experiences of these men.

As a consequence of switching focus and topic, my study literally began from where I was located – sitting in an intensive penal treatment group for high-risk male sex offenders. With few exceptions, sex-offender scholarship is informed by medical discourses and subdisciplines, such as biology, psychology, and clinical studies, that align themselves with scientific positivism, and actuarial-risk analysis based on genetic predispositions and pathologies (Cowburn 2005; Cowburn and Dominelli 2001, 400). Two exceptions are feminist scholar Diana Scully (1990), who interviewed 114 convicted male rapists in American prisons, and sociologist Kristy Hudson (2005), who interviewed 32 convicted male sex offenders over the course of their treatment in one of three British sex offender programs. Both studies challenge dominant media and clinical representations of sex offenders as aberrant predatory psychopaths. Both researchers agree that the social constructions of sex offenders hinder rape prevention and reduction strategies. While Scully reveals revulsion towards her sample of rapists, Hudson engages her participants as knowing subjects and sympathetically explores their diverse presentations of self and strategies for managing "spoiled sex-offender identities." Both studies, however, separate each man's sexually assaultive behaviour from other gendering practices and from the broader material conditions of their lives. Other exceptions to medical approaches are Douglas Pryor's (1996) interactionist life-course study of thirty men who had undergone penal treatment after convictions for sex acts with children, and Pamela Schulz's (2004) social constructionist study of nine convicted child molesters. Both researchers report that their subjects were not particularly different from other men (apart from Pryor's finding of a higher reported incidence of boyhood sexual abuse), and both studies show the human side of the interview subjects by providing the social context in which they committed sexual violations. Although gender, race, and power can be read into many of their men's narratives, the authors do not make these categories the focus of their analyses. In *Nine Lives*, however, James Messerschmidt (2000) centres gender, power, and bodies in life history interviews with working-class white boys who committed sex acts against either female relatives or girls. Messerschmidt draws on structured-action theory and Raewyn Connell's (2002) theory of hegemonic masculinity to argue that sexual offending was a response to their lack of alternative practices for realizing the hegemonic masculine norm. Apart from these studies, to which I will return, the lived reality or embodied subjectivity of the sex offender – and more specifically the adult stranger rapist – have generated little interest from feminist and critical researchers.

Overview of this Book: The Return of the Subject of Rape

Little is known about the lives of men imprisoned for rape or rape-murder. How do these men perceive and make sense of their own transgressions? In what follows, I bring the rapists back into focus and enlist them as agents in the making of their own accounts about how stranger rape happens, what the act means to them, and why they hurt women. I adopt the critical and feminist tradition of giving visibility to people whose knowledge, words, and memories are often muted in expert accounts and institutional practices. Rather than argue for the greater accuracy of my accounts or ascribe epistemic privilege to the subject of rape (cf. Bar On 1993), I argue that each man's account of a life gone wrong disrupts existing simplistic portrayals of sex offenders as monsters (Marshall 1996a, 1996b). I reverse the historical trend in which female offenders are viewed through male eyes by viewing the men in my study with a feminist gaze. I argue that their life histories contribute to theoretical debates about gender, race, and power – more specifically, men's contradictory experiences of power within male-dominated societies (cf. Kaufman 1994). For Canadian penal authorities and treatment experts, the high-risk sex-offender program is predicated on lowering violence and recidivism by instilling individual men with self-management practices for reshaping sexual desire and monitoring risk factors to reoffend (e.g., Marshall et al. 2006). Approached from

another angle, the sex offender program is about persuading men to
re-form masculine practices and perform gender differently. In short,
their treatment regime is based on practicing new ways of being men
and governing themselves (cf. Segal 2006, 1990, 270).

The most widespread and highly regarded contemporary penal
treatment programs in Canada, the United Kingdom, the United States,
Australia, and New Zealand are based on cognitive-behavioural models that deliver relapse prevention in small therapeutic group circles
(e.g., Abracen et al. 2004; Crooks et al. 2007). Sex offenders are pre-
sumed to suffer from cognitive distortions that lead them to make bad
choices. In this view, rape stems from thinking errors and distorted beliefs that can be detected, self-monitored, and corrected (cf. Auburn and
Lea 2003). Understanding past choices and learning how to make responsible new ones are fundamental treatment program objectives. The
program's emphasis on choice and change encouraged the men in the
group I observed to discuss their feelings about themselves and their
conduct. I benefitted from this approach. I found the men willing to talk
reflexively and extensively, not only about performing gender, but also
about the psychical links between their own subjectivity and the forms
of violence they committed, although none used those terms. While penal treatment staff use life histories or autobiographies[3] to produce
therapeutic narratives and knowledge about prisoners availability for
risk management practices, I use them as a research method to explore
the impact of gendering discourses and practices on the choices of those
men who became sex offenders, and who then tried to create new selves
and identities in penal institutions. I explore each man's life story and
emphasize the interactions between specific relations of power and
various discourses constitutive of the men's social location and their
active participation in their own subjectification, what I call "the return
of the subject."

Organization and Chapter Content

Chapter 2 traces the history of the sex offender as a person and rape as
a social problem. I briefly trace the discovery of rape by the women's
movement during the late 1960s, discuss some intended and unintended effects that stem from the politicizing of rape, and summarize
dominant trajectories within feminist rape theories, highlighting the
exclusion of the rapist-as-subject as a topic of research. I set out a perspective for thinking about rape that blends post-structural feminist

theories about gender, discourse, and bodies with critical masculinities about hegemonic forms of manhood. I develop a toolbox to untangle the connections between constructions of masculinity, violence, sex, power, and agency to help analyse my life history interviews with the men who committed stranger rape.

Chapter 3 introduces the federal penal treatment site where I carried out my study. I examine some of the changes in Canadian penal policy and practices coincident with the shift from a welfare to a neoliberal state. In particular, I explore the displacement of the welfare state's docile body and corollary disease models of rape with cognitive behavioural models for cultivating a more active, reflexive penal subjecthood. I study the emergent Canadian rehabilitative sanction and conclude that it is now a set of interwoven and de-structured discourses about individual responsibility, rational choice, and risk management.

The next two chapters present each man's life history. Chapter 4 begins with boyhood and examines my participants' contexts, their lived relationships to men's power.[4] I showcase each man's life and explore the making of gendered subjecthood through their *contradictory experiences of power*. I illustrate how their structural exclusion from higher education, intellectual pursuits, skilled labour, and other forms of cultural capital encouraged them to develop and overemphasize a bodily based masculinity defined by physical performance and biological maleness. Chapter 5 explores how rape functions at a psychical level. I examine stranger rape as performative. I show how rape and sexual assault are intended to reiterate certain effects that materialize different elements of contemporary hegemonic manhood. From the subject of rape's perspective, I consider the lived connections between hegemonic masculinity, embodied subjectivity, and stranger rape.

Chapter 6 discusses common themes in the men's narratives. I review the specific socio-structural and linguistic contexts in which masculine subjectivity is materialized: families; schools; and relationships with women and men, workplaces, and prisons. I consider the impact of two lived definitions of manhood on rapists, namely that *real men fight* and *real men never cry*. I use my participants' stories to suggest that stranger rape is not best-seen as the personification of men's power and control, notwithstanding that rape produces power and control over women. Rather, I argue that stranger rape is linked more to men's experiences of powerlessness or to losing signs of gender. Stranger rape, I conclude, is one contemporary gendering practice that reconciles, at a psychical level, men's power and powerlessness, however temporarily.

Chapter 7 investigates whether or not Canadian men's prisons and sex offender penal programs challenge or reiterate hegemonic masculinity. I describe how gender is materialized in homosocial penal environments. I show that sex offenders do not experience the penal treatment milieu as solely oppressive by highlighting the men's receptivity to performing gender differently. However, I query whether the subjecthood and skills cultivated in penal governance are reconcilable with the lived reality of men's prisons. I end the chapter by summarizing what we now know about masculinity and stranger rape, power and control, and what might be done to circumvent the cycle of abuse documented throughout the book. I argue that race, class, and gender inequalities are the significant sources of violence that must be addressed in order to begin talking about meaningful change and reform.

Finally, a short epilogue continues the life history narrative of one of my participants. By giving him the last words, I underscore the difficult road ahead and the possibilities for change in a world of endless incarceration.

2 The Sex Offender: Every Man, Other Men, and Monsters

[Prisoner] is hostile and afraid of women. He sees women as having the power structure weighted in their favour. (1980)

One factor seems certain ... the assaults were causally linked to his highly charged and confused emotional stance at the time, rather than to negative feelings towards women or to the possession of a violent nature in his personality. (1988)

High Risk Factors: Boredom, Resentment, Sarcasm, Withdrawal, Alcohol usage, Deviant fantasies. (1998)

> Entries taken from one convicted sex offender's
> institutional files over 20 years

There is certainly an abnormality and I hope that the psychiatrists can diagnose and treat and hopefully cure it. I am also going to recommend to the Parole Board that you not be released at the end of the twenty-five year period or thereafter until there is some measure of psychiatric or medical certainty that it is safe to release you. (Canadian Sentencing Judge, 1983)

The actions of the accused could only be characterized as the function of a demented mind and twisted personality ... treatment prognosis is poor. (Canadian Sentencing Judge, 1989)

This, in my view, was really not an offence of sex. This was an offence of violence. (Canadian Sentencing Judge, 1992)

This chapter examines four issues. First, I trace the emergence of the sex offender and the rapist as objects of inquiry. In particular, I historicize the "discovery of rape" and its politicization by the North American women's liberation movement in the late 1960s. Second, I examine feminist theories of rape, and note how each explanation presumes to varying degrees one standard of masculinity – a generic man whose subjectivity is undifferentiated and unmarked by his location within structural relations of power. Third, since gender is not synonymous with women, I contend that feminist and masculinities scholarship needs to incorporate both women and men into their analyses and to examine both the individual subject and social structure in understanding stranger rape (cf. Comack 1996; Scott 1986, 1064–7). Responses to rape ought to be grounded in both the victim and assailant's lived experiences, since as Jefferson notes, the social and psychical are "irrevocably intertwined: both necessary to an adequate understanding [of masculinity], neither reducible to the other" (2002, 66). Finally, I selectively survey critical masculinity and feminist scholarship and assemble a theoretical framework to help me examine stranger rape as both a socio-historical and localized gendering practice from the stranger rapist's standpoint.

Constructing the Sex Offender: Making Up (More) People

While the idea of rape has existed since antiquity, the category *sex offender* has a rather short history. According to Benjamin Karpman's survey (1954) on sexual offenders from 1912 to 1951, the sex offender – as a kind of person or master identity – did not exist prior to 1921. The literature does refer to sexual offending and cases of rape, but not to sex offenders or rapists. Neither had then been constructed as proper objects of scientific study or categories of persons that could be identified, classified, and distinguished from non-sex offenders or non-rapists. Indeed, Karpman claims that he published the first North American article on the sex offender in 1923. His single case study involved a man convicted for writing obscene letters. Karpman (1954, 625) diagnosed the cause as latent homosexuality – stemming from his patient's psychosexual attachment to his mother – and commenced the first psychoanalysis treatment in North American prisons. He noted that the sex offender was mentally disordered and needed treatment rather than punishment, but astutely observed that "[it] will be a long time before courts and lawyers give place to psychiatrists" (656). Even in the early 1950s, the psychological profession did not foresee the coalition between courts or clinicians and the psycho-medical expert's pre-eminent role in regulating legal and penal subjects charged with sexual offences (see Bourke 2007, 284–91).

Karpman (1954, 622–3) expresses "surprise and disappointment" in finding no English journal references to sexual offenders and no public interest in "the sexual criminal" prior to 1921. He says that between 1921 and 1932, only six English language articles dealt with the sex offender, increasing to thirty articles between 1933 and 1941 and to about one hundred articles between 1942 and 1951 (1954, ix). While Karpman does not link the emergence of sex offenders with techniques that study or measure them (Foucault 1990; Hacking 1986, 1995; McCallum 1997), his survey shows that the sex offender – as a way of being a person – emerged in tandem with what he calls the "talking cure" that emerged in North America in the mid-1920s (Karpman 1954, x, 621). For Karpman, Freud created a clinical method that identified the unconscious psychic origins of sexual abnormalities and categorized them into types of people such as rapists and sexual offenders.

Karpman's survey not only corroborates the idea that the sex offender is a modern creation, but also shows that definitions of the sex offender changed historically and incorporated a range of behaviours, attributes, causal variables, and treatment recommendations (see Bourke 2007). Consider the six prison-file excerpts from one participant in my study at the beginning of this chapter. In the set of psychological assessments, the "vocabularies of motive" (Mills 1940) attributed to the offender changed three times during his carceral history. In 1980, his motive to rape stems from violence and misogyny. Ten years later, it stems from an emotional personality disorder and clinicians retract earlier impressions linking rape to his violent nature and hatred for women. By the late 1990s, causal statements have vanished from the diagnosis and are replaced by individualized high-risk factors that need to be managed. The second set of file excerpts illustrate the judges' disparate sentencing rationales. In accordance with dominant clinical and cultural theories of rape, judicial comments shift from medicalized discourse about abnormality and cure during the 1980s to morally charged psychopathological discourses about untreatable deviance or feminist discourses that rape is not a sex crime but a violent offence during the 1990s.

Sixty years after Karpman's survey, the sex offender is a taken-for-granted designation of being a person. The historical and contemporary content of that category was and remains open to modification and debate. From 1923 onwards, "the sex offender" was reproduced and refashioned into new forms and types. A predominant concern with the uncontrollable impulses of the exhibitionist and the homosexual in Karpman's 1954 survey has become a concern with the unmanageable choices of the sexual predator and the high-risk sex offender. I realize, of course, that by deploying the category of sex offender in my analysis I am open to criticism on the grounds of reifying a type of person. In Ian Hacking's (1986) words, I contribute to "making up people." But I also think that the category can be used as a site from which to challenge cultural stories about sex offenders. As we shall see, the men's lives extend far beyond their case management files, diagnostic categories, and high-risk factors, and reveal a great deal about gendering, masculinity, and violence.

Historically, rape under Canadian criminal law was limited to vaginal penetration without female consent. In 1983, the crime category of rape, which had excluded male victims and perpetrators' wives, was abolished and replaced in the Criminal Code by three gender-neutral sexual assault categories, defined and punished according to the degree of threat or bodily harm applied. The threshold test was whether "the sexual integrity of the victim" had been violated (*R. v. Chase 1987*). The *United States Code* also abolished the offence of rape, and currently operates with two types of sexual assault – *sexual abuse* and *aggravated sexual abuse*. By contrast, the United Kingdom's *Sexual Offence Act 2003* contains a gender-neutral offence of rape – defined by penile penetration of the victim's body – as well as sexual assault by penetration and sexual assault through sexual touching. Bourke's (2007, 6) point is eminently sensible: while rape is a "highly ritualized" social performance, its definition has always varied across time and place.

Only two of the men in my sample group had historical rape convictions. Nonetheless, I use the social category of rape and stranger rape instead of the legal category of sexual assault in this study. The specificity of rape or rape-murder is often lost, and its brutality diluted, in the more generic sexual assault crime categories. Without diminishing the seriousness of all unwanted sexual contact, I want to underscore that I am talking about rape or rape and murder against a woman, versus other possible forms of touch that violate a person's sexual integrity. In group sessions and interviews, participants in my study often used the term rape, as well as crime, deviance, and sex, to describe their unlawful behaviour. Only a few referred to themselves as rapists, even though that descriptor distinguishes them from the most disparaged convicts in prison hierarchies, namely, men convicted for sex acts against children. I use rape and rapist for precisely those reasons – to reference men whose victims are adult women versus children or youths. In light of the types of sexual assault committed by the men in my study, my analysis and conclusions are necessarily confined to stranger rape and rapists.

Rival Objects of Study:
Types of People versus Types of Social Problems

Sex offenders and rape do not lack attention from contemporary scholars. The sex offender – as a type of person – tends to be the object of knowledge within psycho-medical literatures, cognitive-behavioural studies, and applied risk assessment research (e.g., Abracen et al. 2004; Hanson and Bussiere 1998; Hood et al. 2002; Marshall et al. 2006; Pardue and Arrigo 2008; Ward, Polaschek, and Beecher 2005; Webster and Hucker 2007). Rape or sexual assault – as types of social problems – tend to be the object of knowledge within historical and contemporary socio-legal feminist influenced studies (e.g., Anderson and Doherty 2008; Bourke 2007; Gavey 2004; Hopkins and Koss 2005; Mardorossian 2002).

Psycho-medical driven accounts produce a one-sided focus on individual deviance and pathology that is bereft of socio-economic, political, and historical contexts (Cowburn 2005; Lea and Auburn 2001), while instrumental risk prediction research absents causal frameworks and focuses primarily on static and historical variables associated statistically with violent or sexual re-offending (e.g., Andrews, Bonta, and Wormith 2006; Bonta 2002; Gottfredson and Moriarty 2006). Both genres see rapists as fundamentally different from normal men. Individual pathology models locate the causes of rape and the locus of rape management strategies inside aberrant male behaviour, and do not examine the gender(ing) practices of a society and the structured relations of power between men and women or among men. Thus, in these accounts, *other* men shoulder the primary responsibility for sexualized violence against women (Greer 2003). By comparison, feminist accounts produce a rather one-sided focus on socio-structural conditions and institutional practices and do not, for the most part, address male agency and choice (Lea and Auburn 2001). For feminist theorists, rape and sexual assault are almost always understood within a historical context of gendered, racialized, and class-based power relations between men and women that privilege men and foster contempt for women as well as ascribed feminine qualities and practices (e.g., Curran and Renzetti 2004; Sokoloff, Price, and Flavin 2004). How the rapist-as-subject experiences and understands the conjunctions between violence and sex, power and gender, and victimization and abuse in his own life is, for the most part, ignored. Explanatory categories of *patriarchal systems* or *male power* tend to erase the complexities of individual circumstances, motives, and meaning, and render all men as bearers of rape.

This disciplinary schism divorces social structure from social agents and macro analysis from microanalysis in knowledge claims about rape and sex offenders. Not surprisingly, stereotypes of the untreatable sex predator – without conscience or capacity for remorse – have become embedded in cultural consciousness (e.g., Cowburn and Dominelli 2001; Petrunik and Weismann 2005; Simon 1998). This image of a new criminal type not only thwarts public support for the rehabilitative goals codified in Canadian penal legislation, but also adds to neoconservative "law and order" rhetoric in favour of more penitentiaries and punitive responses to social ills (e.g., Hudson 2005; Petrunik and Deutschman 2007; Simon 2007). Sensationalized public accounts – generated by writers with no data – are hardly new. Almost sixty years ago, Karpman (1954, 672) declared that:

> The popular articles are mostly rubbish. Here is where we hear about the sex fiends and degenerates lurking around the corner, the thousands of rape cases occurring every year, the danger to *your* daughter, and where we hear the gory details of the most sensational rape-murders. Here we find the pleas for castration.

Concerns about sex offenders have a long history. In the 1930s, 1940s, and 1950s, there were warnings that sex crimes were increasing, claims that sex offenders could be detected in early life, cries that victims were being neglected, and exhortations to develop techniques for distinguishing between potential sex offenders and non-offenders (Karpman 1954, 630–2; Jackson 1939). By the 1990s, the sexual predator was a contemporary target for cultural and political scapegoating. The result has been increased state control of convicted sex offenders (e.g., Greer 2003; Hudson 2005; Petrunik and Deutschman 2007) and the expansion of participation in treatment programs designed to better regulate and manage high-risk sex offenders (Pratt et al. 2005). Today, for example, Canadian penal treatment programs authorize the intermingling of all types of sex offenders by appropriating and decontextualizing a dominant feminist discourse that holds that all sexual offending is about men's power and control.

How, then, are we to make sense of this development of the "classic rapist" or the "rape-myth rapist"? I begin with a discussion of the discovery of rape by the North American women's movement, then track the subsequent disregard for the rapist as a subject of study in much feminist and critical scholarship about rape.

The Feminist Assault on Rape: Disappearing the Rapist

Rape was not recognized as a serious social problem prior to second-wave feminist scholarship and activism. Beginning in the late 1960s, women working in anti-rape movements and at rape crisis centres began speaking out against male sexual violence (Gavey 2004; Levan 1996). They spear-headed a consciousness-raising movement that encouraged women to come together, pool their experiences, and organize to fight for equality (Sarachild 1978, 144–50). Creating a safe social space to talk about rape enabled individual women to discuss rape in a way that de-emphasized it as a personal problem and exposed the oppressive social structures that facilitated it and blamed the victim (see Curthoys 1997). Rape became the paradigm for understanding all forms of male violence within patriarchal societies (Anderson and Doherty 2008, 20). Feminists subsequently linked rape to women's social inequality and economic marginalization and demanded political solutions (Hopkins and Koss 2005). Some suggested that existing structural arrangements, particularly heterosexual marriage, the patriarchal nuclear family, and capitalist labour markets, along with the discourses that produce, reproduce, and normalize those arrangements, make women vulnerable to rape by rendering them inferior at home and in the workplace (see Matthews 1994; Walker 1995).

Empirical research followed the discovery of rape as a personal and social problem. By centring the raped woman as the subject of study, feminist researchers challenged the prevalent myth that rape was a statistically rare event committed by disturbed, psychotic male strangers (Russell 1982; 1984). They repudiated the historically entrenched belief, disseminated through socio-biology, evolutionary theory, and scientific racism, that poor working-class and racialized males were more prone to raping women than white professional middle-class males (Bourke 2007, 100–18). They emphasized the ubiquity of sexual assault. Indeed, in 2008, Canadians reported 21,449 sexual assaults and 2,784 other sexual offences to police (Wallace 2009). Added to these figures are the Canadian government's own estimate that less than 10 per cent of sexual assaults are officially reported (Brennan and Taylor-Butts 2008). While we cannot identify how many sexual offences were rapes or stranger rapes, we do know that most lone perpetrator sexual assaults were committed by male friends, family members, dates, or casual acquaintances of the victim (Brennan and Taylor-Butts 2008). Feminist research also uncovered disturbing statistics about marital rape. According to Diana Russell's (1982) often-cited study, rape by husbands or ex-husbands accounted for 38 per cent of the total number of incidents, while rape by strangers accounted for only 6 per cent. Pressured by women's groups, in 1983, the Canadian government finally amended the statutory exemption permitting husbands to rape their wives; by 1993, marital rape was a crime in all fifty American states (Ferro, Cermele, and Saltsman 2008, 765). Notwithstanding these new legal directives, there is still popular and judicial support for treating marital rape as a lesser crime than other forms of rape (Ferro, Cermele, and Saltsman 2008; Rumney 1999).

Feminists questioned other prevailing myths, for example, that rape was a natural act of uncontrollable male desire that could be provoked consciously or subconsciously by the victim (Scully 1990), or that rape symbolized an attack on "the hostile mother image of [the assailant's] childhood" (Mandel et al. 1965, 239–40). In the 1970s, von Hentig's notion of victim-precipitation dominated theories of rape (Bourke 2007, 71–3). According to Menachem Amir, "the victim becomes functionally responsible for [rape] by entering upon and following a course that will provoke some males to commit crimes" (1972, cited by Scully 1990, 42). Ner Littner, a psychoanalyst, wrote about "professional victims" and argued that they "unwittingly cooperate with the rapist in terms of covertly making themselves available to the rapist" (cited by Scully 1990, 43). Karen Horney insisted that women want to be raped, as "what women secretly desire in intercourse is rape and violence, or in the mental sphere, humiliation … This swinging in the direction of masochism is part of the woman's anatomical destiny" (cited by Scully 1990, 43).

Forty years later, blaming the victim for rape has faded from contemporary theoretical literatures and treatment practices. But discrediting victims still remains the bane of existence for many women and children testifying at sexual assault trials (e.g., Anderson and Doherty 2008, 19; Comack and Balfour 2004). Myths and beliefs about how men and women ought to behave continue to pervade media representations, popular attitudes, and judicial discourse about rape, and subtly shape constructions of the credible rape victim and the real rapist (e.g., de Carvalho Figueiredo 2001; Finch and Munro 2007; Fraink et al. 2008; Smart 1989). These myths continue to guide police officers' decisions about whether or not to pursue sexual assault charges against perpetrators (Anderson and Doherty 2008, 17; Bourke 2007, 395–9). However, feminist thinking has entered into penal treatment discourse for offenders. The penal staff at the treatment centre that I observed forbade sex offenders from voicing rape myths, such as victim provocation, mistaken beliefs about consent, false accusations, intoxication, or uncontrollable impulses that justified rape, trivialized harm to the victim, or diminished the convicted sex offender's individual responsibility for the effects of rape (see Auburn and Lea 2003; Lea and Auburn 2001).

Feminist-informed initiatives centre on criticizing the mismanagement of rape and helping sexually abused women report rape, prosecute their assailants, and recover from the aftermath. Consequently, much of what feminist writers know about rape is framed from the standpoint of the raped woman (e.g., Hopkins and Koss 2005; Mardorossian 2002; Weiss 2010). While the economic and political sources of men's power are acknowledged as key factors in addressing rape, the basic initiatives derived from feminist mobilizations around it tend towards increased criminalization and containment of economically and culturally disenfranchised men. Although women's groups have been divided over the issue of controlling male violence through criminalization, feminist advocates of criminal justice interventions envisioned criminalization as a necessary short-term strategy operating with long-term struggles to transform the structural features of women's dependency and disadvantage (see Currie 1998; Snider 1998; Walker 1995). Feminist lobbying to prosecute rape as a crime of violence and form of assault, rather than as a sex crime, was the driving force behind the 1983 amendments to sex offence provisions in Canada's *Criminal Code* (Boyle 1984; Los 1994). But, as Maria Los (1994) notes, rape law amendments submitted to Canada's federal government by the National Association of Women and the Law were drafted without any formal consultation with women's organizations and interests and the gender-neutral offence of sexual assault is still contentious among feminists who remain divided over defining rape as a form of assault as opposed to a sex crime (Chamallas 2005; Fudge 1989).

Not surprisingly, an early upshot of rape politics was the rapid rise of sex offender populations in Canadian penitentiaries. The broad definition of sexual assault – along with heightened popular awareness and reduced penalties for less serious types of sexual assault – led to increased reporting to police, higher jury conviction rates, and higher imprisonment rates compared to other violent crime categories (Brennan and Taylor-Butts 2008). Between 1989/90 and 1994/95, annual admissions to Canadian federal prisons for sexual offences grew by nearly 40 per cent, from 2,768 to 3,875 (Statistics Canada 1999), and then dropped off afterwards (Boe, Motiuk, and Nafekh 2004). Official reporting rates for sexual assault have also fallen since the mid-1990s (Brennan and Taylor Butts 2008). Despite this decline, the 1997 reporting rate was still 74 per cent higher than in 1983 (Statistics Canada 1999). Canadian convicts with sexual assault-related convictions represented 25 per cent of approximately 13,000 federally incarcerated prisoners in 1997, a number that decreased to 16 per cent in 2006 (Correctional Service of Canada 2006; Motiuk and Vuong 2005). Data from victim-centred organizations, such as Vancouver Rape Relief (2008), do not corroborate official police statistics that sexual assault rates are declining. These statistics, however, do not indicate the extent to which the fluctuation in sex offender populations stems from sexual assault convictions involving adult women complainants. Nor do they tell us the extent to which the rise or fall in the number of convicted sex offenders is due to convictions for assaults on male children, or convictions of poor and racialized men. Indeed, the unintended outcome of feminist lobbying to repeal the crime category of rape has been to "disappear" the actual perpetrators of rape, thereby impeding knowledge production about rape in society. For British feminist Lynne Segal (2006; 1990, 243), traditional feminist analyses of rape remain general because "what feminism has so far been unwilling to explore is why some men become rapists and use violence against women, and some men do not." She writes:

> Although absent from most feminist writing on men's violence, there is evidence that there are significant differences not only between men who commit sexual assault on women and other men, but between different types of violent men – and between different types of violent acts – and their meanings. (1990, 245)

No feminist scholarship questions victimization and self-report findings that rape is predominantly intra-racial and intra-class (e.g., Barrett and George 2004; Carbado and Gulati 2003), and – notwithstanding that feminist research shows unequivocally that every woman is a potential rape victim – no feminist-informed work disputes that women from ra-cialized populations and lower socio-economic positions have the highest likelihood of being raped in their lifetimes (e.g., Barrett and George 2004; Cahill 2001, 213; Chamallas 2005; Curran and Renzetti 2004, 221; Ellerby and MacPherson 2002; Segal 1990, 145). In Canada, for example, sexual and other violent assault rates are higher on Aboriginal reserves than in other regions (Statistics Canada 2004). Some data indicate that eight out of ten Aboriginal Canadian women have been sexual assault victims at some point in their lives (McIvor and Nahanee 1998, 65). Estimates in the United States suggest that one in three urban Aboriginal women will be sexually assaulted during her lifetime. Overall, the sexual assault rate for Native American women is 7.2 per 1,000 Americans, over twice the rate for African American women and three times the rate for white women (Deer 2004). To explain violence against Aboriginal women by men in their own communities, LaRocque maintains that historical representa-tions of Aboriginal women as licentious and dehumanized "squaws," which originated in white racist settler societies, enabled Aboriginal and non-Aboriginal men alike to view Aboriginal women as objects with little human value (cited by Razack 2002, 135; 276).

Paradoxically, feminists steadfastly foreground class and race as for-mative of women's experienced reality as rape victims. Class and race also remain forefront in discussions about institutional biases in polic-ing and punishing men who rape (e.g., Razack 2002; Wriggins 2004). Yet few feminists discuss or study class and race as formative of men's experienced reality as perpetrators.[1] Feminists acknowledge that con-victed rapists within Canadian jail and penitentiary populations are overrepresented by unskilled working-class, poor, and racialized men (Snider 1998; Vancouver Rape Relief 2008). But with few exceptions (Segal 1990, 2006; Taylor 1983), they do not examine the structural link-ages between men's lives and forms of violence. As Segal (1990, 243) observes, "Every conceivable source of evidence we possess on the re-alities of male violence" suggests that class ought to be a significant factor in explaining male sexual violence. Instead, many feminist theo-ries about rape deploy "dominated" and "dominator" narratives around the biological categories of female and male, intimating that all men are potential victimizers of all women. As Kerry Carrington and Paul Watson (1996, 256) note, "This makes every male body a danger zone – a rape zone if you like," which links women to victimhood iden-tities that feminist writers should resist and criticize (see Marcus 1992; Mardorossian 2002). Elizabeth Stanko (2000, 148) puts it this way: "In an effort to forward debates about men's violence to women, we must eschew theoretical frameworks that naturalize women's victimization *and* men's violence."

Feminist Understandings of Rape: Contributions and Critique

Of course, feminist writers have advanced more than one theoretical framework for understanding rape in Western societies, and so I will use exemplars to trace the historical development of feminist theorizing about rape, with the historical subordination of woman within unequal social relations as the common starting point (Bonnycastle 2000, 66–8). Most feminist rape theories were written during the 1970s and 1980s in direct response to the discovery of rape and the desire of second-wave feminists to identify and ameliorate the structural origins of women's oppression (for overviews see Chunn and Lacombe 2000; Hopkins and Koss 2005, 698–707). Perhaps early feminist writers' most noteworthy contribution to the analysis of rape is their general thesis that men use rape as a violent control mechanism that literally and symbolically asserts their power over women (Auburn and Lea 2003; Websdale and Chesney-Lind 1998). The deployment of the categories *man* or *male* in feminist rape theories contrast an emergent position within feminism that rejects a monolithic or generic womanhood speaking in one voice. Spurred on by criticisms raised by lesbians and Black women, few contemporary feminist writers would theorize the category of woman as a unified or stabilized identity undivided along lines of race, class, and sexuality (see Chunn and Lacombe 2000; Crenshaw 1994; Jhappan 1996). Yet despite decades of new theories, no feminist writer has re-theorized rape for over ten years,[2] leaving the terrain open to who Carine Mardorossian (2002, 751) calls "conservative backlash writers."

Susan Brownmiller: Rape as Male Violence against Women

In *Against Our Will: Men, Women, and Rape*, American feminist Susan Brownmiller (1975) theorizes rape as the primary mechanism for securing and re-securing women's social control over women within social arrangements characterized by male patriarchy. In Brownmiller-informed understandings, the rapist's motives are to degrade women and express power and dominance (124–5). Subsequently, fear of rape reinforces women's dependency on men and male-dominated institutions for protection, including laws, criminal justice agencies, and heterosexual family forms. In this manner, rape continuously re-secures women's inferior social status and economic vulnerability (16–17). For Brownmiller, rape is normal deviance and the rapist is the boy next door. At other times, however, she intimates a stronger motivation to rape among men denied access to legitimate expressions of male supremacy. For example, she writes that "corporate executive dining rooms and climbs up Mount Everest are not usually accessible to those who form the subculture of violence. Access to a female body – through force – is within their ken" (194). Brownmiller is at the forefront of early feminist efforts to refuse popular and clinical constructions of rape as an act of sex triggered by men's innate sex drive or instinctive responses to sexually laden stimuli. One of her immediate objectives was to take the sex out of rape and render immaterial the sexual history of the assailant and complainant during rape trials (Cahill 2001, 27; also Smart 1989, 26–49). Brownmiller focuses our attention on men's agency and emphasizes the feminist mantra that men *choose* to rape. In theorizing rape as a violent practice for maintaining patriarchal definitions of women's place in society – versus an aberrant individual male sex act – she contributes to the demise of individualistic, medicalized models of rape, and to the dichotomization of males as rapists and females as rape victims. In her words:

> When men discovered they could rape, they proceeded to do it … From prehistoric times to present … rape has played a critical function. It is nothing more or less than a conscious process of intimidation by which *all men* keep *all women* in a state of fear. (1975, 14–15, original italics)

For her, the original cause of rape is biological and rapists are the front line "shock troops" that safeguard universal male privilege (1, 209).

Lorenne Clark and Debra Lewis: The Price of Coercive Sexuality (1977)

Writing during Brownmiller's era, Canadian feminists Lorenne Clark and Debra Lewis explain rape as an effect of men's historically specific economic and cultural dominance, rather than as a trans-historical technique of male dominance. Clark and Lewis link rape to the devaluation and objectification of women under a specific form of capitalism, and see it as the legacy of two interwoven conditions. The first is women's undervalued economic contribution inside and outside the family in liberal market economies. Rather than fear of rape, as Brownmiller argues, a sexual division of labour produces women's unequal social status and economic subordination relative to men. The second is cultural narratives circulating within patriarchal societies. One narrative allows us to contemplate coercive sex as an affirmation of male power. The other allows us to objectify female sexuality as a resource – a type of male property that can be estranged from a woman's body (Brownmiller 1975, 297) and "stolen, sold, bartered, or exchanged by others" (MacKinnon 1989, 172). Clark and Lewis suggest that without certain material and discursive conditions, existing rape practices would be unthinkable. For them, rape has no transcultural meaning. Rather, it is imbued with meanings provided by prevailing discourses that develop within specific social relations and help support specific social arrangements. Unsurprisingly, given their reliance upon official Canadian crime statistics, Clark and Lewis (1977) found an overrepresentation of poor and working-class men (90 per cent) in their sample police reports of 129 convicted rapists. They provide two somewhat conflicting explanations for this finding. First, they state that this *prima facie* working class bias to rape is an artefact of criminal justice system class bias. But they also insert a secondary sexual motive into their analyses, which contradicts their class-bias thesis. They claim that working class men "lack the purchasing power to buy the sexual property they want ... [accordingly] physical force is the method used by men who lack other, subtler means of sexual coercion" (130). This suggests an empirical relationship between class and sexual violence, as Brownmiller alludes, but provides no corroborating data to support rape as a technique of male power.

Schwendinger and Schwendinger: Rape and Economically Marginalized Men

Julia Schwendinger and Herman Schwendinger (1981, 1982) set out a Marxian theory of rape that also centres the effects of capitalism, but with a focus on unequal class-based societies. Rather than a natural expression of a homogeneous masculinity, these scholars theorize rape as a response to pressures encountered by men who are marginalized within capitalist systems of economic production. Schwendinger and Schwendinger argue that capitalism renders all human beings as objectified commodities of exchange. This enables men who experience an absence of control in the economy to turn towards "the marketplace of sexual relations" and substitute physical power over women for lack of power over the rest of their lives. According to the authors, "The importance of manipulating and controlling women, by violence, if necessary, is elevated ... The cultural portrayal of the 'superstuds' and 'superflies' emerge under conditions of marginalization and the control of women, no matter how precarious it is, is one of the many substitutes that these men use for uncontrollable labor market conditions" (cited in Messerschmidt 1986, 140). For these men, sexual coercion and physical violence against women are the only options for expressing domination and control in a precarious economy. Feminist writers, however, rarely take up this theory, which links "violent, forcible rape," murder, and assault to men's class, race, and gender. Segal suggests that feminist writers' reluctance to pursue this line of investigation stems from concerns over fuelling racist narratives (e.g., Moorti 2002, 56) and letting patriarchal relations "off the hook" for violence against women (Segal 2006, 1990, 241, 246).

Angela Davis: Power, Powerlessness, and the Myth of the Black Male Rapist

The pathological effects of a capitalist economic system are also integral to Angela Davis' (1981) theory of rape. Davis spearheaded critiques against anti-rape movement activists and feminist theorists for contributing to racist ideology. She charges that most thinkers have ignored the historical and contemporary intersection of racism and sexism in Black women's experiences as rape victims of white men, as well as Black men's experiences with wrongful charges, convictions, and lynching for raping white women. She characterizes "the rape charge" and the overprosecution of African American men as racist tactics that reanimate the "myth of the Black rapist," conjured in the post–Civil War American South, as a discourse for controlling post-slavery Black male populations (1981, 176; also Bourke 2007, 100–10). Davis rejects the claim that Black men and poor or working-class men might resort to sexual violence or violence generally to compensate for their structural exclusion from "male supremacy" in the economic order of things (1981, 178). She argues instead that the "anonymous rapist," namely the majority of rapists who are unreported and never convicted, are most likely white men who believe that their privilege gives them license to rape their "social inferiors" and immunity from prosecution (1981, 199). Akin to Clark and Lewis, Davis insists that the causes of rape lie within the class structure of capitalism and women's disadvantaged economic position. She argues that while relatively powerless working-class men, whatever their colour, can be motivated to rape, "men of the capitalist class" have more incentive because of their relative immunity from criminalization.

For Davis, sexual exploitation is an extension of, and not a compensatory alternative to, economic and political power. She also links "the present rape epidemic" to capitalist men's strategies for reconsolidating authority in the face of emerging global challenges to monopoly capitalism (1981, 200).

Debra Cameron and Elizabeth Frazer: Cultural Scripts and Sexual Murder

In *The Lust to Kill: A Feminist Investigation of Sexual Murder* (1987), Debra Cameron and Elizabeth Frazer explore "sex killings" through historical and contemporary discourses that aim to understand such events. They emphasize that historical actions and events did not carry the same meanings in the past as they do today. They explain: "The idea of a killer being motivated by deviant sexual urges, familiar and obvious as it may appear to us, was regarded by many people as recently as the late nineteenth century with astonishment, distaste, and often outright disbelief" (1987, 21). Cameron and Frazer claim that interviewing murderers would add nothing to understanding the connections between sex and murder or sex and violence generally, and instead, their analysis relies on second-hand published confessions and commentaries by sex killers. In their opinion, sex killers and academics alike cannot stand outside their culture, but can only draw on the available resources for understanding human behaviour. To illustrate, Cameron and Frazer use secondary sources featuring convicted sex killer Dennis Nilsen to explore his motives in terms of cultural scripts about irresistible compulsions, external evil forces, cold psychopathic desires, and dissociative states, and to attempt to determine how these discourses both fit and do not fit his conduct (151). They conclude that typical killers are unhelpful to understanding sex killings because the latter can rehearse existing "cultural codes," but can never create new ones. Cameron and Frazer note: "When we attempt to interpret what other people are doing we only have these categories to use as a framework; when we look into our pasts we can only organize them into patterns given by our culture" (152). Nonetheless, they manage to uncover existing cultural codes about sex killers and advance an original argument. Downplaying the sex killer as merely misogynist, they posit a link between masculine subjectivity and sex killings, and conclude that the subject-position of the sex killer is one culturally available subject-position for affirming a masculine identity that may shed light on the topic of rape. Curiously, however, they overlook another explanation offered by Nilsen himself, which appears in his writings and which I will explore in this book: "My offences arose from a feeling of inadequacy, not potency. I never had any power in my life" (cited in Tithecott 1997, 6).

Catharine MacKinnon: Rape as Normal Heterosexual Sex

Nearly a decade after Brownmiller, Catharine MacKinnon urged feminists to retain rape and violence as distinct categories of socio-political analysis. In *Towards a Feminist Theory of the State* (1989), she argues that women's social and sexual submission is intrinsic to patriarchal heterosexuality, and is not historically and culturally specific to forms of capitalism. Although she never claims that all sex is rape, MacKinnon (1987, 88) says that all heterosexual sex contains an element of coercion due to women's unequal status and enforced structural dependency on men, whether for physical protection, economic security, or social identity. Consequently, MacKinnon claims that it is problematic to presume that women are free and equal vis-à-vis men in regards to sexual relationships. For her, rape is a logical extension of normalized heterosexual relations that encourage male sexual and physical aggressiveness and female submission and passivity, and that thus blur the boundaries between consent and coercion, seduction and submission, and sex and rape. She writes: "So long as we say those things are abuses of violence, not sex, we fail to criticize what had been made of sex, what has been done to us through sex, because we leave the line between rape and intercourse, sexual harassment and sex roles, pornography and eroticism right where it is" (1987, 86–7). As she puts it, "pornography is the theory and rape is the practice."

For MacKinnon, then, to take the sex out of rape is to decentre patriarchal constructions of compulsory heterosexuality and deny the effects of a male-dominated culture inundated with representations of women's sexuality as an eroticized submission to a coercive male sexuality (1989, 172). For her, the ontological conditions of heterosexuality are eventually eroticized by many men and women. She observes: "Rape is not less sexual for being violence ... rape may even be sexual because it is violent" (173). Her conflation of male violence and power into sex renders intelligible the conjunctions of men's sexual pleasure and women's terror, humiliation, and pain in some forms of rape (e.g., Caputi 1987).

MacKinnon's praxis centres on challenging the male bias of the law. She points out that white, elite, heterosexual male legislators and judges created rape laws before women were allowed to vote. These people shared, in her words, "a common masculinity" and "masculine norms," and experienced themselves "as affirmed by aggressive initiation of sexual interactions" (cited in Jeffries 2006; also Smart 1989). Feminist-socio-legal studies continue to support this idea of rape as normative heterosexual behaviour by demonstrating how male-centred criminal justice agencies and psychological and psychiatric professions fail female rape victims and, in many cases, effect a second rape on them. Rape is at once condemned and criminalized *and* legitimated and dramatized for popular consumption, whether through legal proceedings that re-victimize complainants, or through events such as televised trials in which rape is fodder for spectacle and entertainment (Carrington and Watson 1996; Jaggar 1983; Smart 1989).

Sharon Marcus: Rape as Scripted Interactions

Drawing on a post-structural framework – that emphasizes discourse and language as explanatory categories, rather than class, race, or heterosexuality – Sharon Marcus (1992, 389) conceptualizes rape as a "cultural script" within which women are always already raped and able to be raped. She sees rape as a "scripted interaction which takes place in language and can be understood in terms of conventional masculinity and femininity as well as other gender inequalities" (1992, 390). Like Cameron and Frazer, Marcus posits a unified homogeneous masculine subjectivity. Men and women alike are exposed and acquire access to rape scripts simply by living in misogynist and unequal social situations. Marcus does not adopt the mainstream feminist strategy of understanding and ameliorating rape by changing materially grounded power relations between women and men, but rather targets discursive representations of male aggression and female passivity as problematic and in need of reform.

Marcus (1992) notes that rape scripts always pre-exist the subject identities of rapist and raped, and circulate freely and independently of individual men and women. During an encounter between rapists and rape victims, these scripts encourage women to recognize themselves as objects of violence and subjects of fear, and never as subjects of violence or objects of fear (1992, 391, 398). For Marcus, rape is a "process of gendering" wherein the rapist "strives to imprint the gender identity of feminine victim on his target." The rapist's power is created by the extent to which the would-be victim submits to his efforts to compel her participation in the narrative of feminine powerlessness. In other words, women are complicit – but unintentional – players in rape scripts. Conceptualizing the relationship of language to rape, Marcus opens up possibilities for women to disrupt a would-be rape by refusing passivity, at once imbuing them with the agency to prevent rape while tacitly saddling them with some responsibility to do so. As she puts it: "To speak of a rape script implies a narrative of rape, a series of steps and signals whose typical initial moments we can learn to recognize and whose final outcome we can learn to stave off" (1992, 390–1).

Ann J. Cahill: Rethinking Rape as Embodied Subjectivity

In an effort to avoid dichotomizing violence versus sex, American feminist Ann Cahill (2001) presents a different post-structural reading of rape in Western societies. She centres the biologically sexed body in order to understand rape "as an embodied experience *of women*" (original italics) that is simultaneously violent and sexual. Cahill (2001, 118) argues that it is the mutually constitutive relations between the body and subjectivity that shape the meaning of rape for women. Since embodied subjectivities are always situated in particular contexts, shaped by intersecting discourses, women necessarily experience embodiment and the effects of rape on embodiment in different ways. Cahill insists that these effects are qualitatively different from the experiences of male rape victims. Rather than using gender as the primary category of analysis in understanding rape, she allows that women's bodies may be racialized and inscribed with other differences, such as social class and sexuality, which shape the meanings and experiences of rape.

Cahill's understanding of rape as violent and sexual iterates existing narratives of men's sexuality as a modality for exercising power that reproduces sexual and social differentiation and sexual hierarchies (2001, 125–6, 139). Indeed, she views the personhood of both the rapist and the rape victim as necessarily interdependent. She writes: "The rapist, who seeks to establish his sexual, physical power over the victim through this particular means (a means that connects him to a history of patriarchal, sexually specific authority), cannot accomplish this goal independently of his victim" (133). Ultimately, the effects of rape are productive for men but destructive for women at the psychical level. Beyond bodily trauma, Cahill argues that rape temporarily destroys, denies, or destabilizes the victim's embodied subjectivity. In her words: "The rapist needs the destruction of the victim's identity in order to construct his being as rapist" (133).

Lynne Segal: Rapists as the Waste of Patriarchy

Although Lynne Segal does not engage directly with Angela Davis' work, she reverses her argument. Segal points out that fear and distrust of police are key factors preventing women from reporting rape. She argues that racialized, poor, and working-class women – whose communities hold more misgivings about police than white, middle-class communities – are overrepresented in the dark figure of unreported rape victims. In light of the intra-class and intra-race dynamics of rape, racialized, poor, and working-class men are also overrepresented among rape perpetrators (Segal 2006; 1990, 245–6). In her research, Segal acknowledges that official crime statistics are, in part, an artefact of racialized and class-based judicial and policing practices that target non-dominant men for state-based punishment. Nevertheless, she places some credence in official police reports and victimization studies and argues that poor, working class, and racialized men – whose sense of masculinity is made vulnerable through unemployment, poverty, and racism – are more likely to commit specific forms of rape, namely, group rape and stranger rape (1990, 248). For her, unlike for MacKinnon, every man is not a potential rapist.

Segal's deduction is informed by her examination of writings on masculinity and manhood by African American men such as Robert Staples. In *Black Masculinity* (1982), Staples argues that the everyday economic and social reality generated by white racism denies Black men the minimal prerequisites of manhood, such as employment and the ability to support a family. These structural limitations, he says, encourage Black men to realize their sense of dominant manhood through "sexual conquest [including rape] and domestic dominance" (cited in Segal 1990, 186). Segal also explores the polarized subject-positions of "Black" and "White" men as portrayed by Eldridge Cleaver in *Soul on Ice*. According to Cleaver, one effect of denying "a mental life" to Black American men is their development of a compensatory "superior bodily existence." Cleaver, writes Segal, prototypes and contrasts the African American man as "supermanual menial" or "supermasculine menial" with attributes of "strength, brute power, force, virility," against the white man's subject-position of "omnipotent administrator" with attributes of "weakness, frailty, cowardice and effeminacy" (Segal 1990, 181).

In her examination of this scholarship, Segal argues that structural barriers that block African American men from realizing a masculine subjectivity through economic and political means reduce them as subjects to "biological maleness." She argues that this resort to biological maleness does not pathologize or relate to the nature of racialized or working-class men per se, but rather to the structure of exploitation and oppression in white-dominated, neocolonial, racist societies. Without denying the necessary involvement of sexism and misogyny, Segal argues that alternative constructions of masculinity, shaped by racism and unequal economic arrangements among men, must be incorporated into feminist understandings of rape. She asks: "Rather than the indispensable weapon used by men to ensure the subordination of women, might not rape be the deformed behaviour of men accompanying the destabilization of gender relations, and the consequent contradictions and insecurities of male gender identity, now at their peak in modern America?" (1990, 240).

Susan Griffin: Rape without Knowing Rapists

Many feminist rape theories have been articulated without input from the men who rape. Feminists continue to try to understand the rapist experientially, through victims of rape, or theoretically, through constructs such as patriarchy and male power (Vogelman 1990, 8). Unlike victims' stories, perpetrators' stories are either never told, or are told in a manner that corroborates stranger rapists as predatory monsters. This discursive practice frames and limits these men's identities to a single moment in a lifetime – albeit a horrific moment that produces consequences extending far beyond their victims proper (Lamb 1999, 108; Marecek 1999, 174). Indeed feminist debates about whether rape is about violence or sex have never been applied to the rapist. As Karen Dubinsky (1993, 34) puts it, if rape is about violence, then "why do men rape women? Why don't they just beat them up?" In re-thinking rape through the embodied experiences of women, Ann Cahill (2001) argues it can have radically different meanings to differently embodied rape victims. The corollary is that different types of rape might also have radically different meanings to different types of rapists. What could the rapist-as-subject approach contribute to understandings of the interplay between rape and men's embodied subjectivity? Would the feminist designation of the rapist as the shock troops of patriarchy resonate with the rapist's lived reality? How do sexual and gendered hierarchies of power shape his everyday world and conduct? To what extent does the rapist draw on interruptible rape scripts in the act of rape? As Nancy Fraser (1997, 211) notes, "social practices do not wear their meanings on their sleeves," and perhaps feminist writers too easily assume that the effects of men's violence on women correspond with the motives of the men who perpetrate that violence (Liddle 1989). In 1971, Susan Griffin – author of a classical feminist text on rape – wrote, "I never asked why men raped; I simply thought it one of the many mysteries of human nature" (cited in Segal 2006; 1990, 231). Decades after rape entered public consciousness, feminist writers have not ventured far beyond Griffin's words. Perhaps too much is also made of a unitary image of masculinity. Segal certainly thinks so, and writes: "There was a time, it seems to me, when feminists would not so readily have lost sight of the significance of [other forms of] oppression for the sake of identifying a universal male beastliness" (265).

Feminist writers correctly note that traditional research has institutionalized the minority perspective of a few men speaking from within a social order that they wish to preserve. These men are also among those who benefit most – economically, politically, socially, and culturally – from what Connell (1995, 79) dubs "the patriarchal dividend." By contrast, feminist inquiry is directed at "challenging the way knowledge is produced ... questioning the monopoly that certain powerful groups hold over information," and producing oppositional knowledge (Kirby and McKenna 1989, 15). Nonetheless, feminist researchers remain uncertain about how to analyse groups of men at the margins of power. I characterize each man in my study as marginalized, based on his economic, educational, and cultural circumstances prior to incarceration and on his penal designation as a convicted high-risk sex offender after incarceration. I am interested in expanding a feminist transformative research agenda to include men who have not been traditionally counted by the research process and in engaging in what Kirby and McKenna (1989, 22) call "researching from the margins."

There is little doubt that *the sex offender* and *the rapist* are constructs that evoke hostility and repulsion in most women. But by ignoring the lives of men for whom the "patriarchal dividend" is all but absent, feminists surrender the political and academic terrain to the clinical gaze of psychological experts and the sovereign power of penal authority. In the struggle for social justice, critical feminist scholarship may be accused of abandoning the men who represent the extreme outliers of privilege and constructed normalcy in our society, thus forfeiting a full analysis of rape and rapists.

Diana Scully: Understanding Motives for Rape

Within feminist research, the study that best analyses individual adult male rapists is Diana Scully's *Understanding Sexual Violence: A Study of Convicted Rapists* (1990). Her data convincingly debunks medical explanations of rapists as psychologically abnormal men who are unable to control their behaviour, which was the vocabulary of motive that monopolized expert knowledge on sex offenders when she began her research in the 1970s (1990, 63). Scully acknowledges the theoretical dilemma that not all men in violent societies rape, and poses the question, "why not?" She interviewed 114 convicted rapists and a control group of seventy-five other convicts in US maximum and medium-security prisons. Scully concludes that sexually violent men are otherwise "normal" (1990, 167), but notes that the men who raped were poorly educated (80 per cent) and working class (85 per cent). Most were employed, but 40 per cent were "frequently unemployed," which she attributes to unequal access to justice and legal resources, rather than to class differences in the propensity to rape women (1990, 64–5). Furthermore, her data show that her rapist sample, when compared to her control convict sample, over-identifies with the "traditional model of masculinity" as opposed to "modern versions of the male role." She concludes that the rapist is driven not by an uncontrollable instinctive drive, but by a consciously chosen strategy for "exercising a singularly male form of power" (1990, 163).

Since Scully's study, critical research has questioned the idea of a monolithic, biologically generic man, and has argued that there are diverse, historically and culturally specific embodiments of masculinities and femininities (e.g., Connell 1995; Messerschmidt 1997, 2000; Newburn and Stanko 1994). In light of new developments in gender theory, contemporary feminist rape scholarship faces a conundrum. By excluding discussions about hegemonic masculinity or diverse forms of masculinities across different social contexts, it ignores both structural and choice differences among men in the explanation of rape. Most troubling, by expelling the rapist as a subject of analysis or portraying him as every man, feminist research empowers the version of sexually violent men personified within contemporary cognitive-behavioural penal programming. Without providing alternative accounts, feminist scholarship inadvertently contributes to pathologizing individual rapists and creating new vocabularies of rape motives, such as cognitive distortions, thinking errors, and bad choices.

Theorizing Masculinities: Social Structure and Social Agency

The foregoing discussion suggests the benefits of pursuing a line of investigation that acknowledges violence occurs in many forms, recognizes differences among men, and asks why some men choose one form of violence over another. Towards this end, I now turn to masculinities studies, a hybrid of critical and feminist scholarship that follows feminism's lead in uncovering diversity and contradiction within the gender category of woman and applies it to men. My aim is not to review the vast body of critical masculinities scholarship, but to highlight the key constructs, methods, and theoretical factors that I will deploy in regard to my own research findings. Most importantly, I take my principal research tool – the life history story – from this genre. Uncoupled from the individualizing clinical case study, James Messerschmidt (2000, 2004) and Raewyn Connell (1995, 89) demonstrate how "theorized life histories provide rich evidence about impersonal and collective processes as well as subjectivity." Life histories reveal the individual's lived experience and practices over time and illuminate the mutually constitutive links between individual action and the historically and socially specific contexts in which all subjectivity or personal experience is embedded.

James Messerschmidt: Links between Stranger Rape and Marginalized Men

By exploring differences among men and talking about specific types of masculinities, Messerschmidt spearheaded challenges to essentialist constructions of masculinity. His early work builds on Segal and Schwendinger and Schwendinger's arguments about the significance of social class in explaining men's sexual violence. Messerschmidt (1986) observes that all men in Western capitalist societies learn from boyhood that they are privileged by sex/gender, despite the reality that many men are removed from economic and educational success and social power. Messerschmidt states that for many of these marginalized men, rape and other forms of physically dominating behaviours are often the only available resources for affirming a heterosexual masculine identity or *performing gender* (Connell 1995; Schwendinger and Schwendinger 1981; Segal 1990; Staples 1982). For Messerschmidt, working-class men and racialized men are the ones most likely to commit gang rape and stranger rape.

Raewyn Connell: Hegemonic Masculinity

The masculinities research genre has adopted Raewyn Connell's (1987) idea that contemporary Western capitalist society produces a hegemonic masculinity expressed through the subordination of women, the suppression of alternative masculinities, and the distancing of men from femininity. For Connell (1995, 77), hegemonic masculinity personifies all the currently accepted cultural practices that institutionalize men's privileged position and power over women – a system of gender relations otherwise known as *patriarchy*. She writes: "Hegemonic masculinity is constructed in relation to women and to subordinated masculinities" (1987, 185–6). Most importantly, it is heterosexual and embodies a "successful collective strategy in relation to women." Whereas hegemonic masculinity can be considered "normative," as it personifies the most culturally glorified way of being a man, Connell and Messerschmidt (2005) emphasize that it is not the statistical norm. They caution that the term should not be used interchangeably or confused with "dominant masculinity." Nevertheless, one of hegemonic masculinity's most successful embodiments is heterosexual marriage and the nuclear family, which naturalizes physical and emotional divisions of labour and galvanizes power hierarchies between men, women, and children (Connell 1987, 185–6). Messerschmidt and Connell enumerate the primary cultural practices and discourses constitutive of hegemonic masculinity as follows: "Work in the paid-labor market, the subordination of women, heterosexism, and the driven and uncontrollable sexuality of men ... practices towards authority, control, competitive individualism, independence, aggressiveness, and the capacity for violence" (Messerschmidt 1993, 82; also Connell and Messerschmidt 2005). For Connell, moreover, the interplay between the body and constructions of masculinity is inescapable. The self, along with other kinds of power, is always constructed and reconstructed through the body. Connell therefore suggests that sexuality is not outside the realm of social and political power, but is instead a major site for its expression and production. Not only is the body the central location of gendered identity, it is historically and culturally coded to exclude certain sizes, shapes, features, and performances as not masculine or not feminine (Connell 1995, 45–66; Butler 1993b; Messerschmidt 2000). Although the mind and body are inseparably linked, dualisms associated with Cartesian philosophy designate man as *mind* and *rationality* and woman as *unruly body* and *emotion* (e.g., Grosz 1994; Lee 2006, 279). Within this mind-body dualism, the thinking subject is classified by not only gender, but also race and class. Thus, for Connell and Messerschmidt, racialized, underclass, and working-class men's structural exclusion from higher education and intellectual pursuits encourages them to drift into and valorize a bodily based masculinity defined through physical prowess, heterosexual potency, and rigorous bodily based work (Connell 1995, 55; 2000).

The irony, of course, is that for working-class men, manual labour is simultaneously at the heart of their masculinizing practices and at the core of their economic vulnerability as exploited wage labour (Connell 1995, 55). The body is the primary resource for asserting superiority over women and subjectifying themselves publicly and privately as holders of power for many working-class, underclass, and racialized men (Tomsen 2002; Seymour 2003; Kimmel, Hearns, and Connell 2005). But it follows that when masculinity is created through bodily-based accomplishments, "gender is vulnerable when the performance cannot be sustained" (Connell 1995, 54). Far from being a homogeneous practice, hegemonic masculinity is better appreciated as an authoritative set of practices that are never fixed or final. By adopting or refusing these practices, individual men may help to sustain or weaken patriarchal systems. While few men embody the hegemonic masculine norm in its entirety, most men consciously or subconsciously know how to compare themselves against that norm and the cultural ideal of manhood (Connell 1987, 184–5; Kaufman 1994, 147–8; Kimmel 2005, 235). Hegemonic masculinity is the configuration of gender practices that sustain men's collective power, rather than what individually powerful men actually embody, and it therefore assumes class- and race-specific styles and practices, and reflects the discursive and material reality of men's uneven access to economic and cultural resources for "making" masculinity (Connell 1987, 185). Connell, for example, distinguishes types of resistance to hegemonic masculinity: "protest masculinities," "complicit masculinities," and "marginalized masculinities," to name but three. Messerschmidt (2000, 110) also identifies "subordinated" and "oppositional" masculinities that develop along with hegemonic masculinity.

My intent is not to map a rapist masculinity, but to demonstrate empirically that gendering practices are choices, even though the options available are always influenced by wider social influences and constraints (Messerschmidt 2000, 86). Like Connell, I want to locate possibilities for changing masculinity within the realm of human agency, however restricted it may be. For me, the most dramatic context was watching men perform gender in a therapeutic medium and at interview sessions, and then watching the same men perform gender in a maximum-security prison. They became different types of men as different contingencies evoked different identities and proffered different behavioural scripts for performing gender and constituting subjecthood (Chunn and Lacombe 2000, 17; Foucault 1994b, 290–1).

James Messerschmidt's Adolescent Masculinities, the Body, and Violence

In *Nine Lives* (2000), Messerschmidt uses life-history research with nine white, working-class boys to examine links between violence and masculinity. His matched sample included three "non-violent" boys and six "violent boys" – three of whom were sexual offenders and three of whom were non-sexual assaultive offenders. Messerschmidt sought to identify the developmental and social patterns that explained why boys with similar class backgrounds had different relationships to forms of violence (2000, 15–17). Using the boys' recounted experiences and actions, Messerschmidt shows how – under certain social conditions and contextually defined situations – boys perceive their masculinity as threatened or challenged. He writes: "Because of its connection to hegemonic masculinity, for many men, violence serves as a suitable resource for constructing masculinity" (2007, 12). Messerschmidt found that the six violent boys were predisposed to using either sexual or assaultive behaviours for "constructing a particular kind of masculinity" that remedied masculinity challenges or otherwise ameliorated their subordinated masculine subjecthood. To varying degrees, the six violent boys grew up in working-class homes that accentuated toughness and fighting among men. Each of the sexual or assaultive offenders was also either a schoolyard bully or victim, and Messerschmidt emphasizes the interplay between home and school as a means of understanding what he calls "the social construction of violent predispositions" towards using forms of violence (83). Messerschmidt describes the assaultive boys as social offenders who perpetrated violence against other boys in public, while the sexual offenders were solitary and assaulted female relatives or young girls in private (89).

Messerschmidt also stresses the importance of the body in understanding different forms of crime. According to him, the key difference between sex offenders and assaultive offenders was that the sex offenders believed that they were unable to access their bodily masculinity to respond to schoolyard bullying and conflict with other boys (Messerschmidt 2007, 104). The three sex offenders constructed their masculinity to manage challenges through heterosexuality. More specifically, they engaged in coerced sex acts with weaker girls. In other words, each boy's sexual offending stemmed from the lived experiences of his body as a site of powerlessness in social interactions. In turn, the key difference between the six violent boys and the three non-violent boys was that the latter grew up in households that embodied egalitarian versus gendered divisions of labour, featured caring parents who emphasized non-violence in social interaction, and instilled alternative forms of communication for doing masculinity. Each non-violent boy had access to legitimate masculinizing alternatives to violence, and consciously refused, rather than appropriated, violence as the central definition of manhood (Messerschmidt 2007, 140–1).

Gendering Practices, Performatives, and Contradictions

The critical masculinities genre rejects a causal connection between biological sex and socially constructed gender. Gender is not derived naturally from male- and female-sexed bodies. Hence, women as well as men can be bearers of masculinity, and vice versa for femininity (Connell 1995, 230). While cultural norms for manhood and womanhood – including power relations between men and women – are inscribed and individualized during childhood, masculinity is not a simple or fixed essence embodied within men's bodies and then overtly expressed (see · Lusher and Robins 2007). Rather, gender is accomplished primarily through practical activities in material contexts that enact and re-enact masculinity and femininity. Messerschmidt (1993, 80) notes:

> We configure our behaviours so we are seen unquestioningly by others in particular social circumstances as expressing our "essential natures" – we do masculinity or femininity ... In this view, then, masculinity

is accomplished, it is not something done to men or something settled beforehand ... Rather, men construct masculinities in specific social situations (although not in circumstances of their own choosing); in so doing, men reproduce (and sometimes change) social structures.

Judith Butler and Carol Smart: Gendering Performatives and Practices

Gender can cross back and forth between sexed bodies through practices that temporarily masculinize and feminize subjects (Atmore 1999, 197; Marcus 1992). As Judith Butler (1992, 142) writes, "There need not be a 'doer behind the deed' ... 'the doer' is variably constructed in and through the deed." By Butler's account, many men's "terror of losing proper gender" (1993b, 238) may connect to more than misogyny or homophobia. If only subconsciously, this fear of being feminized reflects the possibility that any gendered identity – including hegemonic masculinity – is perpetually at risk and must repeat itself to maintain an illusion of a stable, coherent, masculine subject (Butler 1993a, 314). Paralleling Foucault's conceptualization of power, Butler sees gendered subjectification[3] as a practice that:

> "Knows" its own possibility of becoming undone; hence, its compulsion to repeat which is at once a foreclosure of that which threatens its coherence ... coherent gender, achieved through an apparent repetition of the same, produces as its *effect* the illusion of a prior and volitional subject. In this sense, gender is not a performance that a prior subject elects to do, but gender is *performative* in the sense that it constitutes as an effect the very subject it appears to express. (Butler 1993a, 314)

For Butler, the rules, rituals, and norms of compulsory heterosexual or other regulatory regimes *materialize* gender (1993b, 3–9, 18).

Inspired by Foucault's (1972) idea of subjectivity as "subject-position," Carol Smart (1995, 192) coined the term "gendering strategies" to include individual, social, and institutional practices for "bringing into being ... gendered subject-positions as well as subjectivities or identities to which the individual becomes tied or associated." Examples of gendered subject-positions include the rapist, the victim, the sex offender, the serial killer, and even, as Smart notes, man and woman. These are culturally and historically available discursive categories or interpretive possibilities – the effects of specific strategies and knowledge – that exist prior to the individuals that are encouraged to fill them (Smart 1995, 197). By gendered subjectivities or identities, Smart invokes Butler's notion of performatives, which unfold at the psychic level. For Butler, however, subjectification is more than the imposition of fixed subject-positions and the necessity of speaking from those sites. Instead, Butler re-centres human agency in sustaining identity. Individuals choose to identify with a particular subject-position and constantly commit and repeat gendered acts in order to maintain that subject-position. Gendered subjecthood is the result of repeated acts that embody gender norms, and does not exist apart from such acts, which reiterate and stabilize gender at social and psychic levels. This requirement of repetition signals that "identity is not self-identical," but must be "instituted again and again" (Butler 1993a, 315). Despite her conceptual similarity to and overlap with Connell and Messerschmidt, the latter represent pre-existing men and women as "performing gender," whereas Butler argues that there is no pre-existence. For her, gender performatives materialize the performer.

Butler and Smart agree that subjectivity is constructed in and through discourses, but focus on different moments. Butler emphasizes the psychic level by turning her attention to the cultural processes of claiming, elaborating, and reworking interpretive possibilities for individual subject formation. Smart emphasizes the social level by delineating the social construction of distinct subject-positions within institutional sites and their wider relationship to structures of domination and inequality. Together, the conceptual tools of performativity and gendering practices link the gender dimension of subjectivity at the psychic level to relatively enduring and culturally entrenched power-discourse matrices that extend beyond, and shape, the individual.

Rape as Performative and Gendering Practice

In a comment merging her own words with Catharine MacKinnon's, Chris Atmore writes that by accomplishing dominance, rape is something that involves and even creates gender, independent of, or at least partly autonomous from, the bodies of rapist and raped – and thus (citing MacKinnon), "a man is relatively permanently or relatively temporarily, [and/or] a female or a male woman" (1999, 198). Reflecting on male-to-male sexual relationships in prison, Richard Tithecott (1997, 156) concludes likewise that "whatever the sex of the player of the woman's role, masculinity is realized by that player's subordination."

Contrary to some critical masculinities scholarship, this suggests that it is not discourses and practices of heterosexism per se that produce a hegemonic masculine identity (e.g., Mooney-Somers and Ussher 2010). Rather, it is "the power to subordinate sexually" (Tithecott 1997, 154) that masculinizes and feminizes bodies by linking subject-positions to discourses that feminize victimization, particularly sex victims (see Weiss 2010, 277).

It is possible, then, to engage in rape as a practice for feminizing women or bodies in a manner that produces the effect of a masculine subject-position and a masculinized subjectivity (Bonnycastle 2000, 69). In this sense, rape generates masculine and feminine subjectivities at the psychic level, and the subject-positions of men and women at the social level. These effects, of course, are always temporal and always at risk of being undone. As Butler notes, gender is neither an internal psychic state nor a surface appearance, but is instead "the play between psychic and appearance," which allows for a separation of "bodily from psychic formations" and the loss and return of "signs of gender" (1993b, 234, 237). Although no one can choose not to perform gender, embodying, resisting, or subverting gender norms occurs not in conditions of the individual's choosing, but within wider socio-historic relations of "discipline, regulation, and punishment" (Butler 1993b, 231–2), which are always racialized and class-based.

Michael Kaufman: Theorizing Men's Contradictory Experiences of Power

Like other scholars theorizing masculinity, Michael Kaufman writes sympathetically and optimistically about changing men. Whether defined as power over oneself or power over others, contemporary manhood, he says, is commensurate with exercising power and control over something (1994, 145, 159). Indeed, Kaufman argues that the making of masculinities is a dehumanizing process that exacts extraordinary emotional penalties from individual men in exchange for the holy grail of men's power. He writes:

> In more concrete terms the acquisition of hegemonic (and most subordinate) masculinities is a process through which men come to suppress a range of emotions, needs, and possibilities, such as nurturing, receptivity, empathy, and compassion, which are experienced as inconsistent with the power of manhood. These emotions and needs do not disappear; they are simply held in check ... We dampen these emotions because they might

restrict our ability and desire to control ourselves or dominate the human beings around us on whom we depend for love and friendship. We suppress them because they come to be associated with the femininity we have rejected as part of our quest for masculinity. (148)

Kaufman accentuates the disjuncture between historically specific conceptualizations of male power and individual experiences of power and powerlessness. On the one hand, he notes that individual men benefit from the social power accrued simply from being born male. On the other hand, he observes that the discursive and social coupling of masculinity with power and control is also a source of men's pain and alienation. Kaufman explains:

A man's pain may be deeply buried, barely a whisper in his heart, or it may flood from every pore ... Whatever it is, the pain inspires fear for it means not being a man, which means, in a society that confuses gender and sex, not being a male. This means losing power and ungluing basic building blocks of our personalities. This fear must be suppressed for it is inconsistent with dominant masculinities ... The more we are the prisoners of the fear, the more we need to exercise the power we grant ourselves as men ... Paradoxically, men are wounded by the very way we have learned to embody and exercise our power. (149)

Kaufman calls this relationship between men's power and men's pain – which is part and parcel of gender acquisition and subsequent gendering practices – "men's contradictory experiences of power" (142).

Echoing Kaufmann's analysis, Kimmel notes that one of the principal emotions of hegemonic masculinity is the fear of being exposed as less than a man. From boyhood onwards, Kimmel says, men are teased and shamed into repressing their yearnings for love, along with emotions such as empathy, compassion, and kindness (1994; 2005, 42, 485). Drawing on the primary narratives of "real boys" in different social contexts, William Pollack (2000) also reveals the social pressures on boys and men to learn to "build what he calls a 'wall of toughness' and to learn to wear a 'mask of emotional bravado'" that diminishes healthy emotions and leaves them isolated (cited in Evans and Wallace 2008, 485). Together, Kaufman, Kimmel, and Pollack capture the motifs of fear, confusion, pain, and powerlessness associated with hegemonic masculinity and conveyed by all the men in my study.

When feminist analyses root the cause of rape in "the power men have over women" (cf. Matthews 1994, 149), they invoke an essentialist view of men's relationship to power. To avoid this, I draw on Kaufman's notion of men's contradictory experiences of power in their engagement with hegemonic masculinity. I delineate the individual effects of pervasive forms of oppression and alienation in my participants' lives on their gendering practices and performatives, without surrendering feminisms' macro analyses of women's systemic inequality within liberal market economies. In other words, I link local narratives into wider social patterns of gender relations without corroborating the meta-narrative of male power. I am mindful of the penal treatment refrain that reasons are not excuses. By foregrounding the sex offender's experiences of pain, power, and alienation, I am not excusing rape or hypothesizing that men's pain causes rape. Nor am I offering a grand theory of rape and sexual assault, which is too complex to capture in a single theory. Instead, like Kaufman, I hope that:

> An understanding of men's contradictory experiences of power enables us, when possible, to reach out to men with compassion, even as we are highly critical of particular actions and beliefs and challenge the dominant forms of masculinity. It can be one vehicle to understand how good human beings can do horrible things and how some beautiful baby boys can turn into horrible adults. It can help us understand how the majority of men can be reached with a message of change. (1994, 143)

I organize my analysis of the men's life histories along the lines inspired by this last passage. In the chapters to come, I draw out the dialectical relationship between men's power and pain as it pertains to the important subthemes emerging from my research: boyhood, family relations, schooling, work, and the formation of horrific adulthood.

Summary

This chapter began by demonstrating that the sex offender and the rapist are not only new types of people, but malleable subject-positions and sites of competing knowledge claims. I note that the conscious or unconscious representation of the rapist as a biological category that transcends men's structural locations within unequal power relations is predominant and problematic. If the categories of woman and man are relational, and if they are defined only in relation to one another, then ignoring the rapist's subjecthood weakens opportunities to produce a fully gendered theory of rape. Furthermore, this framing of the rapist leads to an easy misappropriation of certain feminist thinking for other political and penal purposes. Untethered from feminist theory and articulated again in cognitive behaviour models, these constructs around power and control, choice, and male accountability now fuel a discourse of sexual violence and prevention centred on the biological or psychological aberrations of *other* men, which I will explore in the next chapter.

To avoid some of the problems associated with feminist theories of rape, the following postulates gleaned from masculinities literatures (e.g., Connell, Kaufman, Kimmel, and Messerschmidt) and post-structural feminist theories (e.g., Butler, Cahill, Cameron and Frazer, Marcus, and Smart) will guide my life-history investigations.

1 Imposing gendered subjecthood is an ongoing practice that must be constantly repeated to produce and stabilize a subject. Gendering strategies and performatives materialize gendered subject-positions and gendered subjects (respectively). They do not emanate from an "always already" gender-inscribed body. Thus, psychic and bodily formations do not always overlap and bodies can lose and regain signs of gender.
2 Men's relationships to forms of violence must be situated within a social and discursive regulatory regime that requires the embodiment of gender norms and yet simultaneously constrains the material and cultural means for stabilizing gender norms for performing gender or "making masculinity," especially along the lines of race, class, age, sexuality, and the body.
3 Hegemonic masculinity is historically and culturally idealized in relation to femininities and all other masculinities. It is materialized in a given situation through practices and discourses that tie individuals to a multiplicity of race- and class-specific masculinizing themes. Given the impermanence of gender formation, subjectivity can be marked simultaneously by dominant, subordinated, and oppositional relationships to the hegemonic norm.
4 Notwithstanding that the exercise of power and control is constitutive of hegemonic masculinity, there is often a disjuncture between social and discursive expectations of men's power and individual men's lived relationship to power. Pain or estrangement from the

social relationships essential to human collective well-being often
coexists in a dialectical relationship with that power.

5 Stranger rape is a subjectifying practice of power for materializing
gender by tying the individual to one or more material and discursive practices formative of dominant masculine subjecthood. This
approach enables us to grasp practices formative of a dominant
masculinity rather than 'always already' men practising or expressing male dominance.

3 Of Mountain Goats and Rabbits: The Penal Context and the Company of Sex Offenders

You wouldn't find this in any regular maximum-security prisons. Here, prisoners have some sort of belief that everybody in this place subscribes to sanctuary. Like, a truce is recognized that nothing bad will happen.

(Kerry)[1]

This chapter discusses the institutional context of my study and my own impressions as a researcher over a period of seven months. First, I provide a short genealogy of the emergence of contemporary penal sex-offender treatment programs. Next, I show how the sex-offender program (SOP) gives participants the discursive and practical tools for linking themselves to neoliberal citizenship, as well as to new forms of hegemonic masculinity.

The Penal Context as a Site of Research

Kerry's observation above was in response to my comment that the treatment centre does not feel like a maximum-security prison. Indeed, sex offenders and other protective custody (PC) prisoners are mixed together with general population convicts, many of whom are transferred to the treatment centre from penitentiaries where PCs are permanently segregated to ensure that other prisoners do not harm them. Despite a lack of overt security, prisoners coexist and share institutional space mostly without major incidents. Most of the staff are female treatment, clerical, or administrative employees dressed in street clothes rather than uniforms. Guards are visible on the breezeways primarily during shift changes and at meal times.

   The treatment centre features both the old and new trappings of the Canadian maximum-security penitentiary. Two fourteen-foot-high steel fences, movement sensors, and miles of razor ribbon wire encircle the cinder-block, two-storey complex. Security vehicles continuously circle and monitor the perimeter road. Staff and visitors enter by passing through six steel doors and gates, four of which are operated electronically by stationed uniformed guards. Behind the walls, prisoners are observed and controlled through camera surveillance, parabolic listening devices, and two tinted, bullet-proof security domes centrally located on each floor. Rifle portals are also strategically positioned to fire down each of four separate corridors, known as living unit ranges. From within these security domes, or "bubbles," guards electronically open and lock individual cells and operate a system of gates and solid steel fire barricades, which independently seal each of the eight ranges in the unit. Each range contains sixteen cells, many of which are double-bunked to accommodate program participants. Cells contain neither toilets nor sinks. After evening lock-up, prisoners must "buzz" security staff to unlock cell doors and open the electronic gate sealing the range from the washroom.

   The treatment centre dining room serves three meals per day, which are identical for prisoners and staff. The eating area is divided into prisoner and non-prisoner sections and seats four to a table. Due to this arrangement, I spent seven months in conversation with a range of staff, including psychologists, psychiatrists, community parole officers, vocational instructors, guards, the Native elder and liaison officer, secretaries, nurses, senior administrators, and treatment program facilitators. Penal authorities issued me a visitor gate pass so I could travel unescorted throughout the centre. Neither prisoners nor staff made me feel uncomfortable, unwelcome, or unsafe. Convicts walked slowly along the breezeways with their eyes focused straight ahead, and did not make unkind remarks or physical threats. Over time, some of the men from the group I was observing greeted me on the breezeway. Eventually, a few participants from other programs nodded their heads in my direction. Otherwise, I felt invisible. Many female staff, however, shared their trepidation about mingling with men convicted for sexually assaulting and killing women. One young nurse who facilitated the violent offender program (VOP) felt that sex offenders were "stalking" her when she walked up and down the breezeway. A clerical worker asked me to accompany her when she walked to lunch, fearful that a sex offender might attack en route to the dining hall. I was warned repeatedly – by women clerical staff members who never interacted personally with prisoners – that the SOP participants were slick and dangerous.

The SOP participants were acutely aware that many of the predominantly female treatment staff feared them. This produced resentment in some men, and embarrassment and self-consciousness in others. In contrast to the prisoners attending violent offender programs, many SOP participants went out of their way to make female staff feel more comfortable around them. They were polite, articulate, and more sociable than other prisoners, though such social graces often backfired and added to female fears. One nurse attributed this difference in demeanour to sex offenders' dysfunctional need for approval. Another told me that sex offenders require highly developed social skills for "grooming" their victims. She was convinced that whenever sex offenders speak with women, they engage in covert deviant sexual fantasies. The sex offenders themselves, however, told me that they are extra polite because they know that many women are uneasy around them. Michel, one of my participants, told me that when we were alone together in a classroom he was careful never to stand between me and an exit. He also said he deliberately matched my rapid stride when we walked along the breezeway so that I would not be afraid of him attacking me from behind.

The only unsettling experience I had in prison occurred on my first day as a visitor. A clinical administrator instructed me not to feminize myself by wearing "miniskirts or see-through blouses." He told me that front gate staff would evaluate my apparel every morning before granting me entry. I found it remarkable that he perpetuated two old rape myths, both of which were discredited as part of the prison treatment program. First, he insinuated that women's style of dress can provoke undesirable, even uncontrollable, behaviour in men. Second, he suggested that women must take responsibility for such reactions by policing their conduct and appearance. Ironically, I de-feminized myself so effectively that, on one occasion, a female guard advised me against wearing my bulky green coat because I blended in so well with the prisoners that "if something went down," I might be "mistaken for a prisoner and shot." On another occasion, I was standing on the breezeway and waiting for my scheduled interview subject to arrive. An older guard approached, and as he pulled level with me, he suddenly did a double-take and laughed; he said he had nearly mistaken me for a transsexual prisoner!

At the time of my study, the treatment centre ran three different intensive SOPs and three intensive VOPs for high-risk prisoners. The eight-month programs had staggered start dates but operated simultaneously. Prisoners convicted for other crimes openly revile sex offenders, and as a result, every prisoner with any historical sexually related convictions is placed in an SOP, regardless of his current offence. To be accepted into the treatment program, prisoners must be able to read and write at a Grade 6 level. The prison also ran a SOP and a VOP with an equivalent, but less cognitively challenging, curriculum for those who did not qualify for the regular program due to illiteracy, head injuries, or impairments such as foetal alcohol syndrome (see Lacombe 2008). Subsequent to my participation, the CSC accredited the National Sex Offender Program for low and moderate-risk sex offenders based on similar cognitive behavioural principles. The expanded treatment centre now includes an intensive domestic violence treatment program.

Even though CSC treatment programs combine men who have sexually assaulted women with those who have sexually assaulted children, the two groups do not relate much to one another. Men with offences against women are usually repulsed by the idea of sexual desire for girls or boys, particularly if a participant has a history of boyhood sexual abuse. In turn, most men convicted for sex acts with children, many of whom maintain that they loved their child victims and did not coerce or harm them, are horrified by the idea of beating, raping, and killing the subjects of their sexual desire. As one participant in my study observed:

> Pedophiles I find are a lot different – they can justify and they can deny and minimize like nobody I've ever *seen* before, [for example] they're "teaching the kid to have sex," "the kid loves it." Some of the things I've heard make me go off my fucking rocker. I ate them alive every day. The facilitators in my first program appreciated that I could identity as a victim and make [group members] face the harsh realities that their actions could have turned kids into people like me. But not everybody acts out who gets abused either. (Cam)

Most of the men in my study felt directly or indirectly coerced to volunteer for more and more programming. Many federal prisoners must complete and repeat intensive programs to satisfy their correctional plan recommendations and garner support for transfers to lower security prisons and forms of conditional release. Although correctional policy states that no prisoner can be treated without his or her freely given consent, a sex offender who refuses to attend recommended treatment programs knows that, as an "untreated" or "unsatisfactorily treated" sex offender, he will stay in prison until the end of his sentence. Consider the following passage from a prisoner's evaluation file:

> Mr. [Prisoner] has done extensive programming in the past including a sex offender program. Mr. [Prisoner] would seem to be of the opinion that he has only to hold the program certificate in his hand and ignores the fact that he must strive to fully internalize the program material. In order to manage his risk in the community, he is required to COMPLETE the Intensive Sex Offender Program. He was told that he was the only one who could take responsibility for his own destiny. He needs to take the SOP or else wait until his Warrant Expiry Date [thereby extending his sentence by almost nine years]. (Assessment for Decision Report 2000, 171)

In other words, a prisoner who declines voluntary required programming will serve his entire sentence in a penal institution.

In the Company of Sex Offenders

Before I arrived at the prison, fourteen group members and their two program facilitators unanimously agreed to allow me to observe their treatment group, which was already in progress. The two facilitators were career CSC staff rather than contract employees; the male facilitator had a master's degree in education and the female facilitator was a registered nurse. Both were attentive to how language shaped and damaged self-identity, and they opted not to distinguish participants by crime categories, as rapists or murderers, but instead identified them by animal icons, as mountain goats or rabbits, by group consensus. When the program ended, I approached each group member individually to request an in-depth interview. I discussed the topics I planned to cover, and gave them the opportunity to ask questions about my research, such as how I planned to use my data. Each group member accepted my request. The men were at ease speaking in my presence about topics they did not routinely discuss with others, let alone with women (see Schultz 2004). Two participants, Bob and Harvey, explained their comfort level as follows:

I would never have talked as much as I did if I was uncomfortable with you being in group. Never one time did I have a problem with you being there. But I would never have been able to do this interview a couple of years ago. I couldn't talk about my crime. (Bob)

It's different with you, Kevin. If you hadn't been in our group the last few months, you probably would have got a lot of us not talking, or [saying], "I don't want to talk about it." But because you were there, we're past that part. You basically know who we are. (Harvey)

I triangulated my methods using life history interviews, group observations, and file data supplemented with CSC sex-offender treatment manuals, instructional group hand-outs, and archival material from regional treatment centres. These documents demonstrated how staff mobilized and articulated the dominant discourse of penal governance, and so gave meaning to the penal context. I also verified data I received from each of the fourteen prisoners. I found no significant discrepancies between their accounts in interviews, in group sessions, and in their official files. Each prisoner knows that treatment staff can verify his story against police reports, judicial sentencing comments, trial transcripts, victim statements, media stories, witness and family interviews, psychology reports, and more. In fact, in interview and group sessions, the men volunteered new, often negative information that did not appear in their files. In grappling with the question of honesty and accuracy, I concluded that those who admitted to rape and murder would have little reason to misrepresent details about their boyhoods, schools, and work experiences.

Beyond triangulation, participants' opinions of each other also informed my research. Most participants offered their beliefs about which group members were, in their words, "real." They pointed out discrepancies and consistencies between others' behaviour in group sessions and on the cell range. Each man emphasized that prison demands a certain presentation of self, and each acknowledged that he wore different faces in the prison and treatment environments. Paradoxically, while saying their own prison personas were not real, many of these men seemed to take those of other group members at face value. Additionally, many participants had been together in past treatment groups. They had served lengthy portions of their sentences in each other's company, and some had grown up together in prison. Their evaluations of each other were thought-provoking and fair, and offered me another layer of evidence that confirmed the validity and reliability of my data.

In the end, I concluded that the men shared their stories with me as honestly as can be reasonably expected of any research participant. While there may be exaggerations or embellishments, they are likely minor, since each subject had little reason to lie or distort the truth to a person they knew could fact-check their narratives. As Stephanie Kane observes:

> Both observer and observed are caught in a web of partial fiction and ambiguous truths … But my participants also had access to ethnographic data in a much more protracted sense than I. It is only the hubris of scholars and fools that attributes more value to the truths arising out of professional visits than those of a good storyteller who has lived her life close to the scene – even if she is embellishing her character. The value of different versions of truth depends on audience and purpose. (1998, 94–5)

In my interactions with the group members, I was by default the person in authority due to my non-prisoner status. During interview encounters the men asked me where they should sit, when they could break for a smoke, when I wanted to interview them next, and so on. Each man walked a half-step behind me, which is how prisoners accompany penal staff. When I observed the treatment group sessions, participants avoided direct eye contact with me. In interviews, they eschewed incidental touching, such as when passing me pencils, paper, or coffee mugs. While intended to be respectful, these gestures were sometimes disconcerting, but were also precautionary. No sex offender can defend himself against a female staff member's complaint that he makes her feel uncomfortable or fearful. During our interviews, many men shared personal experiences that illustrate that they can never forget that they are sex offenders. Cam recounts:

> Staff views us as uncontrollable animals. For instance, we had an older, heavier-set woman working in the kitchen. One day, she had her makeup all done and her hair. I'm not saying it was an attractive thing. But it was beyond her norm of being all wet and sweaty with a flat colour to her face. I say, "You look really good today." And she told a guard she felt sexually threatened and I was grabbed by the guards and called out on the carpet. It hurts when you're not believed and belittled by something that ain't true. If it was true, I would have laughed it off with the guards and said,

"Hey, I'm a lifer, anything looks good." And I'm sorry to say, there was a split second of fantasy in my mind where I could just shut my feelings off and hurt somebody … I could visualize just smashing her head in. We have to learn that we're just fucking animals.

My Sample of Sex Offenders

My data and discussion cannot provide conclusions about sex offenders generally, or stranger rapists specifically. My sample is statistically un-representative, as many offenders or rapists remain neither detected nor convicted (Cowburn 2005, 225). As a result, the extent to which con-victed and non-convicted stranger rapists differ or not cannot be known. The men in my study all came from working-class or underclass back-grounds. My sample included a mill worker, an auto worker, a hospital orderly, a welder, two manual labourers, and several men who were unemployed or never employed. Eight of the men I interviewed were of European descent, five self-defined as Aboriginal (includes status and non-status Natives, Métis, and Inuit), and one was a third-generation racialized Canadian. The overrepresentation of Aboriginal people in Canadian prisons is common knowledge and CSC statisticians report a larger proportion of Aboriginal sex offenders relative to their population. In 2004, Aboriginal prisoners represented approximately 17 per cent of all federal offenders and 23 per cent of all sex offenders under federal jurisdiction (Motiuk and Vuong 2005). My sample over-represents con-victed Aboriginal sex offenders.

My sample is also skewed in terms of the length of sentence served in prison. Most sexual assault convictions do not result in long-term or indeterminate sentences. The Corrections Services Research Branch re-ports that fewer than one in four sex offenders receive a federal sen-tence of two years or more. In 2002, the average sentence length for federally convicted sex offenders was just under four years (Boe, Motiuk, and Nafekh 2004). In large part, the sentence length in my sam-ple is directly related to the degree of harm perpetrated against their victims. Eleven men in my study are serving forms of indeterminate life sentences. Of those, three are designated *dangerous offenders*, four are serving mandatory *life-twenty-five* sentences for first-degree murder, three are serving life sentences for second-degree murder with parole eligibility dates that range from ten to fifteen years, and one is serving a life sentence for attempted murder. The other three men have deter-minate sentences with statutory release dates. At the time of my research, each man had served from four to seventeen years, with an average of ten, in their current sentence. The total time served for all federal convictions, however, ranged from four years to over thirty, with an average of fourteen.

At the time of my interviews, participants ranged from 23 to 51 years of age. The average was 35.5, lower than the federal average of 44. At the time of conviction for their current offence, participants' ages ranged from 16 to 42, with an average of 25.5. Five men were serving a second prison term for a conviction related to sexual assault. Taking prior adult convictions under consideration, the average age for first federal conviction for a sex offence was 23 years, significantly lower that the overall average of 39 for first admission for sexual offences. Taking all disclosed sexual assaults under consideration, the average age for first commission of any form of sexual assault in my sample was 21.

Six of these fourteen men committed interracial rapes, which are statistically less common than intraracial rapes (e.g., Cahill 2001, 213–4). In one instance, a man purposively targeted the ethnic group of the girlfriend who had just broken up with him. In another, a man deliberately targeted women from racial and ethnic groups other than his own to reduce the risk of being recognized, either during the assault or later at cultural events. For the rest of the participants, victims' race and ethnicity were a result of social relations or geographical proximity.

Finally, due in large part to penal treatment programs, the verbal and analytical skills of the men in my sample were more developed than those of sex offenders who had not participated in penal treatment programs. While five men in my sample had no high school education, six had Grade 8 or 9, and only three had Grade 10 or higher, they were all able to speak for themselves and reflect on how penal power worked through them as sex offenders. For example, the treatment program emphasized the alleged affinity between sexual assault and power and control as a way to understand participants' thoughts, feelings, and behaviours. While few men in my study fully accepted that approach, most of their stories were influenced by the discourse of power and control, and each participant illustrated more generally how power and control worked in his own life.

I turn now to an examination of the "conditions of the emergence and operation" of those contemporary penal sex offender programs (Foucault 1990, 73). I examine how certain descriptive statements are considered true, or how a particular discourse is rendered intelligible, while other possibilities and truths are excluded (Foucault 1972, 118–20). In particular, I illustrate how key elements of neoliberal thought have emerged in Canadian prisons and discuss how a new type of penal subject shaped my participants ability to talk about themselves.

The Decentring of Disease Models

From the mid-1930s to the mid-1960s, Canada's penal philosophy emphasized rehabilitation and reform, sometimes referred to as the disease model (Archambault 1938; Fauteux 1956). Official penal discourse centred on individual diagnoses, cure, and treatment, rather than on punishment (Ratner 1984, 146). This focus on psychological and medical discourses represented a break from earlier policies, which claimed that convicts could be reformed through solitary confinement, regulated labour, and religious instruction. Twenty years later, in the mid-1950s, Canada's then-commissioner of penitentiaries described this medical approach to penal philosophy as follows:

> The asocial and antisocial types of individuals who are sentenced by the courts to the penal system have failed through unfortunate circumstances and the vicissitudes of their past life to develop mentally as the average person does ... Reformation ... is the ultimate aim of incarceration. (cited in Griffiths and Cunningham 2000, 54)

This passage highlights one dimension of crime control thinking associated with the former welfare state, namely, that society is implicated in the causes of crime and the state has a role to play in its solution (Garland 1990; 2001). But this may have been more rhetoric than reality. A psychologist in Kingston Penitentiary, which was the flagship for inmate treatment in the 1960s, recalls: "Treatment consisted of individual counselling and occasional group work of an amorphous nature, menial work programs, and extensive use of medication and ECT [electroconvulsive therapy] for psychiatrically disturbed inmates" (Gendreau 1996, 144–5). As this statement shows, not all treatment could take place on the societal level.

By the late 1970s, Western penology had all but abandoned the disease model. However, in the late 1980s and against the grain of other Western penal systems, the CSC underwent massive structural reorganization motivated by the desire for "good corrections." The CSC's new mission document re-inscribed rehabilitation, reformation, and reintegration as its core goals (Jackson 2002, 33–7; Moore and Hannah-Moffat 2004). Yet within the new system, there is no theory of rape or sexual assault that informs treatment practices or risk assessments. On the one hand, the treatment program insists there is a causal nexus between thinking about and committing rape, and suggests it is motivated by distorted beliefs and unhealthy attitudes towards power and control (Blanchette 1996, 50). Arguably, this sounds like a clinical appropriation of feminist discourse about power imbalances between men and women. On the other hand, penal treatment practices also reflect psychopathological theories in which rape is said to spring from deviant sexual preferences and impulses that are scientifically measurable through a penile plethysmograph[2] (e.g., Marshall et al. 2006). In practice, old and new theories work together, as is apparent in one of the program idioms that sex offenders are expected to apply to their behaviours: "I have the power, but no control."

Discourses and practices associated with the disease model of rape are still evident. Some convicted sex offenders, for example, are still adjudged to suffer from organic or mental disorders that cause them to offend. Such a diagnosis warrants pharmaceutical intervention, particularly Zoloft, to reduce sexual arousal. Each man I interviewed was also clinically diagnosed using the DSM IV criteria for psychiatric disorders. The programs that I observed were called the Intensive Treatment Program for Sex Offenders and the Personality Disorder Program. Staff often referred to prisoners as patients or clients and assigned a primary nurse to each. Prison cells were renamed houses and living ranges were renamed wards to emphasize the therapeutic character of care. However, cognitive behavioural models have begun to replace the view that rape is caused by underlying diseases or mental disorders. In this approach, the cardinal directive to sex offenders is that urges do not control behaviour. Rather, giving in to an urge is "an active decision, an intentional choice" for which sex offenders are responsible (Pithers 1990, cited by Janus 2000, 82). One consequence of this approach is that sex offenders who are not mentally disordered, yet insist that "something just came over them," are tagged as either in denial or refusing to take responsibility for their behaviours. Even sex offenders who accept responsibility for their choices, but whose recall is uncertain, present problems for prison staff, as illustrated in the risk assessment report by a prison psychiatrist: "Although Mr. [Prisoner] accepts responsibility for his crime, he used subtle strategies to minimize the impact of his responsibility. For example, he stresses his level of intoxication, the impulsive nature of the act, the patchy aspects of his recall." Under prevailing treatment logic, the most apparently impulsive and explosive behaviours are divided into patterns of consecutive and identifiable decision-making stages. Sex offenders do not simply lose control; in treatment, they mine their pasts for numerous signs that preceded, accompanied, and forecast their crimes. This recognition is now crucial for contemporary penal subjects.

Penalizing Choice and Risk

> I can use my deterrents now. I avoid all fantasies that are high risk for me. I told my parents, "It's all about choices. I didn't have to do what I did. Nobody made me go do what I did." I go through my crime *every* day. How could I have avoided that situation? I didn't experience choice at that time. But that's what I look at every day. The choices I had. Back then I didn't know there was choices. (Bob)

Bob's words illustrate the effects of the techniques that characterize CSC's contemporary sex offender treatment program as a way of governing problems (O'Malley 2006; 2008). This discourse is not penal specific, but reflects neoliberal subjecthood and new practices for supporting specific forms of social order that govern at a distance (Rose 1996, 53–4). Risk, choice, and responsibility are three key constructs that shape this new form of "good citizen" subjectivity (Adamoski, Chunn, and Menzies 2002, 12). The relative decline of Canada's collective welfare state and the reduction of social spending through privatization now require an autonomous rather than a dependent citizen. The neoliberal citizen is expected to refuse a "client mentality" (Rose 1996, 52) and instead adopt self-government practices that call for active, rational decision-making. The good citizen is a responsible subject of risk who is encouraged to create an individual social safety net and, through prudential use of actuarial data, expert advice manuals, and risk-evaluation measures, assume responsibility for preventing future risk. The everyday language and actions of penal authorities and prison subjects alike incorporate neoliberal logic. For example, consider how Simpson, an Aboriginal prisoner completing his eight-month sex offender treatment program, rescripts his life history. His words display an effect of neoliberalism conceived of in penal terms:

The things that happened to me, I took on myself because even at seven or eight years old, I hold myself responsible and accountable, right? 'Cause of the options that were there. I could have run away, but the fear of being hurt was stronger than wanting to run away. But the option was there. The choice. I have the capacity of doing anything in my life that I choose, and I know that now. Instead of making a difference with all these things that make me angry, I chose to become a part of what that is and make *more* of it. I chose to live a life that's dishonoured my grand-mothers and grandfathers. I chose to become a symbol of all that's ugly and shit that exists in the culture. That's a shameful thing. I'm working on my positive power now. I've made a conscious choice to honour my grandfather. (Simpson)

The idea that particular forms of economic and political organiza-tion demand specific types of subjectivity and new techniques of power to promote that subjectivity is not novel. According to Michel Foucault (1979), disciplinary techniques and practices such as drills, timetables, and cellular architectures institutionalized in many Western prisons by the late nineteenth century were strategies to ren-der bodies "docile and useful" (138), especially for the labour require-ments of early capitalism (221). Within the emerging modern prison, discipline created a specific type of individual whose attributes meshed with existing production mechanisms and emerging demo-cratic forms (219). Eventually, discipline based on surveillance, nor-malized judgement, and constant examination became the "general formulas of domination" (137) and spread into the general popula-tion, which led Foucault and others to talk about the formation of a disciplinary society.

However, as a result of shifts from Keynesian welfarism to neo-liberalism (e.g., Pratt 2000), the docile body as an object of power is no longer relevant to neoliberal governance. The latter presupposes an active subject – an individual who can assume responsibility for self-change and self-regulation – and who willingly adopts risk-based techniques. The following passages regarding Michel exem-plify the new neoliberal sex offender who has learned "to recognize and deal with his arousal cues by self-monitoring his thoughts, feel-ings, body signs, and high-risk situations that otherwise could lead to impulsive acting out" (SOP Program Objectives, individualized file entry). Speaking for himself about the official program discourse, Michel elaborates:

I see the progression. I can feel the progression. Even the way I think – the way things irritate me. And then, I start fantasizing about being confrontational with people. The next thing will be violent fantasies. And then sexually violent fantasies. It's a progression I've been through many times. I haven't been through it in a long time because I'm aware of it now, and I make the effort to stop it.

This form of subjectivity is simultaneously an effect of specific penal measures and of wider cultural and political pressures to actively and reflexively practice freedom by taking responsibility for unhealthy, irrational lifestyle choices.

Michel is not alone. Each man I interviewed for this book offers a unique rendition and reworking of his past and present. As we shall see, all fourteen stories are shaped by the key constructs, vocabularies of motive, and helping techniques presented in the sex offender program, which, in effect, enable subject *and* state to monitor individual risk. Consequently, the storytelling combines lived biographical and therapy-constructed realities, and reveals the flow of governance into the recollections and self-awareness that these memories authorize. The men came to learn and speak a neoliberal discourse through the program. Their narratives embody many of the knowledge claims that penal policymakers and cognitive behaviour theorists currently hold. As a result, my life history data cannot be isolated from the understanding my participants derived from the eight-month treatment regime in which they were immersed. Each man had completed at least one eight-month intensive SOP, and several were participating in their third or fourth. Without this common intensive treatment regime, the men's discourse on choice, individual responsibility, power and control, and sexual offending – which anchored each account – would, in all likelihood, be absent.

Neoliberalizing Sex Offenders

In my opinion, Mr. [Prisoner] can reduce his risk to re-offend by targeting the following risk factors in an intensive institutional treatment programme:

a. Explosive violence
b. Rejection
c. Substance use
d. Manipulation
e. Relationships with women
f. Power/Control
g. Self-focus/Callousness
h. Frustration/Anger
i. Accepting responsibility

Following the successful completion of treatment, Mr. [Prisoner] may be a manageable risk for the community if he does the following:

a. Participates meaningfully in ongoing and frequent programming targeting the risk factors above.
b. Participates in counselling with the goal of developing a crime-cycle, detailing his risk factors.
c. Participates meaningfully in a sex offender relapse prevention program with a demonstrated internalization of treatment gain.
d. Remains substance free.
e. Remains open to disclosure with his supervisors.
d. Maintains frequent (i.e., at least weekly) contact with community support persons to ensure close supervision.

This body of opinion was part of a package of recommendations from a psychological/psychiatric risk assessment administered to Fred before his third intensive SOP. The risk factors are interchangeable with those of the other men I studied. There are no references to rehabilitation or reformation; rather, the report highlights the dominance of risk management discourse, objectives, and practices in the penal control of sex offenders and valorizes the necessity for penal subjects to manage their own risk. I will now examine intensive treatment programs for sex offenders so as to provide a context for understanding prisoner's life histories.

CSC's core assumption is that crime is caused by people who think incorrectly and surround themselves with irrational beliefs and distorted perceptions that they then use to justify antisocial behaviour. As Stephen Duguid (2000, 185–6) notes, positing deficits as developmental in origin creates a type of criminality that can be tempered through cognitive retraining. Such retraining is organized around group sessions, in which program members participate in cognitive restructuring exercises designed to identify and confront the core irrational beliefs that sustain their antisocial attitudes and destructive emotions. Participants complete regular homework assignments, such as thinking reports, assumption logs, and feeling journals. They put themselves into discourse, which enables experts to gaze at them and detect and correct erroneous or irrational thinking (Corkel 2003; Fox 1999). The conceptions of appropriate sex and sexuality, of course, are key treatment objectives. For example, the men are encouraged to fantasize responsibly. Michel explains:

Until the end of my third program I was still having, not rape fantasies, but porno kinds of images. And I changed them. I changed what I was thinking about during this sexuality module – orgasmic reconditioning. I didn't *follow* their guidelines, but it gave me a kick in the ass to start changing my fantasies, and seeing what *I* liked. And I was surprised to find out the switch from porno and meaningless sex to meaningful – enjoyable for both her and I – fantasy was actually a lot more enjoyable for me. But I know if I was ever to slip into a deep depression – let myself go – my fantasies would go back to being aggressive.

In their program sessions, each man had to speak recurrently about sex and examine his particular relationship to sex and women. Some program facilitators required prisoners to keep sexual fantasy logs and had staff monitor them for healthy or unhealthy thoughts. Sex offenders were routinely asked about their sexual fantasies, their consensual sexual practices, and their intimate relationships with women. Indeed, their official files were layered with comments about sexual acts and fantasies that transgressed the missionary sexual position and conveyed the message that these behaviours were clinical manifestations of sexual deviance.

The unstated assumptions are twofold. First, if rape resides in specific bodies, then individual rapists' ideas about and experiences with sex and women will yield the truth about rape and provide clues for risk management. Second, rapists are a subgroup of the sex offender classification whose lived and imagined relationships to sex distinguishes them from both violent offenders and all other men. In short, sex offenders don't use sex properly, and sex is therefore a logical site for surveillance, intervention, and self-management. Consider Bob, who learned to micro-manage the sex-aggression inside his head:

BOB: Deviant sex for me, excluding rape fantasies, [*pauses*] would be aggressive sex. Hard. Fast-paced.

Q: Is that always deviant?

BOB: I would have to say yes. But it also depends. Am I doing it because I'm in a shitty mood? That would be bad. Or, if a woman suggested it in real life, and you did it, that might not be so bad. It depends how far you let yourself go. I'm pretty good at self-analysing myself and stopping myself from certain things, so, I might be able to get away with something like that if it's what a woman wanted. But I don't think it would be good to think of it on my own.

In the treatment programs, group facilitators helped the men investigate the causal processes that underlie sexual offences. This was expressed
in language that helped offenders to understand the connections between
their antisocial attitudes and their criminal conduct, and was imple-
mented through having participants write life stories and crime autobiographies and present them orally to their peers for insight. Facilitators
thwarted all socio-structural understandings of group members' lives by
giving them an instructional sheet that outlined what to include in their
life stories. Some treatment facilitators even instructed the men to eliminate events that staff believed were not pertinent to understanding the
origins of sexual offending. In addition, during group sessions, facilitators used a range of discursive strategies that isolated sex offenders from
other men and prevented group members from making links between the
personal and political. Standardized admonitions – such as *stick with your
own stuff; this is about what you did; you're not the victim; you're different from
other men, you raped a woman*; and *life's unfair, deal with it* – reinforced individual responsibility for rape and eschewed wider socio-cultural causes.
James recounts:

> If you don't know why you did it, you don't know how to stop it from
> happening again. My offence was nothing beyond my control. I acted
> without thinking. There's reasons. I'd like it much better if I could blame
> it on something else other than myself. But I can't. I made the decision.

The men, however, did not simply retrieve memories; they worked
on them in therapy to infuse past mental images and events with
emotional dimensions that they could neither name nor comprehend the first time those feelings were lived. To help subjects revisit
their old feelings, facilitators distributed a handout depicting fifty
cartoon faces. Each expressed a different emotion for subjects to label. Consequently, every participant I interviewed displayed good
emotional literacy. In regards to his own emotional development,
Charlie observes:

> If you had asked me how I felt back then, I would have said "fuck you."
> [*Laughs grimly.*] I wasn't aware of any feelings. I just felt I was having a
> shitty life, getting drunk was the only fun thing I had to do, and it wasn't
> all that fun. I would never have said I felt lonely or angry or hurt. I didn't
> even know I was angry. I wasn't aware of any feelings. I have the ability

now – the program has given me some enlightenment about what my feelings were back then.

Throughout the program, treatment staff used interconnected discourses about risk, responsibility, and choice to persuade the men to think in certain ways and to take charge of their own self-regulation. Bear approaches this technique this way:

> I practice being aware of myself – my thinking, my feelings, why I'm feeling. I question myself all the time. It's still a struggle not to go back to that person that holds stuff in. Right now, I'm looking at things I've done and why I've done it to somebody. And I've become aware of things that trigger my anger, trigger my self-worthlessness. It's something that's never going to go away. It's always going to be a part of my life, and that's something I'm going to learn to come to terms with and work on every day.

At the end of the program, participants design individual risk instruments for predicting future criminogenic events and for self-governing their own high-risk factors. The thoughts, feelings, and behaviours that participants recall through life exercises and crime autobiographies are used to build two interrelated risk tools to predict and prevent sexual assault relapse. First, each man must build a crime cycle, a model for reducing a complex, multi-determined sexual offence into a cognitively manageable set of discrete decision-making stages that lead up to sexual assault. At each stage, he must include the cognitive-emotional-behavioural chains associated with each situation. A key assumption of crime cycle construction is that a man in his cycle will advance towards acting out unless he recognizes and disrupts his behavioural cycle with appropriate coping strategies. In essence, the crime cycle creates new choices for the men to manage. Second, after building crime cycles, treatment staff help each man isolate the thoughts, feelings, and actions that make his relapse more likely. Typical high-risk factors or *triggers* include anger, suspicion, shame, alcohol, deviant fantasies, self-pity, boredom, pornography, resentment, sarcasm, frustration, isolation, depression, and low self-confidence. Once identified, participants must devise individual coping responses to manage each trigger. In turn, these management techniques become part of a larger relapse prevention plan that each man must produce, revise, and demonstrate.

From my perspective, these risk tools are rather narrow, and they disconnect rape itself from any general theories of why some men rape. Triggers describe, rather than explain, the subjective conditions that underlie the decision to rape. Once sex offenders are programmed, rape recidivism is no longer a matter of having no control in their lives (which might be true), but rather of choosing not to use one's individual self-control practices. This seems to me to be an extreme form of individualizing responsibility and accountability for rape, and raises at least five questions. First, how and why do such a variety of risk factors produce the same response in men? Second, why are so many emotions high-risk for men? Third, how can such variation across risk factors be remedied by a common set of cognitive strategies? Fourth, when a man is "at risk to relapse," why does he choose to rape a woman as opposed to acting out in other ways? Finally, how does rape come to be expressive of deeper emotional turmoil?

Summary

Individualized penal risk strategies in the 1990s and after demand a new form of penal subjecthood – an active neoliberal individual, rather than a docile person – who, along with all neoliberal citizens, can assume responsibility for self-regulation and adapt customized risk-based techniques (e.g., Bosworth 2007). Within this discursive regime, cognitive behavioural models that emphasize rationality, unconstrained choice, and individual accountability for solving problems and managing risk are eclipsing the disease model of rape that went hand-in-hand with the welfare state. While the causes of criminality remain core objectives, they are not targeted for eradication. Rather, the strategy is to identify dysfunctional behavioural patterns and individual risk factors amenable to self-management practices. While they appear to dovetail with feminist ideas that rape is a choice, treatment experts teach sex offenders to use the language of choice to pathologize their specific actions at points in time, rather than encouraging them to develop a context for choice within wider structural relations of power that link the personal to the political. In doing so, program talk evinces what Scully calls "the rape-supportive elements of our culture" (1990, 166). This includes the structural subordination of women and children, and the marginalization of working-class, underclass, non-heterosexual, and racialized men. Moreover, penal sex offender treatment programs create new choices for performing gender that do not disturb or challenge hegemonic masculinities.

The next two chapters present the life history stories of the men in my treatment group. Of course, each narrative is, in some measure, an effect of penal power and a product of group-constructed reality. These stories are replete with culturally circulating scripts about appropriate fatherhood, motherhood, and family life; ideals of manhood, woman-hood, and heterosexuality; and the character of men's power, since each of my subjects implicitly or explicitly measured his lived reality against social constructions of what he thought was normal in these areas. Penal programs neither explored the feminist question of whether rape is about sex or violence, nor explored links among rape, masculinity, race, class, and gendering practices. Sex offenders were discouraged from linking themselves to narratives of powerlessness; as a result, such thinking rarely appears in their stories. Indeed, the most dramatic effect of penal treatment power that I observed was the eradication of the vestiges of old rape myths from the men's narratives. In contrast to strategies of minimization, denial, and justification that many sex offenders use to mitigate their culpability (e.g., Lea and Auburn 2001), most of my participants emphasized their responsibility by portraying their victims' behaviours as constrained entirely by male agency. While the men in my sample drew on penal treatment discourse to help reconstruct their understanding of their offences, many partici-pants, as we shall see in chapter 7, also articulated points of disagree-ment with the rape scripts and interpretative frameworks that treatment staff provided.

4 Beautiful Baby Boys: Gendering Relationships

There's no major events. Just normal stresses in everyday life basically, but they seemed so intense to me at the time 'cause I never knew how to let it go, or talk about it. And even if I did know how to talk about it, I didn't have anyone to talk with. My dad would have been a waste of time. Not knowing how to express my feelings. And all the hurt. No crying for me – or else I was a girl. Even being taught *not* to feel anything other than laughter or humour or happy. So, nothing specific. Just feeling hurt. My whole life I felt like a victim. I thought, a man needs some sort of power to keep all the assholes away. But I didn't know how I was going to get it.

(Paddy)

I realized around eight years old that women had the power to make me feel good. But, they also had the power to make me feel really shitty. Well, that's not true. I felt shitty about myself, so, what I thought was women are to blame for all this stuff. They invoke all this feeling in me. And to start falling in love, holy cow, that was the worst thing ever. That [*pauses*] scared me. I wanted to open up, and start talking about things, and actually started to a little bit. Then, my god [*laughs*]. She would realize that I was weak. And that would be it. I wasn't taking the chance. I'd just leave the relationship and go to the next woman, and, of course, it's the same, 'cause I'm still the same.

(Paul)

Much contemporary sex offender research seeks to confirm or reconfirm how or why sex offenders are different from non–sex offenders. Typically, these studies seek differences by comparing a population of convicted sex offenders with other men across a multitude of causal variables to isolate statistically significant characteristics. I question the view that all men are bearers of stranger rape or rape-killing, which suggests a potential affinity with this line of investigation. But my objective is not to identify the specific attributes of the rapist. Instead, I will explore the specific circumstances that enabled and constrained each participant's possible links to hegemonic forms of masculinity, and will analyse how each grasped and managed the cultural ideals of manhood in everyday life. I adopt Judith Butler's (1993b, 22) position that the sexed/gendered subject is not a "developmental moment," but is a constitutive effect of power that is "reiterated and reiterable."

Much penal treatment discourse presumes that the sex offender's ideas about power and control are symptoms of aberrant beliefs or cognitive distortions. Some feminist writers argue that men's power derives from existing socio-structural arrangements that reproduce and perpetuate unequal relationships by privileging men and reinforcing patriarchal definitions of women's place in society. This chapter's opening quotations illustrate a third possibility: men's power does not necessarily coincide with individual men's experiences of power. Men may live what Kaufman calls a contradictory experience of power, where they "come to suppress a range of emotions, needs, and possibilities ... experienced as inconsistent with the power of manhood" (1994, 142, 148–9). In both cases cited above, the men's lived experiences of powerlessness produced devastating effects for women whose lives were never connected to theirs. Both examples highlight the need to understand men "at the level of their lived experience, which may include feeling powerless," notwithstanding that men have more power than women (Crooks et al. 2007, 220).

Many gendering relationships and practices are individualized and shaped – but not fixed – early in life. My participants' boyhood life-stories, below, illustrate how such practices were formed and shaped the effects of their lived relationships to men's power. I asked questions about what it was like for them growing up and what it meant to be a man or boy rather than a woman or girl. I asked them to tell stories about themselves as victims and aggressors and to talk about specific physical, sexual, and emotional abuse and racism. I cite verbatim passages of their texts throughout my study, and I balance between "letting the data speak for itself and using abstracted categories" of analysis. I strive to represent my participants' lives without doing violence to their realities (Acker, Barry, and Esseveld 1983, cited by Lather 1991, 67). I conducted all my interviews after the penal treatment program had ended. The tape-recorded interviews were informal, semi-structured, and averaged 11.5 hours each. I came to each session with a topical interview guide and specific research questions. Since the men were familiar with discussing their lives, I suggested that they begin telling their life-stories in their own words and I would ask questions as they arose (e.g., Mullaney 2007; Schultz 2004). These stories, along with group discussions, served as an interpretive framework for their institutional files. My participants knew that I had access to their files, and that I reviewed them before and after our interviews. Doing so gave me an opportunity to examine my reactions to the details of frightful sexual assaults and allowed me to understand those acts in the context of entire lifetimes. I opted to present the raw violence shared with me. The men's narratives were no more gruesome than mainstream televisual representations in programs such as *CSI* and *Criminal Minds*. I also wanted to avoid minimizing both the harm perpetrated by men on women, and also the violence inflicted on them as boys and young adults. I wanted to avoid silencing these men by sanitizing their lives and deeds. As one participant reminded me:

> Staff try to provoke me to talk about stuff, but when I do, they eventually shut me off 'cause it's too much for them, you know? Maybe it's too *frightening* for them to look at the truth of what some people's life has been. They know it exists. But it's like, if they admit it, all of a sudden, *they* have to be responsible somehow and that's not what this program is about, right? (Cam)

Three sources framed my life history interviews or "con texts." First, the men had previously told their life stories in treatment and had been interviewed frequently by clinical staff. Many participants spontaneously offered me additional information routinely sought by treatment authorities. Second, the men answered questions that were informed by feminist and masculinity scholarship, field observations, and studies of penal governance. Finally, the men recounted stories that neither prison staff nor I thought or cared to ask. My fourteen histories are an amalgamation of what penal staff wanted to know, what I wanted to know, and what sex offenders wanted to tell me. Many men brought early boyhood family pictures or albums to the interviews, which gave their stories a poignant visual dimension. The boyhood representations of their lives were the most humanizing moments in the research process and drew me into their memories, opportunities, and failures, with human relationships the common thread.

As a way of managing 3,000 pages of transcribed interview data, I concentrated on gendering relationships, performing gender, gender performatives, and losing signs of gender. In this chapter, I examine how each man learned to re-embody masculinity (a) within his family and other institutional sites; (b) through forms of bodily based masculinity, including male-on-male violence, physical labour, sexual practices, and female stranger rape; and (c) across penal and treatment sites. While recounting past events often left many of the men melancholy and anxious, most participants categorized their disclosures to me as good or necessary practices for taking responsibility for their choices. When I mentioned he looked sad, Michel put it as follows:

I told you about my *crime*. When we first talked I asked you, "Do we talk about our crimes?" and you said, "Not necessarily – that we can talk about everything but, leading up to our crime." You didn't ask for details, but I ended up telling you from start to finish. [*Very dejected tone of voice.*] I like to be very aware of statements – just one single little sentence – that could minimize or justify anything. I feel if I just give a little bit here and there it's like I'm bullshitting you. [*Pauses.*] But it's not really *what* I told you – 'cause it's true – it's just the fact that I told you. It gives me an idea of what it's going to be like down the road when I have to eventually disclose to people around me what I've done. It's the specific feeling I had. It gives me an idea about what it will feel like to tell a woman [*pauses*] it doesn't feel good at all. I don't think it will ever be easy. [*Pauses.*] When I first came in I could barely tell another man what I did. It's a feeling to do with being self-conscious. Just ashamed I guess – all kinds of different feelings. I know I'm never going to get away from what I did [*pauses*] maybe twenty years after I get out [*pauses*] It's okay. I chose to tell you [*pauses*] it's good practice [*pauses*] it's not going to be the last time that I have to tell it. I almost wish – and I know this is bad – I wish I had more excuses, 'cause I really didn't have that hard of a life.

Penal staff unconnected with the treatment group sessions often asked me if I felt victimized by the men's stories about rape. I struggled with the opposite feeling: I felt that my interviews and presence in group were more akin to victimizing *them*. I asked men to relive and recount experiences as victims and offenders that still evoked shame and pain. The following are two rather typical responses to my concern that I was causing harm. They show how participants took the interviews seriously and expressed the truth to the best of their ability:

It's emotionally tiring. I thought it would be easier – coming and talking to you, but *holy* shit, you know? I thought it would be easier talking about my stuff because I had dealt with it in group. All that stuff's still there. And now I'm happy that I got to do it – talk about it. Even though it was sad and hurtful and I was angry. It's a step. It feels damn good for a guy like me who's quiet, eh? And spent his whole life stuffing. You get so used to stuffing it – survival, doing the drugs – you get so used to it. I felt a little vulnerable telling you, but in a way, I felt some trust, like it was okay. I don't know how to explain it. I guess I wanted to help you. (Brian)

After I expressed to you about my sexual abuse I went home, listened to music. I felt, in my mind, I didn't do a very good job of telling you. I felt that I was dancing around. I felt I was avoiding. I really didn't want to be there, you know? I was fighting with myself in myself. So then, I was thinking, "I should have said this. I should have at least went into detail about it." So, this morning, I went in the shower – I take a shower, I pray, I thank the Creator – I prayed to him that I'm coming down here to talk with you, and asked him to help me express myself with honesty and be honest with myself. Not to exaggerate or whatever. And then, if I feel I expressed myself well to you, I'm going to feel good about it. [*Pauses.*] I have to trust you. To say I don't trust you is just denying my chance of expressing myself to you, which is something I thought I could never do with a woman without her hating me. I have to trust you. And to tell you about my life, about my abuse, about my sexual abuse, and for you to get to know me, and why I'm feeling angry, negative, 'cause sometimes [*whispers*] I hurt. I go there and use it as an excuse. (Bear)

This life history focus, of course, raises the issue of whether a small convenience sample can establish the validity of "doing masculinity" and be seen to be representative of rapists. On the one hand, since no one can choose not to perform gender, doing masculinity and gendering practices can be explored in a single autobiographical account. On the other hand, a larger, randomly chosen sample would surely make for more reliable results. However, the fourteen lives I discuss in this book provide depth to lives lived in a way that larger surveys are not normally able to do. They permit a genealogy of the self to emerge that connects structure to agency and reveals the complexity of meaning behind stranger rape and the men who do violence to women.

The rest of this chapter takes up Michael Kaufman's invitation to consider men's lives and their gendered subjecthood through the dialectic of men's power and men's pain. This approach avoids reproducing a one-sided feminist focus on only men's power, or perpetuating penal treatment assumptions about the core pathology of sex offenders. Life history narratives shift attention to the preconditions of choice by providing the social and psychic context for understanding rape as a moment in a historical process of gendered and gendering power relationships that are connected to other structures, events, and processes. Together, these fourteen accounts help to illuminate the contradictory experiences of power in creating, stabilizing, and subjectifying gender and masculinity in the context of eventually committing stranger rape.[1]

Brian's Story

Brian is an Aboriginal[2] man in his early thirties, and has been incarcerated for the past seventeen years for first-degree murder. At age three, he and his younger brother were adopted by a poor white couple that emigrated from Western Europe shortly after World War II. Brian recalls his life as a litany of events that shut him down emotionally: "We have all these survival techniques – these ways of keeping it in – 'cause you've got to be a man." Brian felt disempowered within and beyond the home. He struggles in his simple, hushed voice to convey how domestic events affected his self-identity as a man. Foremost was his fear of his abusive adoptive mother. Brian recounts that she washed his hair in the kitchen sink, and yelled at him and held his head under the water for long periods of time. In his six-year-old mind, his own mother was drowning him. To cope with her anger, Brian learned to shut down:

> Our house is full of boards and cement. You can hear her walking, hey? When she gets mad, you can hear it by how the house squeaks. [*Pauses.*] She's a heavy-set woman, and when she gets mad her lips go like this [*demonstrates a contorted face*]. There was a lot of that growing up – always – she was always fighting, screaming, yelling. She can't communicate. She just gets mad and hits you. She was always fighting my dad or hitting us kids for something silly. She was an angry woman. She'd hit me in the face [*pauses*] with pots and pans. Sometimes there were whippings. She'd belt you and you'd have bruises across your back. [*Pauses.*] She'd hang you from your hair and just punch you. [*Pauses.*] She didn't have to hurt you.

That's the hard part. After I got beaten or something, I'd cry. But after a while I shut down. I shut down lots. [*Pauses.*] It's hard to get it back.

Brian praises his father's hard work ethic, but notes that his meagre education restricted him to "dead bottom" railroad jobs. Their home embarrassed Brian. He recalls his basement bedroom was "dark, cold, and creepy – just a bed and a blanket to divide the cement room." He remembers that other children ridiculed him for wearing "silly $1.49-Day clothes." He was picked on for wearing leg braces and special shoes for his pigeon-toed feet for four years. He resented that his mother took him and his brother shopping in child harnesses, "like we were dogs." He failed kindergarten and Grade 1, and his younger brother caught up to him in school. All that, Brian says, "affects you." Despite his father's traditional gender role as the primary breadwinner, Brian portrays him as a quiet man, powerless within the household, "whipping" his sons only to obey his wife: "You got to understand, ma controlled everything." Brian blames wartime experiences for his father's inability to communicate with or hug his sons, and his failure to "lay down the law" with his wife. Watching hockey or hiking in the mountains bonded father and son in what Brian calls "quiet old ways." Yet, he did not respect his father's passivity and silence. He believes that if his father had been less "compassionate" and more "aggressive" – in regard to usurping his wife's power – then "maybe none of this would have happened" to him.

A trilogy of sexual abuses imprinted his boyhood. At age ten, Brian's Catholic priest offered to make him head altar boy. The priest began to pick Brian up from school, cook him dinner, and give him wine and money. Over time, the priest raped and masturbated him. Brian remembers five separate incidents: "For some sick reason, I liked it. Maybe that's because I was getting attention from him. Maybe that's why I came back for all those other times. I didn't know nothing about it at all – what it was. I thought it was normal." Brian remembers an earlier sexual abuse committed by three adult female cousins when he was eight years old. The women entered the washroom where he was bathing and, laughing and joking, masturbated Brian and inserted a soap bar into his rectum. He was confused, mortified, and aroused: "In some sick way I liked it." Nonetheless, he shut down. Unlike acts sanctioned by a priest and "men's power," Brian expresses overt hostility towards his female cousins, who in his eyes embody another misuse of women's power: "They were adult women; I was a boy."

Brian characterizes his first sexual abuse, also at age eight, as "the most devastating of all." He was a Cub Scout sleeping in a tepee full of children during an overnight winter outing. Talking for the first time about this incident, Brian struggles to communicate memories encoded only in a child's brain. He stammers: "I'm cold," "it's smoky," "I'm scared." He was cold, and everything was dark. He remembers "smoke": the air was filled with smoke from the wood fire that heated the tepee, and there was smoke in his eyes. Someone was crying, and somewhere, a child screamed. He felt "something heavy above me" and "afraid." In our interview room, Brian's face contorts with pain and confusion as he searches for the words to flesh out an experience that, at eight years old, he did not know how to describe or remember. When the priest raped him two years later, Brian was less confused. He says that "it happened before so it was nothing." Brian's subsequent attempts to cope through desperate assertions of subjecthood now frighten him:

I had temper tantrums, but it took me a while to build it up. I'd smash things. I lit fires and burned things. Grass fires, garbage, I was bad. I used to shoot animals in the leg to make them suffer or get a dog, and beat him in the ribs with a shotgun, and throw him over the bridge, [*pauses*] trap gophers and cut their tails off and sell them. It scared me, Kevin, when I seen stuff [later] on serial killers. A lot of serial killers have similar behaviours. I could have been one of them. It felt good starting fires, you know what I mean? I wanted to watch something burn. A lot of people would come around and I would stand in the back – if only they knew it was me. You've got to understand, I was quiet – it was shameful. I always hid in the back with my bad posture – always had my head down.

Brian's mother remained ever-present in his life, and accompanied him everywhere. He dreaded such outings, and resorted to self-injury. He smashed his wrists and head against walls to avoid her company on the way to school and Sea Cadets. By age thirteen, he was big enough to free himself from her physicality. This marks an early moment of engagement with hegemonic masculinity. He retaliated against her blow to his head at the supper table by "smashing her." He "kick[ed] her about ten times" as she lay on the ground, her husband watching silently. He then ran away for three months. From that point onward, Brian took "no shit" from his mother. He recounts:

First, I had fantasies of killing my mom. That's sad to say now. Then, at age ten, I had [non-maternal] rape fantasies. You've got to realize, from age ten, after that priest did that thing, you know, you're just learning about sexuality. I saw a pornographic movie at a stag party – whew – that stuck in my mind, too. Deviancy. I started stealing a lot of magazines. I had over 200 of them stashed in my fort, and I'm reading all this garbage. That was a big part of who I was then. I was quiet and I had fantasies. Looking at women, those thoughts were always on my mind at school – this affected me. (Brian)

At age thirteen, Brian began his only romantic relationship with the only Aboriginal girl in his school. Brian was out of shape and, in his words, "geeky looking," but Elizabeth[3] liked him. He recalls: "She was the best thing that ever happened to me." They began to skip school, leave home at night, use alcohol and drugs, and incur more and more disapproval from Elizabeth's mother. Brian says he "became a quiet kind of rebel." Too uncomfortable and nervous with women to "do it naturally," he and Elizabeth had sexual encounters while both were "high." He was too shy to try any of the acts depicted in his pornography. Brian denies abusing Elizabeth: "She made me feel good," he remembers, but then he admits, "I had to have control – that's abuse in a way – telling her what to do or where we're going to." For two years, the "fat, chubby, Indian kid" savoured the status of having the best-looking girlfriend in school. Claiming "he didn't understand that he wasn't white," Brian was confused by the nickname "Chief," but otherwise did not sense racism. By age fourteen, he had two newspaper routes and worked part-time at a grocery store, but he also supplemented his earnings with "a lot of B&Es and selling things." He drank whenever he could, and snuck alcohol from his dad or bought it from a bootlegger. Unexpectedly, he arrived at Elizabeth's house one day to find it vacated and sold. He felt "lost," then "depressed," and finally "angered" when she failed to return to him. To Brian, Elizabeth was "taken." His primary masculinizing practice with corner store pornography surfaced even though his dreams of power over women starkly contrasted with his everyday social and sexual self. Brian recalls:

Even though I was with Elizabeth, I was still watching women – scanning them. Doesn't mean I was going to lash out. Women intimidate me. It's hard for me to talk to women. Since age thirteen, I had fantasies of tying women up and raping them – threatening them with a knife and taking control away. Fantasies of kidnapping, then killing them. I didn't know the word "fantasy," but I had lots of them. And they got violent. They were getting violent, especially after Elizabeth left me. That's all I was doing. Then you see a woman, and you think, [*pauses*] you see, at that time, I thought it was all normal. It was part of my whole life, and hitting puberty fuelled it more. I learned masturbation from the priest – even though my cousins did it to me. And I did a lot of that too – reading all that garbage. I thought reading that stuff was normal. You got to understand, I thought everything was normal. My mom beat me – I thought that was normal. But I hated it. To be honest, I had a lot of hate for women. In prison, I learned about gay and pedophiles, and then I got angry at the priest. (Brian)

Brian continued to fail school, and was much older and larger than his classmates. He was an aggressor with a reputation for fighting, and was suspended from school several times for fighting male students in class: "I would never talk, but if someone got on my case, I'd build it up and hit him with a chair or something. Or I'd beat them up and take their lunches." At the age of seventeen, his school awarded him Grade 9 just to move him out of junior high. That summer, Brian killed a young woman who lived on his newspaper route.

Harvey's Story

Harvey is a white man in his early twenties, nearing the end of his five-year, six-month sentence for sexual assault with a weapon. His boyhood was "chaotic." His mother married five times, and moved her family – Harvey, and his younger half-brother and half-sister – fifty or sixty times. Harvey even recalls living in a tent. He says his mother "wasn't a regular mom" and often took "men's jobs," such as operating mine derricks and driving tractor trailers. This kept the family financially stable, but it meant she was frequently away from home. Harvey recalls that he spent much of his boyhood tending to his siblings. He identifies, yet understates, his mother's poor choice in men; with a chuckle, he says she preferred "dominant," "rugged," "rough," long-haired men who were drinkers, bikers, and partiers. The smallest, Donald, was six-foot-three and 230 pounds. Harvey's boyhood father figures were violent and brutal towards him, his mother, and his siblings. Harvey often sustained injuries that forced him to miss school, and once he spent three months in a hospital with broken ribs. With a man in the house, violence was an everyday event; otherwise, his family life was "awesome." He recalls that "[mom] took really good care of us when there wasn't a man around," which he also remembers was rare. Even so, Harvey describes a home life filled with alcohol, drugs, and fights among his ever-present aunts and uncles.

Harvey disliked his mother's fear of being alone, which in his eyes made her emotionally weak. He sensed his mother's loneliness, but remains puzzled to this day by the contradiction between her choice in men and the qualities she tried to instil in her sons. She could criticize her many partners' fusion of masculinity and violence, but she could not prevent it. Harvey elaborates:

> My beliefs are strange considering the life I come from: being raised by a strong woman who preached very strongly about the way men should treat women. My mom tried valiantly throughout my life to instil the values in me that men are to treat women like gold. You don't swear in front of women. You don't become physically aggressive. You don't be angry. I'm supposed to have this shoulder for women to cry on. I'm supposed to be understanding. Compassionate. Funny. And, she used to tell me all the time – and this is a big one – you never hit women. A valuable belief, but that belief is really contradictory because of my crime. She also instilled that women were fragile, not in a physical way, but in the sense of the heart. She also tried to instil in us that sex was something very special, not to be taken lightly. And that is not a belief that any of us picked up on. We all had our own kids before we were seventeen.

Yet Harvey's mother refused victimhood. He recounts, with admiration, watching his five-foot-one mom "take out" Lance, her six-foot-eight, 270-pound husband, with a cast-iron frying pan. Once, she landed six upper-cuts on the jaw of her own six-foot-four, 230-pound son after Harvey challenged her authority. He points out quickly that he was shocked, not hurt. But then he adds, "she could be quite the physical person." In fact, Harvey's mom and his sister represent his ideal type of woman – "very intelligent, very firm, very aggressive, or very emotional when need be." He credits his mom for attempting to do something when her partners' violence got out hand. Nonetheless, Harvey himself feels powerless with women. His mother's choices and counsel undermined his sense of physical safety and psychic manhood. Harvey elaborates:

Growing up, I used to think, "*man*," it seemed to me that I *knew* what had to be done. I'm just a kid, but I know what had to be done. I *knew* that we had to leave this guy. But, it was like I was powerless to do anything, no matter how much I talked to my mom. All my life I felt very powerless to women. I know that comes from conflicting beliefs – the belief that I can't be aggressive – verbally, physically – I cannot make a woman's life hard, right? And the belief that I *know* what has to be done, but I can't do any-thing about it. Because of the other belief, right? So, I felt – especially around women – I felt very vulnerable. I only knew one way to deal with things and that was through physical or verbal violence, and I couldn't do that with any of the women in my life. I couldn't feel like a man. At times I did feel like a man. My mom used to specifically call me her little man. I *thrived* on it. Very much so. It always followed a responsibility, like "look out for your brother and sister, you're my little man." Even as young as eight years old, I remember her saying it, and that *feeling* of overwhelming pride. But then that would change, and I wasn't the little man any more. And now I'm powerless because she's making choices that are affecting my life that I have no control over.

Despite his mother's best counsel, Harvey was enamoured with images of hegemonic masculinity. He saw his uncle Henry as "the ideal man":

He was very tough physically, quiet, not mean looking, but intense. He did ten years in Edmonton Max. He has the front down pat. He was a protector. He didn't go out of his way to cause conflicts, but if it was brought to him, it was dealt with very quickly, very physically. He worked hard. He and some of my uncles are racist to all other than heterosexual whites – a belief that I don't share.

Though Harvey saw women's tears, he never saw his uncles express emotion, and things rarely seemed to bother them. On serious occasions, they responded with "massive anger dealt with in a physical way." Harvey adds that a man who can't fight is not a man, and jokes that men's heads are for "head-butting." He observes: "Men's minds are more in tune to seeking respect and dominance, whereas a woman's mind is on the level of harmony and making things comfortable and bright … Does that make sense?" He reflects on his experience with power:

Program-wise, you can be a man if you have no power. But honestly, I don't think so [*pauses*] a man is supposed to be powerful. I guess I umbrella everything under ways of getting respect. A man gets power from another man physically. Fighting. That was my belief as a teenager, and even today, I felt the guy across the hall this morning had taken some power from me by his comment. I didn't physically hurt him, but I made it very clear that if it was to happen again, there would be a physical altercation and he would lose. Now I got that power back.

As a boy, however, Harvey was far-removed from his uncle Henry's ideal of manhood. Harvey suffered humiliation and panic attacks in his home, at the hands of brutish stepfathers, and in school, where schoolmates ridicule him for being overweight. Not until his later teens did he cultivate a hegemonic masculine persona as "the strongest, the biggest, the heaviest drinker, the heaviest pot smoker, the best football player, and the most promiscuous." At age fifteen, Harvey's first of three sons was born. As he peered into the hospital nursery alongside his mother, he resolved to teach his son *his* sense of respect and survival. Irrespective of his mother's advice, Harvey wanted to teach his son that "women are weak" and to "never be controlled by them."

Another woman Harvey felt disempowered by was his sixteen-year-old female baby sitter, with whom Harvey and his younger brother had their first sexual encounters. Harvey was ten at the time, and describes her as very dominant. Though he suspected that sex was supposed to be enjoyable, he was aroused and confused because she physically hurt him. At the time, Harvey believed she meant to punish him and his brother because she always used physical discipline. The boys made a pact to tell no one. Although Harvey couches his story in humour, the incident contributed to his brother's nervous break down, and Harvey wonders if it taught him that sex and pain go hand in hand. Otherwise, he cannot explain his adult sexuality, which he characterizes clinically as containing "sadistic" elements. At seventeen, Harvey and his twenty-seven-year-old wife Lauren were "very involved with S&M." During sexual encounters, they took turns being the administrator of pain, even though they both hated being the recipient. In these encounters, he says that to get what he enjoyed sexually he had to give up his power and partake in his own sexual objectification and passivity: "I didn't like the loss of power. Being tied up, and I'm tied to the bed and there's *nothing* I can do. There were times when she'd hurt me physically to the point where enough is enough. It pissed me off. I'm not enjoying this anymore. I *hated* it."

At age fifteen, Harvey had no career prospects. He was failing school. In class one day, a male English teacher kicked him, and he thought, "This isn't happening," and retaliated in class. He was expelled from all provincial public schools, and attended an "alternative" school, but felt demeaned in the company of slower learners. His son's birth was his escape from formal education, and at the time, he thought: "Screw school, I'll be a labourer, whatever." Notwithstanding his vulnerability in the labour market, Harvey temporarily accomplished gender through the physicality of his jobs and through fatherhood. But these gender performatives did not make Harvey feel like a man:

> My uncle Henry taught me concrete finishing. It gave me a very proud feeling. I felt very confident about myself. My uncle said I was a natural. The money was beautiful. But the work was seasonal. Then I went to work on a gas line. This was a manly job too. I was a seventeen-year-old kid working alongside thirty-year-old men. When I'm doing physical work, I love it. I zone right out. It's my thing. That job put me on cloud nine. You know, the power I had at work? I was lead hand. I became very egotistical and my head swelled large. The respect I got from people was just phenomenal. Plus, in front of other men, it was like, "Hey, I got two boys," you know. But, in the grand scheme of things, it was stress, and it was pressure. And I told myself, "I'm not man enough to deal with this stuff." But I never said that to anyone else. To anybody else, I was very in control – a very, very good man. That's the face that everybody saw. Inside I was going nuts with all this responsibility when I didn't want to be there. I put myself there. But I didn't want to be there. Then the plant was finished, and everyone was laid off. My third son was born now.

Harvey started to party and depleted his and Lauren's $15,000 bank account. Finally, with less than $400 left, Lauren told him that she and "his boys" were leaving him until he straightened out his life. He recalls:

> I lost it. I never laid a hand on her. But I got very loud – ignorant. I turned around to leave and she smoked me in the back of the head with a two-by-four. She's [pause, smiles] tough. I spun around. Right at that moment she could see that I could have very well hit her. She took it for what it was, and walked away. I left.

At age nineteen, Harvey returned to his mother and latest stepfather. After one week, his stepfather told him to take his $2,800 income tax refund cheque and get out. He advised Harvey to live on that money and seek employment in a new gold mine that was opening up north. Harvey left by bus that evening. Twelve hours later he was in jail, charged with sexual assault with a weapon against a woman and attempted murder against her husband.

Marvin's Story

Marvin is a third-generation racialized[4] Canadian in his early forties. He has served seven years as a dangerous offender. Marvin grew up in a "real nice" house in a "nice" neighbourhood. His childhood personifies the deliberate estrangement of a boy from family relations, friendship, communication, and human touch. His subject status was affirmed only by his power to observe life through a picture window, and his pleasure in "watching" and "looking" eerily foreshadowed his adult voyeurism. Marvin's involuntary containment within the household was matched by his voluntary withdrawal from the public domain in the face of overt racism. His boyhood subjectivity was shaped at the crossroads of private and public disenfranchisement. Marvin remembers:

> No one talked to me. And I mean *literally*. I was locked in my room from Grades 1 to 5. There was just [a] table and a bed in that room. And there was a huge window. That's where I basically spent all my time. I sat on my bed, with the table in front of me, looking out that window. In between our house and the neighbour's house, I can see a little bit of the street. I can see a baseball going by, and I know the kids are playing. On weekends, a regular routine for [my family] was going downtown, shopping, and eating. Then they would visit people. I was left outside on Saturdays and Sundays. I rarely ventured beyond our yard because I was called racial names. The other times I was locked down – that term comes from prison.

From boyhood, Marvin was denied the "natural" gender privileges and higher status bestowed on boys in his culture, and this norm violation compounded his outcast status. His older and younger sisters were permitted to play outside, join sports teams, invite friends home, receive allowances, wear new clothes, own bicycles, and keep toys. Neither sister was punished physically. Marvin observes that his parents knew how to care and provide for children. But inexplicably, his mother seized his Christmas and birthday presents from aunts and uncles and gave them to other children. She nicknamed him Vargo and Nuncio, and implied that he was "mentally retarded."[5] Marvin did not appear in any family photos. He was literally an untouchable in the family:

> If I accidentally touched my mom like this [*gestures on his arm*], she would take her other hand and go like that [*wipes off his arm*]. I'd always see her do this. Every time. And, it bothered me of course. My older sister copied my mother. If I accidentally touched my sister's hand, she would wipe her hand. Then, as I got older – people in stores, if they had to hand me my change? I'd put my hand out. They would just drop the money, and it would hit my hand and fall all over the place. They just didn't want to touch my skin. I think they were just racial. Why my mother and sister did that, I don't know. I couldn't make sense of it 'cause I was a kid, hey?

Unable to comprehend his parents' behaviour, Marvin exercised some control over his life by monitoring routines. Alone in his room, he learned to predict his mother's and father's attacks on him. Marvin estimates that his mother beat him with wooden spoons at least four times a week. Before each attack, he heard the sound of metal utensils clashing in the cutlery drawer as his mother searched for a wooden spoon, "and I *knew*." Then she would burst into his room and lash out without cause for one or two minutes, often breaking the spoons on his wrists as he shielded his face. His father's routine was equally predictable: "Return from work. Shower. Change clothes. Drink at a neighbour's house. Return home drunk." Then, his father unlocked Marvin's door and took him into the basement. Marvin elaborates:

> He'd tell me to go find a piece of wood, and then he would put it in a vice and cut it. Just his look. He's looking at me. His dirty looks. His *angry* looks. After it's cut, put the saw away, and just smash, smash. I don't know why they did it. It was *so* predictable. I never gave them any reasons to do it that I know. And it happened frequently.

Marvin's father only spoke to him when he was drunk. On some evenings, he allowed Marvin to join him in his own room to play country and western records. But even here, he belittled his son. In the face of such oppression, Marvin could only exercise power and defeat his parents' sense of agency by refusing its effects on him:

What became routine when he was drinking was me playing his old favourite records with him sitting there cutting me down. He'd just look at me and swear for no reason. But I would sit there. I would play those songs because – even though it's wrong what he's saying, I'm a kid, and that's still my *dad* talking to me. I wanted him to accept me. Besides, it got me out of that room. I can't tell you how much I hated that room. Sitting on the floor in the dark just whacking my head against the wall [*pauses*] I cried a lot. I wouldn't let them see me cry. I didn't want them to think they were affecting me. I didn't want them to think that they were really hurting me. I tried to put this front on for them that "yeah, I can go in this room and stay there." They never saw me cry.

Marvin blames his mother more than his father for his mistreatment because she was always sober: "She knew what she was doing." He attributes his father's distance and violence to alcoholism and bi-polar disorder. His father was unable to form a close relationship with his son because he was ill. His mother's behaviour, however, violated Marvin's portrait of white middle-class femininity. Women, he thought, were "supposed to be" soft and more affectionate, caring, and loving than men. His mother actively contested his father's authority, and Marvin cleaned up the aftermath:

It was a constant struggle. You know, the *fights* that they had. Fist fights. *Knives* pulled on each other. It's just terrible. Oh yeah, mom would fight back. She would just go after him. Seeing all these fights became a regular thing. It was so predictable. My dad seemed to go to my mother's plants first because he knew she liked them. He'd throw her plants all over the place. There'd be dirt all over the stove, the countertops, the floor, the tabletops. Just everywhere. It would remain there. My mom wasn't going to clean it up because he threw it at her. So, I'd get up in the middle of the night and clean it. That's kind of followed me to this day. Even my crimes were spotless.

Marvin adapted to the situation by suppressing his need for human companionship. After six years of confinement in his room, he couldn't carry on a conversation and, on trips, often wandered off to sit happily in empty train cars. Accustomed to being alone, he began to choose solitude and closed spaces. He was unable to participate in sports, and found a baseball diamond's green expanse unsettling. He recalls that "even as an adult with my wife, I used to eat dinner and go into my room at seven in the evening." At age fifteen, Marvin joined a street gang. He recalls:

> I couldn't build relationships with other guys – I'm talking about guys who follow football, guys who played sports, guys who knew how to swim, ice-skate. I didn't know anything about football or baseball. I didn't know how to do any of those things. So, I didn't fit in with those kind of guys. I never fit in with the good guys. Gang life was so different. It demanded respect. Respect came with it. I could relate to those people because they were like me. They were able to express their anger – they were already angry at their parents. They came from dysfunctional families, so I was able to build relationships with them.

As a gang member, Marvin participated in masculine activities centred on "turf wars" and "power and control." Before he turned eighteen, he was stabbed twice and received a six-inch scar where his throat was slit. After he graduated from high school, he severed his gang ties. His father helped him get hired at a mill, where he met the woman who would be his common-law wife. He was smitten after he observed her through an office window, and began to plan their first meeting. He began to watch her. He learned her routines, knew her car, and let out the air from one tire in order to appear by chance to assist her. At twenty-one, Marvin settled into a pattern of dominant masculinity with her and their son. They each held steady, well-paid jobs. Marvin was able to rise above his own childhood experiences, befriended his son, and took him to soccer practices and hockey games. He says, "I never hit him. I never hit him." Surprisingly, Marvin's parents were attentive and loving grandparents.

Marvin, however, was not committed to monogamy. He basked in the power from "parading a pretty girl" around in front of men and women alike: "It's a nice feeling when other guys are envious" and women are asking, "What's going on with this guy that this girl is with him?" Marvin recalls:

> I had relationships with other women when I was with my wife. When I was out there, women were, to me, someone that you have sex with, but also someone you showed affection to. I wasn't just there for the sex. Some of these girls that I dated, I didn't have any sex with them because I didn't want to. That was very typical for me. I just wanted to go out with a nice-looking girl. It was also very hard for me to do a normal sexual act.

By "normal," Marvin means sexual intercourse with vaginal penetration, the staple act of compulsory heterosexuality. After their son was
born, Marvin's partner no longer enjoyed sex, drinking, or dancing,
which Marvin attributed to her new status as a mother. Despite his requests, she stopped "making herself look nice" for him, and he was
upset. She consented, however, to masturbate him, an act that became
the basis of their future sexual relationship. Until age thirty, Marvin
relied on female sex workers to satisfy his desires for fellatio and the
erotic leg and foot fetish he developed as an adolescent.[6] During adulthood, Marvin also derived sexual pleasure from watching woman at
bus stops and gazing into ground-floor apartment windows. He masturbated while he sat next to lone women and gazed furtively at their
legs. He began to monitor the routines of women as they boarded and
disembarked at bus stops. Soon, he began to follow them and engage in
what he calls "seeing without being seen." Characterizing himself as "a
peeping Tom," he insists he did no harm:

> Other than my victims, the only woman that I ever mistreated was my
> common-law wife. When I say mistreat, I said that, because of these crimes
> that I was doing. I would maybe start an argument with her. It would give
> me a couple of days, right? I don't have to talk to her and I can go and do
> what I want to do and come home and not be asked anything about where
> I've been. I guess I was victimizing her, but I didn't realize it. I didn't *care*
> at that time. I really didn't care.

The clandestine sexual relationships between Marvin and the objects
of his gaze shaped and confirmed his masculine subjectivity and evoke
the archetypal male "looker" in Western culture (Cameron and Frazer
1987, 154–5). Marvin's acts of sexual agency became progressively more
frequent and bold. At age thirty-six, he was arrested and charged with
over ten counts of breaking and entering women's ground floor apartments and forcing them to participate in his "deviant sexual practices."

Cam's Story

Cam is a white man in his mid-thirties, and is five years into a life
sentence for first-degree murder. He grew up in a blended family of
eight sisters and two brothers with his birth mother and father. He
was the youngest boy, but had two younger sisters. Cam's father,
Glenn, received a fourteen-year prison sentence for sexually assaulting

all his children. Cam embodies the resort to hegemonic masculinity as a result of enormous physical and sexual violence his father perpe- trated against him. Refusing victimhood, Cam used oppression to cre- ate and recreate his own agency and exaggerated masculinity. His father, he says, established a type of undisputed patriarchal rule at home that included a right to sexual services from all family members. No erotic boundaries existed in the home. As a child, Cam loved and felt loved by his father. Each time Glenn was arrested and charged, his wife and children rallied to protect him and denied all wrongdoing. For Cam, intrafamilial sexual practices were mostly a source of pleasure rather than pain:

> It started with me around six years old – full penetration, shit like that. It's not like you'd look at it and think something was wrong. Everyone was going through the same thing. If you wanted his attention, or to be part of the family, you had to go along with this. There were many times he made the kids perform different acts on each other, and he would watch and ei- ther join in, or masturbate along with it. [*Pauses.*] Just so much of it. It went on seven days a week, all the time. Anything you can imagine was done. It wasn't so good at first because things hurt. But after you got used to that kind of stuff, it started being pleasurable. Everybody liked it. And going through puberty, this was a great thing. I had a hard time coming to grips with that. I had eight sisters, and a lot of times a lot of that stuff felt good, better than letting my father do this to me or me doing this to him.

Absent traditional practices of heterosexuality, Cam's family was nonetheless a site for recreating extreme gender divisions of masculine dominance and feminine subordination. His sisters' sexual availability affirmed some sense of sexual subjecthood and agency. Cam and his brother Tim raced each other home from school for "first choice" with their two younger sisters, which allowed the boys to transcend their status as homosexualized objects. To young Cam, Glenn's sexual ex- ploitation was simply another privilege that embodied male power. In contrast to women's biological destiny, men have what Cam terms "op- tions." He explains:

CAM: In my family, girls are just there for fucking.
Q: So were you.
CAM: Yeah. But it would be different for the guys. I don't know how to explain that because the guys in the family would have more support than

the girls. Girls were just going to be wives and stay home and have kids. That's all they're good for. To explain the sexual part of it, that was just an extra option that's open to guys. It was all part of being a man and who you were, and having different avenues of travel than women. Obviously, Glenn liked boys and girls. It wasn't necessarily what the boys in the family liked. But it was just maybe three or four times a week I'd be treated like one of the girls.

At an early age, Cam learned to shut off his feelings and separate sexual practices from sexual identity. His sexual practices became resources for exercising economic power over other men. Before Cam ever com-modified women's sexuality, he commodified his own. He explains:

> I can shut my feelings off. I've been in situations living on the streets where I had to sell myself to gay men for money. I knew I wasn't gay. You did what you had to do to survive. Because I have a cause and I know why I'm doing it, doesn't mean I'm accepting that's who I am. You're just used that way. You're a piece of meat, but there's a pay-off. For me, men are not in the same category as women. As a child, I've done the acts I had to do because I was put in a position where I didn't have a lot of choice. And when I did have a choice as a young person, or even as a young man in prison, it was for financial gain and survival. My relationships with men have always been very limited, like, I never liked the hugging and kissing and the shit like that.

Cam has relatively happy childhood memories of growing up on their farm – horseback riding, fishing, hunting, skidooing, and dirt-bike rid-ing. He sees these "good times" as the children's "pay out" for cooper-ating with their father, even though Glenn combined sexual acts with most family events: "To us, being kids, they were all good times. There was no bad times really, except when the violence would start. You were beat so much all the time on a regular basis that you were more than happy and willing to go along with anything different." Glenn beat every family member, and his fury was often unpredictable and uncontrollable. During most of these violent incidents, Glenn was so-ber. Cam says: "Glenn would just scream, *run, run, run!* because he knew if he caught you, he'd kill you." Cam, then and now, cannot fathom Glenn's rage. He sounds almost cavalier as he recounts these violent encounters:

I had my eye kicked right out of my head. My eyeball actually [*laughs*] come right out of my head. I was getting beat from him one time, and he knocked me to the ground with a punch. He was in his bare feet and underwear. He went to kick me in the stomach, and I covered up. His big toe caught me right in the eye. Just little things like that.

Cam admired his brother Tim's ability to steel himself emotionally against his father's physical abuse. The ability to endure "vicious fucking beatings" without displaying emotion became a model for performing gender in the household. Like Tim, Cam refused passivity and powerlessness, and each witnessed the other's resistance and masculine performativity:

I looked up to my older brother Tim because he could take such vicious fucking beatings from Glenn. Like, *man*, Glenn sitting on his chest and beating him with the fists. And Tim wouldn't show no feeling. He would lay there and take it. You couldn't make him cry. Today, you see Tim? He's brain damaged. We tried to look out for each other. Like, if Glenn was on [Tim's] chest beating him, I'd take a ball bat and I'd attack Glenn. Then I'd get a licking. Then Tim would attack Glenn and everyone would end up getting a beating, but maybe he'll tire out, and slow down. It usually worked. Glenn could only beat you so long. After fifteen or twenty minutes of beating somebody, you're winded. We got pretty good at being able to attack, then get on our back on the ground, cover up, and wait for the blows to come.

Cam's mother remains in the background of his narrative, and emerges only when I question him directly about her: "My mom's responsibilities were to keep the house clean, clothe the children, try to keep the home together, cook, and take care of Glenn's sexual needs." She worked full-time as a nurse and was aware of her husband's activities in her absence. One daughter even had Glenn's child. Despite her economic role as breadwinner, she was utterly powerless in the home: "We seen mom beat. Badly. Hospitalized. Oh fuck, he would kick the shit out of her, stick a gun in her mouth. He done her so much harm for thirty-seven years." His mother's voice was the only compassionate sound Cam heard during childhood. Still, he holds her "just as accountable" for the violence and abuse, and for staying with Glenn rather than recognizing her "maternal duty" to protect her children. He says: "Mom knew we were being abused" but she coped "by allowing [Glenn] to do what he done, never disagree with him, and support him." Cam adds:

> Besides, where would they rescue us to? Would they lock us up? Take us away from the only family we know? That was our only way of knowing and understanding what love was about. And, I don't think any other normal feeling could have replaced that once you learned that. If you were to put us in other homes, we would have started sexually abusing whoever we were with because you're going to do what you're taught. And even with dad gone, the abuse wouldn't have stopped because I had two older brothers that are just as guilty as him, and they're loving every minute of it, too.

Glenn worked as a mechanic, and brought his children into his trade by teaching them to steal auto parts to use or sell. Cam learned to strip down cars, change serial numbers, and break and enter: "We were a really deep-rooted, serious crime family." To win his father's approval, Cam also preformed an exaggerated masculinity without concern for injury to himself or others. From age thirteen, he began to discipline his mind in order to kill. He sat on the barn roof and watched Glenn through the scope of a loaded rifle, and by doing so, affirmed himself as the ultimate subject of violence and object of fear. He tells me, "I always knew I could kill any time I want, and I could do it without a feeling." Crime and fighting materialized corporeal and psychic formations of masculinity that Glenn also highly valued. Cam explains further:

> You have to have a certain amount of heart and intelligence to even do them crimes. The adrenaline rush – and that was just part of the family. Some of the older kids would always get more attention than I would, so my way for getting the attention was I had to outdo everybody. I had to be the meanest, the violentest. My dad would brag all the time to everybody, and he'd pump me up so big that I had to live a certain way. If someone knocks you down to the ground in a fight, you can't lose. You got to be the crazy one. So, if it meant picking up a brick or a club or whatever, you'd smash him with all you got. You don't think of whether you're going to hurt him. I would be acknowledged for that. It's hard to explain. It gave me power and recognition.

Cam left home and school at fourteen. From age seventeen, he was in and out of jail for stealing cars, theft, and narcotics trafficking: "I had a real thing for cars and changing serial numbers. I was good at it." At age twenty-two, Cam married and then divorced, experimenting briefly with working-class hegemonic masculinity. He took pride in being the sole breadwinner for his young wife, and enjoyed the physicality of his work:

> Everything was beautiful for a year. I bought a double-wide trailer and worked on the rigs. I had to work like a dog – it was rough cold work. It was very profitable, so that the work, no matter how hard it was, really paid off. My wife doesn't have to work. I preferred that she didn't. I needed someone at home to watch my dogs. Work gave me a sense of responsibility and taking care of my wife.

Eventually, Cam was arrested and convicted for possessing stolen cars and driving getaway vehicles during two bank robberies. While serving his six-year sentence, he married Charlene, his second wife, who was eighteen years his elder. Cam remembers: "I liked her to begin with but I didn't know then what she was worth." After his parole, Charlene's money allowed Cam to begin his own auto shop. Cam says that "she owned me," and he resented her power over him and planned to kill her. Charlene was "of a proper upbringing" and was unaware of Cam's troubled family life and unorthodox sexual practices:

> Before Charlene, I coped with my abuse by being in relationships similar to that kind of background, where I can identify the same feelings. You may not want that consciously, but subconsciously that's exactly what you're getting and finding. You're going to look for something that feels of the norm to you, not something healthy and new. You might be able to keep it under control for amounts of time, but it's going to come out somewhere. People identify and find people that they are comfortable with. [For me, they] happened to be prostitutes.

Cam's auto business was next to a prostitute stroll. In our interview, he diagnoses himself as "highly addicted" to the services of the trade. He purchased sex from approximately 200 women during his three years living with Charlene. By the time he met Dee, the bar waitress he eventually raped and killed, Cam was almost delusional. He believed that "there isn't anybody, there isn't anything out there I couldn't have if I wanted it."

Charlie's Story

Charlie is a white man in his early thirties. He has completed seven years of a life-fourteen sentence for second-degree murder and an unrelated sexual assault. As a child, with an older and younger brother, Charlie's mother wanted him to be a girl. She was mentally ill, and dressed Charlie in female clothing and took pictures. During boyhood, Charlie used punishment and pain as gendering strategies to refuse his mother's efforts to feminize him. As a marker of his own agency and masculinity, Charlie was proud that he could force his mother to punish him more severely than his siblings. He explains:

> My mom was [*pauses*] strange [*pauses*] mentally incapable. One day she could be passive, and the next, violent. But she had some serious mental problems. Mom said that all her pain was coming from me. It was my fault for not being born a girl. She let it be known every time we scrapped and argued that I was supposed to be a girl. And I fought it. I was the exact opposite. Big-time male things. Bleeding all the time. Constantly getting hurt. Getting punished. I never seen my mother hit my brothers in the face. That was saved for me. I was proud of that. [Later] I always wanted to please [my parents] and I felt ashamed that I couldn't. I can describe it now, but back then I couldn't. I could never put a name to it. But it was shame and guilt. 'Cause I believed her sometimes that I had the choice to be a girl.

The relationship between Charlie's birth mother and father was strained. Nonetheless, Charlie witnessed few arguments and little physical violence between them. He believes now that he was the one "wearing" the effects of their deteriorating relationship. Charlie's father was an angry man who punished his sons with custom-designed tools. By age eight, Charlie reworked his coping responses to such abuse into an effective ritual that linked him to manhood:

> He liked to show his friends that his boys don't cry. I could put up with more than my brothers could. I can't remember when I stopped crying. The less crying, the better off you were. In front of his friends, he'd put my hand on the table, pull out a knife, and play chicken. Stabbed me right through the hand once. [*Shows me the scar*.] Didn't flinch. When I wouldn't cry, I felt I was in total control. I was strong. I listened to a couple of dad's friends say there's no way they'd do that. That made me feel more powerful. They're admitting they couldn't put up with it, but I could. I was stronger than some men. The more pain I could put up with, the more of a man I was.

Charlie's family was relatively well-off until he was nine years old. At that point, his parents finalized their divorce. Left with their mother,

Charlie and his two brothers learned about poverty, life on welfare, and Salvation Army clothing. Charlie does not know whether his mom worked outside the home, but he would go days without seeing her: "She was out with her boyfriends." There were relatives who supervised, but Charlie avoided them because his uncle "liked to play sexual." The family moved constantly and lived in "the worst hovels imaginable." Charlie emulated his mother's independent qualities and learned how to cook for himself, clean the house, and do laundry. His happiest times were alone. To entertain himself, he built log forts and pretended he was a trapper, and often stayed out overnight. He was never missed. Charlie reinforced his separation from other people by repressing and denying emotions that challenge or reduce his ability to control himself. He explains:

> I was not an emotional kid. I learned how to turn them off very soon in my life. And, if they were off, they weren't there. Or, they were so minor, they never affected me. I coped by keeping everything to me. A lot of things never bothered me. Or, at least, I thought they never bothered me. I seen things between the ages of six and eleven that most people just never see. I found a woman who had hanged herself. I saw a man beheaded – the top of his head and half his shoulder cut off – in a car accident. I watched my first knife fight in Grade 1. I didn't have compassion for people back then, or empathy for others. But I wasn't a cruel kid either. I just couldn't be bothered with other people. But I liked to watch them – it was exciting.

While eight-year old Charlie lived in an unsettled household, an eighteen-year-old man, Clifford, befriended and sexually abused him. Charlie's uncles also sexually abused him. He recalls: "I never knew what was being done to me. I never knew about homosexuality until I was sixteen." Charlie refused victimhood, which he saw in gendered terms as feminine and weak: "*Victim* and *women* all seem to be the same to me." Instead, he tried to turn his victimization into choice. As Sharon Lamb (1999, 124) notes, this interpretation affords some people some control over their world because *they* instigate their own form of abuse. Charlie remembers:

> The truth is, even as children, we had choices. I had a choice between two evils. But I still had choices – sex over beatings. My sexual abuse was sort of a conscious choice, on my part, as a kid. To accept the sexual

abuse over the physical, [*pauses*] I could handle the sexual abuse. It didn't hurt. I could handle a lot of physical pain, but it's not like I went looking for it. If I could avoid it, I'd definitely avoid it. And I started avoiding it – by going to people who were sexually abusing me. They didn't beat me up. And I knew I was choosing it too. So, I made the choices, but with the knowledge I had. At the time, there was no such thing as shelters. At least, not heard of.

When his father divorced and remarried, Charlie joined his new step-family. Within five weeks, he had been hospitalized for nine months, and needed painful skin grafts and tendon repairs, because his two new stepbrothers set him on fire. His father and stepmother told him to tell the doctor that he tripped over a log and fell into a campfire, and afterwards he returned to his mother's custody. Charlie spent a year learning to walk again. He sums up his experiences bluntly: "We never had a TV. It wasn't until I seen it from other people that I realized there was no motherly nothing in my life."

Charlie does not remember much of school. He believes he was an average student, and remembers that other kids did not want to social-ize with him. Schoolmates avoided him for his "funny looks" and his older brother caused trouble when he told them that Charlie was sup-posed to be a girl. He remembers: "I fought that so much, it was incred-ible – I was not a girl. I was a boy." As Charlie grew older and bigger, he relied on physical violence to assert himself publicly and psychi-cally. Fighting channelled his embarrassment and fear into a gender-acceptable practice. He observes:

I fought a lot in school. I was good at it. I wasn't sadistic, but when I got into a fight I was mean. Fighting was a good release. I fought whenever I perceived any challenge or embarrassment. I believed it had to be physical punishment. When I fought, I had power – enough power. Without power I got hurt – physically and mentally. My whole life revolved around weak-ness and strength. If you weren't strong, you were weak. And yes, I thought women were passive and weak. Men were aggressive and strong. Mind you, I thought a lot of men were weak.

In Grade 8, Charlie was banned from school. He recalls thinking educa-tion was an "inconvenience" and that his skills, such as stamina and physical strength, were best brought to the labour marketplace. Charlie personifies the constitution of masculinity through bodily performance as discussed by Connell (1995, 54). He explains:

> By the time I was six years old, I knew how to drive a tractor and a cat. I've never been a really intelligent person, but I can *master* equipment. I think I liked the power. Plus, I grew up with "be a man" and "men aren't afraid of this and men aren't afraid of that." I was a pretty strong kid. By the time I was fifteen, I was six-foot-one, 180 pounds, and mean. Oh yeah. I used to push hay every summer all summer long. I once picked up a motor block and threw it over a tailgate of a pickup – by myself. I worked in the bush – logging. I could run up and down the mountain all day. I did a lot of construction work. I moved bricks. I kept two brick layers working all by myself. I love non-stop physical going. Work made me feel good about myself – accomplishing something. I put everything into it. I didn't think about life.

Charlie classified himself as a "bona fide manual labourer." Rather than a form of alienation, manual work and physical embodiment helped him transcend everyday life. When he was not at work, he drank and used drugs; when he mixed both, violence invariably followed: "I knew what I was doing – I wanted those feelings." Removed from work, Charlie saw himself as worthless, unless he was fighting: "I was worth something in a fight." Anger camouflaged his embarrassment, low self-esteem, and shame, and destabilized his otherwise stoic masculine performatives.

Charlie's relationships with adult women demonstrated misogynist themes. In our interview, he voices both repulsion and resentment towards women. Repulsion derived from Charlie's fearful response to his own boyhood sexual abuse. He reveals:

> My sexual abuse didn't cause me to go to the extreme where I had to have sex all the time with women just to prove that I'm a man [*pauses*] I was also afraid of having sex. I was big time afraid of being touched. I seen sex with a woman as [*pauses*] not very good [*pauses*] disgusting is the best way I can put it. I didn't *like* it.

Resentment derived from his experienced helplessness and rejected sense of manhood as a perceived result of women's power. Charlie explains:

> My opinion of women through my school years is that women are so fucking lucky because they get to choose anyone they want. When you dance,

going steady, getting married, having sex – it's all the woman's call. It's never a man's choice. Most women that I know can walk into a pub and pick out who they want to be with. Guys can't do that. We try – but we just can't do it. I could never do it. Guys can lie to you about it, and be the man, but the truth is – I've listened to it a hundred times. The woman always has the choice. He does not. A man asks who he thinks he might get. When a guy comes up and asks a girl to dance, he's giving her all his power and control – all of it – just by asking that one simple question. Do you know what a man has to do mentally to get himself to come over to ask a woman to dance? A fuck of a lot more than [a woman does] to say no. And it's incredible how polite women are about taking away men's power and control.

These stories in Charlie's narrative disaffirm hegemonic masculine themes and dreams of men's uncontrollable sexuality and power over women. Instead, he dreaded female sexuality and rejection. He had few qualms about beating up men. Beating up women, however, was not a masculinizing practice, because he believed that "women are too weak" to fight. Nevertheless, Charlie killed the first woman he hit.

Kerry's Story

Kerry is a white man in his early fifties who has served ten years as a dangerous offender. Previously, he served ten years for rape and inde-cent assault, committed only months after his full parole from a life sen-tence for murder, of which he served eleven years in Arkansas.[7] Kerry personifies the conscious unmaking and re-making of masculinity to survive life in a brutal prison. Consequently, rather than discuss gender-constituting moments from his boyhood, I focus on his private and pub-lic strategies for masculine performativity in a violent homosocial penal world. His poignant narrative illuminates the fluidity and temporality of gendering relationships. Because Kerry's American prison ordeals pre-date his sexual crimes, treatment staff gave him the opportunity to explore the relationships between his lived reality in prison and his sub-sequent practices of sexual assault. His prison experiences, while ex-treme, differed from other group members by degree. However, it is important to note that others in the treatment group did not consider prison's effects on their own subjectifying events or high-risk triggers.

Kerry's experiences in prison began at age eighteen when he was jailed for his first car theft, which he hoped would force his release from the Canadian army after three attempts to walk away failed. Attracted to what he calls "that kind of lifestyle," Kerry considered becoming a professional car thief, but was not very good at it. He received one year for his second conviction but escaped to the United States. To make money on the run, he and a hitch-hiker began robbing men at knife-point outside downtown nightclubs. A tragic incident on one such night led to Kerry's life sentence for murder. He recounts:

> We tied one man up because we were going to take his car and use it, and we wanted time to get out of the city. And he died of exposure. Apparently he was diabetic – we didn't know it – and he didn't have the strength to roll – he was one hundred feet from the road. We used his own clothes to tie him up, so he was exposed to the elements. It was a terrible thing. Like, I wasn't even a kid who got in fights. That was a profound experience that completely shook my whole sense of self.

During his first night in an Arkansas county jail, Kerry was gang-raped. There was no safe place to express his pain within the hegemonic masculinity that he knew he must perform to avert future sexual assault. He could not defeat the attack on him, but he could defeat some of its effects by refusing to identify as a victim. Kerry explains:

> In the beginning, I wanted to call myself a victim. Like, I really wanted to tell my mom – what they'd done to me, and how I feel, and how much it hurt, and that I didn't know what to do, and that I really felt helpless. And I think I would have told any sympathetic person immediately afterwards. It wasn't that I didn't want to tell. You can't be a victim in prison. Not unless you want to be a victim every day of your imprisonment, and I knew I couldn't live with that. I remember a kid got raped on the Rolley Unit. I felt very uncomfortable around him because he was what I was trying to hide. My method of dealing with my victimization was I wasn't a victim, and to hide it. So, anybody else who didn't do that was very threatening because that suggested I was doing it wrong.

Kerry attests to how rape created gender independent of the sexed bodies of both the raped and the rapist. While male on male rape violates hegemonic masculinity's heterosexual imperative, Kerry's sexual subordination created masculinity in his assailants and femininity in him. His experience indicates that rape's effects depend on all players participating in cultural ascriptions of "power as the domination of women, or the *idea* of women" (Tithecott, 157, italics added). He remembers:

The men who assaulted me were [*sarcastically*] real men. Real tough men. Part of my mind thought that. Because it's the antithesis to what I thought about myself – which was that I wasn't a real man. I wasn't strong. I must be weak. I should have been able to stop [*pauses*] all this leads to conclusions about who they are. They must be the opposite of all those self-judgements. And I *hated* that, you know? That I thought that about them. It's the nature of the act that's unmanly. It's sort of like being branded. Like, I don't know what it means to be genderless. I always felt like *something*. But what is a man who's been raped?

At age twenty-one, Kerry deliberately began to suppress feelings that he believed linked him to femininity. These emotions not only restricted his ability to brace himself against compassion, but also imprinted him with "the idea of woman" and connected that idea to vulnerability and rapeability. Kerry's control over emotional display was his link to the hegemonic masculinity found in American penitentiaries. He reveals:

I shut down that part of myself that I felt was feminine. I believed that's what was attacked. And that was only because of the sexual assault. If I had only been physically assaulted, I wouldn't have made any gender association. I became a very silent person. I used to be really expressive. I didn't express that part at *all* after the event. I was looking for what made me different than the other people in that cellblock. And what I came up with is I reacted to things emotionally. So, I began to look around me at what I perceived to be masculine – which was silence – the willingness to be violent, and shut down anything that I thought was sensitive or emotional because the only acceptable emotion was anger, actually, sort of a rage. Even anger wasn't acceptable because that was a loss of control. And even rage had to be somewhat controlled. That's what I put together. Don't show pity. Don't show concern. Don't show any of those kinds of things – 'cause that's a sign of weakness. Like, you should be able to see somebody get their brains bashed out literally in front of you.

Within a homosocial penal environment, direct displays of physical violence are a key resource that materialize and maintain a public masculinity. Rather than an individual need to "feel like a man," fighting is a collective masculinizing practice for "the eyes of other men." Kerry is clear about the gendering effects of male-on-male violence:

It's in the eyes of other men that I know that I'm a man. What makes you a man in prison is an ability to hurt other men. I had to acquire the skill to do that through practice, without acquiring the need and desire to do that. And I sought out people who knew, who *really* knew. And they taught me. You got attacked a lot in the first few years. I had a lot of beefs. A *lot*. I had broken ribs, teeth knocked out. My defence to myself was that I never attacked another human being. But I never turned down a challenge. And that can be a look. I deliberately changed who I was so it wouldn't happen again.

The gendering effects of gang-rape inscribed heterosexual sex acts with new dangers for Kerry and rendered his old sexuality as a site of weakness and emotional vulnerability. To make sexuality feel safe again, he reconnected his fantasies to emotions of domination and control, and consciously fused his (hetero)sexuality with control over the object of his desire. He recounts:

After being raped, I was asexual for probably two years. I was twenty-one when it happened, so, the hormones are still flowing. It's got to go somewhere. I'm not making an excuse. I'm just saying, in order to feel those feelings, I felt like I needed to have control in the fantasy. They became more controlling. Like, before that, sexuality is like surrendering to someone else, but it's really neat, you know what I mean? Well, the idea of surrender was completely *unbelievable* to me. I couldn't see myself ever surrendering that part of who I am 'cause I had mixed my sexual assault with sex.

The role of consent in his sexual fantasies changed after his prison gang rape. His resulting indifference to women's consent and his focus on control stemmed more from his thoughts and feelings about himself as a man, rather than active disdain for women. He explains:

My sexual fantasies were non-consensual. But not non-consensual in that *that* was exciting. Consent wasn't required or needed or sought. And that is different than the sexual fantasies I used to have, where consent was very much an issue. I can remember that it was the idea that my partner – whoever I used when I was an adolescent – *was* consenting. The idea of the consent was very much a part of the fantasy. I remember fantasizing about Marilyn Monroe, but we had a relationship and consent played a role. I mean, to have sex with Marilyn Monroe, and she didn't *want* to have sex with me, would not have been a pleasing fantasy to me at all when I was a kid. There's the element that she would *want* to. Well, that was missing after that because consent, I believe, has to do with self-worth and self-respect. And it was strikingly absent in my sexual fantasies following that.

Kerry buried emotions that could not be expressed safely within prison social practices. He traces the origins of his three post-release rape scripts to culturally produced television dramatizations. Once again, he says his conscious intent was not to control women's sexuality. Rather, the erotic qualities of his rape fantasy stemmed from the pleasure he derived from controlling his own uncontrollable sexuality. He reveals:

I shut my emotions down one by one. Which means I buried them deeper and deeper because they were untenable, because they were out of control. My fear was out of control. My anxiety was out of control. My guilt was out of control. My shame was out of control. All those feelings were uncontrollable for me, so I clacked them down, and imposed intellectual control over them. And some of them were deviant intellectual control. Expressing my sexuality in a deviant manner – it was masturbating to deviant fantasies. I remember seeing a rape scene on TV. I'd never thought it out that way before. And, I thought of it only in the fantasy sense. That's because I never thought I'd be out of jail in my life. It was a visualization [*pauses*] I remember almost fixating on it. Running it in my mind over and over again. And I wasn't thinking, "I'm afraid." I wasn't feeling panicked. I was just *feeling* pleasured and excited. And of course, I reinforced it.

Working in the prison hospital, however, gave Kerry an alternative avenue beyond physical force for a gender-affirming practice that, in his words, "builds up pride." He became a lab tech, then the prison's ECG, X-ray, OR, and EMT tech, and was finally certified and registered to work within the United States as a physician assistant. This marked his relationship to work as a primary gendering practice that affirms a provider masculinity (cf. Messerschmidt 1993). He explains: "Until this last period in my life, if I'm not the provider, if I'm not a father, if I'm not a regular job holder, if I'm not a taxpaying citizen, I'm nothing as far as a man goes – my feeling of what a man was. So, there was a fair amount of turmoil about that – internally."

At age thirty-two, Kerry returned to Canada on a prisoner-exchange program, and was granted parole after seven months. He began to live with his stepfather. The transition was not easy: "My panic" about working and living in society "was now out in the open. It's not hidden down deep any more." He adds:

> I think if I had been able to pursue that [physician assistant], I don't think I would have ever reoffended. Because, I felt good about that. When I returned to Canada, of course, we don't have such a thing. I've worked since I was eleven. Work was my one path to appreciation from my stepfather. If I worked hard, I could get silent approval, and take silent pride. That's the only time I was his boy. I was Arnold's boy if I worked really hard, and did a good job. I was a sissy and my momma's boy if I didn't. Now I'm being taken care of by my stepfather, undermining whatever self-respect I might have every single day. I'm a supplicant.

Kerry found work as a hospital orderly. Three months later, he sexually assaulted two young women on one night, only hours apart.

Simpson's Story

Simpson is an Aboriginal man in his early thirties. He has completed six years of a fifteen-year sentence for aggravated sexual assault and manslaughter. Simpson and his older sister grew up on a reserve in a small fishing village. After the only cannery closed down, unemployment, poverty, and drinking were widespread. Simpson drank by age eight, and his father was the first person he got drunk with. His childhood was difficult. He remembers:

> I considered myself a different class than white people. My sister and I were made fun of by white kids and natives for being poor. I'd be called "Stink," or, "Doesn't your mom know how to clean your clothes?" I ran around the school gym in bare feet when all the other kids had brand new runners.

Simpson's father built boats for a living, and was a frightening patriarch who inflicted extreme violence on his wife and children:

> My dad would drink anything to get drunk – aftershave, vanilla extract. He drank for two or three weeks sometimes. We'd go without food for a couple of days. Very abusive, my dad was very abusive with my mom and

us kids. Mom left us numerous times. She wasn't allowed to talk to any-body. She wasn't allowed to work. She stayed home *all* the time. Dad would be fooling around with women. Dad was king of the house. I seen dad slap mom, throw her around, punch her with his fist. I seen my dad raping my mom at knifepoint – a kitchen knife at her throat. I was about nine. I remember mom screaming and asking for *anybody* to help. I kinda chickened out. I stayed hid under my bed.

At sea, however, Simpson's father was a gentle, caring man. He spoke his traditional language and taught his son ancestral skills. Simpson, who knew little of his parents' past, could not comprehend this dichot-omy. He observes:

As mean as my dad was, when he was sober enough to go out and get food for us, he was the kindest person. Hey, out on a boat? Really gentle out there. He would teach me how to hunt and fish, and make my own traps. I'd wonder how many of my uncles, relatives, have been there at the same spot. He'd teach me how to set a long line for halibut, how to set up crab traps. He was a totally different person out on the boat. He'd call me *"son"* out there. He'd lend me his jacket when I was cold and let me steer the boat. Back home [he called me] a stupid Indian.

In obedience to a grandmother's dying request, Simpson's father suddenly became a Pentecostal minister. Though he quit drinking and forced his family to attend church, his beatings and abuse did not abate, and he incorporated physical punishment into religious events. Simpson's father-as-minister would summon his children before his congregation and "lay it right on me and my sister for horse playing. When we got home, he gave it to us worse." Violence in the family was not a sharply gendered practice. Indeed, Simpson's father encouraged similar relationships to violence for his son and daughter:

My sister had it just as tough as I did. My dad beat her up quite often too. It didn't matter. My dad taught me and my sister how to fight. We both fought. He told us, "Somebody hits you, then hit them back twice as hard. If they push you, then push them back twice as hard." Back then I'd fight girls too. That was kinda a normal thing to fight girls.

Simpson recalls that his father's parents were also "very, very strict and very religious," as well as physically abusive. Simpson has little good to say about Christianity and insists that it contributed to enforced cultural alienation for him and his family:

> Honestly, I think the church was a negative influence in my community. As a boy, I wasn't allowed to learn how to dance the way our people dance with our button blanket regalia. I don't know how to speak my language. I don't know any of our traditional songs. I do *now*. Dad still doesn't want no part of traditional ways.[8] He'd rather open the Bible and preach. Honestly, I think he's ashamed. His favourite line to this day is "pray and let God take care of it."

On the one hand, Simpson's preacher-father inculcated his son and daughter with an actively defiant subjecthood formed and affirmed through physical retaliation to interpersonal violence. On the other hand, his father articulated and displayed a surrender of cultural identity to Christian values. With no meaningful alternatives for making masculinity, father and son personify the after-effects of neocolonial agendas to secure Aboriginal women's and children's subordination through Christian marriage, corporal punishment, and gender ideologies based on male supremacy and European dominance over Aboriginal peoples (e.g., Lawrence 2002; Razack 2002).

At age nine, Simpson's older adult cousins (one male and two female) forced him into sexual acts, and made him at once an object of homo and hetero sex practices. During three years of sexual abuse, he reclaimed some sexual agency of his own: he chose to be the instigator of his own abuse and pleasure and sought sex with his female cousins. Although Simpson's body was a site of contradiction for validating heterosexuality, his lived experiences embody the link between masculinity and sexual agency. He recounts:

> My cousin Francis raped me. Tied up my hands and tied my legs together. He was about six years older and bigger than I was. This went on for a long time. It got to the point when I went to the washroom for what you would call a bowel movement, I used to get erections. I started questioning my sexuality because when he abused you, that's what it felt like – having a bowel movement. But when his older sisters started doing it, I *enjoyed* that. They didn't hurt me. These sisters used to baby sit us. They never tied me up. I got so comfortable with these women doing this to me, and what they'd get me to do to them, instead of waiting for them to baby sit, I'd go and see them. That went on for three years, till we moved away.

At age twelve, Simpson responded violently to his mother's attempts to punish him, heeding his father's counsel to hit back hard against aggressors. His father, however, used that occasion to reaffirm his own right to inflict familial punishment, along with both age- and gender-specific divisions of power in the household. Simpson remembers:

> Sometimes mom hit us, but we'd just laugh at her. I hit my mom one time. I'd stayed away all weekend. When I got home my mom started hitting me with a broom and calling me stupid. I punched her right in the mouth as hard as I could, so hard I broke her false teeth in half – top and bottom. When dad came home, he lifted me right off my feet. He punched me in the face and knocked me out cold. When I came to, he hit me in the same place, and knocked me out again. He knocked me out three times. The third time I came to, he grabbed me by the hair, and threw me across the living room. He said, "If you even look at your mom wrong, I'm going to kill you." Only dad could hit mom.

Despite severe beatings, Simpson admired and feared his father's physicality. By contrast, he read his mother's nurturing qualities as passivity rather than moral agency:

> My dad's a very powerful man, physically, to this day. I wanted to be like my dad. I don't know of anybody that's beaten him in a fight. He's very feared to this day. He just don't back down from nobody. He likes a good fight. My mom's a very passive person. You ask her to do something – even if it's out of her way – she'll do it. She'd do anything for dad and us kids.

As a young teenager, Simpson began to sing and play guitar in his father's church, which drew attention from girls his age. He recalls: "*Immediately*, I wanted to have sex with these girls." By age fifteen, he imagined that every girl was "my possession to do whatever I wanted to them, whenever I wanted to." From then on, Simpson's masculinizing practices centred explicitly on pursuing, dominating, and controlling women's sexuality. His routines for finding female partners constituted troubling gender and social practices. Simpson saw women as weak and vulnerable objects for his predatory sexual agency:

> I preyed on these kinds of women. They were from homes like mine. I always ended up with these girls that I knew were vulnerable. They were all so easy to control. I watched for weakness. And when I seen it, I took

advantage. When I was fifteen, they were older women. If they had just broken up with their boyfriends, I knew they'd be in a vulnerable state, and I'd move in. I'd be the shoulder – anything I could do just to have sex with these ladies. And it was always just sex. I'd do anything to meet my own sexual needs. I even had sex with my mom.

At age fifteen, Simpson's mother left the family. Simpson quit school in Grade 8 and fled the home to escape beatings. He became a ward of the court, and was shuffled among institutions and programs for troubled youth, though his age and reputation deterred prospective foster parents. Deskilled and powerless on the labour market, he began to live with much older women in arrangements that satisfied his basic needs for shelter and food, and reaffirmed a masculinized subjectivity through his power over women and their seemingly unlimited sexual availability. These relations provided mutually exploitative and advantageous elements. Simpson explains:

> I've lived with women since I was sixteen. I was happiest drinking with older women and them giving me all the attention. They had daughters and sons the same age that I was living with them. I'd just meet them at a party. Sometimes I wouldn't even leave their house. I'd end up with their daughter. I'd start with the mother, right to the daughter, the cousins, everybody in the family. I've done that many times. I was asked if I ever forced any woman to have sex with me. In all honesty, I have. I used drugs and alcohol. Even with my male friends. I'd get them drunk so I can fool around with their wives somewhere.

Men and women remained legitimate targets for Simpson's physical aggression as an adult. However, he does not express shame or pride in exploiting and beating women. Rather surprisingly, Simpson has no adult assault convictions. His body and mind were disciplined to inflict and receive pain, which enabled him to restabilize a dominant masculine selfhood. He notes:

> I've always beaten the shit out of anybody that was there. Man or woman. At the time, I didn't care. And I'd laugh about it: "See what happens when you fuck with me – man or woman, you don't get loud with me. I don't care who you are." I didn't care how big you are or how tough. A statement that still comes to mind is "if you can give a good beating you can take a good beating." And boy, I used to get good beatings. And I could sure dish it out.

Simpson drew on a "phallocentric framework" of beliefs (cf. hooks 1992, 94) and practices of sexual conquest to affirm his cultural ideals of hegemonic masculinity. He had eight children with five women, but he explicitly rejected fatherhood and a role as a domestic provider. He left his partners once they became pregnant, but was unable to surrender his need for absolute control over them:

> I remember being very jealous and possessive with Denise. All her time was devoted to me. When she got pregnant, I thought I was happy about it. I didn't have a job. I didn't have anything. I always stole to make a living. I was good at it. Will was born, and I became jealous because now all Denise's time was with Will. It got to the point where I wanted to kill them both. I was going to kill my son because he was taking up all Denise's time. I could not get all of Denise's time any more, so I ran out on them.

Simpson resorted to brute power when emotional pain interfered with his need to dominate the people in his relationships. He "didn't give a shit about anybody," which he says was a blockage to unwelcome emotionality. He explains:

> Nobody controlled me. I didn't let nobody get close. If there was anybody going to be hurt it wasn't going to be me. I remember telling myself, "Nobody's going to hurt me. Nobody's going to leave me." I always thought, everybody's going to leave. I'm going to hurt them before they hurt me.

In a context of economic marginality, Simpson established and reproduced gender through his interactions with his female partners who, in turn, reinforced and repeated arrangements that reaffirmed women's social and cultural subordination to men. By the time he raped, beat, and killed a woman, Simpson was performing gender through a consciously chosen predatory masculinity. He puts it bluntly:

> Women were just there to meet my needs – my sexual needs. Clean up after me. Cook for me. They were weaker than me. I'm not that intelligent of a person. Every girl that I've gone with has been smarter than me. But they were easy to manipulate. I wanted to take advantage of every woman I could. Men too. Coming into the federal system, I picked on vulnerable punks in jail – forcing them into buying drugs and giving me their

canteen. Back then I was an animal. I preyed on vulnerable people like a wild animal preys on weaker ones.

James' Story

James is a white man in his mid-thirties. He has served sixteen years of a life-twenty-five sentence for murder, an offence that occurred five months after his release from an eighteen-month sentence for attempted rape. As a boy, James was found guilty for indecent assault three times; today, he acknowledges many more. The process of his alienation from family, friendship, and receptivity to others was subtle and was more visible in its effects than in its method. His masculine self remains rather unfixed: "I don't have a real sexual identity – never had." James was an only child, adopted by a middle-aged white couple of Eastern European descent. His mother was Canadian born. Nevertheless, she and her husband spoke Polish[9] together because James' father never learned much English. James, however, never learned Polish. Linguistic and cultural barriers isolated him from the private and social worlds of family relationships. As an early mechanism for coping with exclusion, James withdrew into what he calls "his world." He explains:

> Mostly, they spoke in Polish to each other. When there were problems, they spoke in Polish. I never knew what they were saying. All of their friends were Polish, so that was the language around me. When conversations came around I usually left. I never learned to speak the language. I resented being out of the conversation. I didn't feel a part of anything. I saw kids on TV would run up and get big hugs and kisses and all this. And there was a lot of resentment about not having that kind of intimacy. I basically started doing my own thing. During these times I went to play with my toys in *my world* – fantasy worlds that I would create.

His parents were uncomfortable outside the Polish community and restricted James' movements outside the home. Cultural and generational differences added to his everyday estrangement from his peers. His parents' powerlessness to communicate with or protect James heightened his sense of helplessness:

> I was always unable to communicate with kids my own age. Because of this I stayed home a lot. I became aware of why the other kids teased me about my parents. My parents were out of step with fashion so this made

me a target for other kids. I was never able to tell [my parents] that there were problems with other children. Only when I came home crying or beat up could they tell. Once, when I was five, two kids my age held me while another pitched rocks at me. My parents never once went to deal with the parents of these children. I hated them for this.

Economically, James' parents gave him much of what he wanted, and he was not a recipient of or a witness to violence at home. His father worked in a forestry camp and returned home on weekends. Even though they did not share father-son rituals such as "playing catch and wrestling around," James knew he controlled his father. James' mother was kind, gentle, and always at home. He never once saw her angry or tearful. James was impatient with her "over-protectiveness," but adds, "that's not a bad thing." Nonetheless, his mother compared unfavourably "to all the moms I saw on TV. I'd always see *Brady Bunch* holding their kids." Media-constructed images of motherhood gave form to James' desire for expressive displays of what he calls "love and affection." To the best of James' knowledge, his only experience of intimacy and reciprocity occurred at age five. He did not then recognize or pursue these context-specific bodily interactions as general social practices:

The first time I knew that girls were different than boys was kindergarten. Twice a day we had naptime. This girl didn't have a blanket so we shared mine. We wound up fooling around under the blanket. She undid her pants and let me touch her, and I let her touch me when she asked. Later, we were almost undressed under the blanket. We did that for an entire school season during naptime. I associated that kind of touching with closeness and intimacy – I didn't know that then. I just knew I got that good feeling. I liked being this close and holding her. I wanted that. I never felt scared. She was the first kid that didn't seem to hate me. So, that was my one and only good experience with a female. [After kindergarten] I let the event slide to the back of my mind.

Thereafter, school was the primary site of James' distress and eventual social alienation. His own conduct and the reaction of peers distanced him further and further from others. He was a slow learner – the "dummy," "the strange one," and the "granny's boy." He failed Grade 5. He was miserable at sports but refused efforts to make him quit. He was called ugly because of his "very, very horrible acne." James fought back, but his pugnacious assertions of self deepened his estrangement from others. He caused reckless accidents, antagonized his antagonists, and told "everyone to go fuck themselves." He sheltered his ego by actively refusing to allow others to effect him: "I tried not to care what others thought or felt." Often friendless, James gravitated towards younger children. He explains:

> When I was around the younger kids, I was able to control the situation a little more. I'm the older one. And I was able to be the boss, so to speak. Little kids made me feel good and confident. They never resented me because they didn't know me. It didn't matter whether I knew math. *They* didn't know it either.

At age eight, an unknown man molested James after they worked together hauling gravel. To this day, James interprets that experience as enjoyable. But the incident also rekindles past memories and created new gender-specific meanings for James. He recalls:

> He didn't do anything that hurt me. I still don't consider it a bad experience. But I can see the whole evil of the thing because he said, "This is what you do to girls." I associated it with the act that he was doing. He undid my pants and slid them down. He was rubbing himself against my bum. It wasn't confusing because he was holding me gently. I can't get angry over it, 'cause I can't get that close attachment out of my mind – that it was something I was wanting in me to be held. And I remember holding this little girl in kindergarten. From that point I saw girls differently.

From ages nine to eleven, James revived his kindergarten practice of producing intimacy through genital contact. His interactions with girls created a gendered subjectivity, which was not then informed by the masculinizing themes of sexual coerciveness and dominance over women. Later, however, James started to molest girls:

> I never thought of doing it to a boy. I related it only to what the man had said you do to girls. I molested ten or fifteen girls. I never had one refuse. I asked them to come with me. I knew some of them. I talked to them and persuaded them that this was all right to allow me to touch them. There was never any physical violence or coercion. They were all usually

two years younger than me. I exploited their trust of older people. I was holding them close to me. My genitals were against their bums, but I wasn't exposed. We'd do that for ten or fifteen minutes and then I'd leave. I was aware this was wrong. But I liked the good feeling I got too much to stop.

James achieved psychic empowerment by dreaming and imagining worlds where he commanded authority. But he never combined his conceptualizations of power with sexual acts. He reflects:

I thought about the children I touched and kept playing the event over in my mind. I also still had my own little world and I used my dinky toys as the medium. I would create this world where I was someone in charge – military, construction, fireman – and people treated me like an equal. During these fantasy trips I never included my sexual acts in them.

Finally, one girl reported James, and a police investigation followed. His court-assigned social worker told him that being eleven was too old for "sex play." His parents said nothing. Undeterred, James returned to his original practice after viewing culturally prescribed images of consensual heterosexual sex. He recalls:

I found a *Playboy* magazine. Prior to this, I never really touched their genitals. Never even thought about it. But now I see these guys with their pants off touching women there and here, and other kinds of touching that I didn't know – obviously didn't understand. My next victim I had *completely* naked. This time it was without her consent. She didn't resist at first, but I think she was scared. I was twelve. She was nine or ten. I was touching her genitals. I was unsure of exposing myself. I was unsure of any form of oral sex. But there was a strong desire to do that. But I never did. What I kept doing is rubbing her genitals.

At puberty James reframed his intimacy needs as sexual in character. His body's agency gave new meaning and direction to his private and social conduct. He explains:

With puberty I became more aware of why I liked the feeling. I started to get a sexual response. I now wanted a sexual release more than the intimacy of the act. There was no violence against any of my victims at this point. It was still only touching, and then when I was alone I masturbated.

I would relive these assaults till it stopped being good. Then I would go and find another girl.

At age twelve, James once again became known to the police, and was put on probation after he was formally found guilty of indecent assault. His school expelled him for aggressive sexual tendencies. He reoffended and his probation was extended. James eventually became a ward of the court, and for two years he cycled through six-month foster home placements, private tutors, and psychiatric counsellors. His clinical sessions focused exclusively on his parents and entirely ignored the fact that James liked what he did and "didn't care what anyone thought."

Even though James knew that men are supposed to have real power, he appropriated power only in his imagination. James elaborates:

I have two types of fantasies – the sexual and my old fantasy world fantasies. The sexual fantasy is my own sexual gratification – no rejection, the women give me what I want, when I want it, no conversation – just sex. There was no violence in them. My fantasy-world fantasy goes with my other feelings – the anger, the hurt, frustration, the fear – all of that will lead me into my fantasy world where I don't *have* any of this nonsense. Nobody's making me angry. I'm in control. I act out of vengeance, if you will, in different ways. So, I have sexual fantasies and violent fantasies, but the two are never linked. Like when I'm angry at a particular woman, I don't fantasize about raping her. I create a war fantasy where she will be killed.

At age sixteen, James returned to his parents' care. His primary frustration now was physically sexual. He believed, however, that female children were not capable of giving him what he wants. Besides his fantasy worlds, James lacked any obvious material masculinizing practices. He observes:

As a man, I felt I needed to be strong and independent. I guess, most of the time, I didn't feel very much like a man. I had low self-esteem. I began to believe some of the kids, calling me stupid, ugly. I still had very bad acne. Girls my own age wouldn't have anything to do with me. Though I was sixteen, I still didn't know what I wanted to do with my life. I spent my free time wandering around alone. Most of the time now I was in the fantasy worlds I created. My parents didn't throw out my toys so I went right back to them.

At age seventeen, James tried to rape a fifteen-year-old girl whom he happened upon while wandering alone in the woods.

Paul's Story

Paul is a forty-year-old Aboriginal man. He has served ten years of a life-seven sentence for attempted murder. That incident happened thirteen months after his statutory release from a seven-year, nine-month sentence for rape, unlawful confinement, and assault causing bodily harm. Those events occurred while Paul was on probation following a sixty-day sentence for trying to abduct a woman off the street. Paul's narrative conveys his lived experiences of powerlessness with women. On his first birthday, his white birth mother divorced his Aboriginal father and married a white man. Paul grew up with a baby brother (who also eventually served federal time for sexual assault) and two younger half-sisters. Paul idolizes early memories of his mother and says he spent his boyhood years watching media images of women. He remembers:

> My early years were just me and my mom, 'cause my dad was a commercial fisherman. It seemed like everything was really cool. She taught me to read even before I went to school. We used to watch the Rock Hudson and Doris Day movies. I still like the Audrey Hepburn-type woman, who's independent and cheeky, but loving and caring. And smart. Intelligent. Talks back. I like cheekiness. It's more challenging. That's what my girlfriend is like. Straightforward. I enjoy banter. My girlfriend's got a graduate degree. I enjoy debating with her.

At first Paul admired his big, strong father who, like Paul, was a quiet, humorous, playful man. Paul was keenly aware that his skin was "a way different colour" from his sisters'. At age nine, Paul learned about his "real dad, his real name, and his Nativeness," and began to refuse his stepfather's authority and friendship. He interpreted his mother's apparent emotional distance as part of a process of difference, which filled Paul with a sense of self-worthlessness:

> Our house was almost like a halfway house. We shared it with five other adults. Plus us four kids. I had a real close relationship with my mom, and now I can't even see her with all the adults. "Where's my mom?" [*Laughs.*] I'd stomp my feet jump up and down, but I'd just get some kind of downer to calm me. When I couldn't get the attention from my mom that I had

before I started school, it was like, now, I'm not so much *different*, I'm just kinda worthless. That's how I *thought* about it: "Ah, she doesn't love me because I'm not worth it. I'm different."

Fourteen years after her death, Paul is still ambivalent about his mother. On the one hand, he says, "You love your mom – she's your first relationship." On the other hand, he acknowledges she frustrated his boyhood belief in his own agency and power. To this day, Paul feels helpless and exasperated by his apparent failure to obtain his mom's care and affection. He reflects:

I loved her very much, but I really thought she didn't love me. And I tried everything. I started smashing windows, stealing things from the store when I was six. But I found out getting into trouble wasn't worth it cause they disliked me even *more* [*laughs*], 'cause now I was a little troublemaker. So I thought, maybe if I'd be good, then they'd start to love me – I actually *was* thinking that. So I was into everything, trying to do the best I could – cub scouts, earning my badges, cleaning up the house, school choir, baseball team, volleyball, track and field, gymnastics. Maybe she did notice. In Grade 7, I remember winning the best twelve-year-old athlete-of-the-school. I came home all happy. Mom just told me to go play: "Go away." Holy shit. What did I have to do?

Paul responded to his mother's growing indifference with his own apathy. From age twelve, pot, LSD, MDA, cocaine, and alcohol helped him exercise some sense of control over what he calls his "inner turmoil." At age thirteen, doctors prescribed Valium to calm Paul; however, he mixed drugs and was often out of control. Once a curious student who enjoyed learning and excelled in school, Paul no longer envisioned a hegemonic masculine future of a marriage and a career. At age fifteen, his school expelled him. Afterwards, his fears and needs for emotional expression and receptivity surfaced only when he was "high." Paul explains:

I just gave up. From then on I said, "I can't wait to get out of this house." You know what they said? "You have to wait until you're sixteen." When I got into Grade 8, I was disruptive. I eventually quit – I got kicked out. In grade school, I wanted to be a doctor. I had it all planned out. I would get married at twenty-five. I was a good student until we started moving all over the damn place. After the doctor, I didn't want to be anything. I just wanted to get high and party and that's how I lived. I spent my whole life high. I mean, I took drugs and alcohol so I wouldn't *have* to deal with things. Only when I got drunk would I talk. Long conversations with anybody. I had a feeling that I wanted to talk and tell somebody what I felt like. I felt really shitty and, I guess, I wanted to ask people around me, ask my parents, "am I okay?" "Am I loveable?" "Am I worth something?" 'Cause I never felt myself worth anything.

Paul began to embrace "doing Nativeness" as part of his gender identity. At age fourteen, he and a friend made a romantic attempt to "live off the land for the weekend" and "go back to the old ways," but were defeated by the weather and the failure to find any food: "Maybe we can't be Indians after all." Paul resolved his ambivalence about Aboriginal identity by consciously choosing not to live like "a bad Indian." He connected his racial difference to his mother's inattention and later to fights with other boys, and acknowledged both pride and shame in Native identity. Paul elaborates:

After my friend moved, I went to visit him. That's where I ran into some prejudice. It was a poor reserve. There was a lot of alcoholism. It was just terrible. In the town, you couldn't walk on one side of the street – you'd get shit. All he had to eat was potatoes. I wasn't used to that so I took him out for supper. I had to show the restaurant guy my *money*! That I had money. And I've never been treated like that in my life. I did feel ashamed there. "How can people live like this?" I remember thinking, "it's not where I was *from*," but I was also thinking, "my people." I was ashamed of my people. That was the only time in my life that I ever thought about my heritage, really. I put it all behind me and said, "That's it. I'm not going to live like that." [Later], this one [Native] woman says, "Oh, those must have been the bad Indians." And I thought, "Oh, that makes sense, there's bad ones – they're the ones that give that stereotype, [*laughs*] the ones that don't care." After I moved to the Prairies, I had a little more sense of pride out there. It was kinda cool being a Native out there.

In treatment, a program video triggered new recollections about his early sexual abuse. Seeing and talking about the video helped Paul re-script his past. He explains:

In my last program there was all these pedophiles. So we all had to watch those kinds of images. I'd never been so angry in my life. I don't like any sexual crimes. But I don't normally get that angry – it was like a moral outrage. I could feel the rage in my chest. I could hardly speak. This guy committed suicide shortly after. Mom's all crying and upset about him. I never said anything. That kind of put my life together for me. I have no male role models. No close male friends. Plus, as a teenager – I spent my twenties and thirties in jail – I thought the more girls I go to bed with the better. Maybe I was trying to make up for something. I don't know. Maybe I had to prove myself as a man. Maybe I was more needy and felt I needed more attention from my mom. But she was just getting pissed off at me for smashing windows and shoplifting. Getting into so much trouble when you're only six years old. I can remember myself as a little kid – just being a sweet little kid – really enjoyed helping, then, just blowing up. Sure, anger at my mom but … I have stuff to work through.

Paul's immediate family, however, was the primary site of his perceived disempowerment. Interestingly, the causes of his fear and helplessness are more difficult for him to elucidate than their effects on him:

I always thought that there was nothing in my childhood worth talking about. I wasn't beaten up or abused by my parents [*pauses*] but hearing other people talk, I felt the same way. I may not have got the crap beat out of me, but I sure as hell felt the same way. There was tension between my parents I guess. I never knew why. The tension – the fear I felt – was because of, not the *threat* of violence, but you know, there's a tension in the air. You get scared. *Nothing* would be talked about. When I would get picked up by the cops for stealing a car, they'd bring me home and tell my parents. Nothing would be said. Not a damn thing. That was the hard part [*pauses*] that was so hurtful. My mom didn't say a thing. I felt really helpless. Really. I didn't know what the hell to do to get my parents to love me, so, I felt helpless.

His stepfather's masculinity was not defined by dominance or assertiveness over his wife. Rather, his passive resistance and silence seemed to mirror Paul's own sense of helplessness. Even though Paul refused his father's authority, when his mother did the same, he saw it as an illegitimate challenge to gendered power divisions:

She would flip out on him. Not yell and scream, but "rar, rar, rar, rar, rar, rar, rar you should be home." Mom used to bitch at my dad constantly. 'Cause, he's quiet. He's like Al Bundy after work. He'd sit like this in front of TV. But they never really fought. I mean, she'd nag him, and he would take it. I lost some respect for him for that. 'Cause he'd just sit there and take it, and I'd be thinking [*pauses*] actually, I'd be thinking bad about my mom: "What a bitch. Why is she [doing that]," you know? And then I'd be thinking, "He's just sitting there and taking it. Stand up for yourself."

Paul eventually appropriated a version of his familial power relationships into his own romantic endeavours. He refused all overt forms of aggressiveness towards women and adopted his father's passivity. Rather than striving to control or ignore women, Paul distanced himself from any relationship that invoked his boyhood powerlessness to find love and be loved:

I couldn't express the anger towards my *mom*, and I think one of the values that I learned was you don't talk to women like that. 'Cause my dad, he never said anything. All you do is take it, and swallow it. You don't express it. I never hit a woman. With women, *any* bad feelings, I'm serious, *anything*, any argument or nagging, and I was gone. It didn't matter how little. It reminded me too much of my mom. I would start fooling around and never express any anger towards women at all.

By contrast, Paul was not averse to hitting men. He reworked a self-defensive response to his racial difference into an aggressively masculine persona. Paul was a resolute fighter, and refused surrender in all his battles. His public display of hegemonic masculinity belied his private sense of helplessness and fear at home:

I hit guys all the time. And I wasn't really mad at them. I'm a serious fighter. I am. People don't think I am, to my advantage. I grew up fighting all the time. I started fighting in school. I learned to fight protecting myself. I mean, in the first six years of school, I remember running into one other Native person. I didn't understand what Native was. I remember saying, "No I'm not [an Indian]." The only thing I learned, somewhere, was all Indians are just drunks on Skid Row and that was it. The fights were after school. I'd never give up. I'd fight three kids at once. I remember when I was ten, our landlord saying, "Why don't you just fight them one at a time?" I said, "I'm okay. I'm not going to give up." And I never did.

Paul's sexual practices with women were imbued with the masculinizing theme of sexual conquest. By his own words, however, he equated sex with love and used sex to reaffirm himself as "worth something" and "loveable." He frames his affairs with married women in the language of stealing another man's love rather than possessing sexual property. Paul knew, however, that the materialization of masculinity and femininity through sex, love, and the body is always transitory and time limited. He explains:

> The initial romance stuff was cool. I'm lots of fun. I'm a romantic. I've never taken anyone to a fancy restaurant. For me, it's more romantic to have a candlelit dinner at A&W in your car. I remember midnight picnics in [the] Park. Of course, I never really had a car. That stuff never bothered me at all. [*Pauses.*] I would *like* to have a nice car, don't get me wrong. I did kinda prey on, I don't know if it was weakness, but – this is kinda stupid – but I thought I could fulfill some need – [*pauses*] I've had lots of affairs with married women. It was like I could sense something missing in their life. Romance. Excitement. I also thought that if I could steal somebody else's girlfriend, she definitely loved me more than anybody. But then I would think, "If I could steal her from him, who's to say someone can't steal her from me?"

Since boyhood, Paul believed that women had the power to make him feel good or bad. In his lived reality, women possessed the potential to remove his control over his suppressed emotions. With little sense of his own agency and power, Paul explicitly blamed women for eliciting feminizing feelings of fear and vulnerability in him which, if unleashed, threatened his sense of self. Paul elaborates:

> I was eight when I realized that women had some kind of big power over me – and in a tender moment, I might be caught off guard, and I'd be spilling my guts. [*Laughs self-consciously.*] I was scared to let anyone know I was so angry. I always thought that if I started talking about everything that was inside of me, [*pauses*] it's like, I have all this stuff in me, and if it all started coming out, I'd be left [*pauses*] just hollow and empty, you know. [*Laughs self-consciously.*] I always thought that. I was scared. And I always blamed women for bringing that kind of stuff up in me. It's like, after all the romance, getting closer in a relationship, you get the feeling of wanting to share everything. [*Pauses.*] If I was with a woman I really enjoyed *talking* with, it was even more scary, because, it's like I knew I wouldn't be able to help myself. I'd just start talking about everything, and that scared me. [*Laughs self-consciously.*] That added to women's power over me, 'cause I didn't think of it as my *fear*. I did have fear. I knew

I was afraid, but I was angry at women for being able to *pull* that out of me, you know what I mean? Like a trap. I somehow blamed women … [for turning] my vulnerability into anger.

By leaving school at an early age, Paul marginalized himself on the labour market. His economic vulnerability created another sphere of powerlessness, which distanced him from traditional hegemonic masculinity and denied him economic independence. Like others in this study, his fighting skills were an alternative means to obtain money and a link to a male persona:

I had to move back home a few times. I had no idea how to survive in the real world. I was sixteen. After the party was over, "how the hell am I going to pay the rent? Where do I get a job?" I have no experience – do nothing. I didn't have a trade. By this time I was worried. Between sixteen and nineteen, I'm feeling even more worthless 'cause I didn't *have* a job. Feeling useless really [*pauses*] so I'd move back home, then get the hell out of there. I moved in with a friend of mine. He'd lure someone home with him and I would rob him. Beat him up and take his money. After punching them in the head, they're more likely to give you money.

At age nineteen, Paul committed his first of six stranger rapes or attempted rapes. He appropriated and internalized rape as a private practice to cope with his personal crisis:

Before my first [sexual] crime, I had about four or five relations kinda going. It's like, I can't get enough or something. And then I get lost in everything. Nothing is fulfilling. And the women in my life know I'm not serious, so they pull away. And then I'm thinking, [*mocking voice*] "Nobody loves me." [*Laughs self-consciously.*] "Why can't I have a normal relationship?" When, you know, I started the problem in the first place. That's what happens my whole life really. My head just spinning – trying to stay stoned to deal with it. Gets into a total mess. I get all pissed off. Blame it all on women.

Paddy's Story

Paddy is a white man in his late thirties, imprisoned over sixteen years for first-degree murder and an unrelated rape and attempted murder.

Paddy's repeated failure to convey a programmatically compelling autobiography puts him at odds with group members and program facilitators alike. They suspect him of "keeping secrets," "limited insight," and "refusing to confront all his issues." After five programs, Paddy could easily introduce new memories or emotions into his storytelling: "I know what [CSC] wants to hear." But he stands by his story and refuses to rewrite his past in treatment discourse.

By his account, nothing horrible stands out in his boyhood. Paddy spent his first ten years with an older and younger brother in their parents' fishing resort lodge, which was run primarily by his mother. His father was a logger, a former high-school track star and ex-biker who told Paddy that he "won" his mother in a biker fight. His father emphasized a brand of rugged manhood centred on toughness and stoicism, and taught Paddy how to hunt and fish and "not to be weak." These masculinizing rituals earned Paddy praise, and yet frightened him. He was taught to see sadness and fear as effeminate and believed that he could win his dad's affections by reiterating the gender norm of male toughness. He recalls:

> I remember being taught to swim. I was taken way out in the lake on my dad's shoulders. He dove under water and swam back to shore. He yelled, "You better learn to swim." And swim I did. Later, he told me and everyone else that he was proud. But I was frightened. He never hovered around to make sure I was safe. The quality I associated with being a boy was tough. No crying, or I was a girl. I was a disappointment to dad anytime, *anytime* I cried. Anytime I cried. "You're weak. You're just a little baby. You're never going to be a man."

Paddy's father controlled his family members through physical and verbal force. Even though Paddy never witnessed overt physical violence against his mother, gendered messages about men's power were unambiguous. In the face of what appeared to be her voluntary subordination to his dad, Paddy's early admiration for his mother's strength gradually became a thinly veiled disdain for her weakness:

> Mom's five feet flat. Very athletic. She played all the sports I played. Mom was pretty feisty. She was tough, 'cause she put up with him. When they fought, mom didn't back down at all. A lot of screaming and yelling when they did fight. Mom would run out of the room crying, and I'd attack my

dad. I was six years old, but I would see red. And dad would just back-hand me. But, it *wasn't* like a constant. I think there was some hitting, but it was behind closed doors. I don't know how much she got hit. After age ten, she seemed to fall in line and back him up. I guess she was eventually cowed by my dad and just gave up. It came to the point where she just became weak. Later on, mom took his side, or, I *felt* that she always took his side against me, and I got in fights with her too. Never physical. My dad always taught me never to hit women. Except in my second crime, I never did hit a woman. Never once in a relationship.

Paddy was more successful than he realized in living up to his father's ideals of manhood. He disciplined his emotions and body against public displays of weakness and channelled his needs and feelings through humour or anger. Any other emotions hindered his ability to control his tears:

> A man's got to be able to take it and dish it out to other men without being an enemy. I tried to live up to dad [*pauses*] I could never measure up [*pauses*] and I wanted to. I didn't feel like his son. I *hated* him. Later, in school though, you couldn't get a tear out of me if you wanted to. They could hit me with the strap until my hands bled. But they wouldn't get a reaction of me. The only emotions I knew how to express were humour or anger. And anger usually led to violence. The others – loneliness, pain, fear, guilt, shame, embarrassment, usually led to me crying. And that was not allowed, right?

Even the expression of his anger was muted and furtive. After Paddy's arrest for murder, his mother discovered a note hidden under his mattress, written at age twelve. It read, "One day I'm going to kill mom and dad and [older brother]."

By twelve years old, Paddy weighed 200 pounds. He was an object of ridicule for his classmates, but his sheer physicality gave him an edge in sports and a fear-based form of control over other boys:

> I had to play sports. Had to. To fit in. I got teased about my weight. By the time I was twelve, I was very heavy – close to my adult weight. I never really thought about my weight, but everybody else did. Both girls and boys ridiculed me because I was fat. But I remember thinking *then* that women don't have the right to tease me because I could defend. Girls were weak and they must have seen how I treated the guys that teased me. A lot of boys were afraid of me. If I ran into them, they're flat. I was constantly in fights with kids. So, girls should have known better.

Beyond taunts and boredom, school was a place of physical punishment. Paddy estimates that he was strapped on twenty occasions for fighting boys.

In Grade 12, Paddy left school to work for his father, who by then owned a logging company. Paddy's father routinely fired him "a couple of thousand times," then re-hired him. For the next five years, Paddy logged for his father seven months per year, and the rest of the time he moved back and forth between low-skilled manual labour jobs and entry-level manager trainee positions in retail. Paddy's opportunities to create a gendered subjecthood varied across different work sites. In the masculine domain of logging he was "his own man," self-affirmed by the transcendent qualities of independence, freedom, and power over nature. By contrast, he felt limited and abused in department store manager training positions, where he saw himself as an object of authority, subordinated within power relations where feminizing deference was more valued than male physical performance. Paddy explains:

> When I'm working, there aren't enough hours. Sometimes I wish I could go without sleep. And I loved logging. 'Cause you're in the middle of nowhere. I guess there's a power to take this great big tree and just waste it. I look back on it, it's kind of sad [*pauses*] I liked being out in the woods. It was fresh and clean and I was my own man. I made really, *really* good money. [One of the times] dad fired me; I got this job as a manager trainee for [a department store]. The guys above me were totally inadequate. They were telling me that I should do it this way and I should do it that way. I had to crumb to them to keep my job. I don't like brown-nosing. I actually despised it. I felt abused by it. I think my actions and work ethic should speak for itself.

Paddy recalls being fired by his father for "doing the same thing everyone else was doing," and forced "to crumb" in front of incompetent retail managers. Through these school and work interactions with his family, teachers, school mates, employers, and later women, Paddy claims he learned his own victimhood: "Most of my life I felt like a victim. No control." Paddy's words illustrate the disjuncture between the hegemonic masculine ideals that he valorized and the actual material resources available to him for exercising forms of men's power:

> Back then I figured that a man has got to have the car, the motorbike, the speedboat. A man had to have possessions so he could look good to

other people. You got to be tough. You got to work. You got to have money. You've got to have the girlfriend. You have to be able to take punishment and give punishment. I always thought that a man needs some sort of power – so he doesn't have to crumb to asshole bosses. I didn't know how I was going to do that. I was never able to do the quick money turnaround ventures.

Paddy remained puzzled by the power dynamics that characterized his sexual practices with women. He speaks about media-based sexuality and the cultural expectations of male sexual aggressiveness. Pornography, he says, confirmed his father's messages about women's weakness and inferiority, and gave him visual representations for "doing" men's power through specific sexual acts. He explains:

A thousand different pornography books just kind of shored up the be-lief system that my dad taught me, which is that women are weak. Here were these books saying that this is what they like …. [That they like] aggressive men. Different sexual positions – mostly male-dominated po-sitions. Anal sex. Women want to be forced – well, dominated – by men in bed. This is a belief system that's all over the place, I mean, even in parts of the Bible, women are subservient to men. That makes women an acceptable outlet for men's anger. But I also learned that a man protects the woman. From other men. It makes us feel like men, right? So, that's contradictory, isn't it?

After high school, Paddy put these images into practice in his encoun-ters with older and more sexually experienced women who initiated and normalized these sexual acts. By enacting rituals of male domi-nance and female passivity, Paddy and his partners created specific masculine and feminine subjectivities:

PADDY: I learned about sex from older women. They told me how to do things. And I got some confidence. But it solidified my beliefs about women that came from the pornography. So, my experiences with women at that stage were they wanted to be treated this way, you know, in an aggressive [*pauses*] not hitting or anything like that, but held down, dominated. And I found that most of the women after that were very much the same, or, they didn't say anything. They never complained. One woman, she wanted me to hold her hair from behind while we had sex. I had one girlfriend, she wanted to be raped – she wanted to be overpowered and the whole fear thing. I thought, if I give them what they want, maybe I'll get what I want.

Q: What did you want?

PADDY: I don't know. Not that.

Paddy felt pressured to enact male sexuality in terms of control and agency, yet he also desired forms of intimacy centred on reciprocity rather than difference and dominance. However, he was unable to communicate an alternative to any of his partners because he feared they would laugh at him for departing from conventional scripts of sexual assertiveness. Sexuality was a site of contradiction, dissatisfaction, and frustration for Paddy, and a site of disdain for his female partners, who participated in their own subservience:

I don't know how to describe it. I never felt satisfied afterwards. I didn't feel fulfilled. It was kind of empty. I felt I was doing the right thing because they seemed to be enjoying themselves, but the thoughts that ran in my head were, "You're nothing. You're just a slut like every other woman." Back then, I honestly don't know if I could have sex with a woman and respect her. I didn't respect women before I had sex with them. So, sex wasn't going to change that. I thought there should be more to it than just sex. I can't explain it. I thought it should be mutual. But I never had the ability to communicate that. Well, I had the ability. But I figured if I communicated that, I would get ridiculed and teased. That's kind of what happened with my wife. This is jumping ahead because I married her in jail. I think I just wanted to be [pauses] just cuddling. Companionship is what I wanted most in life. But my wife couldn't understand that. She said she did. But she was hurt. She thought she wasn't pleasing me. It was embarrassing.

Paddy was unable to relate to women other than through an aggressive, albeit consensual sexuality. In turn, consensual "aggressive and dominating" sex became one of his coping mechanisms for dealing with life's conflicts and stresses. He adds, however, that "I hated everyone" then and "put a few guys in the hospital."

At age twenty, Paddy lived hundreds of miles from his hometown. He was recently separated from his girlfriend, and worked sporadically delivering pizzas, framing houses, and installing pools and hot tubs. The first and only time Paddy broke into a dwelling with the intent to steal, he also raped and killed a woman he had never met.

Bob's Story

Bob is a white man in his early twenties. At age seventeen, the courts raised him to adult status and convicted him for second-degree murder. At that time, his life-ten sentence was the maximum penalty allowed for a youth. Growing up, Bob aspired to be a NHL hockey player and a serial killer. His role models were Wayne Gretzky and Ted Bundy. Bob bespeaks the contextual character of gendering practices and identity. He remembers:

> It's weird looking back. Thinking about raping and killing women serially, being a person like Ted Bundy. Because I also wanted to become a hockey player. Wayne Gretzky was my hero. I was raised to play clean hockey. On the ice, I was a totally different person. I wasn't aggressive. I very rarely got a penalty. I was no good to my team in the penalty box. My strength was my skating. I was a good player. Damn good. I never thought of being a serial killer while I was playing hockey.

Bob and his younger sister grew up in a nuclear family with conventional divisions of emotional and economic labour and power. Bob's father was a mechanic who built backyard ice rinks in the winter and taught Bob to skate and play hockey. Father and son interacted through other "man activities" like hunting, fishing, and camping: "There were no verbal messages about how men should behave. It was all visible." Bob's family evinced the unchallenged authority of the father, and family members indulged his temperament. Bob's father projected an aura of masculine violence that scared Bob "shitless." Even so, he insists, "we had a great relationship":

> I loved my dad, but I feared him dearly. I didn't see much emotion from my dad. I seen him cry once. *That's* strength. When I was five years old, I seen him punch a hole in the wall. I thought he was angry. [Recently] I found out he was just joking, and it was a thin cardboard wall. But I kept this image of my dad as huge and tough and strong. A guy who could BAM! Put his fist through a wall. A man – when you get angry, you have to punch a wall. I never seen my dad *physically* abuse us. My dad has other ways. When he came home from work, you'd say something to him, and, if he lost it, you knew something was bothering him. Then, me and my mom and sister had to walk on *eggshells*. We had to watch what we say, and what we do. He would just go down into the basement and work on something. He'd get frustrated, throw a tool. I was scared shitless of my dad.

Bob also defined his masculinity against his mother's passivity. On the one hand, he calls her a "great mother, always there, doing laundry, cooking dinner, doing anything for us." On the other hand, he refused her any authority: "I disrespected how weak and passive she was – how easy she was to control." From age twelve to seventeen, "we were at each other's throats maybe four times a week." Bob's mother often drank prior to their verbal brawls. On such occasions she mocked his speech impediment. Restrained by cultural imperatives against harming his own mother, Bob felt helpless. He could only perform gender through frightening displays of rage and frustration. Recently, during family counselling sessions supervised by penal treatment staff, Bob's mother admitted that she often feared for her life. But Bob claims his anger was a controlled display of violence:

> We got into some serious, serious fights. She was a great mom when we weren't fighting – when I was younger? She used to take my sister and I to the lake. She used to make us popsicles. She used to make our initials out of pancake mix. She used to have water fights with us. I knew then that she loved me, but I thought she provoked fights because she enjoyed them. She was drinking – that's when most of our fights would start. She's really annoying then, and very obnoxious and sarcastic. I used to stutter a lot, and she would mock me when we were angry. She would go, "ah, ah, ah, ah, ah." I felt powerless with my mom in verbal arguments. She couldn't hurt me physically. She was so small and weak. But I couldn't match her verbally with my stuttering. But I could never lay a hand on my mom because she's my mom. I respected the mother part. I used to punch walls and doors and cut my knuckles open. I'd destroy my room – toss my bed, smash my head on things. I couldn't hit her because she was my *mother*. Not because she was a *woman*.

School was a demoralizing place for Bob. He was defined institutionally and socially as dumb, and the classroom exposed his stuttering. His own friends mocked his speech defect and called him stupid. In our interviews, he often laughs off his embarrassments rather than reveal his true emotions. He earned poor grades: "I always got five 'D's on my report card." He had tutors, who helped "a bit," but "I *believed* I was stupid – that I wasn't smart enough. When it got hard I stopped trying." In Grades 6 and 7 Bob grew faster than other boys, and became "athletic" "muscular," and "good-looking." He drew on his physicality and quick temper to materialize a combative enforcer masculinity. Through fighting and crime, Bob affirmed himself psychically as a subject of violence and an object of fear and intimidation. He finished Grade 9, but his school suspended him:

> The anger, the temper, the fighting. My friends seen that a lot and they were scared of me. I never saw myself as a bully, although, sometimes my reason for beating a guy up was, "I don't like the way you look." Or I find out a boy called my sister a name. So, I'd hit him in the head. I used to tell my friends that if I knew I wouldn't get caught, I would kill somebody. I was a very dangerous person. We weren't considered a gang, but my school principal called us "the untouchables." We stole hundreds of cars just to joy ride. High speed chases with cops. Doing robberies. When it came to stealing or violence, it was always about respect. I always held the gun when we walked in. If I had to, I would have used it. But it was only a silver pellet gun. That was a rush. I enjoyed it big time.

By age thirteen Bob was physically and emotionally abusive with all his girlfriends. He tells me, "I got my control back [from my mother] in my relationships." Like his father, Bob did not hit women, but he used "anger and violence to intimidate them to have sex when they weren't in the mood." Bob's physical and discursive practices for sexual and social control over women worked in tandem with his girl-friends' apparent acquiescence to coercion and control. Their interactions re-created extreme dominant masculinity and submissive femininity. Even though Bob never witnessed his father emotionally abusing woman, his father and uncle actively encouraged him to sexualize women and nurtured his belief that "women were for one thing only – and that was sex."

> I was a very jealous, possessive kid. My girlfriends weren't allowed to associate with their friends. They weren't allowed to talk to males. They had to explain where they were going, where they *were*, and how long they were going. I told them, "If you leave me, you're going to be alone. You'll never find anybody." I don't know where I got that from. I never heard anything like that from my dad. I seen him, like out driving around and a good looking woman – "check her out" – *sexualizing* her, [*pauses*] "he's a breast man" kind of thing right? But I never seen him emotionally abuse women. Sexualize? Yeah. My uncle did too. My girlfriends were willing to give up their friends for me to always be with me. Lynette still loves me today, she says. She still wants a relationship. She calls my parents "mom

and dad." I dated Cindy three different times on the street. She still comes to visit me when she breaks up with a boyfriend. She told me when her and her boyfriend fight, she would walk away. He wouldn't grab her and throw her down like I did, so she didn't feel loved. He wasn't abusing her, so she broke up with him. That type of codependency used to attract me. It's so easy to control.

Yet Bob understood that his everyday power over women was unstable and his dominant masculine subjecthood was fleeting. His sexual partnerships had confusing and contradictory effects, and constituted both confidence and insecurity, pleasure and anxiety, and control and fear. Bob observes:

I know I had low self-esteem, intelligence-wise, and stuttering. But I also know I'm a good-looking guy. I knew I could get any girl in the school. I didn't even have to approach women. Most of the time I'd get a note from a girl. I always had a fear of them leaving me, though, which is weird. I always thought I wasn't good enough for them. When my girlfriends talked to guys, I would think that he had something better than me. That he was nicer looking or had a better body. But I also thought I had complete control over my girlfriends. So, that didn't make sense.

In his imagination, Bob attained total control over women. To cope with a boyhood rejection he began to eroticize extreme male action and extreme female helplessness in rape fantasies. His private desires threatened to cross over into real-life practices. Bob recalls:

When I was twelve, I had a crush on an East Indian girl. She was seventeen. She didn't want nothing to do with me. I was too young. That's when I started fantasizing about raping East Indian women – breaking into their homes and tying them up. I did a paper route. I remember actually placing my hand on doorknobs; I wanted to go into those houses so badly. There was no murder, no beating. It was about taking something I couldn't have. The power and control was definitely there. Having that control. But I also was a very sexual kid, so sex was always there too. Does that make sense? It's weird. Thinking I could get any woman that I want, but also wanting to rape women.

Ultimately Bob's dreams of empowerment were embodied in cultural renditions of a real-life serial killer. Although Bob had not seen or read any serial killer documentaries or biographies, and can name only Ted Bundy and Tim Manson, he knew what serial killers were supposed to accomplish. Fantasy and everyday life blurred and imploded as Bob disciplines himself to kill a woman to get away with rape:

> By the time I was fifteen, I fantasized about being a person like Ted Bundy. I'm still thinking about rape. But now I'm thinking, "What if I got caught?" So I was murdering to get away. Burying bodies. I remember riding my bike to Ravine Park, looking in the bushes and thinking, "This is where I could bury bodies." I cruised for hookers or hitch-hikers – both will just jump into your car. I fantasized about raping and killing them. I'd have the shovel hidden somewhere. Then I would bury the body. When bodies would start being found – probably by dogs and people walking in the park – I'd have to find a new place. This is how serial killers have done it before. But I never thought of how to get away with killing.

Bob believed that his desires and fantasies distanced him from normal men. While he was unfamiliar with Ted Bundy's *modus operandi,* he recognized that he could disguise the sinister in normal conduct. For Bob, Bundy provided a masculine subject identity that meshed everyday ordinariness with serial rape-murder. He explains:

> Sometimes in my fantasies, I wasn't even raping. I was simply referred to as Ted Bundy. He was the popular one growing up, hey? The Bundy thing is just – I was the boy next door, the clean-cut guy. Even when I had my mediation with my victim's daughter, I told her about myself. And she says, "You're so normal. You talk so normal. How can you think those things?" Just like Ted Bundy. He was attractive. He manipulated women big time. The nice boy next door. I thought rapists were scum. But myself? I was a closet rapist. I grew up thinking I was weird and demented. I thought I was the only one who fantasized about raping women. I thought I was the only one who masturbated to fantasies. I thought I was different from everyone in the entire world. When I came to the system at seventeen, I was asked about my masturbation. I said, "I don't do it." I was so embarrassed.

Bob's gender-specific fantasies of violence were context-driven and focussed on men as well: "When I'm in an angry, vengeful mood, I want to hurt somebody and I fantasize about it. Sooner or later I'd be in prison – if not for raping a woman, then killing a man." He adds:

> I also fantasized a lot about hurting men. Knocking their teeth out and breaking their fingers, and watching them try to pick up their teeth with broken fingers. I still do that when I'm in a hateful mood sitting on the [prison] range. The guy doesn't even have to piss me off. On the street, if I got into an argument with a male friend or male teacher, the fantasy would be about hurting *them*. I don't go off and start fantasizing about hurting women.

Bob provides two accounts that indicate his will to rape and include several masculinizing themes. First, he viewed women as "sex objects," and displaced rape on to any woman. He recalls:

> Three months before my actual crime, an opportunity occurred. I picked up a lady hitch-hiking. Found out she was a hooker. That fed right into my fantasy. I went twenty minutes out of my way to drop her off at a bus station. The only reason I didn't attack her was because I was in my dad's car. There would have been a lot of blood. She even talked about her daughter. That didn't even faze me. A daughter waiting for her mom and, if I wasn't in my dad's car, I would have done it.

Second, Bob viewed men as competitors, and bolstered his performative dominant manhood by taking private and sexual property. But Bob did not simply transfer his aggressiveness onto weak and powerless men. He also attacked bigger and stronger men and affirmed himself as the creator of weakness, powerlessness, and social and sexual object-hood in others. Bob remembers:

> The Halloween before my crime my friends were supposed to pick me up to go to a party. They didn't show up. I was *choked*. I was walking down to the store. I seen two people. One was big. One was short – my height. He had really long hair. I thought he was a woman. I followed them. I was going to beat up the boyfriend, steal his leather jacket, and rape his girlfriend right in front of him. It was important that the boyfriend was there. He [would be] powerless. He couldn't do nothing. But they ended up being two guys. I made a big stunt that they were picking on my little brother. I took the jacket anyway. I got arrested. Convicted for robbery and assault.

At age seventeen, Bob returned to school after working for one year in a car lot. He loved work. He loved hockey. At school, he was still considered "stupid." He persistently tried to reunite with an ex-girlfriend: "She kept on saying that she's leaving her boyfriend for me. But she's not. I was jealous. Angry. Frustrated." One morning, Bob decided to skip school. A few blocks away, he made his fantasies of power come true: "I *felt* I had no control over my deviancy. If I *thought* that I could talk about it with my parents without them judging me, ridiculing me, I don't think I would have raped and killed Lynda."

Michel's Story

Michel is of white and Métis descent and is in his mid-twenties. He has been in jail for the past eight years while serving a fourteen-year sentence for aggravated sexual assault and a three-year young offender manslaughter sentence.

Michel's childhood was quiet, and he insists that "I kinda caused my own problems by refusing help and refusing rules. I'd feel better if I had some abuse to tell you about." He was raised in "a pretty nice place" with his older sister and two older brothers. When he was seven, his Métis father died. When he was nine, his mother married Eddy and "starts getting *drunk* all the time." She belied nurturing, caring, and feminizing practices, and Michel saw her as strong-willed, fearless, and un-affectionate: "She doesn't put up with anyone's shit." Remarriage altered the emotional links between Michel's mother and her children:

> My mom's affection towards us kids were completely gone. It was like her social life was more important than us. She was only my mom now because she punished me – grounding me to my room, the wooden spoon. Other than that, she wasn't really anything to me. I didn't know how to *show* her I loved her. But she didn't know how to either. Or, maybe she knew, but she just didn't do it.

During supervised family counselling sessions, Michel's older sister recalls his pain over their mother's sudden emotional disappearance. But she also says that Michel's rage began far earlier, and was provoked by archetypal older/younger brother power imbalances. He recollects her words:

> I can't *remember* any hugs from anyone. There was a lack of that at home. Over time, that made me angry and resentful. That's what I thought. My

sister [recently] told me – I didn't really like what she said – even before dad died, I had pretty bad temper tantrums. She said it was like I was a bad seed from the start. It kind of hurt when she said it. I can't explain why I would have temper tantrums at such a young age. The only thing I can think of is my parents were never at home. There was only my brothers, who did nothing but tease me, and make fun of me, and embarrass and humiliate me. My brother and his friends would tickle me until I pissed my pants. They'd all laugh and point, and I'd go into – it was like a rage. I'd go break a window or smash my sister's bike.

Michel refused Eddy's authority and his efforts to "buy" him with video games and money: "I instantly hated him no matter what he did." Yet Michel soon appropriated Eddy's embodiment of manhood as his own as he began to drink and fight:

Soon the [male-on-male] fighting in the house and the boozing was incredible. Eddy had a good sawmill job. He was a fighting Irish man with huge fists on him, but he was five foot nothing – big beer belly, short stubby legs, going bald. He was a happy drunk, until he got fighting with men. I liked him better when he was drunk. When he was sober, he was a miserable asshole. No affection that's for sure. Just telling me what to do. I'd say *"fuck you, Eddy."* I didn't like him until I grew up. He could understand getting drunk with the guys, but he couldn't understand having a man-boy talk. Once we got older, we'd drink together. He'd take on four or five bouncers in every bar we went. He'd come back with a broken nose, but he took out two of them before he went down.

At school, Michel was unable to "add up to the other boys." As a ten-year-old, he was so fat that he broke the schoolyard swing twice and was an object of ridicule. But his physicality eventually transformed him from a fearful to a feared male. He began to respond to teasing with a power-based gendering performative, and this constant fighting connected him to a dominating masculinity that he calls his "nature." He elaborates:

I was angry now in school. I was being teased because I was pretty fat. I had no friends. I didn't want to be there. I didn't want to be *anywhere*. I would mouth off to teachers. There came a time I started fighting back. The kids who were teasing me – for being fat – I remember the very first guy I lost it with. I beat the crap out of him. I didn't think I had it in me. The reason I did have it in me was because I was so fat. I was able to beat up guys like they were nothing. And it made me feel powerful. They all shut up – they didn't say anything to me anymore. And that felt good, not being the one scared and picked on. But I went too far. I kept doing it. And I got kicked out. This is Grade 5. The first person to test me at my new school was the first person I punched out. I'm going around punching [boys] out. I kind of taught myself to use violence, but it became my nature. When I was thirteen, I was banned from the entire school district for fighting.

At age thirteen, Eddy physical assaulted Michel and his mother for the first and only time. Michel fled to a neighbour, refused to return home, became a Ward of the Court, and moved between foster homes for three years. Michel used crime as a tool for negotiating respect from older males and for financing his autonomy from his foster care placements: "I'd show up to get a good night's sleep, eat, do laundry, and leave again." He adds:

As much as I was a rebellious kid, I was still *overwhelmed*. I thought I was tough, but I wasn't ready for the kids who were there. They all knew the drug scene and B&Es. And that's what they taught me during my first six months under the government's care. It was a bad time in my life. I went to jail soon after. I already drank, but it was more experimenting. I started drinking more, and hung out with these older guys. They taught me everything. I looked up to them. I wanted to be accepted. They used me to sell their drugs at the transit station. And they taught me well how to do B&Es, 'cause I never got caught. I did over a hundred of them. I did that until I was sixteen. I made lots of money. I supported myself, but I spent it all on booze and drugs, food, and hotel rooms.

From age twelve onwards, Michel's relationship to sex was shaped by hard-core heterosexual pornography: "These are the images I'm using." Such images taught him that "sex is something that's very powerful for a man." He craved girlfriends, but was too "shy and insecure with sex" to date. In his everyday reality, he faced less-abstract embodiments of men's power. State-sanctioned fusions of masculinity, violence, and the abuse of power created gendered hierarchies of dominance. Michel explains:

Getting beat up by the cops was just part of the game. You learn it when you are young. I've had the cops beat me without ever having laid any charges against me, just because they know I'm guilty of something. I *hate* them for it, but, after a while, it's not unexpected. When I went to juvie the first time, I was thirteen. If it weren't for this one guy I knew from group homes, I would

hardly have had any food. That's the way it is for the young. They take all
your milk. They take all your desserts. They take your best meals. They take
everything. And if you don't give it up readily, you just get beat on. And some
guys got beat on anyway. I actually looked up to these guys doing it. There's
one guard who brought in steroids – some of the kids then were just huge.

Michel learned to celebrate aggressive manhood and used unremitting
violence against males to publicly and psychically stabilize a masculine
self. His subject status was an effect of his power to evoke fear and inflict pain: "I needed to *feel* powerful. I guess I got power from hurting
people – people fearing me." He adds:

For years, me and my friend Greg victimized people. Instead of respond-
ing, we started being the aggressors. We pretended we were cool in our
Mack jackets and jean jackets and pick on people. We never lost, even
against four guys. We were so mean together. Half the time, we looked for
violence. Everything I did was for power. In Grade 8, even the older grades
were scared shitless of us. Nobody fucked with us. Once, they got a re-
straining order to keep me one block from the junior high. All that stuff
just fed me, like, "Yeah, I'm bad. I'm bad." I wanted to be bad. I wanted to
be powerful. I wanted to hurt people. I did it everywhere I went. And it all
fed me, and it just got worse.

Michel's resort to violence was not entirely unexpected, and in addition
to being performative, it released what he calls "an inner rage": "I just
felt I was having a shitty life. I would never have said I felt lonely or
sad. I didn't even know I was angry." However, even when provoked,
he never beat up women. He explains further:

It's boys I wanted to be revered by. We didn't pick on girls. I've never beat
up a woman. When I was thirteen, I was teasing a girl in group home. I
pulled a barrette out of her hair and she broke my nose. I got up, kicked her,
and I guess there's a split-second decision – girl-boy – can't beat her up. If a
man had done that, and I was tougher than him, I would have beaten him
until he begged for mercy. If it's a guy, I have to prove to that guy and every
other guy around, that I'm not going to be messed with, so, I go into a rage.
It's a calculated rage, but it's also an inner rage that's coming out in me.

At age fourteen, Michel nearly killed an eighteen-year-old man whom
he stabbed seven times (one time punctured his lung). He remembers

his feelings at the time: "That really fed me because he almost died. And I got off for self-defence." Officially, Michel received seven youth assault convictions; unofficially, he "hurt someone bad once a week for no good reason." At age sixteen, Michel found a well-paid telemarketing job. He refrained from any crime for an entire year, and neither assaulted nor was assaulted by anybody. However, one night, an elderly night watchman challenged his presence in a dark hotel parking lot and Michel accosted him and kicked him twice in the head. The man died that night. Michel was convicted for manslaughter and received three years in youth custody. His "sexual deviancy," he says, developed in jail as a coping response to sexual failures with women:

I had opportunities. I've had disappointments with three different girls. First of all, it was hard to get an erection. I'm extremely nervous with these girls. Very anxious. Then, it was premature ejaculation, almost immediately. And it was embarrassing. It was downright humiliating. The girls didn't say anything. I automatically assumed they were thinking bad about me. I met the last girl in juvie. She used to be a prostitute. We hooked up on a weekend pass. She was visibly disappointed. I remember hearing this big sigh. The next night was the same thing. I thought my head was going to explode from embarrassment. [*With disgust*] I'm *twenty* years old.

Michel's anger and aggressiveness increasingly melded with his sexual frustration. A prison guard provided him with visually explicit images that gave form to his fantasies about having power and control through sex with women. In a subsequent rape, Michel adopted these practices as his own:

After that weekend, I'm sitting back in juvie. That's when the anger started coming into my sexual fantasies. Over a six-month period before my crime, I went from having regular fantasies to getting more aggressive. Finally it was just full of rage. I was one angry person. I always was. There was a guard in juvie who brought me dope. He turned me onto anal sex. I didn't have a clue what it felt like. But he gave me a complete mental picture – the speed, the lubrication. He described the woman that he was having anal sex with as experiencing an intense, painful pleasure. Of course, he wasn't talking about rape. I latched right onto that, and, because I was getting more sexually frustrated, and more sexually angry, that was easy for me to go with. A positive sexual experience would have changed everything, I think. My confidence would have been up 90 per cent.

Michel's fantasies of male sexuality contradicted his lived experiences with sex and his beliefs about women. His motivation for rape was not explained by either women-hatred or rape myths. Nonetheless, he evinced the masculinizing desire to exercise power over women's sexuality by silencing their agency and subjectivity. Michel insists:

> I didn't have the beliefs that most rapists have. You hear them talk in group about past or current beliefs that all women are sluts; all women are there to be used. I didn't think that way. I might think that about individual women sometimes, but it was never a blanket thing because women did pretty good things for me in my life. Most of the staff that I got close to was women, so I couldn't say that. Before I started fantasizing deviantly, women were like gods to me. Something I couldn't have. I didn't hate all women. But in my fantasies, the woman who's there – which is usually one I just made up – I'm mean to her. I'm powerful. The only quality I give her is she knows she's going to submit and do whatever I say. They don't even try to fight back. It's my assumption that they're weaker than me – that's why they're submitting. It makes me feel powerful, even sexually confident. My fantasies have just as much to do with sex as power, 'cause in my fantasies I can go and go.

However, Michel soon connected his masculine identity to heterosexual sex acts. Prevailing motifs of male sexual adequacy shaped and directed his sexual anxieties and insecurities, and penetration and performance became the norms against which he measured his relationship to cultural ideals of heterosexual manhood. He elaborates:

> I didn't feel like a man. My own ideas about sex involved penetration – the only satisfaction comes from penetration. I judge some of my worth as a man on what I know I can do with sex and lovemaking. And I can't help but judge some of my esteem in that respect. And I know society does too. It's something you can never get away from. For me, I had the stupid idea that because I'm taking a woman against her will, I have no worries about performance. I don't have to worry about if she wants it 'cause I know she doesn't, and I didn't care if she was satisfied. That's what I thought.

At age twenty, Michel went into a long depression. Three months before his release, he awoke "thinking about my miserable existence, my pathetic life." He resolved to rape a woman and then kill himself. He left prison on a day pass, and did not return on time. Ten days later he turned himself in to prison authorities. He thought, "I'm fucked in the head. What am I thinking? You can't go out and do that to a woman. You can't off yourself." Michel left prison again on a pass but this time he did not return: "I knew what I wanted, but I knew I didn't want to do it either." Thirty days later he committed rape.

Fred's Story

Fred is a forty-year-old Aboriginal man who has served eighteen years of a life-fifteen sentence for second-degree and attempted murder. A white couple, Ruth and Doug, adopted him when he was six months old. Fred joined an older adopted white brother and lived with two other younger white sisters, who were adopted later. He spent most of his first twenty years in his boyhood home, which was located in a white working-class suburb. Although Doug was the sole provider and household head, Ruth's severe mental illness undercut her ability to fulfill traditional gendered divisions of domestic and emotional labour. She created and circulated racialized and gendered subject-positions for Fred, which he variously resisted and internalized. At one extreme, Ruth's outrageous and abusive manic behaviours frightened all family members. At the other, her near-comatose moods made her unable to manage her personal hygiene, let alone her family. As Ruth became stranger and stranger, Doug detached from his family and fatherhood and began to drink and spend more and more time in bars. He exercised his own version of men's privilege by ridiculing Ruth's intellect at social and family gatherings, and by parking in the family driveway and sleeping in his camper. He preferred to play no active role in child rearing. Fred recalls:

> I never knew Doug. He rarely spent time with us. He never acknowledged me as his son. Whenever we spoke, he had a disinterested, disgusted, angry, or indifferent tone and expression. I can't describe him as abusive, but he was neglectful, irresponsible, and distant. I could never gain his approval. He never could accept a Native as his son. I never made Doug laugh or feel any pride. I could only be a cause for his disappointment or anger – often for things I hadn't done.

From his early years, Fred was an outcast in his family and elementary school for his race and chubby physique. His body carried the signs of subordinated masculinity. He felt helpless against his brother and classmates, who labelled him "fatso" and "Indian." He played alone in his room or out in the bush. At the dinner table, Ruth encouraged Fred to eat everyone's unwanted food: "I was the family *dog*, [but] it gave me some status." His boyhood identity was shaped outside hegemonic subject-positions of whiteness and middle-class ideals of family and home. Fred observes:

> I saw how families were supposed to be on TV and you see it with your friend's parents. I'd get invited over to my friend's for dinner and I'd watch how his family interacted. They acted like a family. They even carried each other's features in their faces. My family all looked different. Plus I was brown. Not only did I not look like the others, I was treated differently. Not just by my family, the other kids at school tormented me about being Native. I knew there was something wrong with me. I remember kids [*claps hand to mouth and mimics*], "*woo woo, woo,* where's your bow and arrow?" And the knot in my throat. I could never defend myself against name-calling. I would sit stiff-backed and try to hold in the tears. It hurts. You try not to show that it hurts. But inside it hurts.

As Ruth's mental illness began "to best her," Fred was subjected to cruel, frightening, and illicit behaviours that subvert cultural ideals of motherhood. Ruth exercised maternal power over her son through physical, psychic, and sexual abuse. Fred notes:

> Ruth could be a scary woman. She'd play with me as a child by sitting on me and tickling me until I couldn't breathe ... By the time I was ten, I was being awakened in the middle of the night by Ruth tickling my genitals. When I'd push her hand away in fear, she'd slap me hard across the face, saying, "Now you have something to cry about, you little bastard." I taught myself to sleep on my stomach, even to this day.

Fred's boyhood subjectivity was created at the crossroads of dominant discourses about race, masculinity, and family:

> I can't show anyone my feelings. If I don't show how I feel, no one will know that the things they say hurt my feelings. Boys don't cry. I'm too emotional. I'm too sensitive. I wish I didn't feel everything. No one loves me. No one wants me. I wish my mother didn't give me away. I'm a mistake. I'm a dirty Indian. Indians are no good. I'm stupid. I'm fat. I wish I were white. My family is wrong.

Despite his biological maleness, Fred was acutely aware that his size, shape, and lack of athletic ability prevented him from creating masculinity through typical body images or practices. He hid his bare chest after a schoolboy ridiculed him:

> No matter what I did, I wasn't as good an athlete as the popular boys. I didn't get involved in high school sports because it entailed getting undressed in the boy's change room. No other boys had the same chubby chest as me. I had more in the way of breasts than some girls. I was also quite small compared to other boys my own age at that time.

Fred experienced his adoptive mother as a frightening and pathetic figure. Her erratic mood shifts, a consequence of severe manic depression and electroshock therapy, affected all family members: "We learned to adapt," and "we all did our best not to anger Ruth." Doug never used physical violence or threats to control Ruth in the home. Instead, he disappeared from the household. Fred recounts:

> Doug stayed out of everything. Ruth was constantly goading him with, "What kind of a man are you? You're as useless as tits on a bull. A good for nothing drunk." Doug would tolerate the insanity for a while, then go to the bar. Ruth had strange behaviour cycles. They'd start with her being giddy and laughing hysterically. The next stage, I'd walk into a room and find Ruth bawling her eyes out or bursting into tears right out of the blue. I'd feel sorry for her and ask, "what's wrong mom?" She'd say, "everything." After a few weeks, she'd go into her violent stage where she could be extremely dangerous. Doug would often place her in [a mental institution] and she'd be medicated involuntarily and given electroshock therapy.

Fred's only caregiver was in dire need of care herself. Although Ruth and Doug had many brothers and sisters, none intervened to help Ruth or protect Fred. As a boy, no one ever explained to him "what was wrong with Ruth." He adds:

> When Ruth returned from the hospital she was a zombie. She'd breathe heavily through her nose and move about the house in her sweat sodden nightgown and slippers with an emotionless expression. Her face, arms, and legs were covered in boils due to improper hygiene. She wouldn't change her clothes or bathe. She smelled of urine. She wet herself and her bed. She was taking lithium and gained enormous weight. Sometimes she

asked me if I wanted her to make me a sandwich. I was disgusted and ashamed of her.

Fred was never a good student, but he aspired to be a lawyer until his teacher told him that he was not "smart enough." By Grade 7, Fred was the focal point of Ruth's bouts with dementia and was drawn into daily arguments with her. These episodes escalated in terms of frequency, profanity, and stupidity, and had a cumulative deleterious effect on Fred. He says:

> It's difficult to recite specific instances because there are so many and they were so stupid. She'd start arguments about anything. If I was sucker enough to take her bait, I'd soon be in a senseless, directionless argument. Ruth always called me "teepee creeper" and "sucky Susie." I didn't know what they meant. She'd use them as a last resort during the hottest part of a dispute until they held a hateful meaning that could hurt me. She found nastier and nastier things to say: "Dirty little Indian, good for nothin' Indian." Her most hurtful line was I was "a dirty little bastard that no one would love or ever want," or else, "a little bastard that no one had ever loved including my whore, slut, squaw of a mother." She'd argue nonsensically, saying utterly unthinkable things until I was stymied. Then she'd sing, "I won, I won, I won," or, "See, you little bastard; I got the last word in so I win."

Fred focused on his relationship with Ruth even though Doug was the first family member to call him a "teepee creeper." Ruth mimicked and augmented Doug's debasement of Fred. She materialized her own sense of agency and power at Fred's expense by subordinating him to maternal violence. His helplessness in the face of such violence was demasculinizing. He explains:

> Ruth would argue until she had enough, then she'd slap my face or hit me with a wooden spoon. At thirteen, I was big enough to block her slaps so she upgraded her weaponry to a steel stirring spoon that didn't break when I blocked her. I started hiding it. She started grabbing the electric fry pan cord. That hurt more because it would wrap around my arm or leg and leave thick red welts. I started hiding *that*. One day Ruth ran for her utensils, found everything gone and grabbed a big Jason knife. I ran the wrong way. There was no escape except through the plate glass window. I froze. She ran up to me and raised the knife. When Ruth saw my fear she began to laugh insanely. I thought she was going to plunge me. She just

walked away. Her scariest threat was: "Don't go to sleep tonight you little bastard. I'll come in there and cut your balls off." I remember propping chairs up under the doorknob to my bedroom. If I ever told Doug, he'd say, "That's just bullshit."

With no sympathetic adult to consult, Fred used alcohol to cope with his pain and shame. His drinking, in turn, unleashed embarrassing public displays of unrestrained emotion. He remembers:

> By Grade 8, school wasn't important. I'm spending less time at home. My friends discovered alcohol. I remember little of these occasions because I'd usually drink until I blacked out. My self-esteem was very low. When I was drunk, I didn't feel pain. I wasn't self-conscious over my behaviour or how others perceived me. The bad part was I'd cry like a blubbering fool in front of my friends. I ruined parties with my anger or depression.

Throughout his adolescence and into his twenties, Fred's subjectivity was interlocked with his adoptive mother's madness and violence where disturbing bodily based performatives trumped reason and logic:

> From thirteen until I first left home at sixteen, these vicious arguments and name-calling sessions were a daily occurrence when Ruth was not medicated. There was screaming, profanity, physical violence, property damage, and threats of death and maiming. She became disgustingly vulgar. I always thought I was dismantling her reasoning and on the verge of getting her to admit that she was wrong. I remember one time – she must have felt that she was losing the argument. This crazy look came into her eye and she blew a wad of lime-green mucous into her bare hand and began chasing me. When she finally cornered me, she just cussed me and walked away. Many of these arguments would end with her running into her bedroom and flinging herself upon the bed. She would lift her nightgown and expose her genitals and scream, "fuck me, fuck me, fuck me! I know you want to!"

After a mortifying public experience in which he was unable to defend himself against a smaller aggressor, Fred decided to train his body to fight. He strapped weights to his wrists and practised boxing, and soon became a proficient fighter. Puberty streamlined his once-pudgy body, and his new body, along with physical combat in public spectacles staged for schoolmates and, later, for bar and nightclub patrons, became his primary tool with which to materialize manhood. Although he preferred not to fight, Fred understood that his class and race position and his reliance on his body to communicate created and constrained his options for performing hegemonic masculinity. Fred recalls:

> In junior high, I was too shy to talk to women. I wasn't a jock, so I couldn't meet cheerleaders or sports-minded girls. I wasn't a bookworm, so I couldn't meet library-smart chicks. I wasn't a rich kid, so I couldn't meet rich chicks. I was a stoner and hung around with scrappers and tough guys. We were not really desirable, but we received admiration for our rebelliousness and respect for our stand-up-for-ourselves attitudes. I didn't like fighting, but I played the role of someone who did. It made me friends and kept enemies away.

Although Fred and Ruth never stopped fighting at home, Fred finally hit back and ended years of physical abuse. He announced that whenever Ruth slapped him, he would slap her back, "so you might as well just slap yourself," he told her. Ironically, such expressions of power in public emulated Doug's detachment from conflict and pain, as well as Ruth's unpredictable displays of power, uncontrollable aggression, and emotional pain. Fred remembers:

> I became verbally abusive to people outside the family at probably age sixteen. Sarcastic. Unpredictable. Destructive when mad. I'd punch holes in walls, pound mailboxes with my fists, smash bottles. I'm fighting with strangers or friends and insult people whenever I take offence to anything. I'm angry and aggressive one minute and crying the next. I drink until I black out. I'd wake up with a fat lip or black eye and not know how I got it.

Fighting linked Fred to men's power and male domination, and let him release unwanted and unfocused anger. He quit school, joined the manual labour force, and entered the illicit economy:

> I was failing school. I had hooked up with a hip crowd of kids that liked to party. I quit school, started buying and selling LSD and delivering drywall part-time. I'd go to the bar, drink, and get into fights. I'd actually go to the bars and look for fights. I'd go out of my way to create fights. But winning a fight didn't help resolve my anger and losing a drunken brawl was even worse. I know that it's that kind of anger that allowed me to do what I did.

At age sixteen, Fred accepted his uncle's invitation to live with his wife and two children. Fred's aunt, ten years his senior, seduced him, and their sexual relationship ended after Fred was overcome with guilt, confessed to his uncle, and punished himself by slashing grooves into his face. He moved back home with Ruth and Doug. Thereafter, heterosexual sex became Fred's key gendering performative. He took more and more pride in his sexual prowess and believed that sex was a site in which he had superior abilities to men and could exercise power in relationships with women. Fred says:

> After age sixteen, my self-esteem is derived through people I was involved with romantically or socially. I moved from place to place, going to parties, bars, cabarets. I slept with as many girls as I could. I had a lot of one-night stands and even started to make a list to keep track of their names. I took pride in having so many names on my list. Women always said I was the best [sex] they ever had. Sex with women made me feel powerful. I also thought that if a woman slept with me she must love me. Physical acceptance is love. Once, I was with a prostitute and afterwards I thought I loved her.

Outside the sex act, however, he was unable to build genuine relationships with women. He felt insecure, worthless, and ashamed. Unable to sustain a romance because of his jealousy, possessiveness, and infidelity, Fred internalized Ruth's claim that he was a "dirty little Indian that no woman will ever love." He observes:

> Overall I had a lack of control over my life, whether it be in interpersonal relationships, employment, family members, or lifestyle. I had a lumberyard delivery job that I didn't like, but I stayed because I needed it. I was having car troubles, but I didn't earn enough to have someone repair my car, let alone the fact that I wasn't mechanically inclined enough to fix it myself. I'd fantasize that I would do great things in life and excel to great heights of wide recognition, but I knew that I had an insignificant future ahead of me. I believed I wasn't smart enough to ever have an important social status.

When Fred met Emily, a woman ten years his senior, he believed he finally had love in his life. But he soon worried that Emily was too beautiful, that he was not good enough for her, and that he would not be able to "keep her." He wanted to marry her, but was troubled that she actively flirted with other men whenever they were together in public.

Fred located his subjectivity outside the gender norms of a provider masculinity based on monogamy and he experienced lived powerlessness in his relationship with Emily:

> I really felt as though I loved Emily. I loved her but I didn't think she loved me. Emily liked to argue and would never give in to the way I saw things when her friends were around. She also had a very good job. She didn't let me share rent, even though for all intents and purposes I had moved in. She preferred to take care of necessities. I didn't trust her, but was pretending I did. Three months later we had a disagreement. I went out to a local cabaret. I wanted to hurt Emily by having sex outside our relationship.

Fred says that he did not "have murder in mind." Regardless, he raped and killed a female hitch-hiker whom he picked up while driving home from a cabaret.

Bear's Story

Bear is a forty-two-year-old Aboriginal man who has been incarcerated for the past seventeen years. The courts designated him a dangerous offender after he committed rape six weeks after he served a three-year rape conviction. Aided by therapy metaphors about "wearing masks" and "building walls" to block true emotional reaction and receptivity, Bear has developed an uncanny understanding of the performative quality of *all* social identity. In our interview, he paraphrases a program handout: "Please hear what I don't say. Don't be fooled by the face I wear, for I wear a mask. I wear a thousand masks that I'm afraid to take off, and none of them are me."

Bear's parents raised their children on a small island reservation with no electricity that was linked to the mainland only by radiophone, private boat, and chartered plane. Bear had one older brother and four older sisters. His family was a social site that produced and reproduced female subordination to male power. His sisters left home "the first chance they [got]," and fled their father and his unremitting violence. On one occasion, Bear saw his father disfigure his oldest sister's face: "Rose did just one little thing wrong cooking and he beat her up. I remember her going down. If you see her today, her eye is screwed up." From ages six to nine, Bear witnessed his father's enormous violence against his mother, who attempted to use Bear as a human shield. In the process, she transmitted her own helplessness and fear to her son:

I started seeing my mom get beat up. She would use me for a shield. Put me in front of her hoping that dad wouldn't hit her. I remember hanging onto her neck and crying. And the blood of my mother would sometimes be all over my clothes. I [was] really [*pauses*] you know [*pauses*] scared? It's like he would never stop until his anger was over. I was afraid for my mother. He'd be calling her names: [*snarls*] "You fucking bitch." It's like he totally hated her. And I couldn't understand that. And I'd be crying. She'd be bleeding at her mouth. Or her nose. And she'd be trying to change my clothes. Sometimes we'd fall asleep together. I can hear her justifying: [*softly*] "Oh, daddy's just drunk. He'll be all right once he sobers up." And, it would happen again.

Bear's father was the sole wage-earner, and supported his family by logging in work camps. Bear recalls: "When dad was gone, all the fear just went away." Bear's sisters would visit and "the house would come alive." Bear says that he wanted to "feel dad's acceptance and feel that he loved me." While his father was a good parent to his brother Richard, he repeatedly called Bear "a stupid, fucking Indian" and trained him to stifle and fear emotional expression. Bear elaborates:

When I'd cry, he'd lock me in the attic: "You stay there." Told me, "You want to cry?" And he'd tell me that crying is weak. And he would express it real angrily, like [*contemptuous voice*] "You fucking baby. You fucking crying." Sometimes I'd cry myself to sleep in the attic, and wake up, and feel really ashamed when my sister would come and get me. I felt I'd done something bad. I remember feeling that embarrassment and really [*pauses*] hurt. [*Whispers*] I'd be afraid to go downstairs. He'd be sitting there looking out the window. As I come down, I'd glance at him. And he would look at me with that really mean look. It caused me fear. And I always wondered why mom would never say anything. I thought about it as I took programs – [*whispers*] mom was afraid too.

At age nine, Bear watched his dad cripple his mother. For three years afterwards, he returned from school every day to help her cook and care for her. Bear failed Grades 4 and 5. His mothers's exercise of maternal power and Bear's own efforts to cope with fear and abuse in the family connected him to her disempowered identity: "It was hard to see her always, always in pain. It really made me feel helpless." Bear's father, however, never hit his wife again:

I remember the last time my mom was able to walk. My dad was swearing at her on the stair landing. He was calling mom a fucking whore: [*spoken with vehemence*] "You fucking bitch. You don't fucking love me, you never did." I remember my dad says, "You fucker you. I'll fucking kill you." And mom says, [*defiant voice*] "Go ahead, I'm better off dead, you fucking ass-hole." Boom. My dad hit her. She came tumbling down the stairs. I seen her hit the floor. I remember running over there. And I say, "Mom, get up." I was crying. Grabbing her hand, pulling at her before dad gets down the stairs. As he got close, I took off. He says, "Get up!" and kicked her in the belly. She would go [*groaning sound*], and he'd kick her again [and say] [*groaning sound, then snarling voice*] "get up you fucking bitch." Then he kicked her in the face three or four times – hard, with his work boots. I could see blood coming from her mouth, from her nose. I felt really help-less. I ran out to get my mom's sister. When we got there, dad was sitting in his spot at the window. He didn't say nothing. Mom was still laying in the same place. Blood all over, [*pauses*] all over her hair.

At age ten, Bear's paternal grandfather began to counsel and console him. This anchored Bear and gave him a different perspective on fam-ily: "When dad was doing this stuff, I put up a wall. I ain't going to let nobody hurt me. Grandpa came along. He opened that door, and I let him in." His grandfather taught Bear "the ways of living in the forest and eating off the sea." He also provided an alternative to the gender performatives Bear saw in the rest of his family. His grandfather's paci-fism, nurturance, and deference to women contrasted Bear's father's contempt for women and use of corporal punishment to enforce patri-archal rule. Bear elaborates:

All the time I knew my grandpa, I never seen him get angry. I could never understand – he was totally different from my dad. Sometimes I look at it, and I see my dad as really bitter, angry, hiding his feelings. I never really knew my dad. He never expressed himself. He didn't know how. But I knew my grandpa. My grandpa was somebody that I wanted to be like. When my grandma would tell him to do something, he would never ques-tion it. He'd nod his head: "Okay, I'll do it." And he would never curse or mumble. He never pushed people away. He respected my grandmother. Man, it's something to see because, today, I know what my grandpa was doing. Today I see other Elders telling me the only doorway to come into this world is through a woman. That's a gift that person gives. I regretted not going the way my grandpa was going. I strayed when he passed away.

After his grandfather's death, Bear felt disconnected from his cultural roots and braced himself against emotional pain by "shutting the door again." Without his grandfather's spiritual strength, everything crumbled. Bear used his grandfather's death to do what he calls "stupid things," and began to drink, sniff gas, and skip school. Despite his love of education, Bear stopped dreaming about graduating and "having a good living." At age twelve, two separate sexual assaults by two different uncles negated his sense of agency, power, and manhood:

> My first one, it seemed I had nothing to fear because I'd been around him before. He gave me stuff, like my grandfather. All of a sudden, this person turned into [*whispers*] my father. He asked me if I want to do it, and I said "no." And then he hit me. And I remember, from the fear of what I seen my father do, I let the fear come over me. And I remember crying. And I remember that part of me, [*pauses*] like I had just died or something, [*pauses*] I remember feeling really helpless and feeling hurting. He said, if I told, that he would get me. I remember sitting there, my pants half off. I remember crying. I was afraid to go back into the village. So I sat there. I cleaned myself off, and wandered all around in the bush. [*Pauses.*] Hurt. Angry.
>
> The second time, I felt afraid because of what happened before. Then I thought, I got nothing to fear of this guy. Then it's like [*pauses*] being a nice person, then all of a sudden he got rough with me. He come over, and he put the knife here on my throat, and he says, [*growling*] "You fucking move, I'll cut your fucking throat. You tell anybody, I'll fucking kill you." Then, you're fucking standing there. I couldn't fucking move, you know? I couldn't move. I couldn't run. It's like I was a fucking statue. And this fear going through my body. He told me to pull my pants down. I didn't want to and he hit me on the head. I remember laying on the ground looking at him. Then he got more aggressive, like, he jumped on me, and he put the knife at my throat again. He says, "When you don't do what I tell you, I'll fucking kill you right here." I thought I was going to die. And [*exhales loudly*] then he started undoing my pants, and he took them off, and he raped me. I sat there for about a half hour, crying. I didn't know what to do. I was just afraid.

After these incidents, Bear says, "I got really dysfunctional." He joined a gang of young men "to fit in." There, he learned and honed a hegemonic masculinity to counter the feeling that he was "weak, just like mom." He remembers that "we were kinda feared." He began to drink regularly and broke into homes on his reservation. He was shipped to residential school, but the priests expelled him four months later for partying and drinking. His reservation offered few alternatives to such behaviours. An Aboriginal social worker's memo in Bear's file confirms that his reservation was tolerant of sexual offenders. But the file does not record that the federal government relocated the community twice and destroyed its traditional institutions of social control. This relocation caused by colonialism, along with the community's geographical isolation, separated reserve residents from police, child protection, and victim services, and in all likelihood added to the collective resort to sexual violence.

At age twelve, Bear aided a rape by luring a young girl for an assailant. At age fourteen, his own gang members beat him unconscious because he rescued a teenage girl during a gang rape. At age fifteen, Bear raped a young girl who for years after was raped by so many other men that she committed suicide. These rapes, and others, were known on the reserve, but were either unreported or not prosecuted. The rape of the weak by the strong appeared to be normalized social behaviour: "Nobody laid out a hand to help nobody. I thought, nobody cares. Nobody does nothing." To cope with his own rapes, Bear avoided human interaction. He felt "worthless" and powerless to express his emotions, and so he suppressed them instead. He explains:

> I hid all the hurt. All I could do was bury it, but it would come up in different ways. I was this angry and bitter and hateful person. I felt like nobody, nobody could help me with [my sexual abuse]. I couldn't tell nobody. I'd have nightmares. The image of my uncle floating down. As he gets closer he pins me. And I can't move. I can't do nothing. I was all confused. Feeling lost, feeling alone, feeling worthless. I really wasn't aware of that, but I was aware of the feeling? It really hurt. It was like a depression just wearing me off. I would be exhausted just being that way. Couldn't express myself. With my sexual abuse, the fear came of someone touching me. I'd freeze.

At age fifteen, Bear accompanied gang members on a break and enter. The occupant was home and swung a pipe at him: "I went berserk. I took it out on this man. And [he] had done nothing wrong but put fear in me." Bear beat him to near death. The next day, Bear's father sent him to a province-run home for troubled boys. There, he revised hegemonic masculine ideals, as the custodial culture encouraged him to settle conflict through controlled violence. On one occasion, Bear scared himself by choking a boy to near death. He deployed his father's behaviours into gendering rituals to discharge his own anger:

> It was mostly white kids. I treated them like punching bags – the way my dad used to treat my mom. If you wanted to fight, you had to go see [staff]. They would take you into the gym. You could pick whatever you want. If you wanted gloves, or "everything goes" – kicking and punching, whatever. I fought this one kid. I tried to choke him to death. I wanted this guy to feel what I was feeling. The next thing I know, guys are pulling me off. After that, I never wanted to fight. I got scared some day I might kill somebody. I never fought again 'till I came to a regular prison. But guys that I hung with? Whenever I felt abusive, I would punch them, or push them, treating them mean.

Bear eventually rejoined his family, which had relocated to the city. Once again, he became his mother's primary care-provider, but he felt overwhelmed in the face of her pain, dependency, and violence. To sever her control over him, he left. Bear elaborates:

> My mom still was always, always in pain. She always depended on me to care for her. Everyday, it was hard for me to hear her crying and moaning. I had to get out of there. I had to get away from mom. I started living with my sister Mabel. All because I didn't want to stay with mom because of her handicap – because [*whispers*] it hurt too much to be around her. That's why my sister Rose is angry at me today. For leaving mom when she was the only one that cared about me. Mom would take pills now that would get her drunk really quick, and she would just – boom. Nobody wanted to be around mom when she was angry, even though she couldn't walk. She had these crutches. She'd hit you with them, and it was like she was going crazy. We had to take those crutches away from her because, now, she was beating *dad*.

From age sixteen onwards, Bear was in and out of provincial jails for property-related convictions. He had two daughters by two common-law arrangements. Bear viewed women as "sexual objects" and "weak," yet he actively refused his father's practices of control over women: "I still hear my mom tell me that if I ever get a woman, not to treat her like she's being treated." Bear adds:

> I stayed with Marnie for nine months. That's the longest I was ever out of prison. But I'd never allow her to hold my hand or hug me. She tried one

time and I went like this [*snatches his hand away*]. I never thought about beating Marnie, or being angry at her. I never was jealous of Marnie. I never tried to control her. I wasn't, "do this, do that." She was her own person. Like, she was very intelligent. She had her Grade 12. And me, I only had Grade 6. I used to always wonder why she wanted to be with me. It seemed like we had nothing in common except going to bed. I didn't deserve her. She deserved better. One time she accused me of fooling around. She hit me, and I got angry. 'Cause somebody *hit* me. I threw her against the wall. In my mind, I said I would never be like my father. When I had her against the wall, I seen my dad. It scared me. I let her go. Didn't say nothing.

Bear coped with his frustration in performing gender by identifying himself with two embodied subject-positions that he experienced as "two different people struggling." One was "cold and uncaring." The "outsider looking in" evoked Bear's alienation from self and others, and encapsulates how he hid his hurt and pain to perform a hegemonic masculinity that allowed him to go to "wherever I wanted to go." The other subject-position, inspired by Bear's traditional grandfather, wanted to express himself truthfully but did not know how to do it. Bear explains:

That hurt – [*pauses*] it's something that you push away. But it's not gone – it's always there. But somehow I numbed that feeling. I hid it with two people – the person that hides and the person that's honest and open and kind like my grandpa. The person that's cold – that uncaring person? Is angry, bitter, hateful, and very hurt, and has a lot of fear. When things get too difficult, he gets all confused. He gets all lost and doesn't understand why these feelings are coming up. He's safer when people are away. [*Whispers.*] He's afraid to get too close to anybody. He's the outsider look- ing in. So he's sad. That's how I see that. I didn't get close to nobody, in- cluding my mom and my dad. That's the way I was with everybody. Don't get too close. And [*pauses*] I struggle, going back and forth. I want to go back there and be that person over there, 'cause it's much safer, and I don't have to express myself to nobody. To express is a struggle of fear.

Bear's Grade 6 education contributed to his economic vulnerability. He could not complete application forms or meet basic bureaucratic information requests. Government employment offices intimidated him. He feared questions that he was unable to answer, such as "about

my birth certificate and social insurance number. I couldn't give them."
Without a job, he felt "worthless," and was not "getting anywhere." He
was in prison when his mother died. Penal authorities waited five days
before they granted Bear's urgent request for a compassionate escorted
temporary absence to visit her in the hospital. She passed away the
morning they approved it:

> I never said goodbye. I was this zombie at her burial. When I got released,
> there was nothing out there for me. In my mind, I thought mom was still
> there. I remember walking into the house thinking, she'll be happy to see
> me. But it was totally different. I felt lost. I just hid the pain, just like be-
> fore, just numbed it out, never expressed it.

Two months after his release from prison, Bear committed rape.

5 Good Human Beings Doing Horrible Things: Stranger Rape as a Gendering Practice

I've lived for years and years with many, many men who committed sexual crimes. I know that everyone's story is different. Just because I have raped doesn't mean that I understand everybody's story when I hear it. Lots of times I'm sitting there going, "Huh?" I have figured out that there are different drives. What somebody who has never raped before can't understand is the actual crossing of the line. Somebody who's never crossed that line will find it, I believe, at some level, incomprehensible as to actually how that takes place. And, perhaps frightening. Because, if they can't understand, then there's a possibility that it might happen to them, or somebody they care about.

(Kerry)

When I talk to you, you also carry what I express to you, like the frustration, the anger, the confusion, and the negativity. It doesn't just affect me. It affects you. And I don't want you to go home feeling this. You have to cleanse yourself of what you carry after we talk. In our ways, we go into a stream or a river and take a cedar bath. Rub ourselves with cedar boughs. Pray. Talk to the Creator. Ask the Creator to take all this away. Take it down the stream. Wash it away. I remember my grandpa doing that. You have to clean off the layer of bad so that the good can return.

(Bear)

The gendering relationships, practices, and discourses I discuss in this chapter focus on the objective and subjective moments of stranger rape from the rapist's perspective. I will examine how stranger rape and rape-killing unfold, what these acts mean to the fourteen men here, why they want to hurt women in this way, and whether sexual assault embodied what each man intended. Kerry's comment above indicates that stranger-rape practices defy a single process, common objectives, or shared intelligibility, even among rapists undergoing similar treatments. In treatment programs, the men were counselled to provide the thoughts and feelings that accompanied their behaviours. They were not discouraged from documenting the horrors of their crimes or from minimizing the harm that they perpetrated against their victims. They were encouraged to signify their individual responsibility for rape and its effects. They did this by focusing on moments of choice and decision. At times, the imagery is brutal and graphic. The men know that hearing stories of rape produces vicarious trauma in listeners; thus, they told their stories uneasily in respectful, tentative, and sombre voices. It is difficult for me to convey the tonality of the session transcripts and the tape-recorded interviews, except to remind the reader that unlike other practices that materialize a masculine subjectivity, such as sports or work, stranger rape and rape-killing are intended as private, not public, iterations of gender (see Messerschmidt 2000). When a rape occurs, the public effects on the victim are devastating. They may also demasculinize and dehumanize the rapist, and cast him as unmanly, cowardly, and monstrous. Marvin puts it succinctly: "I hate what I did, Kevin. I'm embarrassed by it. My crimes make me less of a man. They're despicable. When I look at my crimes, that's very dirty, unnatural acts, and I have to live with that. And I have a hard time with that."

In Canadian prisons, rapists are not celebrated as front-line shock troops who safeguard patriarchal privilege. To the contrary, sex offenders try to hide their "bad beef" from other convicts. While rape narratives may reproduce the social power of rape, they disconnect rapists from the power that men ideally use to protect and provide for women and children (e.g., Cowburn and Dominelli 2001). If Foucault is correct that "power is everywhere" and one is always inside power (1990, 93, 95), then saying that rape is about power does not take us very far. Using rapists' accounts of their motives and actions, I explore how rape works at a psychic level and reveal how it forms around biological maleness and social constructions of masculinity. I do not deny that there may be other approaches to the topic. I offer one understanding of rape as a gendering practice that subjectifies power. I argue that rape is located at the crossroads of men's contradictory experiences of power and that such gendering practices produce the effects of a dominant masculinity and femininity that structures male actions to do violence against women.

I continue the life histories in this chapter. Once again, I give prominence to "contexts," to the voices of the fourteen men, and interject with analytical connections between rape, masculinity, power, powerlessness, and control only when necessary. I pick up their stories in this chapter at the point at which they anticipated they would commit rape, or would commit rape and murder.

Brian's Story Continues

BRIAN: I always thought my crimes were sexual. That's what I thought. But [treatment staff] said, "No, they were violent. You were aroused by violence on the PPG." That was true. And I had to really think. Maybe it was violence. [*Pauses, wondering tone.*] Violence. The sexual part just happened because I was into it. [*Pauses.*] Do you know what I mean? I guess I got off on the violence. My crimes were control [*pauses*] and the power. I was reading deviant books and stuff – fantasies – the sexual part was just there anyway. I think I was more into the controlling part – the violent part. I really don't understand it myself.

Q: If it was the violence that was arousing, why didn't you just beat her up?

BRIAN: That's true. Maybe, I was going to take it out on her, *and* I was going to rape her. Maybe it's all in one. I mean, the sexual was there. But they say I reacted to the violent tapes. I know the power and control was part of it, but I know the sexual was there too because I had thoughts of rape and fantasies … You know, I can have all these concepts and look at all these things, but I just knew that somebody was going to pay.

Q: A woman.

BRIAN: A woman [*adds quietly*]. And she paid. [*Pauses.*] I still don't understand it.

When his girlfriend, Elizabeth, left him, it angered Brian, and made him feel lost, depressed, and hurt. He turned to his rape fantasies to give concrete form to his anger. After six months, Brian purchased a small pocket knife to carve a hiking stick. He says, "I think subconsciously I knew what I was going to do – go attack some woman. Somebody I guess was going to pay for [my] pain. Any female would have done … any young woman." Brian felt driven by unbearable rage and fantasies about raping women. He speaks to me in the program language about choice, and uses terms that relate to intent and automatic action: "I had a choice of not doing it. Something held me back from stopping it. I was sixteen. But I knew exactly what I was doing." Brian selected a young woman by happenstance, and watched her every day as she arrived at the school where she worked. For one week, he disciplined his mind to the act: "I was building myself up for it. I was going to rape her – that was my intention – threaten her with the knife." Even though Brian drank regularly to "numb" his feelings, he was sober, but angry, during both of his offences. Nevertheless, his attempts to "take women's control away" failed. Brian remembers:

> The day came and I rode my bike over there. I just walked right up to her and threatened her to take her clothes off [*pauses*] and she did, 'cause I was angry and threatened her. While she was, I was touching some of her private parts, and I can see that she was cold, so I told her to put her clothes back on and warm up. I guess I liked the power of it. [*Emphatically.*] No. I *know* so. I thought I had control, and I liked it. When I seen that she was warm, I told her to take her clothes off again.

The woman, however, startled Brian by bolting: "She ran away naked." Brian returned to the school later that day to play football. Suddenly a truck drove onto the field carrying two men "who look a bit like cops." They glared at Brian:

> I thought, "They're looking for me," and, "I got away with this." After that, I thought, "The bitch got away. The next one is not going to get away," so I was planning the next one. [*Pauses.*] This is where it's hard. [*Pauses, whispers.*] I knew I was going to kill my next victim. [*Pauses.*] I didn't want to get caught. [*Pauses.*] Down deep in my conscience, maybe I wanted to kill her anyway. Maybe that thought was already there. I built myself up all night to do it. I didn't know who I was going to do it to.

Brian set out the next morning on his bicycle, and the first woman he saw, one he recognized from his newspaper route, became his target. He knocked on her door and then showed her the pocket knife. Brian elaborates:

> I was yelling, "Take your clothes off." She wouldn't do it. I was really threatening her. She's calling my name out: "No Brian, no Brian, give me the knife." I was getting real frustrated. But I'm also getting real angry. She was trying to grab the knife. This was going on for twenty minutes. I didn't act out till she says, "My daughter's on the phone with my mother." Right there and then I thought, "Well, the cops are coming. They can hear us,"

and I thought, "I'm going to kill her so I don't get caught." That's when I blew and started attacking her, stabbing her in the neck multiple times. [*Pauses.*] You know [*pauses*] she fought, [*whispers*] she fought for her daughter. I was bitten, scratched. I cut myself. [*Pauses.*] And then when she fell down I started kicking her. I kicked her and kicked her and kicked her.

Brian acknowledges that his lethal rage was sexually arousing. Death and dying, however, weakened his desire to rape. In a quiet voice, he says:

It seemed like minutes I was in a rage and when I came out of it, here she was, the ground covered in blood, blood everywhere [*long pause, whispers*] horrible mess. [*Pauses.*] My sexual part. I was aroused. But I didn't want to rape her then. It was too bloody. I can see that she's dying. I touched her [breast and vagina], and I know I got to get out of here. I had this thought that the cops were coming and I walked to the back door and I seen her daughter crying on the table, and I jumped the fence and I rode home.

Brian heard about his murder on the radio, but was in denial: "I couldn't believe it." He returned to the crime scene and stood at the back of the crowd. Police officers followed the trail of blood from Brian's sliced finger to his house and arrested him that day:

I lied about it. I made up stories. [*Pauses.*] I didn't really understand what I did. I lied in court. The only thing I was worried about was my freedom. Maybe subconsciously I felt something. But I sure didn't care. Eleven years ago I wrote a poem about it. I called myself a freaking animal. The sad part is, her mother heard everything.[1] [*Pauses.*] The sad part is, her daughter is rebelling now – drinking, doesn't like her stepmom. That affects me. The sad part is, I told my group, if I didn't get caught for that one, I would have done it again. [*Pauses.*] I feel like crying. [*Mumbles.*] The shame.

Brian's first penal program facilitator questioned his misogynist desire for power by providing an alternative view point. She raised the gender norm of wanting to control women's sexuality, and told him that he symbolically assaulted his girlfriend and killed his mother. Brian remembers, "I actually disagreed with her. I was just learning in that program, but I still don't think she's right." The feminist debate over whether rape is about sex or violence is part of CSC discourse, and PPG technologies now measure whether a sex offender is aroused more by images of sex or images of violence. Penal experts told Brian that their scientific data proved that his crime was about violence, which negated his experienced reality of sex and suggested that the violence, sex, and power in his rape could be casually untangled and ordered.

Harvey's Story Continues

> I was very angry. And I'm very clear in my mind on what I want. And the whole thing is I want to humiliate? To [*pauses*] induce pain. Physical, emotional, intense pain. And degrade. And all through it, that's what I'm thinking. I never hit her. I instilled massive fear in her, no doubt. Like, I wanted so intensely to know that she was being hurt by what I was doing, and degraded, and humiliated that I was forcing her to *tell* me that this was happening, and *tell* me everything that was going on, right? And it still wasn't enough.

Harvey resented his mother because she supported her husband's decision to oust him from their home without a word of protest. He recalls, "being the *good* mother that she is – she understood this had to be done." At the time, however, Harvey believed that his mother chose her husband over him. Treatment staff told Harvey that he suffered from "chronic feelings of emotional abandonment by his mother," but he is still sceptical: "I don't believe it. It's in the paperwork. You can't erase it once they write it. But I don't have to believe it." Harvey remembers the aftermath of this departure from home:

> Riding the bus, I felt panic. From here to here [*gestures to his chest*]. It's tight. It's – I can *feel every* beat of my heart, and it's almost like I can see it, like, my chest is *bouncing* to the beat, it's so intense and strong and very deep, like *loud* breathing. It's – I sweat. And it's warm, very warm, very *hot*, and it's like chaos in my emotions. And my fears are *right* through the roof. At that point, I'm afraid of everything. The specific thing is loneliness. Riding that bus is probably the most alone I've ever been in my life. I don't know *anybody*. I ain't got my parents for emotional or physical support.

In his hotel later that evening, Harvey counted his money and discovered that only $940 remained of the $2,800 income tax refund he used to leave home. He had spent the rest in the hotel bar on drinks, tips, and cocaine. Harvey's memory of the early evening is blurred, and he can only recollect it retrospectively through testimony sworn by the bar patrons. In his room, however, he was sober enough to count his money and reflect on his options. His feelings of fear and powerlessness transformed into a desire to "show women" he had power, even though Harvey's stepfather was his primary antagonist:

> Then I laughed out loud. Very loud. And I remember my thoughts specifically are, "I've done it. I've given myself a way out." 'Cause there's no way I can stay at this hotel for a month until I get a job. I can't afford it. And then instantaneously, my thoughts are, "Oh fuck." Now they're at the exact opposite end of the spectrum going, "Well fuck, I can't go home. He won't take me." And now I'm fucking screwed. And I cried, [*quickly clarifies*] not much. A couple of tears. Then I started going over my whole life. I started thinking of my mom first. About that morning at the table when she didn't say nothing. And then I remember every other woman I believed I felt powerless against. And I remember the exact moment that the thought came into my head that I was going to show them. I was going to show women period what I thought. And ten minutes later [*soft voice*] my offence was started.

Harvey's last thought before he resolved to "victimize a woman" was about Melody, the fifty-two-year-old front-desk clerk who Harvey says treated him "very disrespectfully" when he entered the hotel wearing cowboy attire. Harvey had no plan of attack. He buzzed the night desk and asked Melody to assist with his room key. When she came up, he drew a boot knife – a parting gift from a friend that day – and pulled her into his room. He elaborates:

> I didn't push her to the point that I would do any serious physical harm, but I made it very clear that I would out-power her by a great deal. She's talking out of fear because the threat of her life is following everything I'm asking. She was doing exactly what I told her to do. See, if Melody would have *fought*, I don't know if I would have killed her, but there would have been some definite damage done physically. Like I said, I didn't have a plan. I see a link between having deviant fantasies and acting out, definitely. Because, without the fantasies that I've had in my life, at the point when I committed my crime? It wouldn't have been against a woman. It would have been – I'd be doing time now for killing a man. I may not have sat there and thought about exactly what I would do, but for the last six years in my life, the fantasies that I've had essentially were like a plan in my head. About hurting women. Specific women.

At this point Harvey felt very angry. He did not want to kill or beat Melody, but instead wanted to induce fear and humiliation. Rape did not have a fixed meaning for Harvey, and so he needed constant verbal assurance from Melody that he was creating the intended effects. Even though Harvey forced her collaboration through death threats, their interaction created the transitory and temporal effect of masculine power and feminine powerlessness. But it still was not enough for Harvey, who had difficulty with his erection and retreated into the bathroom, leaving Melody alone. While she waited for Harvey to return, her husband came up to the room, and Harvey's restrained anger was unleashed and transformed into a gendered form of violence. While his desire to produce fear in a woman motivated and structured his sexual assault, fear and pleading from Melody's husband "[made] it into his conscience" and extinguished his anger. Harvey could not gain further gender currency by hurting a man who so demasculinized himself. He quietly puts it this way:

> He tried to be a man and physically subdue me, but unfortunately for him, he wasn't physically capable of doing it. I didn't really hurt him. I chased him and grabbed him. All the anger – I don't even know where this anger comes from, but this anger just *flooded* my mind when I seen him. But we were looking eye to eye, and I had it in my mind that I was going to stab him. But he started crying and all he said was, "Please don't hurt me." But, I actually *heard* that. It made it through all that anger, and made it to my conscience, and that was the end of my crime. I let him go, dropped the knife.

Harvey grabbed his luggage and ran. He forgot his money, and when he returned for it, he was unable to open the door to the room. Outside, he heard police sirens, and sat down on the sidewalk and waited to be arrested. The arresting officer recorded that Harvey was remorseful. He also provided physical evidence about the crime and voiced his desire for help and treatment. He ultimately plead guilty. Harvey recalls:

> All my life my mom preached to me, you *do not* mistreat women. So, *especially* rapists – I thought lots about how despicable they were. In [treatment] group, you hear people saying that they became the thing they hate most. I said that a lot. I committed the very thing that I believed was the worst thing in the world. Shame comes very heavy with that.

Harvey's narrative reveals his lived experiences of men's contradictory relationship to power. He lacked alternative means to contextualize his beliefs and feelings about women's collective liability for men's problems (cf. Scully 1990, 139), or to think within the theoretical framework provided by treatment staff, and so Harvey identified his mother as the origin of his powerlessness. Penal staff encouraged Harvey to rethink his relationship with his mother as a high risk factor, and said he needed to manage his thoughts more effectively and incorporate her into his crime cycle. Harvey concludes:

> At the time of my crime, I believed that I did it just to inflict pain on somebody else. I didn't understand why. But now I understand why I felt those feelings. I understand where they came from. I also understand where all my beliefs came from, and how different beliefs contradicted each other, and my own thoughts about being powerless. I understand how it all tied together to create what I eventually did. And my understanding now isn't that I was hurting all women who had hurt me, as much as I was specifically hurting my mother. I was hurting her for all my powerlessness around women. It was her beliefs, not mine, about how to treat women, how to act, how not to act. So, she, in my mind, was essentially responsible for all those feelings. She's hurt by it. Which is natural – she's a *mother*. And confused. But I wouldn't expect *anybody* to understand the process. I barely understand it.

Marvin's Story Continues

> I didn't enjoy seeing these women scared. Them being afraid had to be a part of it because this was force. I wanted them to comply. Not to resist. I actually had to stop threatening some of them, calm them down. Then I *had* to scare them again. You have to calculate and gauge whether you're scaring a woman too much … My actual motivation, I guess, was just self-gratification – a sexual release. It was about being there to make this person take part in my deviant behaviour. It was about sex. Sex played the major role. At the same time, it was a rush to pick a beautiful woman. Knowing you were going to have a strange woman do that to you became [*pauses*] erotic, I guess. If that type of a sexual act was a natural act between a woman and a man, then [my crimes] probably wouldn't have happened. I don't know.

Marvin emphasizes the sexual dimension of rape. He began to assault women to gain access to a form of pleasure that he believed would disaffirm a hegemonic heterosexual masculinity in the eyes of consenting female partners. During his assaults, Marvin did not attempt vaginal or anal penetration or inflict physical pain. All his victims' reports confirm that Marvin's sexual acts focused invariably on their legs and feet, and "when the media started talking about this *rapist* who was attacking women in my neighbourhood, I didn't know it was me." Marvin himself despises his own sexual desires and links them to abnormality and homosexuality. He observes:

> That's embarrassing to ask for. Very much. Because, to me, it wasn't normal to *always* do that to your partner. You know, to go out with a girl, and ask her to do that. Maybe a person will start doing that, but it leads to ... she's expecting something else, and then you're not doing that. It's kinda, "What is this guy? Gay?" To me, it's not normal. And it really affected me.

Marvin transferred his childhood practices for obtaining and exercising control in his life to sexual assault. He monitored his potential victims' behavioural patterns for weeks, and broke into their apartments while they were away. He used their names and personal information during his assaults. His desire and techniques for control amazed even his treatment group peers, one of whom tells me, "*That's* power, that would freak a woman out." Marvin puts it this way: "You have to be comfortable to do this kind of a crime." His quest for control extended far beyond surveillance over his potential victims. Marvin would not act until he had total control over the entire city block. His power was co-extensive with his local knowledge of the target area. He acknowledges the tenuousness of his power, and notes that his victims could thwart him by simply altering their routines:

> I can't tell you how well-planned these crimes were. Before I committed a crime, everything had to be perfect. If I follow the victim, and I knew her pattern for a whole week, then, if there was a light on a city block away that shouldn't be on, I wouldn't commit my crime. I knew who lived where. I knew who had boyfriends, husbands. What time he was coming home from work. The woman's name. I had all that information. These women had *such* a routine. Coming into their home. Turning on the same certain lights. Going to have their showers. Not even locking the door. And then opening the patio door and laying down watching TV and falling asleep. Sounds like I'm blaming them. I'm not. It's just common sense.

They could have protected themselves. I never broke windows. I can't tell you how many single females do not even lock their doors.

Marvin trained his body to the task of rape. He kept his weight at 145 pounds by running in the park "in case I had to handle myself with a boyfriend." He vacuumed his clothes before his offences and read books on how to evade capture by police or citizens.

Marvin's sexual assaults did not issue from the certainty of men's power, or even from his own physicality. He had to create the effect of his power, which illustrates the performance of rape. He depended on surprise, familiarity, a visible weapon, and a scripted threat to create the subject-positions of the powerful rapist and the vulnerable victim, and knew that both could be contrived through overt display. Even his anger towards women was feigned. Through practice and emotional identification with his victims, Marvin learned how to calculate the optimal level of fear to maintain control. He explains:

I'm taking myself back to when I walked to a victim's bedroom. Now, I know the whole house layout because I planned it for weeks. I know where the end table is. I can *walk* to her bed in the *dark*. I wake her up. Put the knife under her throat. I'm able to be instantaneous with my anger. But the *anger* is something I portray, okay? She doesn't know that. She doesn't know me. She can't calculate my anger. She's petrified from being awakened by a stranger. She's petrified from feeling a knife at her throat in the safety of her own *home*. She feels weak and she thinks she's going to die. I know different. I know that she's not going to die. The anger I portray is so controlled. It's all part of the crime. You don't really know the person. How can I be angry at them? I've broken into their house. That person could be the nicest person you ever met, but you don't want that person waking up and running … screaming or calling the police. So you try and scare 'em. I used the same horrible string of threats. They're made up to apply anger and fright. It sounds sick. But that's what happened and I don't know how you can sit there and not dislike me.

Two incidents suggest that Marvin's anger or desire to humiliate women did not motivate him to rape, and illustrate the illusory nature of his power. In the first case, a victim who seemed to want to have sexual intercourse with Marvin frightened him. Marvin says he did not want to violate a woman by raping her:

One of my victims *wanted* me to have sexual intercourse with her. And it really threw me for a loop. I couldn't understand why she wanted me to do that when all she had to do was this. I didn't view [my] act as something that was going to leave them really terrified because there was never any penetration. When it came up that one time, I didn't want a part of it. I was actually sitting on the bed, and I said to her, "No I don't want to do that." She had this heavy accent, but she knew what I meant and she still wanted me to do this. And you know? I became sort of scared. 'Cause I'm thinking, "Why would a woman want to be violated in that manner?" She scared me.

In the second case, which was confirmed in the women's written statement to the police, Marvin retreated from rape when the victim resisted:

An easy victim wasn't really my motivation, because none of these ladies were easy to take advantage of. But I found women easy to overpower and manipulate. To say that I found a victim easy to overpower, I never hit any of my victims. There was one lady who – she got out of her bed and she wanted to fight me. And I'm standing there with a knife in my hand. I just turned around and left. Because, I never hit a woman.

Even though his elaborate planning indicates the deliberate nature of his offences, Marvin is less convincing about his ability to control his behaviour. Sometimes his discourse conceals his agency and suggests that his crimes are spontaneous: "What happens to me is, when I'm peeping or when I find a potential victim, the sexual arousal starts to take over. Because of all the planning stages, I have to wait before my crime happens." For Marvin, sexual assault is about sex, albeit fetishized sex. He contrasts a "normal guy" with a "sex offender," and applies the latter type to himself:

MARVIN: A normal guy driving a car down the street sees a pretty girl. He might look at her and whistle, and just keep going. After a few minutes, she doesn't even register. He can go home to his wife, hug his kid, and not think twice about that woman. A sex offender who sees her, he *won't* whistle at her. But he wants to follow her. He wants to drive around the block and park quickly in a fire zone or [handicapped] spot, and he will run up behind her and follow her. He may even follow her *home*, all the while fantasizing. I fantasized about the act all the time. Just cruising alone was very time-consuming. If I was to see a pretty girl, then it would be hard for me to have a fantasy about a *normal* love-making session. My fantasy would be about me holding a knife to her. It would be about me forcing her to do this act. My self-talk was, "What the fuck am I doing?" I had no answers. My self-talk was, "No more." But, before long, I'd start following another woman to learn her patterns. I always knew I had a choice. But I chose not to. Would I have stopped? No. This was a sexual release.

Q: You can get that without attacking a stranger.

MARVIN: [*Reluctantly*] Yeah. But not the same way. Not the act itself. A woman wants a full encounter.

Marvin's cat-and-mouse relationship with the police is further external confirmation of his need for power and control, and it is the only occasion in his narrative where he says explicitly that he felt powerful. He watched the watchers as part of his practices of control to rape. He usurped and reversed customary power relations by monitoring the police officers assigned to detect and arrest him. Marvin explains:

It became a game for those police officers. It made me feel *very* powerful that the cops couldn't catch me. I didn't make any mistakes. [For years] the police had nothing – no hair. Nothing. They had my whole neighbourhood cordoned off. But I kept getting in. It was sort of my territory. They used to try and find my footprints. I'd walk on the edge on my shoes, [etc.] … The police weren't very smart. And I'm not trying to be funny. I had all their vehicles and licence plates written down. Like, I started watching *them*. I know they exchanged their [ghost] cars every three months. Beating the cops and committing the assaults went hand in hand. It came out in court that they were following me for months. In my car, I had a sheet with all the descriptions of their cars.

All Marvin's victims testified at his trial. He denied all the charges because "they were so terrible and I had some family at that time," but the Crown convicted him on all counts.[2] His two-and-a-half years in pre-trial detention evoked boyhood memories: "Being locked in cells wasn't so *awful*. I'm used to this. I was locked in a cell before." But Marvin was piqued when treatment staff suggested that his anger was real and that he enjoyed scaring women: "I've said, I am a serial rapist. You are not. You *can* calculate if you're scaring a woman too much. And I'm talking through *experience*. So I can interpret my feelings about it. She [the facilitator] can't disagree. She can't. How *can* she?" However, Marvin is less convincing when he describes his motives through a series of treatment reflections. His formulaic account of his actions ignores his experiential testimony that he actually enjoyed the act of offending on a sexual level and feared that his sexual desires distanced him from heterosexual normalcy. More to the point, his official therapy-induced account belies the fact that the first man Marvin had a relationship with also mistreated him in "every imaginable way." Speaking from the discourse of penal therapy, Marvin surmises: "I guess the anger had to go somewhere. I wanted someone to feel how I felt, that's violated. Being mistreated in every imaginable way made me hate the first woman I ever had a relationship with, and that's my mother."

Cam's Story Continues

> The prostitutes were meeting needs in me because this was my way of being a *man* – it was part of being a show-off, too – having any woman I want, or that I could buy. It created sexual problems for me because I'm using women only for sexual purposes – that's their only purpose and basically they're all little low lifes. I mean, I can go out and buy whatever one I wanted. And I was proving that's the way it was, and that's what I came to expect. I never had a rejection – until Dee. I thought I could buy this person because I'd never found anybody I couldn't buy.

Cam was still on parole when he went on what he calls "one of his binges." He began to drink tequila in the morning and did not stop, though he insists: "I can't use alcohol as an excuse because I remember every detail. I may not be able to walk proper, but the brain don't stop working." Cam became enamoured with Dee, who had recently began to waitress in the bar that he patronized with his friend Rob, and gave her between $400 and $500 in tips over a two-day period. He believed through his life experiences that he could buy people. Even though Dee was married, Cam thought he was "winning over her affections" and that her behaviour signalled her sexual availability to him. He blames Dee for inciting his sexual interest:

> I had eyes for her and I wanted her. I was attracted to her beauty and her accent. It went beyond the desire of wanting her. I was thinking of a relationship. I was thinking, why couldn't I have a life with someone like that? She was overly friendly, and being overly friendly showed me that she had an interest. I mean, how am I supposed to read into that? I would have had her working at [my] car lot within a month. She was greedy. Greedy

people are vulnerable. Given that she acted cheap, and threw her body around, and flirted, and stuff like that has nothing to do with the right of killing her and raping her. I understand that too.

Dee, however, rejected his sexual advances. In treatment, Cam admits to team staff that he and Rob planned to abduct and rape her after her shift, though in court, Rob testified for the Crown against Cam and denied any role in Dee's rape and murder. Cam's rape was about sexual access and conquest: "Sexual assault is having something that you couldn't have if you were trying to have it the right way." As Dee drove home after her shift, Cam and Rob "chase[d] her down" in Cam's van. They pursued her for miles, flicking the headlights. After some time, "I guess she finally got nervous and pulled over." When Dee rolled down her window, Cam forced her out of her car and threw her in his van:. He remembers: "I went right into a rage. Something came on me like, 'you just fucking wiggled your little ass around me all the time, just to keep me interested in you so you could bleed me out of my money and tips.'" Cam and Rob raped Dee. Cam does not claim that Dee enjoyed it, and instead, he contrasts a narrative about rape with the reality:

> I never pictured rape like that. I pictured it as a little bit of a struggle in an aggressive manner. I know they're saying no, but all they need to be is turned on first, and then they would be willing. It had a completely different effect because what I heard was a pleading, crying person. I'm thinking, "This person don't want you." And it was too late for it to come out in a positive manner.

Cam's decision to kill Dee was calculated. It was not about a more extreme extension of rape, but rather was a deliberate and separate act to keep Dee from going to the police. Cam also describes his motive to kill as a gender performative, as he did not want to "lose any face" with Rob, with whom he anticipates committing a "serious violent. robbery" in the future. In his words: "I'm leading this guy and I'm trying to show power and force and control of the situation." After Dee's execution, Cam and Rob buried her body in the rural countryside. Cam elaborates:

> The realization came that I just kidnapped somebody off the highway in her vehicle. I'm carrying weapons. I'm on parole, and that's fifteen, twenty years right there. And I thought, "holy shit." And all I can think

of in my mind is, "How am I going to cover this up?" Knowing that this person is going to go to the police. There was no other alternative. [*Pauses.*] Don't get me wrong. There was an alternative, but I wasn't willing to make that alternative. It was too costly. There was no turning back 'cause the damage was done. I wasn't willing to go to prison for a sexual assault. I wasn't willing to go to prison for a kidnapping. And I sure the hell wasn't willing to go to prison for murder. I put two shells in the back of her head.

In our interview, Cam uses clinical language to convey rape as out-of-character for him. In contrast to many of his peers, Cam says he "never had the thought pattern of acting out sexually." While Cam portrays rape as idiosyncratic, he acknowledges killing as representative of and consistent with his own self-image. He does not claim that emotional problems led him to rape, but he was transfixed with fear in the aftermath of Dee's death: "I thought it would be no different than killing an animal." His anger surfaced *after* he raped and killed Dee. One year later, her body was discovered:

I don't know where it came from, but I always knew I could kill any time I want. And when the time came, I did it without a thought. It was a stranger. I had desires for her. I didn't know her, but [*pauses*] it was rough. It wasn't rough to a point where I could have just stopped and went in a different direction. Something inside me drove me to complete the whole thing, but it was rough enough that it had to be covered up [emotionally]. That's hard to go out and dig a hole and bury the body. To fight my fear, I had to cover it up. I can't show any kind of fear. My way of covering my fear was anger. Anger was a good protection for me all my life. And that's what I did. I brought the anger out. But I always knew that this is going to haunt me. This is going to come back and kick me in the ass. I'm not getting away from this one.

Cam talked about his murder to two undercover police officers who contacted and then contracted him to kill two prospective court witnesses. Cam dug two graves and layered them with lime. He was arrested by the undercover officers to whom he inadvertently confessed. After his conviction, Cam confessed to a sexual motive for his crimes, which legal and penal authorities are suspicious of but cannot disprove. He says: "To learn to live with what I have inside me, I came forward and labelled myself a sex offender."

Charlie's Story Continues

> I outright reject that my crime was sexually motivated. Sex had a lot to
> do with *how* I did my crime, but it wasn't my crime. A woman's sexual-
> ity is her tool for power and control. Why do women wear tight skirts?
> It's not because they're comfortable. And that's what I wanted beaten.
> When you attack that, you eliminate her power – it's beaten, gone. I
> don't know of any other way to explain the sex part in there. Raping a
> man is trying to turn him into a woman. Raping a woman is because she
> is a woman. For me, back then, it was my way of saying I was better
> than she was. I can take something from you that you can't take from
> me. You know?

Before his current convictions, Charlie served a three-year sentence for
sexual assault. He refuses to discuss the assault with me or his treatment group. I offer this information in order to understand why Charlie
says he feels like "a piece of shit" a lot of the time. He elaborates:

> At the time of my murder my dominant emotion was embarrassment.
> About who I was. I honestly thought I was a piece of shit. I wanted to be
> away from who I was more than anything else. I wanted to escape. And
> drinking took that away. Like I said, I only got violent when I did both
> drugs and alcohol. I'm not saying the violence wasn't always there. But
> using one or the other, I needed an excuse to be violent. With both, I didn't
> need an excuse – it was automatic. Anger was a great way to cover my
> embarrassment. A great way to hide.

Charlie insists that neither of his sexual offences was out of character.
Although he was never charged with physical assault, Charlie admits
that he was "fighting constantly and consistently with other men." On
one occasion he caught his girlfriend engaged in oral sex with a friend,
but he says that "beating up either one didn't run through my mind."
He describes the effects of this event as losing signs of gender (cf. Butler
1993b, 237):

> I grew up believing that if a girl rejects you, it's because you're a disgust-
> ing individual. And when a man already has low self-esteem, rejection just
> heightens it. We fear rejection from women. I feared rejection, but we can't
> be afraid because men are supposed to be so tough and so strong. We're
> supposed to be men and act like men.

His choice of words convey his lived experience that masculine subjection is often based on repeated acts of rejection. Charlie knew that part of his loss is his subject-position as a man: "It's a male thing. It has something to do with how we were brought up. If something's yours, you should be able to keep it. You fight for it. We're taught that. What is a man if he loses it? If someone comes in and takes it away from him? You're no longer a man."

Ten hours after he discovered his girlfriend's infidelity, Charlie committed rape and murder. He does not say that he *chose* to kill a woman, and can only salvage his agency retrospectively: "I can remember making the choice that I didn't give a shit about anybody." Drugs and alcohol affect Charlie's memories but did not affect his behaviour. What he calls his "venting" may not have been premeditated, but after viewing pictures of his victim Charlie agrees, "that was something I would have done." He beat his victim's face and head and broke her neck. His official file records that there was "no sexual trauma." However, a DNA test identified Charlie's semen on his victim's pantyhose and established the existence of sexual arousal, beating, and killing, but not, it seems, a clear relationship between the three acts. Charlie's file indicates that forensic experts could not "determine when the beating and asphyxiation took place in relation to the semen deposit." Charlie says:

> My murder was a venting. To this day, I can't say what the truth is, 'cause I was gooned. I left with my victim. I don't know if sex was intended. I believe I was giving her a ride home. I believe that the blow job was consensual. There was no other sex. All I can think of is that act was a reminder of what I had walked into. I remember punching her in the head. But I can't remember how many times. I might have kicked her. I probably did. She died of asphyxiation. I don't remember how. [They say] I could have smothered her with her skirt. I don't remember how we got to the spot we were at. They said there was no struggle outside the car. She was found about forty feet away from where any vehicle could have parked. It sounds like I picked her up and carried her there. My theory is that I beat the shit out of her and killed her. I don't really want to know what happened. No matter how you look at it, her death is my fault.

Charlie surrendered to the police. He was charged with first-degree murder and tried to plead guilty, but the judge declared a mistrial. He was released on his own recognizance, and found work despite being "pretty fucked-up 'cause of my murder beef." A new trial date was set. During the five-month interim, he raped a woman who worked as a prostitute. They initially agreed to sex, but Charlie also raped her anally and threatened to kill her. When the police arrived, he dumped her purse contents on the ground to get his money back because he "wasn't pleased with the product." He adds:

> She kept coming into the pub where I was drinking and hitting on us. I finally had sex with her right there in the parking lot. At the time, I had no use for her whatsoever. My rape against [her] wasn't sex. Men don't rape women because we're horny. Sex is just a weapon when a man is beating up a woman. It's a venting. You feel the violence coming, and so you push it to where you can vent. I've always known I could punch out men. But, even in school, the girl – the biggest insult was to degrade them. I used sex as my perfect tool for degrading. [*Referring to his killing*] hit them where they live – their looks. And I've always known that.

Charlie avowed only the violent and aggressive element of rape. Sex, he says, is just another option – "a weapon" – available to men for committing violence. For Charlie, rape was a way to create gender. His experiences as both a victim and a perpetrator of sexual assault gave him the view that rape inscribes femininity and inferiority on the rape victim (whether male or female) and, by extension, masculinity and superiority on the rapist. In his second trial, the Crown accepted Charlie's guilty plea.

Kerry's Story Continues

> My sexual assaults were my attempt to fulfil my fantasies. I was after the control, not the violence. My crimes don't reflect a level of angry violence at all. They do reflect a strong level of control, and that's what, I guess was the most exciting – the idea that this person was in control, and in control of what to me, was a very uncontrollable part of myself – my sexuality. There were no *unknowns*. There is no *risk*. It's scripted, you know, it's such a script. Each of my crimes just enacted that script every single time.

Kerry's sexual assaults all began with him travelling in a car "looking for a victim." In his words: "I actually took them [to my] home, but grabbed them from my car, or inveigled them into my control." The emotions at play were not anger at women, but despair, guilt, and worthlessness, which led to "a sustained state of panic." He convinced his first victim to stop her car by flashing his headlights. Two hours later he returned her to her car and then "abduct[ed]" a female hitch-hiker. He took her to his home but left her bound and gagged while he picked up his fiancée from work and drove her home. He then returned to his own residence, raped the second woman, and then drove her home, too.

Kerry's says he wanted control, not violence. He achieved this by threatening the women with a knife and putting them in state of helplessness by gagging their mouths and tying or handcuffing their arms together. Kerry did not inflict physical pain beyond the force needed to commit his assaults and restrain his victims. He self-consciously choose a role to perform and an identity to display in the act of stranger rape. Each sexual assault re-enacted the television rape scenes he saw while in an American prison: "There is nothing more controlled than a script." He adds:

> In a sense, my fantasy did mesh with the reality. My first victim was very frightened. But she became very, very cooperative. And that fed my sense of that fantasy very much. So, yeah, fantasy and reality meshed for that period of time, forty-five minutes, an hour. And that was quite powerful. That's the one that I've had the most difficulty looking at. It was almost too powerful to look at. It was too much to happen in the real world. She's also the victim who is the angriest. I kind of understand. That's the most that a person can be invaded.

Kerry transformed a fantasy into a practice that affirmed many masculinizing themes mentioned earlier in this book. His rape acts enabled him to "express sexuality" and "be in control of the sexual part." But in order to be masculine, he had to bypass the normal social stages and human interactions "to get to the sexual relationship." Kerry says his motives transcended "the real world" and the ordinary constraints on his "normal wants, desires, and needs." Instead, each of his crimes was about "trying to leave myself behind." This perspective positions women as objects rather than as social and sexual subjects. Kerry raped only anonymous women. He strove for the temporary and psychic effects of what he calls "fantasy rape," which he contrasts with control over his actual everyday world. He observes:

I could never have sexually assaulted a woman who I knew because I'm what I would call a fantasy rapist. That's my own way of making sense of it. It needs to be somebody who's not in the real world. Because it's very much about a fantasy that's going on in my head. The less reality that enters, the better. So a stranger is a part of that pattern. Power rapists tend to want to get to know the person, or it's somebody they know very well because that's what they're trying to do – get power over the real world. So, it's useless to them to go after a complete stranger. They get a feeling of power from taking control of what's in their world.

Kerry's victims were strangers and not part of his real world, and so he told them stories about his "real me" that he shared with no one else. Speaking to his victims was a subjectifying act that reinforced his need for control, and he compelled them to listen:

What I am trying to achieve is the fantasy, in the sense that the fantasy has taken control of my wants and desires and needs that I would normally have, and the way I would normally express myself. After [the sexual assaults], I would talk and talk and talk to the women about, "I was in prison in Arkansas, etc." I wasn't looking for sympathy. I was looking for an ear. And I never talked about that to anybody else. That scared the hell out of them. I mean, it just made it that much worse for them. I didn't mean it as a threatening thing, or a "feel sorry for me" thing. It was a "this is the only place in the world where I can talk about the real me." How do I make sense of it? I honestly don't. I know those things were going on in all three. The same dynamic in all three.

Kerry's rapes did not mirror the brutality of his own gang-rape. Yet he knew from his own experience that rape is performative and that sexual subordination creates gender. Kerry apologized to all three victims, offered to drive one woman to the police station, and gave another one a written apology (confirmed by the victim's statement in his official file). Kerry explains:

My crimes were not wanting to go to prison, but wanting to get out of life. All my victims went to the police. I just waited for them to come and get me. It's over for me after the crime. I always plead guilty out of, I think, a desperate desire to make up for what I've done, which, of course, never works. I'm probably the only person in Canada who's ever pled guilty to [being] a dangerous offender. There's no procedure for that. I'm not one of those people who can do something, and then live with it, and forget about it afterwards. I need to be punished and make sure that I am.

Kerry received four years concurrent with his original life sentence for murder. During that sentence, he completed his previous three-year sex offender behavioural modification program at a regional psychiatric centre. After nine years, Kerry was paroled again. He worked and dated the woman whom he has since married. Within five months, however, he re-enacted his rape script, and once again his sexual fantasies were a prelude to rape. Kerry does not acknowledge his agency, but instead casts himself as the object of transcendent forces that compel him to do things beyond his control: "My thoughts were: I'm going down the tubes. I experienced that I could not stop it. It was awful." Clinically, he says that he "knew his crime cycle was reactivating." But Kerry also viewed himself as among the most successful in the sex offender program. He did not want to admit that his "deviant fantasies" had returned and bested him: "I was thinking, if I could just somehow drive this out of my mind. Then, I'd get some beer, do some drinking." Kerry's third offence was not spontaneous, but was planned and calculated. He purchased handcuffs one week before the rape and even attended a community-based sex offender group the evening of his offence. He elaborates:

The last crime is over the longest span of time. But, I never completed the assault in the sense of a sexual completion. And it was like. [*Pauses.*] It was a very strange feeling. It was kind of over in the middle of the crime. I just kind of stopped it. It's just like, the point of it all – whatever it might have been – was gone. [*Pauses.*] I mean, it was so elaborately planned in my fantasy, you know? And it just didn't make any sense.

Kerry embodies the program idiom about having the power, but not the control. This formulaic framework prevents him from developing his earlier insight that without certain gender-affirming practices, such as being a provider, "he is nothing as far as a man goes."

Simpson's Story Continues

I considered myself an animal. Didn't give two hoots about anything or anybody as long my needs were met. If I hadn't been caught for this offence,

I'd probably have a few more deaths on my hands. Sexual offences too. I honestly enjoyed that power that I felt from taking a life [*snaps his fingers*] just like that. I felt that power. Treatment staff talk about power and control. At that time, I had no control. But I had power. I felt that power. I honestly think I would have continued because of the power that it gave me.

Around the time of his crime, Simpson estimates that he drank "a forty-ounce bottle and a couple of flats of beer every day." He was also angry, and one day, he fought with his common law partner, Lucy, and passed out. Later that evening they attended Dolores' nineteenth birthday party. Simpson had seen Dolores before, but did not know her because she was from a different reserve. He was still angry with Lucy: "I flirted with her sisters that I've already fooled around with." They drank from seven until two, and then went to a series of house parties. Lucy's cousin saw them walking to the next party. Simpson says he was "getting pretty physical with Lucy, slapping her around, pushing her," and Lucy's cousin pulled her into the car and drove away so Simpson could cool off. When Lucy did not return, Simpson assumed it was because she was "seeing somebody," and her imagined sexual infidelity enraged him. He began to make phone calls to find Lucy, "yelling at people, calling them a fucking liar." He eventually left the last party at five in the morning.

Soon after, Simpson saw Dolores walking along the road and tried to "pick her up." She refused and resisted him with strong language. Her remarks, which threatened his sense of male authority and superiority, animated his anger and rage: "There was a fear there. I'm thinking, this woman did this to me. No woman should do that to me." He describes beating Dolores to death as a conscious decision to physically punish her:

> She was drunk. I thought, "There's an easy target right there." I knew she was weak. I tried to take her home. And she started swearing at me. She told me, "Fuck you, go back to your own reserve, asshole. You don't belong here." A few minutes of that and I just exploded. She started to run and I chased her. I knew I was going to hurt her. She kept saying, "I'm sorry." But I wouldn't listen to her. I wanted her dead.

For three years afterwards, Simpson claimed that he had been too drunk to recall anything. Six months into his first treatment program, he told his group that he "can remember every detail." He underscored the deliberate nature of his acts. Simpson's recall was, in part, a consequence of the treatment program. Penal staff dissuade prisoners from using strategies that minimize responsibility, such as blaming alcohol or omitting details of their crimes. Simpson describes the event this way:

> As drunk as I was, I remember *everything* that happened quite clearly. I remember I could hear the raindrops dropping off of the leaves in the woods. I could smell the cedar. I could smell the ground. The smell of wet ground. And I could hear the wind blowing in the trees. And it was cold. I remember that. I'll never forget. I still got it pictured in my head. I can still see her. Every time that I hit her with my fist, her head bounced off the ground and you could hear the echo in the woods that we were at. [*Pauses.*] I kept beating her and beating her and beating her until both fists were too sore to hit anymore. Then I beat her with my elbows. She kept passing out. I beat Dolores until her head was like a Nerf ball.

After Simpson finished beating Dolores, he wanted to degrade her. Simpson separates his motive for beating her from his motive for raping her, even though both avow his right to punish all challenges to his authority and link him to men's power and gender performatives. Although raping Dolores gave Simpson sexual access to an unwilling woman, misogyny, and not sexual desire, was the basic element of his motive. More specifically, he wanted "to show what I thought about that part of a woman's body by destroying it." He continues:

> I degraded her before she died. I raped her. I wanted to use her, degrade her. I didn't care how. I just wanted to meet my own needs and walk away like nothing happened. And that's what I did. This was a physical need and sexual. She kept telling me to get off her. Then she was unconscious. [*Pauses.*] I found a tree branch a little thicker than my thumb and I rammed the branch into her as hard as I could. I walked away like nothing happened.

Dolores died after she inhaled blood from an internal mouth laceration. The police suspected Simpson because of his badly swollen knuckles, and he confessed. His community took collective responsibility for Dolores' rape and death. They argued that Simpson's behaviour was symptomatic of a social, cultural, and economic malaise that transcends individual behaviour and responsibility. The Crown reduced his first-degree murder charge to manslaughter and aggravated sexual assault.

In our interviews, Simpson offers a cultural narrative of himself as an animal, which belies the intentional, self-conscious quality that he ascribes to his motives. Simpson was empowered by the general act of taking a life, rather than by the specific act of killing a woman. He explains his behaviour through the penal program mantra that "he had the power but no control," even though his narrative defies such determinism. His account reveals how he used violence and sex as two separate, deliberate responses that recreate his sense of male power in the face of perceived threats. Rather interestingly, Simpson confounded penal science when his PPG testing revealed "no arousal to violent [sexual] stimuli."

James' Story Continues

> I guess I sort of always figured that the only way I'm going to get sex is take it. I didn't feel comfortable going to a child who I knew I could control without violence. A child can't physically do that. My sexual crimes were driven more by a sexual need than anger. And the rationale that, if girls won't even talk to me, there's no way they're going to want to have sex with me. I wanted to know what it was like to have sex. 'Cause I heard other guys talking about it. But I never thought of doing anything violent.

James' words emphasize his intent to "take sex," though he never once used the word "rape" in his narrative. For James, rape is sex. He rules out children as sexual partners, but not because of morality or lack of erotic interest: he says that children are not physiologically ready for sex with an adult. Yet James voices confusion about the main focus of his sexual desire. He reveals: "I don't know where I stand. I can go different ways. I've never had sex with a woman. My sexual identity is still not set. My PPG results show that I can be aroused to basically anything and I have a sexual preference for women with no pubic hair."

James' first attempt rape was unplanned. He describes his attack on a young woman as "instinct," although he admits he acted only after he determined that they were in "a secluded and isolated place." He notes: "I had a choice, but I was committed to taking sex." Even though James was not that big or strong he imagined feminine powerlessness in stranger rape. He believed that men have more physical strength than women and that his intended target would recognize the discourse of male power and comply. He recalls:

I thought she would cooperate. My intention was to try the same thing as when I was with little kids. Pull her off to the side and say "do this," and then, because I was bigger and stronger, they would comply. She didn't. She started hitting me. Then violence ensued. I didn't even hesitate. Just started strangling her. I could have just run away. I've always done that with physical confrontation with guys. Part of my belief was I'm bigger and stronger than her. She's the weaker sex. I didn't want to be afraid.

James tried to have sex with his unconscious victim, but "it [did]n't happen." Then she regained consciousness. She suggested that they go to her house because her parents were away. James believed she was sincere: "I actually gave her my full name." He let her go. His explanation suggests that he prefers consensual sex and intimacy, not rape: "I felt good because somebody was accepting me, and was willing to do this with me. And, I never thought she would lie. That never even went in my mind. I was very happy. And then a cop car pulled up. Two years less a day [for indecent assault]."

Five months after his release from jail, nineteen-year-old James lived on a foster home farm. He was target shooting near a school-bus stop. He remembers, "I still felt I was missing a big part of being a man. I obviously knew the kids got off the bus." That day a fifteen-year-old girl got off alone. James decided to take her into the barn and rape her and "that would have been the end of it." He recalled that his last victim "beat him up," and was "determined not to let the same thing happen. That's why I had the gun. My confidence was up that she would cooperate when she saw the gun. I had no intentions of hurting her." He continues:

I told her to come with me. She ran away. I just reacted. *Gone*. I chased her down. Then I shot the gun. I still had the desire for sex. I took her into the barn. She was dead – shot in the middle of the chest – right through. I had to remove her clothing and I could see the bullet hole. It wasn't disturbing. There was actually very little blood. The coroner said it all stayed in her chest cavity. It was still sex to me at that point. The fact that she was dead didn't even come into context. I tried to complete the sexual act. I couldn't. [*Softly*] I became extremely angry and I mutilated the body. The knife was there because it was in an area that we butchered animals. I grabbed the knife and whack, whack, whack, started slashing. [*Pauses*.] It changed from simple anger-mutilation. I saw that her stomach was open. I wanted to see her internal organs.

James rejects the view that he engaged in an expressive act of rape: "I don't use sex to express rage." In our interviews, he describes sex and violence as mutually exclusive for him. He outlines his psychic relationship to sexual desire and violence/anger during his attempted rape, murder, and mutilation:

> There was a part of me that just didn't care. I wanted what I wanted. There was no struggle in my mind. She was dead. She wasn't going to feel anything. Why not? And, *gone*. I went from angry – which is when I shot her – to sexually aroused, to angry again, and the sexual arousal was completely gone. There was no sexual arousal with the slashing, my erection was gone. Sex was completely gone from my mind. When I'm sexually aroused, my emotions aren't angry. The anger started when the sex was gone. When the sex was there, I wasn't angry. I don't use sex to express rage. I don't get that way. I can't link violence with sex. I either see violence or the sex. If I see the violence, it doesn't do anything for me sexually. But, if I *only* see the sex, I can get sexually aroused.

Although James says he does not fantasize about rape, he links his acts to practices of objectification that distance him from the crime and the person. He believes that his sexual fantasies about "faceless body parts" enabled him to attempt sexual intercourse with a dead woman and cut up her body: "I didn't care if it was a person. I didn't see a person. All I saw was something I wanted."

The police arrested James at the farm. He confessed. Given the opportunity to make a final statement in court, he stood for ten minutes with his head bowed. Ten years passed before James was willing to even consider his offences: "I didn't want an explanation. There were no nightmares, no thoughts." To cope, he tried to forget, though he now says "you can't." His acts embodied the ultimate destruction of the female body, but James repeats that "there was no sexual gratification or pleasure" taken. He offers his own account, which goes against cultural and expert consensus that such an act is prima facie an erotic act or substitute for sex.[3] The path of least resistance was to concede a "sadistic sexual necessity," and his treatment group pressured him to acknowledge this outcome. James, however, resisted this interpretation because it did not mesh with his lived reality. Instead, he speaks of a sense of power from examining a human body as an object to study. His mutilation was an act of self-affirmation that resembles popular ER and OR television documentaries more than clinical constructions of sexual sadism. James explains:

I'm a very hands-on person. In school, no hands-on with chemistry and biology was boring. I know all the organs. But knowing and actually seeing them – there was always, with me, a desire to actually do the things. I wanted to actually see it. The desire to actually see the internal organs, to see inside an engine. When I was seven, I took apart my dad's chainsaw because I wanted to see how it worked. One of the cuts penetrated her abdomen. And, when I saw her intestinal tract, then that put me into another mode where I remembered the biology books, and wanting to see this and do that. As soon as my curiosity and desire to see the internal organs kicked in, the anger's gone. I didn't care about anything else. We butchered animals in that barn. That was very exciting for me. I didn't find it disturbing at all. I could feel my heart pumping, and the adrenaline rush enticed me more. 'Cause I started wondering, "is a human the same way?" There used to be a TV show called *Operation* that dealt with actual surgery. That fascinated me too. That's the only way I can figure it out. My theory sounds too simple – that my desire to know more was my only motive.

Jeffrey Dahmer, who was convicted for killing and dismembering fifteen male victims, offers a near-identical account of the non-sexual pleasure taken in gazing at bodies as potential objects of mutilation. As a young boy, Dahmer cut up fish he caught because "I want to see what it looks like inside. I like to see how things work." Later, in the affidavit sworn after his arrest, he affirmed that he cut up his male victims' corpses "to see how they work" (cited in Tithecott 1997, 97). Certainly both men's acts were extreme practices of objectification that reaffirmed themselves as "the subject, the looker, [who looks at] his Object" (Cameron and Frazer 1987, 155). Both men admitted a sense of power associated with such degradation, but James insisted that his arose from transcendent experiences, not embodied gratification:

I do understand the theory [mutilation as a sexual act]. But I'm more of a watcher than a doer. And it's not even a sexual thing. So, watching and looking are arousing, but not sexual. The guys in the group are thinking that because I watch movies with blood and guts splattered all over the place, there's a connection to my crime. But, no, no, for me there isn't an actual connection. One of the facilitators believes I'm still keeping secrets about the mutilation.

Paul's Story Continues

I had this thing that sex equals love. It was easier for me to have sex than love, so sex equals love to me. My crimes, it sounds kind of stupid, but they were more about love than sex. It was like, I felt so worthless, [*mocking voice*] "I want someone to love me." So maybe I can make someone love me. And how do I express love or get love, it's through sex. So, it's kind of – they go hand in hand. That's kind of the motivating thing behind it, and then anger is the trigger. My life is so fucked up and out of control that I'm desperate. Like, I need some love, and I'm pissed off at everybody around me and it's all women's fault anyway, and I'll just get my love however – take it or steal it. [*Pauses.*] I don't know where the link between anger and sex came into my head, at what point anger and sex were connected.

A break-up with a serious love interest was the prelude to each of Paul's six rapes or attempted rapes. Rather than physical or verbal exchanges with his partners, he displaced his emotions onto other women. Before his crimes, Paul says he felt "so worthless" and "out of control." His words convey powerlessness and desperation. Although Paul says that he was desperate to get love, he also admits that "women have some kind of big power over me." His words in the quotation below suggest a link between anger and sex. For Paul, "taking or stealing sex" is a gender-specific practice for dominating women and creating and recreating his sense of power. Raping a woman is analogous to assaulting a man, but he adds that raping a man and assaulting a woman also defeat and degrade the perpetrator. For Paul, neither practice accomplishes the effect of masculinity at the psychic level. At bottom, both are what he calls "unmanly" acts:

Raping a guy would be degrading for him for sure. But the manly thing to do would be if you could beat him *up*. I mean, our main fear is being dominated by other men. It's a man thing, where, if you have a fight and beat up another man, then he's defeated, kinda degraded. But, with a woman, you can't [*laughs self-consciously*], this is going to sound retarded, but you can't *beat* up a woman. You can't have a fistfight. There's lots of men do it, but you don't even think of it as the thing to do. So, what can you do? What other power do women have? They have the right to say no. So, when you *take* that power, see, it's a *power* thing, since women have the right to say no, and the power and all that. You take that away, and that's the same thing, I think, as beating up a man.

While Paul hoped to get love through sex, he stabilized gender – and a dominant masculine subjectivity – by usurping cultural ascriptions of woman's power through rape. However odd and unrealistic his rationale might appear, Paul's conscious intent was to have mutually consenting sex. He assumed women's implicit compliance because he was not often rejected by them: "I can only remember maybe a couple of times where anyone said no to me. But I never used force. I'd just whine." Not surprisingly, his victims' refusals and resistance always shocked and angered him.

At age nineteen, Paul's first marital engagement ended unpleasantly. Months later he rode his bike home after a dance that got violent, and on the way, he stopped to talk with a woman. He says:

> As I was leaving, I just turned around. I remember thinking [*incredulous voice*] "naw." I thought, "maybe I should say something," but she looked pissed off. So I said, "Well, I'll force her." I *tackled* her basically. Right there on the lawn, right beside the road, right under a streetlight. I don't recall thinking anything about her or what I was doing. More focused on the act itself, like, I was having sex. I knew it was wrong. I think I was pissed off at her for resisting. She eventually stopped, and then talked to me. It was like someone I picked up at a party almost. When I was arrested, I was a bit angry, really, thinking, "Why?"

His reputation as a man with many girlfriends helped raise reasonable doubt about consent in the legal case against him. Paul was acquitted, but he admits that he then had deep-seated abduction fantasies:

> I never had rape fantasies. Nothing out of the ordinary, like bondage or rape. I sort of had abduction fantasies. Like, when I had a fantasy, it wasn't like, here I am, going down the street, grab her, and all these things. In my fantasy, I somehow had an idea that I had abducted her, but I never really thought of the means. It was more like I've abducted her, and now I'm in control. And she basically does whatever I wish – there's no force. She's just a passive participant, and I use her body in which ever way I desire. That's what my fantasies were.

Months later, Paul tried to abduct a woman off the street. He had been drinking and blamed his girlfriend for his emotional turmoil:

"Everything is falling apart." Paul drove around in a stolen car and felt "just pissed off." He saw a woman walking with a child and thought: "Well, [she's] like a substitute. Maybe I can have *her*." She escaped his attack and reported him to the police. He served sixty days in jail:

> I just thought, "Well I'll grab this woman off the street, and there should be no problems." She freaked out and got away. When I've done that, for some reason I've always been surprised, do you know what I mean? Like [*mocking himself*], "wa, wa, wa, why isn't this working?" It comes as a surprise when the woman isn't cooperating. For some reason, it never entered my mind that she would resist.

Then after his release from prison, his second fiancée ended their engagement. A month later, Paul was leaving a bar. Still on probation, he tried to rape again. His first intended victim escaped. Two hours later, he found a second woman and raped her. He says:

> In my second rape, I don't remember anything. I remember running, running down the street. But I got no shoes on, and I'm thinking [*rapidly*], "I got to get away." I stole a few vehicles to get to where I'm going. I kinda *knew* that it was a rape. I came from the bar. At the time, she was seventeen. Followed her down the road, then almost the same thing as the first one. Got her, raped her, then took off.

According to police reports, both assaults resembled his first earlier rape. While Paul did not remember the events, he pled guilty. He is not especially remorseful, but he is confused about what happened: "If I knew the truth, it would be easier to lie. It's hard to make up stuff if you don't know what happened. I had the feeling that I had done it." His words illustrate the moments of automation and agency within his assaults, and explain his bewilderment and anger. He explains:

PAUL: I saw this woman come out of the store [and thought], "I'll try it again." She was driving. So I followed. She pulled over and I pulled over. Then I tried to get her out of her car into my car. I don't recall thinking a whole lot about anything. It was like, I get drunk and go on automatic. Like, now I'm a wild fucking animal or something, you know? I'm just doing, you know? I punched her hands to get them off the steering wheel. By this time, there's such a commotion. She was yelling, and I'm still thinking, "why isn't she cooperating?" And I'm getting pissed off and – it's not like we were out in an isolated area. There's people coming out of their houses. Somebody yelled, "Hey, what's going on?" That's when I thought, "What is going on? What are you doing? I got to get out of here." I remember being scared afterwards. And a bit surprised really. When that guy yelled [*pauses*] it's almost like it snapped me out of whatever.

Q: Are you suggesting you were dissociative?

PAUL: No. No. I was half-drunk, but I was aware of what was going on around me. And I made a conscious decision to abduct this woman. And I knew that I was going to have sex with her. I was going to get her in my car and go somewhere. But aside from that, that was my focus. I wasn't aware of anything else going on around me. Like, where I was. The fact that other people could hear or see what I was doing. None of that ever occurred to me in any of my crimes that I've committed.

Paul was sentenced to seven years and nine months. Thirteen months after his release, his then-girlfriend ended their relationship. One week later, he targeted a woman who was of the same ethnic background as his now ex-girlfriend: "I took out my anger on this woman who was walking by herself." He pulled her into his van and asked to view her passport. Paul elaborates:

It's kind of stupid, but if I had done a lot of fantasizing about it – the abduction and rape, I think I'm smart enough that I wouldn't have got caught. I mean, my present offence was even more stupid. Really. I mean, like nine on a Sunday morning. There were lots of witnesses, people that got my licence number, people that even chased me, seen me plain as day. I definitely wasn't thinking. My present crime is a nightmare. Definitely. Not a fantasy. I mean, I don't want to go thinking about it, but, it wasn't planned, that's for sure. Like, I had no idea *why* I was doing *anything*. At the time, I wasn't thinking, "why did I do that?" I was thinking, "I'm in some serious trouble, I'm going to jail – what's wrong with me?" – that kind of thing.

In her statement to the police, the victim remembered Paul saying over and over that "he want[ed] her." She refused consensual sex, and he became angry. Paul hit her in the face with a pipe and threatened to "smash her" if she shouted. He dropped the pipe. She grabbed it and hit the top of his head, which split open the skin on his scalp. Paul then hit her face with the pipe. He raped her repeatedly, vaginally and anally, and inserted the pipe vaginally and anally. Paul's victim fell from the van while he tried to elude pursuit. In the rape report, a police officer wrote that "short of death, it was the worst case of human abuse I had ever witnessed."

Paul pled guilty to attempted murder, and in exchange the Crown dropped the sexual assault charges. He recalls, "I had no intention of killing her. It was like impulsive – a spur of the moment thing. But there was serious, serious rage, I think." A verbatim extract from Paul's statement to arresting officers conveys that he "had no idea *why* I was doing *anything*":

> I didn't say to myself that week or that day or that night, or, as I left my friend's place. I never said, "I got to go find someone to beat the fuck out of" … I don't know why. I don't know, have no reason at all. Might be okay if there's no chance of getting out. If, in the future, there's a possibility of release [*pauses*] I didn't plan this. If I get out, it may happen again. Next time someone may get killed. I don't know – they seem to get more violent.

During his first federal sentence – prior to his current conviction – Paul completed a penal sex offender program. At that time, his nurse told him that his problem was that he did not talk with women and that his relationships with them were only sexual. While in the program, Paul worked on his communication skills: "I think I learned there how to be more charming – talking with all the young nurses." But Paul also believed, then and later, that his problem was drugs because his assaults occurred while he was intoxicated. Despite the fact that Paul's assaults were typical of rapists, he did not experience himself within the subject-position that matches his conduct. He elaborates:

> My stereotype of a rapist was some geeky guy that jumps out of the bush. Someone who was inept and couldn't get any women at all – a social outcast. I didn't think of myself as a rapist. I was *confused*, really. I committed a rape, but I'm not a rapist. I mean, I'm not the stereotype person that I think of, and I don't even know where it came from. It wasn't even something that I dreamt about. I didn't grow up wanting to be a rapist or, you know, "I'll move to [this province] and become a rapist." I was really confused, even after my second offence. I thought, "What the hell? Why?" It was always similar circumstances.

Today, Paul believes that he carried anger towards his mother from relationship to relationship: "It just kept getting *bigger* and *bigger*." But he adds, "acting out doesn't get rid of anything or solve anything else. I needed to get all that stuff out of me." In the face of the program's axiom that "I had the power but no control," Paul's admission of his fears of women's power over him were dismissed as cognitive distortions. He now says:

> In all my relationships, I never trusted anyone. I was scared to let anyone know I was so angry. I thought I might be rejected. I have no idea why. No one actually ever rejected me. I more or less pushed people away. It's easy now. I can stop and [*pauses*] it's because I'm getting bits of awareness [*pauses*] so much trouble. It was nothing anybody ever did to me. It's all stuff that I thought about though. Feeling inadequate, or unloved, or scared, and then – took all that out in anger.

Paddy's Story Continues

> For me, I don't think sex was the issue. It's a sex offence because rape was involved. I think my crimes were about trying to be a man. But not having any control in my life. I'd get angry and express it through anger or domination – dominating men by fighting and women by aggressive sex. Aggressive sex makes me feel in control. I'm dominating her. I guess [*pauses*] because I'm feeling less of a man before sex, right? I get that back through sex. My crimes are the truest sense of the most power I've ever had. Of course, looking at it now, it wasn't very powerful. But at the time, I felt [*pauses*] the whole time I had a sense of "yes, this is what it feels like to be powerful."

Paddy had been drinking in a motel bar before he committed assault because "I needed more money to get drunker." He describes his emotional state as agitated, but not angry. He rode his bicycle behind the motel and started to look into guests' rooms. In one, he saw a purse on a table through the sheer curtains of an open sliding-glass patio door. Paddy entered the room and grabbed the purse: "This is the first time I had ever done any kind of break-in." He tells me:

> A woman walked out of the bathroom with no clothes on. She was little – a diminutive woman. She grabbed the purse, too. I just yanked the purse and she came flying with it. She hit her head on the edge corner of the table. I looked back. I saw her lying on the floor. I saw her forehead was bleeding. I was scared. I put her up on the bed and tried to stop the

bleeding. She opened her eyes. She said, "I'll do anything you want." That's when I got the idea to rape her. I was not aroused before that point. But I told her, "Of course you'll do anything I want." Her eyes stayed shut the whole time. I told her to and she did. I knew what I was doing was rape. But it did cross my mind that she said this is okay.

Paddy suspects that penal treatment experts did not believe that his initial intent was to rob and not to rape. But Diana Scully's (1990, 141–2) study shows that a surprising number of rapists are motivated by robbery. Rape, she says, is an afterthought, "an added bonus," which closely matches Paddy's narrative.[4] In such situations, women may cast themselves as rape victims and accept rape before it occurs, which gives men the power, though not the consent, to rape (Marcus 1992, 388–9). Paddy insists, "I would not have done my crime if she had not grabbed her purse, and then made that statement. See, it sounds like I'm trying to blame her, right?" It is difficult to know if Paddy blames his victim because no empirical research exists that explores rape as an intersubjective phenomenon. There has been little research into how rapists and victims accept, negotiate, or refuse the violence and sexuality of the event (Cahill 2001, 128; Marcus 1992, 390).

Although Paddy refuses the narrative that he was overcome with emotion, he acknowledges that "no woman could ever fight me off in that context. And that's a powerful feeling." He forgets details of his rape, such as that he destroyed his victim's eyeglasses and inserted a curling iron into her body. Yet after raping her, he recalls "cleaning everything that I touched," forcing his victim to walk naked into the forest with her suitcases, and tossing her briefcase into the river. At that time, he says, "I'm not thinking of killing her." He brought her into the woods to get her away from the phone and to give himself time to escape. Her suitcases, however, were found open with clothing strewn everywhere, which indicates serious rage: "She should have screamed. I would have booked it." Instead he struck her head with a brick "to knock her out." His three blows killed her.

Paddy returned to his hometown, and two years later he raped a second woman. He remembers more details of this second rape: "My second crime was much more brutal. I beat her." He met her at a party and she offered him a ride home. As Paddy exited her vehicle, she asked, "Is everything okay? Do you need any help?" Paddy became enraged: "I was pretty loaded, and for some reason I'm thinking, 'who the hell are you to offer *me* help.'" Similarly to his first sexual assault, this rape was an unplanned response to a recognized opportunity.

However, in this case, murder was a deliberate strategy to keep the victim from identifying him to the police. Paddy sounds like he blames this victim, too: "She shouldn't have looked at me. She shouldn't have picked me up." After five treatment programs, Paddy knows that experts think that *blaming the victim* is a form of denial that increases his risk to reoffend. Perhaps Paddy wants to express that rape and murder were not foregone conclusions in either encounter, and to suggest that they were the result of a contingent series of interactions, decisions, and discourses about male power in which the women are not really passive players. Paddy elaborates:

> I took her back to my parents' place. [The rape] was over six hours. I put gauze over her eyes and tape. I eventually tied a rope around her wrists and went to sleep. When I woke up, she was still there. My thoughts were, "fucking idiot. How am I going to get out of this one?" It wasn't my intent to kill her until the end. My thought was that, she saw my face, and I would be toast, and I'm going to jail. I took her to a construction site and hit her over the head with a piece of cement. She had kept looking at me – like she was trying to memorize my face. I think if she hadn't of looked [*pauses*] I don't know what I was thinking – she picked me up on the side of the road, so she saw me clearly, right? [*Pauses.*] She should never have picked me up. It was a dark night in the middle of nowhere.

The woman did not die, and identified Paddy. After fingerprint evidence linked him to his first victim as well, he confessed to both assaults and murder. Paddy struggles to offer a coherent account about his motivations to rape: "At my arrest, I had no understanding why I did it." He suggests: "I wanted her to feel the exact way I am feeling," "it was a control thing," "I wanted to demean a woman," and, "anger came over me." Paddy finds the "*how*" of his offences easier to explain than the reasons behind them:

> The understanding I have now – that a lot of people who are trying to understand seem to miss – is that there is no rational reason. You can't make sense out of something that doesn't make sense. Very, very hard to explain [*pauses*] most people try to understand it based on their own morals and values that they were brought up with, and their feelings about offences like that. Like, "how could someone do that?" Because it goes against every facet of humanity. There's no empathy. There's no feelings at all during those offences – feelings that would stop me. I'd agree with that.

That's *how* I could do it. *Why* I did it was because it was available at the
time. And I was frustrated enough and angry enough – my beliefs about
women and people in general. I don't think that sex was the issue. Part of
my intent was to hurt, was to cause pain. And how do you demean a
woman? For me, it's sex, right? That's my thought. I still kinda think that
way. But it wasn't just women – it's safer to assault a woman. No chance
of repercussions. It was everybody. I *hated* everybody.

Many of his comments about his conduct come back to "trying to be a
man," but lacking the hegemonic gender markers of "control over something." Rape temporarily links Paddy to men's power, or, as he puts it,
gave him the sense of "what it feels like to be powerful even if it is only
for minutes or hours." Other comments of his, such as "I'm feeling less
of a man before sex," also conjure sex and rape as a gender performative
that restores his subject-position and male identity. His narrative explicitly shows that hegemonic masculinity is the *effect* of rape.

Bob's Story Continues

It would have to do with my moods whether rape was about sex or violence. I had fantasies where I tie women up. For control. If she's tied up,
she's not really moving much. It's the rape. If she's tied up, sure it's a violent act. But it's not as violent as some of my fantasies where there are
some pretty brutal beatings. I'm raping them *and* beating them. Those
ones are about violence definitely. But, in fantasies about tying women up,
it was just the sex and the rape that I wanted.

Bob awakened on the morning of his offence knowing exactly what
he was going to do. Lynda, his victim, lived fifteen houses away. He
was vaguely acquainted with her, as he had briefly dated her daughter,
and he gained entry to her house by asking to use the phone. Raping
Lynda was about sex and control, not violence and anger: "My anger
had nothing to do with it. I was dead cold. There was no anger during
that act." He continues:

I pushed her over the couch. I grabbed her by the throat. We wrestled to
the top of the stairs. And we ended up falling down the stairs to the landing. She tried to run out the front door. I grabbed her shirt. And then I was
choking her. Her body went limp. She came back to consciousness, and I
choked her again. I closed the door and locked it. I didn't know then if she

was dead. If I thought she was dead, it probably wouldn't have mattered to me. I was sexually aroused at her being unconscious. That put it right in there with my fantasies. I pulled all her clothes off and I raped her.

Bob relives the sexual element of his offence in therapy and in my interviews with him. He says, "I used to think, why did I rush it so much? I could have went through it more than once. I could have tied her up, raped her, left the room, come back, and do it again." Bob was aroused by the passivity of the object of his sexual desire. Lynda never regained consciousness, and Bob took no pleasure, sexual or otherwise, in the deliberate act of killing her. But neither does he hesitate to hide his lack of remorse: "It's sad to say, but I took someone's life just to hide my appearance." He recalls the details:

My immediate thoughts afterwards were to kill her. I felt her pulse. I don't think she was dead. The reason why is, I filled the bathtub with water. I dragged her over, and I leaned her over the bathtub, and stuck her head under water. She blew bubbles. They found water in her lungs. I pulled her out. I tried to feel for a pulse again. I couldn't make sure if there was one. I went upstairs and grabbed a kitchen knife. Grabbed the blanket off of the downstairs bedroom and put the blanket over top of her. I didn't want to look at her. I cut her throat. I stuck my hand underneath the blanket. I thought about stabbing her, but I couldn't do it looking at her.

The coroner concluded that all three traumas Bob inflicted were sufficient to cause Lynda's death. Bob's fear of getting caught for the crime was greater than his remorse for it. He says:

I walked home. My mom knew by then that I had skipped school. I went downstairs and threw my clothes in the washing machine. My sister came down. I was crying, and she asked, "What's the matter?" I told her that I was in a fight and I think I hurt him really bad. My mom and my aunt came down. I told them the same story. I had a shower and kept on thinking, "This ain't happening." My mom said I laid downstairs on the couch with a blanket covered up to my neck. I don't remember. That night I asked my sister to sleep in the same bed as me. She wouldn't do it. Every noise I heard I went and looked out the window.

Bob's first rape and murder did not affect him the way he intended. He did not feel empowered, but was "scared shitless" and overcome with unexpected emotions. He knew that his guilt, shame, and anxiety sepa-rated him from what he calls a serial killer subject-position. He explains:

> I probably would not have been a good serial killer. I was scared shitless after I committed my crime. I couldn't even look at her. I didn't think I'd feel that way after. The guilt and the shame – I didn't think I'd feel. I think my guilt and shame *got* me caught. I couldn't hide it. My parents and my sister suspected me before I was even arrested.

Yet at other times, Bob was adamant that he could have normalized killing and repeated it. During the first years of his sentence, he chron-icled and reviewed his mistakes. He concludes: "If I could have just been calm and relaxed, I could have been there all day. I could have lived one of my fantasies out." He portrays serial killing as a practice that requires more mental and emotional discipline than he expected. Bob draws on treatment-based crime cycle presumptions and envisions his future as a repeat killer:

> I would have done it again. I don't doubt it one bit. Even though I felt the way I felt, I would have went through a period of paranoia and guilt. I would have adjusted and calmed down. I would have realized that I was capable of doing it now. I would have done it again. I know it. I think there would have been a lot of dead women out there. I just put myself back in that mind space of that kid. I couldn't imagine turning myself in. No way. There would have been a period of adjusting to what I did. And knowing that I'm not going to get caught. Then [*softly*] I would have done it again. There would have been a new build-up stage.

Bob rejects simplistic Freudian ideas about his mother and his desire to rape women, but he accepts general psychoanalytic or popular cul-tural narratives about mother-hating leading to woman-hating (see Tatar 1995). In Bob's view, his mother bears the chief responsibility for raising him as a near-serial killer, but he also suggests that his father was responsible for teaching violence. Bob at once blames his parents and evinces his own agency and choice:

> Psychologists always ask me, did my victim look like my mom. Yeah, she did. How does that sound? [*Agitated voice.*] I was *never* thinking about my mother. I never seen my mother's face. I never thought about my mother *during*. I never thought about my mother after [*exhales loudly*]. I tell them

that. My mom feels extremely responsible for my crime – my relationships with women and everything. My mom was a woman, and all I learned was to fight, to argue. From my dad, I learned how to deal with my emotions – stuffing. And how I dealt with my anger. That's what I learned in my relationships. I tell my parents, though, it's all about choices. My parents didn't make me go do what I did.

Michel's Story Continues

I didn't have any anger towards women. But I was intimidated by all women. I more or less feared them. I had two motives. One was power and control, and one was sex. I was an angry person. I always was. And I had a sexual frustration alongside my anger. They were never together until I was twenty years old. Then they kind of merged. I don't know if that makes sense. I was always so shy and insecure with sex, and so aggressive and angry with everything else.

Michel materialized gender primarily through power relationships with men and "doing crime." He tells me that he thought about rape when he was most removed from those primary masculinizing practices: "It's normally when I'm straight, alone, and depressed that I think about rape." His failed heterosexual performances led him to conclude that women hold all the sexual power, and can confirm or disaffirm masculine gender identity. He repeats the lived incongruence between psychic and bodily formation in his narrative about rape: "I didn't feel like a man. I wanted to get some [power] back." He believed rape would give him physical and psychic power over women, in part because he would not worry about pleasing his partner. Michel elaborates:

Rape is about power. I agree. I can't help but say every single rape involves some sort of power for that person. Back then, power and control was a feeling I wasn't able to label. It was like a gratifying feeling from the fantasy. It's hard to explain. You're taking what she's not giving, and you feel powerful. As for why I wanted to have power and control over a woman, I think I held the belief that women have the sexual power. I felt they had something I could never have. They can also make men feel bad about it, and after while, I suppose I did. It's hard to remember my *beliefs*, cause I never explored them then. In juvie, I had lots of power in my life. It was just, in the sexual aspect of my life,

I had no power, or – power might be the wrong word – and I wanted to get some of it back.

His victim lived in a basement suite in the house that he had been visiting. He tells me, "her name is Becky. I don't know if I want to use her name – it doesn't sound right." For Michel, his victim had to be a perfect stranger: "I couldn't hurt somebody that I cared for – I was still capable of caring." Becky fit his profile, because "she looked like she wouldn't be able to fight me off and wasn't sexually unattractive." After he saw her for the second time that day, he resolved to rape her. When the family upstairs left for the evening, Michel broke into Becky's suite to wait for her: "It was a very tense, long hour." He says he consciously tried to distance himself from his intended victim:

The old B&E artist in me looked around thinking about value. It didn't take long to realize there wasn't any. I remember seeing a collage of teddy bears. It's almost like I made myself *not* look at it – 'cause the teddy bears were very sweet. Now I'm in the kitchen, and I see the fridge is covered in magnets, and under them are positive affirmations – the kinda things you hear in therapy. Maybe she's been to therapy. And they were on the wall too – professionally done. I had no idea what a woman was about. I think that's why her suite kinda amazed me. I looked at everything. It sounds stupid – I mean, *odd*, that I would look around and think, "So this is the apartment of a single woman." It was kinda pathetic – it was a small place.

Michel was not motivated to humiliate, hurt, or "make someone feel what I'm feeling." Notwithstanding that rape is always intersubjective (Cahill 2001), Michel wanted to produce a power effect in himself rather than in a woman. He explains:

Then, my thoughts turned to, "How am I going to get control of her?" I didn't have a single *thought* about her, how it would hurt her, or how she would be affected. Looking back, I realize all I had to do is grab her, kick her door shut. If she screams, no one will hear. In my mind then, I'm thinking I have to get instant, utter control. I'm going to do it by knocking her out with something. I already had a knife in my hand – a Wiltshire Stay-Sharp knife from her kitchen. The initial plan was to point a knife and say, "Do what I tell you." I found a Teflon and a cast-iron pan. I picked them up. The cast-iron was very, very heavy. I took the Teflon. I heard her car pull up. I remember having second thoughts, but I was determined. "I haven't put myself through all this *shit*" – I'm suicidal, and I don't really care. I dropped the knife and I picked up the pan.

Like other rapists, Michel assumed that rape would unfold like a series of pornographic fantasies. But "sex" did not give Michel power and control over a woman, but rather amplified his sense of ineptness:

I hit her with the pan, just above the forehead. It didn't do anything. It was Teflon. I don't know what I was thinking. It just bounced. She just screamed. I hit her again. The pan had twisted in my hand and she got the sharp edge. A cut opened just above the hairline. The blood kinda freaked me out. I was expecting a blunt blow that would knock her out. Whatever I wanted to do wasn't happening. Basically, I took her to the bedroom and attempted to rape her. I couldn't get an erection. I tried three times. Between the second and third time, I took her to the bathroom. She wasn't bleeding a lot, but the blood was getting to me. I told her to wash up. She was actually quite smart. Instead of trying to stop the bleeding, she tried to make it bleed more with her hairbrush. [*Sighs.*] But, she cleaned herself up. I tried one more time. I did penetrate her anally for about three seconds, and I gave up. I was very angry at myself. But when she threatened to scream, I put my anger onto her. I punched her twice in the stomach.

Afterwards, Michel needed cash for more drugs. He decided to get Becky to drive him to a bank machine after dark and enter her personal identification number. He remembers, "I had to kill time. That was the weird time." Even though "she [was] scared for her life," the conversation between them turned casual and polite. At times Michel interacted with Becky as if she were a date with whom he had just had sex: "I started telling her about myself." He even told her his name. At other times, he replayed his performance as "the rapist" and Becky's as "the rape victim" to reaffirm these subject-positions. He used language rather than physical force to recreate the effect of his power. Michel elaborates:

There were times I felt powerful, but once my pathetic attempts at sex were over, I was more or less trying to figure her out as a woman – looking at her apartment – talking to her. Every *once* in a while, I would say something mean or threatening – to kinda *remind* her I was still in control, you know? She was being nice and I was being nice back, but I knew I shouldn't be, or I *thought* I shouldn't be. So every once in a while I would say something mean, just to remind her that I'm still the guy who's raping her. [*Pauses.*] Why are you smiling?

Becky began to scream in the car on the way to the bank, and Michel had to decide whether or not to use the knife to silence her: "A threat and actually doing it are two different things. I just said *fuck it*, and let her go." Michel describes his psychical and physical relationship to power and control during rape:

> The *power* and control I had over her was obviously something I was looking for. But, at the same time, I had tinges of guilt, but not overwhelming. Like, when I seen the pain in her eyes when I punched her in the stomach. The teddy bears. When she was cleaning up. But they were quick and gone because I *pushed* them back and told them to fuck off. The sexual part was very [*pauses*] unsatisfying. The power and control that I had was what I wanted, but it didn't feel the same way as in my fantasy. The real thing didn't feel the same as I thought it would, *probably* because it was a real person. Maybe I'm completely wrong on that, but I didn't enjoy the power and control side as much as I thought I would. I thought by raping a woman I wouldn't have to think of her satisfaction. I thought that the power and control would be arousing. I can't say I wasn't *aroused* by it – I was. But it didn't change all my insecurities. It didn't automatically give me an erection – I had to concentrate on it. It didn't come automatically.

Michel's story emphasizes his agency and the deliberate nature of rape. Yet, Michel also sees himself as an object of psychic forces beyond his control. He was arrested and convicted, and has completed four programs in prison, but he still wonders how he turned out to be, in his words, "some sexual sadist" rather than a "normal" man:

> I had so much going for me in juvie. If I had just continued on the way I was going, instead of turning into a sexual deviant, I'd be a fucking carpenter right now. Could have been anything, but sure as hell wouldn't be here. My fantasies – there was no stopping them from getting worse. There's lots of twenty-year-olds out there right now who are virgins – not because they *want* to be, but because they haven't had a chance. And they're not angry rapists – and, I know you can't answer this – but why didn't I turn out like *that* [*softer*] and just become normal, then become some sexual sadist. They gave me that label from the disclosure of my fantasies, not from my crime.

My fantasies dealt with power and control and domination – I got pleasure from those fantasies. I didn't get any pleasure from my crime.

Fred's Story Continues

My offences are more about anger. One could say they were about power, but the power to do what? To overcome what? Everything about my life made it hard for me to feel that I fit the bill of what society determines is a man. I was powerless to do anything to make myself feel more like a man other than using sex and violence. When I desperately tried to be a man with [my victim] and she rejected me, I believe now that I answered my need to not feel powerless and worthless the only ways I knew how – with sex and violence, but this time I used them together. My rape was also about control, but not for control's sake. Restoring control alleviates fear and the alleviation of fear dissolves the anger.

After a three-month "romantic and stormy" relationship with Emily, a seemingly insignificant event preceded Fred's first sexual offence. Against Emily's instructions not to discipline her son, Fred lightly swatted the youngster's backside. Emily reacted with the silent treatment, which epitomized Fred's failure to "make his relationship work" with her. He retreated to a nightclub to play eight ball, and drank and danced with women to forget "his hurt." Fred acknowledges the relationship between heterosexual practice and embodied masculinity. To re-secure a viable masculine subjectivity, he indicates that he needed to enact gender norms associated with hegemonic maleness:

I believe that all the stresses in my life built up to the point where the silent rejection of my girlfriend made it absolutely imperative that I be able to feel like a man. I went to the bar to do man things. Having sex with women and beating up men were the only man things I knew how to do. I thought I had obliterated my feelings of shame and rejection with alcohol and cocaine.

Fred recalls "having a good time" at the nightclub and feeling neither angry nor sad that night. He snorted cocaine with a friend and drank liquor until the cabaret closed: it "seemed as though I couldn't get drunk, although I felt quite high." As he drove home in the rain, Fred picked up a cabaret patron by the name of Anita who told Fred that she did not want to go straight home. Although Fred's rape was sexual, he says he did not pick up Anita for sex:

> I feel terrible saying this. My victim wasn't very attractive. The witnesses at my trial remembered her because she wore a low-cut and revealing dress in a [bold] pattern. But she wasn't very pretty. When I saw the picture of her later, I was surprised. I just picked her up to give her a ride. I would have done whatever she said – if she said, "Let's go have sex," I'd go have sex. If she said, "drive me to [a city miles away]," I would have done it. We agreed to go to a park and drink beer.

They talked, listened to music, and drank beer. Fred believed that Anita's willingness to park in a dark, secluded area with a male stranger signalled her receptivity to consensual sex. He touched her leg, but Anita slapped his hand, and he erupted in sudden anger and says an explosive compulsion came over him. He broke three vertebrae in Anita's neck and raped her:

> The instant that she slapped my hand away, my hands were around her throat. I remember watching my hands strangle her as though they were acting independently of my mind or body. I recall a feeling of not being able to stop it, as though I were a spectator in a dream that I had no control over. I don't recall undressing her, but I had a recollection of lying atop someone and beside someone on the ground. I remember no pleasure in the act. I remember throwing her body into the river.

Fred's next memory is being awakened by Emily's kiss. He slept on her couch, but cannot recall how he got there:

> I was stricken with the most baleful feeling. I knew something really bad had taken place. Images and pieces of the night began to return. I remember the strangling. But I didn't think I was capable of killing anyone until I found her black purse smack in the middle of the passenger seat, a pair of high-heels, and pantyhose on the floor of my car. I freaked and started hiding everything. I have hardly any independent recollection of events that took place in the next days.

Over the next month, Fred tried to comprehend his acts. He struggled to culturally understand himself as a "rapist" and "killer." His words to me suggest that he felt lost and unable to comprehend his apparently motiveless actions. Fred's sense of being out of control simultaneously amplified his lived powerlessness and yet, in his mind, exonerated him from full responsibility for his conduct. Fred describes a psychic and bodily experience akin to being catalyzed by evil. He elaborates:

> I remember looking in the mirror and feeling frightened for not knowing the person in the reflection. My self-talk is, "I'm dangerous. I'm sick in the head. I raped that girl. I'm not a rapist. What the fuck's wrong with me? I know I didn't mean to commit this offence. I'm not a killer." I knew I was a murderer. But I didn't know what that meant. To be a murderer. I was deathly afraid of losing control and attacking someone else. I remember picking up a woman hitch-hiker. She recognized me because I picked her up before. I knew I had to pick her up. The whole time I was driving I was terrified that I would kill her. The whole ride I was praying that I wouldn't kill her. I was a killer and that's what killers do.

Fred's lived reality of disempowerment stood in stark contrast to the cultural empowerment experienced by sexual murderers discussed by other authors (see Tatar 1995; Tithecott 1997). Over time, Fred tried to reconstruct and re-stabilize himself through heterosexual sex and contrived normality. He explains:

> I am emotionally unstable and burst into tears for no reason. I'm living with Emily but I'm afraid I'll hurt her. I go for long walks to secluded areas to provide whatever's out there the opportunity to kill me the way I killed Anita. I'm more polite and friendly with people to avoid more conflict and stress inside my head. I'm staring off blankly and unaware of people trying to get my attention. I inflict wounds on myself. I punch myself in the head. I can't get what I did off my mind and at any given time an image of my victim's face with my hands around her throat pops into my head. I continue to work. How can I stop myself from hurting anyone else? Eventually, I get back to my regular behaviour. I go out at nights drinking. I'm promiscuous. I begin dating a woman outside my relationship, looking for that ideal relationship that will help me get back on track so I never hurt anyone again. I believe that I'm going to kill again. I'm terrified, but I pretend that everything is normal while I try to figure out what to do.

Fred concluded that it was the cocaine that enabled him to rape and kill, and decided to abstain from it and live as though "nothing had happened." He convinced himself, rather conveniently, that "turning himself in won't bring her back." One month later, however, he attacked Julie, whom he had never met. She was asleep on a couch in his friend's basement, following a house party that Fred had not attended. Fred remembers little about the assault: "I probably made a sexual advance and upon seeing her reaction, strangled and beat her." Although there was no precipitous fight with Emily, in hindsight, he believes the same dynamics were at play. Fred's violence was ferocious but according to forensic reports, he did not sexually assault her. He took Julie from the house, transported her in his car, and abandoned her on the roadside. To destroy evidence, he cleaned his car and laundered his clothes. Fred's attack left Julie severely disabled. He recalls: "When Doug [Fred's adoptive father] told me they had found Julie, badly beaten, I was full of fear and shock. I believed I had done this but I didn't understand why or how. It was hard for me to believe that I could do that. That I had that cruelty in me."

Fred relied on external controls in his struggle to regain power over himself. He confessed his first rape and murder to his friend Darryl, and shared details that only Anita's killer would know. He told Darryl "there is something wrong with me" and "I don't know if I'll do it again," and asked him not to turn him in "unless someone else gets hurt and [Fred] is near when it happens." These events were confirmed in police and court records. Fred did not tell Darryl about Julie, though Darryl suspected he was behind her attack. Fred hoped that his pre-arranged capture would deter him from hurting more women. Darryl contacted the police, who arrested and charged Fred. Fred pled not guilty by reason of insanity. The jury convicted him of first-degree murder, but he was retried and pled guilty to second-degree murder.

When Fred recounts his attacks upon both women, he invokes two forms of consciousness connected to the acts. One is shaped by discourses about men's power, dominance, and pain, and the other is formed by his lived experiences as a racialized subject, "a dirty little Indian." Fred explains:

> In hindsight, my desire was for power and dominance – to get over the lack of control in my life and rejection. The way I was feeling inside. My anger. In my relationships, I kept feeling like I couldn't be loved. I was raised to believe that no one would ever love me – my mom [and dad] kept telling me that my entire life – I was a dirty little Indian. I thought I really loved Emily. It was the most important relationship in my life – it

could make me or break me and it broke me. She kept playing little games – she wasn't aware that she was doing these things to me, but she wasn't ready for a serious relationship. I went out to meet someone else.

Bear's Story Continues

When I was a kid I thought I wasn't going to be like dad. Yet, I was. I lashed out at women in a different way. I *choose* to victimize somebody. I knew it was wrong, but still did it. Didn't care. My *dad* didn't care about my mom. My sister's husbands beat them up too. They were objects – sexual objects, weak. Nobody laid a hand out to help anybody. The thought ingrained in my head was that this was okay. I had a quick glimpse of right and wrong, but my arousal weakened my belief. 'Cause, in my thoughts, nobody cared about me, so why should I care about that person?

In his reflection on his life, Bear links his two post-carceral rapes of adult women to his early boyhood model of masculinity, which sanctioned constant male violence against women and children in the home. After his release from prison, Bear felt alienated from self and others, and faced psychic suffering over his mother's death:

The feeling was feeling alone. Couldn't fit in. Ah, unloved, nobody seemed to care. [*Pauses.*] I felt the only person who really cared for me was gone. And I never told her, never showed it to her. So this is how I'm thinking: "If only I did this for her. If only I told her." I started dwelling on myself as a person. Not knowing who I was. Feeling confused, feeling worthless, feeling lost. How I'd cover all that up was by drinking, you know, numbing it a bit. But, it was always there.

As noted earlier, Bear and his male relatives committed crimes to supplement social assistance. One of these occasions provided him with his next victim. He notes:

The opportunity happened when this friend of mine broke into this apartment. He came back and then *we* went there. This woman was sleeping alone on her bed. She never even knew that four of us were in the house. She left her balcony door open. We took her stereo, her speakers, and her table. About a week later I thought about this lady. I knew she was alone. Then I went through the cycle of feeling alone, feeling unloved, putting myself down, going into self-pity. I had thought of raping this woman. I was running it through my mind. Like, dwelling on it, and fantasizing about it. Nothing could distract it.

Bear returned and raped her, and was later arrested after she spotted him in a local shopping mall. He pled guilty to rape and served a three-year sentence. His ascribed status as a sex offender further alienated him from ideals of hegemonic manhood and haunted him more and more. Bear elaborates:

> I had no remorse for what I did to that last woman. It was like – you did something? And boom, you forgot it. Like, you knew it happened, but you never thought about it. It's just like when you are a kid. Like, when you seen mom get beat? You forgot about it. You never brought it up. Somehow, that became a way of dealing with things. But it was always still there. It would make me feel shamed. It would make me feel worthless. I went through all these feelings that I could never be trusted, you know? I could never care. No one could ever care for me. I couldn't look at myself in the mirror because I always see that person – I categorize that person as a sex offender.

Six weeks after his release from prison, Bear raped again. He seemed unable to sustain a life-affirming identity, let alone a masculine one. His gendered subjectification was shaped at the crossroads of unemployment, social isolation, and race. He was tied to the racialized subject-position of "stupid Indian." He recalls:

> I was feeling those feelings when my sister started talking about my mom, just before my last offence in '82. It started that morning when I went to see my dad. He told me that he didn't want me to come into his place, 'cause he didn't want the police around. I felt hurt. I went to the employment office. I looked all through these jobs, and I was still feeling hurt inside. Felt alone, felt lost, felt rejected, felt that no one cared. No one understood me. I'm looking at all these jobs – but they were Grade 10, Grade 12 – grades I couldn't match, which made me feel stupid – I'm not good enough. I'm this worthless person. I'm a stupid Indian just like my dad says, and I'll always be this person. So, I left.

Although Bear portrays himself as uncaring and unfeeling towards his two rape victims, his decision to rape also resonates with emotions associated with guilt, remorse, shame, and anguish. For Bear, the function of rape was more personal than political:

I walked back to my sister Mabel's. I was exhausted, but I was still hurting. I put on this front. I put on this mask, and sat down. I was drinking from four-thirty. After an hour my brother-in-law drove us to see my sister Lorraine. She was passed out. I tried to wake her up. I wasn't sitting there twenty minutes, and Mabel started bringing up my mom. She was telling me in anger that I should never have been in jail. I should have been by mom's side. I should have, I should have, I should have – telling me, "Mom said this, [*whispers*] mom said that." I left. I went down to my nephew's. I was restless. After ten minutes, I said "I got to go." Boom, I left. Caught the bus. Went back up to Lorraine's. She was still passed out. And Mabel started saying more things about me being in jail. That mom wanted to see me. She was making me feel ashamed, guilty, that I didn't care. I remember sitting there with my head down. I left. I went back down to my nephew's. After ten minutes, boom, "I got to get out of here." Boom, back up. I felt lost. And then boom, I caught the bus down there, and then caught the bus back up. Then Mabel – she started in on me again about mom. That's when I left. That's when I had that little glimpse of choice. I had a glimpse of right from wrong. I *did*. Whether to not do it or whether to go ahead with it. I believe it within myself because I *seen* it. I *had* that choice.

Bear acknowledges his moral agency and his choice to rape to include any woman. He describes his decision to rape an elderly woman as an outcome of bodily arousal and an attempt to communicate his pain rather than his power. He conveys rape as his only available choice for action:

I *knew* what I was going to do. I started walking. If I went to my left, I would look for a victim. If I went to my right, and caught a bus, I would just go home. There's the choice I had. And the choice of going to my right was much weaker than going to my left. Because I knew the urge of the offending, the feeling, the arousal, um, the loneliness, feeling alone was there – the hurt, the anger, wanting somebody to feel what I was feeling. I'd had a taste of it already, so I know what it's like, you know? Didn't care who it was. Boom. I just started walking to my left. I'd made up my mind. I *knew*, walking to my left – I was going to be looking for a victim. That was my intent. 'Cause I could see it in my mind already. I went to light a cigarette. There was a little breeze blowing – so I turned like this [*gestures*] and I went *chew*, and I seen the door open with a screen door. I walked onto the lawn. I walked up the stairs. I looked in the door. I seen an elderly woman. I looked around – didn't see nobody. I thought up a lie to get into the house, and pressed the button.

For Bear, sexual desirability was irrelevant to stranger rape. The woman who answered the door was over seventy-nine years old. He consciously called up a dominant subject-position. He distanced himself from his victim's pain the same way that he learned to block his own. He made himself up into an angry rapist. Bear explains the process:

> Out of all the nerve of adrenaline, I didn't care whether the door was open. I worked up this person that didn't care. Worked him up, and asked him to be angry and her to be fearful. And then, she was totally terrified and scared because, all of a sudden, this was happening. I forced her into the bedroom. She didn't want to go, but there was nothing she could have said to stop [me], 'cause I had already made up my mind. I told her to lay on the bed and [*pauses*] she was crying. It never hurt listening before, but when I went through it in my crime cycle, I started hearing this voice saying, "Why are you doing this to me?" And she said that many times. I shut that out. It's like, you don't hear. It's like you're stubborn, you know? I didn't care whether she was an elderly woman. To me she was just an object. And then I forced myself on her.

Although Bear makes no attempt to exonerate his conduct or mitigate his responsibility, he emphasizes that he was "this other person that had no feeling," which suggests a separation between his self and the rapist subject-position that he constructed and dramatized to create fear and submission in his victim:

> They say I was there for two hours, but it didn't seem like it, you know? And I remember I had a hard time, um, ejaculating. I didn't ejaculate. She was still pleading with me. She was crying. And then somewhere in there she asked me to go to the washroom. And I let her get up. And, she went and I sat on the bed and waited. Still didn't care. I was this other person that had no feeling. And it wasn't long before I asked her if she was finished. I didn't give her a chance to answer. I showed no remorse for this person. I pulled her out of the bathroom and on to the bed again. And then proceeded to have intercourse with her.

By raping an elderly woman, Bear publicly disgraced himself, and this psychical shame alienated him in perpetuity from the fundamental teaching of Aboriginal cultures to respect one's elders. Bear elaborates on his arrest and the aftermath:

> It wasn't long after that I heard somebody at the door. I went to look. And there was this guy standing at the door. Somebody else came in, and he told him to go call the police cause a guy had broke into the house. I just gave up, and stayed there. The cops came and stood me out on the walkway. I had to wait there. They were all looking at me. I was feeling shamed and embarrassed. And so was she, you know, because I totally humiliated this person. It's been twenty years. Whenever I'm with Elders I still feel that shame. Whether it's white or Native. That's something I will always feel. Because, in our culture, we respect our Elders. It's something we believe in.

6 Men's Power and Men's Pain: Gendering and Gendered Violence

Most men are intimidated by aggressive men. Most men don't want to compete physically. If you're going to get beaten by another man, it belittles you. And it opens a big door. When men see my kind of hostility and aggression, they stay away. But women like an outlaw kind of aggressive man that will stand up for himself – a rugged kind of man. Most men are babies. They look at that shit and it scares them. There's not a big majority of men that are actually violent out of Canada's population. The amount of males in prison for violence – we're a small percentage.

(Cam)

In the passage above, Cam links himself to men's power and hegemonic masculinity. He claims that aggressive physicality is not a normative gendering practice among men, and insists that only a minority of men have the predilection and bodily formation for this form of gendering. Cam echoes Elridge Cleaver's representation of white men's subject position as frail, cowardly, and effeminate (cited in Segal 2006; 1990, 181), and believes that most men shirk physical conflict with other men because they know that gender can also be undone should their physicality fail them. Yet it is Cam's rugged, combative, working-class, aggressive masculinity that is identified as the prototypical male in much feminist work on systemic male violence against women (Segal 2006; 1990, 264–5). Unfortunately, this portrayal is too simplistic. It obscures the fact that the category "men" contains a multitude of identities and bodies; variable forms of physicality; diverse propensities, abilities, and opportunities to use that physicality; and different ideas about suitable channels for the deployment of physical force. A unitary prototype naturalizes male physical violence and ignores how the interplay between social inequalities and discourse about men's power shapes each man's relationship to violence (Stanko 2000, 153). Paradoxically, this representation valorizes the rugged aggressive outlaw as a cultural measure of manhood and as a subject-position for materializing a masculine identity. At the same time, it locates some men's deviant bodies outside existing philosophical categories that define the masculine in terms of rationality and intellect or the transcendence of mind over supposedly unruly feminized bodies and emotions (Butler 1993b; Cahill 2001).

I agree with Cam, however, that the participants in this study are not most men. Such a characterization might minimize or trivialize the violence and pathos of their life stories. But neither are my participants *other* men or monsters. Rather, their narratives reveal ordinariness and indicate dramatic experiences well beyond the ken of many men and women, especially those whose lives are sheltered by economic, educational, and racial privilege. That said, most men with similar circumstances and disadvantages as my participants do not rape or kill anonymous women. In fact, similar events – most notably physical, emotional, and sexual mistreatment – produce different gendering effects among even my own sample of participants. At one extreme, Cam, Simpson, and Charlie normalized boyhood serial physical and sexual victimization and transformed it into a weapon that fortified their sense of hegemonic manhood. At the other extreme, Bear, Kerry, and Brian's sexual victimization, while less extensive and severe, produced vulnerability, weakness, and passivity that tied them to feminized object-hood and cycles of psychic suffering. Yet all these processes and events, however momentary, presented mechanisms and obstacles for creating a coherent masculine identity. Collectively, the narrative conveys multiple layers of private pain and suffering and illustrates the complex emotional discourse that underpins violence, victimization, and gendering in men's lives (see Jefferson 2002). Their narratives raise the issues of how men's pain and victimization fit with feminist narratives of patriarchy and men's power, and how men's power and hegemonic masculinity fit with narratives of penal governance.

These life histories illustrate some of the interplay among gendered power relationships, social discourses and practices, and everyday life whereby masculine subjectification is inscribed with controls over emotional expression and with the ability to accept and inflict physical harm and pain. While social and individual practices of stranger rape are enabled by hegemonic masculinities, those masculinities do not necessarily determine rape. I do not claim that any one of those social relationships caused stranger rape. No man is fated to rape a woman. But I do maintain that those relationships and life events help to illustrate how fourteen men could transform strangers into spontaneous or deliberate objects of extreme physical or sexualized violence, and how some of them could create the emotional contexts that caused the deaths of human beings without apparent conscience or remorse. I use the gender-neutral term "human being" deliberately here to emphasize that these men had far fewer qualms about hurting men than women.

This chapter uses Diana Scully's (1990) research on convicted American rapists and James Messerschmidt's (2000) life history findings on working-class boys to organize and discuss themes from my participants' life histories. To interpret the rich and complex data was an enormous task, and different tools of analysis from different theoretical frameworks could certainly be brought to bear on these stories. But to my mind, Scully's study is pivotal (see Mardorossian 2002, 751). Her major thesis is that "rape is an acquired behaviour, an act of normal deviance, found in societies or culture groups whose social, economic, and political structures support sexual violence through the subordination and devaluation of women" (1990, 63). My objective is *not* to dispute Scully's socio-structural framework or other feminist writers' insistences that there are links between sexual violence, systemic power relations, and women's subordination. Indeed, my life history data corroborates Scully's findings that even the most powerless of men can deploy sexual violence to exploit structurally produced gender relations of dominance and subordination. Instead, my intention is to locate these fourteen men and their practices more precisely within the relations of power and domination that Scully and others discuss. To that end, I incorporate concepts and ideas from critical masculinities and post-structural feminist theories to identify and analyse distinct practices that are formative of a hegemonic masculine subjectivity, rather than to assume a universal form of male dominance. There are places where I disagree with or revise some feminist theories of rape, including Scully's. Her data suggests four motives for rape: (a) revenge and punishment, (b) sexual access, (c) impersonal sex, rape fantasy, and pornography, and (d) what she calls an added bonus to other crimes such as robbery. Yet the discourse of power and control never arises in her participants' accounts of their rapes or in Scully's analysis of the data. This absence confirms Cameron and Frazer's (1987) observation that available cultural representations for making sense of rape at a particular historical moment influence how the rapist understands his own behaviours.

Twenty years ago the feminist-inspired argument that violence is a construct of power and control was not a dominant discourse or cultural code in society. By contrast, the subjects in both my study and Messerschmidt's – all of whom had encountered contemporary forms of clinical interventions – draw repeatedly on power and control discourse to explain their conduct. Each of my participants, for example, filtered their reasons for rape through this conceptual lens. While feminist-based theories of rape and men's violence concentrate on power and control as historically specific and materially based acts, cognitive behavioural penal treatment programs use the power and control framework to describe individual thinking errors or cognitive distortions that happen independent of any material context. Neither perspective, however, considers the lived effects of power and control on men as both a discourse and a practice. That said, my findings do confirm the value of some of Scully's original categories and suggest a measure of thematic stability in men's expressed motivations for rape over three decades. This similarity is striking, since Scully's research subjects had not been exposed to treatment regimes or clinical rape narratives for making sense of rape. However, I must add three qualifications to Scully's categories. First, her categories of analysis are deployed simultaneously but I think they may also occur sequentially. Second, the rapist's motivation and objectives are not always predetermined and stable, but shift as each unique social situation unfolds and especially as victims contribute to defining the situation. Finally, her categories and my analysis as a result are historically specific and, as Cameron and Frazer (1987, 125–7) note, change over time and offer new ways to see and think about rape and rapists.

In what follows, I locate my fourteen subjects structurally. Next, I summarize how constructions of masculinity interacted across family, school, heterosexual relations, and workplace. I deploy Messerschmidt's (2000) concept of practised definitions of men's power to anchor my analysis of boyhood. During the adolescent portion of my subjects' lives, I compare their stories with Messerschmidt's six "violent" boys stories, and examine the effects of the gender norm that "real men" confront interpersonal challenges through fighting. Then I review and analyse my participants' life histories through Michael Kaufman's (1994) notion of men's pain or contradictory experiences of power. I examine the effects of a second ubiquitous gender norm and definition of men's power ignored by Messerschmidt, namely, that real men do not cry or express weakness. Finally, I advance an alternative understanding of stranger rape from the standpoint of the rapist, and build on and beyond feminist and critical theories of rape.

Locating the Men Structurally:
An Overview of Similarities and Differences

Scully has difficulty answering the questions of why not all men in sexually violent societies rape, and why some men become rapists. She does not look for similarities and differences in men's lives, but homogenizes men as a category and concludes that otherwise "normal" men rape "because they have learned that in this culture sexual violence is rewarding and low-risk behaviour" (1990, 159). However, the men in my study revealed that diverse themes figured prominently in their motivations to rape. Nine of fourteen men learned first-hand that sexual offending is punitive, hurtful, and destructive, rather than rewarding. They perceived many commonalities in their lives as teenagers and young adults. As Paddy notes, "We've all had similar feelings, similar upbringings, similar thought processes to reach the violence and stuff like that, similar relationships, past beliefs about women." Fred adds:

> You sit in a group and start to see that other people that went through similar circumstances do similar things. We're all different people, but we're affected by these events of our lives in similar ways [*pauses*] – how we deal with and how we're affected is often different, but not so different that we're unique.

The men in my study were born and raised in five provinces (see Appendix on page 293). They came from white and Aboriginal communities, and lived in both urban and rural areas. Two men grew up in abject poverty. Otherwise, none recall feeling materially deprived as children. Yet the men were mostly undereducated and most were often unemployed or underemployed. Each man who worked for wages was unskilled or semi-skilled and followed or fell below his parents' working-class economic circumstances. Only Marvin completed Grade 12. Otherwise, formal education ranged from Grade 5 to 11, with an average of just under eight years completed. Eleven men failed one or more grades. For some, failure was due to constant family relocation and the absence of educational stability in their lives. For others, a mixture of emotional chaos, drinking, fighting, and abuse within family, schools, and community cut short formal education. Ten men began to form and affirm a hegemonic masculinity through physical conflicts with other male classmates and teachers. School authorities responded with suspensions and corporal punishment, and seven boys were expelled temporarily or permanently from school. For some, leaving school was an economic necessity and often coincided with leaving their boyhood homes to escape physically or emotionally abusive circumstances. Others saw education as irrelevant and an obstacle to their future occupations as manual labourers. Most left school feeling stupid, frustrated, or bored, and were relieved to move on to other activities.

By leaving school early, each man faced economic vulnerability and experienced powerlessness in regard to work. Other than Simpson, who characterized himself as a good thief, the rest supported themselves financially by working part-time in low-paying, unskilled, or seasonal jobs. Given their gender, age, and education, their only marketable asset was physical strength and endurance. Only Michel's telemarketing job and Cam's auto-pawn-shop job – financed by his wife – emphasized any degree of intellect over body. Except for Charlie, Marvin, and Cam – the latter two men benefiting from their partners' income – no one managed to achieve financial independence from family or social assistance. To supplement their licit incomes, ten of the fourteen men shoplifted, sold illicit drugs, stole vehicles, committed residential break-ins, and robbed. As a result, each of these ten men already had a criminal record prior to his first sexual assault conviction. Cam and Kerry had served federal time (prison sentences two years or longer) and seven men had served provincial time (prison sentences under two years). For example, Marvin, Fred, and Bob had served probation and paid fines and Michel had served multiple sentences in closed youth detention centres. Only James had youth convictions for sexual infractions.

Finally, race and class had different impacts for the five Aboriginal men. The two men raised by their biological parents in isolated First Nations reserves bore the brunt of intergenerational violence, alcohol abuse, economic impoverishment, and cultural devaluation engendered by nearly four hundred years of European contact and Canadian governmental policies that had the goal of assimilation (e.g., Lane et al. 2002; Paul 2006). The three other Aboriginal men were raised in white households. While these three men fared better economically and educationally, each experienced enforced transcultural exposure in their white communities, internalized his difference as inferiority, and struggled with identity (see Walmsley 2005). Whether the Aboriginal men grew up in Aboriginal or non-Aboriginal communities, all were estranged from their cultural histories, traditions, languages, and ceremonies until they entered federal prisons (see Ellerby and MacPherson 2002; Waldram 1997). All five Aboriginal men heard, and to some degree internalized, culturally racialized stereotypes about Indians as "inferior," "stupid," "lazy," and "drunks."

Men's Power and Women's Weakness

The men's stories indicate that patriarchal-style family and compulsory heterosexuality are primary social institutions and discourses that reproduce hegemonic masculinity, women's inequality, and youthful expectations about men's power (e.g., Lusher and Robins 2007; Mooney-Somers and Ussher 2010; Renold 2007). Each of my participants was raised in a family characterized by traditional gendered divisions of labour. Except for Cam's mother, a full-time nurse, fathers earned the primary income in the household. Mothers provided childcare, house work, emotional labour, and, in four instances, part-time incomes through unskilled and semi-skilled labour. The nuclear family arrangement with a father provider and mother caregiver was the boyhood norm. Charlie was the only man with an absent father during boyhood. To different degrees, each family differed from the media-constructed middle-class family form as it conveys affection and belonging. In most rapist families, gender and generational power inequalities erupted frequently in abuse and physical violence against weaker family members. Government, family, or community rarely intervened to help the boys or other abused or abusive family members. Kerry and Cam acknowledge that women and children's economic dependency and the discourse about familial privacy and husband's (or father's) rights enabled physical and sexual abuse in their lives:

> Remembering back, the first time my stepfather ever physically lashed out against my mother would not be tolerated today. But my mother at that time had *no*where to go. She was *required* to keep his abuse towards us secret and to assume responsibility and blame for my stepfather's actions towards us. I was taken back again and again by the police. It wasn't *his* fault. It was my fault. You don't find an eight year old boy 150 miles away from home on the *highway* in inclement weather without there being a darn good reason. After age twelve, I was old enough to realize that I didn't know where to go. (Kerry)

Everything [my father] does has a perversion play. He acts like that in public. He would pinch my sisters' nipples or their privates and stuff like that when they were just growing. He thinks it's humorous, and people usually do laugh because they are embarrassed. How do you react to something that's so far beyond the norm? You either laugh along or you make a big scene. And most people don't want to make a big scene. They think, maybe he's just being funny. But the reality is, underneath it all, a lot of hidden things are going on. You just don't act like that. And he's done it for so many years. He believes there is nothing wrong with it, you know. Those were his kids and he had the right to do whatever and no one outside the family ever said nothing different to him. (Cam)

Messerschmidt (2000, 84) notes that each of the six violent boys in his sample of nine male youth was raised in a "non-egalitarian" or "non-democratic" family characterized by "a *practised* definition of masculine power." The families in my sample were also non-egalitarian. Each father and mother conformed to traditional patriarchal divisions between men's and women's work. However, four of my subjects (Paul, James, Fred, and Brian) had non-violent father figures who did not personify masculine power in the home by active control over women or other family members. Indeed, Paul, Fred, Brian, and Marvin had mothers who contested male power through disparaging remarks and behaviours towards their husbands, or displayed physical and verbal violence against their sons. Practiced definitions of male power in the home were lacking in four of my cases. However, each of these men was mindful that his father deviated from a patriarchal norm and each derided him for not "laying down the law" with his mother.

Messerschmidt (2000, 88) also notes that violent boys received and accepted advice from their fathers "that 'real men' solve their problems by physical violence." Most fathers in my sample certainly encouraged their sons, explicitly or implicitly, to manage interpersonal problems through aggression and violence. But I found that this hegemonic masculine practice extended to other institutional sites. For example, the state-run group home that Bear attended actively promoted supervised fighting to resolve disputes between individual boys. The public school system inflicted corporal punishment on many of the men in my sample. Men who had served prison sentences recounted incidents of physical abuse by some penal staff. As Michel recounts, getting "beat up by the cops" was "a normal thing" during his many arrests and police interrogations. By contrast, Paul and Paddy's parents condemned their sons for fighting. Fred, Brian, Bob, and Marvin's mothers, more than their fathers, displayed physical violence against them (but never their sisters). Aside from Cam and Simpson, my participants' fathers voiced approval for hegemonic masculine qualities such as toughness, strength, and stoicism. Similarly to the experiences of the violent boys in Messerschmidt's study, no significant adult in my sample imparted alternative practices for resolving interpersonal or intergenerational strife. Consider Bob's recollection that "everything [in my family] was always fight, fight, fight – that's how you dealt with everything in my family" Paul also recalls: "When there was conflict or tension between my parents, instead of talking they just avoid everything. Nothing would be talked about. Nothing would be said at all. Not a goddamn thing." In spite of their ambivalent or antagonistic relationships with their fathers and their different experiences of familial power relations, each man in my sample ultimately embodied a version of his father's masculinity. Bear elaborates:

> Thinking about the way mom was treated, I used to say, "I'm not like dad." But I am. I just acted out in a different way. I am like dad inside. It's hidden. The way I looked at women, the way I treated women. I was so much like dad. I didn't want to believe it at first. I looked at women as weak objects. I grew up seeing dad treat mom this way. It seems like everywhere I went – I went to my sisters' homes – they were treated the same way. They were abused like my mom. And nobody, nobody laid out a hand to help my sisters, help my mom, [*pauses*] help me.

The social and economic conditions that shaped my participants' families interacted with cultural gender norms to produce women's inequality, subservience, and dependence on men. But no single prototypical mother or mother-son relationship existed. Brian, James, and Paul's recollections suggest matriarchal rather than patriarchal households: "ma controlled everything," "dad always turned his pay cheque over to mom," or "my dad never stood up for himself against my mom." Yet at the same time, familial social relations were structured so that women served men and cooked their meals, washed their clothes, and cleaned up after other family members. Only Cam's mother, a nurse, had any stable economic status outside the family. Strikingly, most of my participants interpreted their mother's adherence to gender norms, such as compliance to male authority and physical power, as manifestations of women's inferiority or lack of agency. The adjective the men most often used to describe their mothers was "weak:"

My mother's fear of being alone – I didn't respect her at all for that. I thought she was weak because of it. Because, when there wasn't a man around Life was good. So, physically *and* emotionally, women were a lot weaker. Like, my mom, my aunts, when there's a problem? A lot of crying, you know. With my uncles it was a massive anger right now and it was *dealt* with – in a physical way. (Harvey)

Yet, Brian, Michel, Paul, and Marvin, for example, found fault in their mothers because they lacked nurturing qualities, refused their husband's rule in the home, or deployed forms of power traditionally associated with men. They viewed their mothers as proactive rather than passive in the infliction of physical and emotional boyhood injury and harm. This power relationship, however, was contingent and temporary, and was reversed as soon as the boys realized that their biological maleness gave them the physical strength to define their masculinity against their mother:

I disrespected how weak and passive my mom was – how easy she was to control. In the teen years, I wasn't scared of mom no more. She'd tell me, "go to your room Bob," and I wouldn't. What could she do? She's not going to do nothing to me. Even if she would have hit me, it wouldn't have hurt – she's five-foot-four, maybe one hundred pounds. I also knew I can't hit her. Maybe I knew my dad was coming home and I would get it from him, but I knew I couldn't hurt my mom. (Bob)

Brian, Fred, and Simpson recall the exact moment when they ended their mother's physical abuse by striking back. Thereafter their mothers respected this new gendered power hierarchy. Paddy says: "It came to the point where women just became weak. My mom and dad's qualities Looking back – she's [*pauses*] weak. The man controls and she puts up with him. The man's the boss. Women cook, clean, take care of the house, take care of the kids." Later, some men appreciated their mother's choices and behaviours as culturally constrained based on their economic dependency. But seen through boyhood eyes, most mothers in the families in my study were eventually defined as inferior, weak, and victims.

Each man's story emphasizes the effects of women's subjectifying power as mothers and women's agency in shaping boyhood subjectivity. With some exceptions (e.g., Ashe and Cahn 1994; Simon 1994), feminist scholarship concentrates on mother's transformative and enabling power as nurturing caregivers, and ignores that some mothers and other women exercise power on boys in a harmful way. Only Kerry, Bear, and Harvey admit to an affinity with their mothers. Paul and Michel yearned for their mother's love and attention, but felt physically and emotionally abandoned. Marvin, Fred, Brian, and Bob's relationships with their mother evinced extreme psychological and physical mistreatment and open antipathy. Other men describe their mother's care as undemonstrative, unreliable, and inappropriate. Each participant's gendered interactions with his mother produced lived experiences of powerlessness, whether powerlessness to protect their mothers from violent partners, to interact verbally with their mothers in emotionally charged situations, or to elicit maternal affection and attention. Many of the men were critical of their mothers' rather than their fathers' departures from idealized visions of parenthood. Marvin provides a typical example of how he and his cohort codify women and mothers in gender terms:

MARVIN: Being mistreated in every imaginable way made me hate the first woman I ever had a relationship with, and that's my mother.

Q: Your dad was brutal too. Did you hate your dad?

MARVIN: A woman is supposed to be soft. A woman should show more affection and caring and loving than a man. And a woman gives birth to her child. And you have to nurture and guide that child and give him love, apart from the shelter. There's something about being a mother. How could a mother mistreat her own child? I blamed my dad's distance on his alcoholism and mental illness. He was unable to get close to me, [*pauses*] although he was able to with my sisters.

Their fathers' silence, violence, and steely stoicism personified hegemonic working-class manhood, but their mothers' conduct contradicted dominant constructions of motherhood, whether through failing to protect their children from male violence, or through inflicting forms of violence against them.

Violence, Masculinity, and Schoolboys

Messerschmidt dismisses one-sided explanations of male adolescent violence that focus exclusively on dysfunctional families. He argues that physical aggression is a legitimate and oftentimes preferred masculinizing response to perceived attacks against the self in working-class communities more generally. In his words, relationships in the home and in "the culture of cruelty" at school intersect in social constructions of violent masculinity (2000, 137). My life stories also confirm that boys began to fight at school as a gender-appropriate response to different forms of peer conflict. Nearly all my subjects were derided by school mates for various forms of physical and social difference that distanced them from hegemonic and gendered constructions of cultural normalcy. Paddy, Michel, Harvey, Fred, and Brian reported that the most common source of ridicule was weight-related; each of these boys was very fat (see Tager, Good, and Morrison 2007). Bob was mocked for his speech impediment, and both he and James were repeatedly labelled "stupid." School mates denounced Charlie and James because they had "funny looks" and "ugly acne." Fred, Marvin, Simpson, Bear, and Paul encountered racialized stereotypes, taunts, and challenges from classmates as well as their own parents. Taken together, most of the participants in my study experienced ostracism over their failure to measure up to the other boys at school.

Messerschmidt also notes that three of the adolescent boys in his study engaged in sexual offences because the shape and size of their bodies prevented them from developing the masculine self-esteem to fight back against male tormenters at school. In my sample, only James confirms this finding. While he figured out that he was supposed to fight back in the face of taunts, bullying, and ridicule, he also knew his body was too small and fragile to defeat his male antagonists. James lacked masculinizing practices and social peers, and so he turned his attention to younger boys and girls over whom he could "be the boss." He began to manipulate younger girls into sexual touching, although he says he did not identify or experience this behaviour as sexual until puberty. By late adolescence, most of my subjects had made the transition from victims of violence and ridicule to active purveyors of violence and abuse, not unlike Messerschmidt's (2000) physically adept assaultive boys who chose physical aggression against males rather than illicit sex acts against girls as their key masculinizing practice. But why did each man in my research sample also sexually assault women?

Male-to-male fights featured prominently in my research subjects' everyday lives. Fighting was never merely a gender appropriate practice for resolving interpersonal male conflict; it was equally a way to materialize a masculine persona and link it to male power more generally. All my subjects agreed that a man gets power from another man physically and all regarded fighting as an activity in which they had superior ability over other men (see Connell 2000, 218). While one man claimed that fighting was "his nature," most denied that it was an uncontrollable impulse. Instead, they saw fighting as a situational response to cope with vulnerability and weakness or with actively refusing victimhood, which the boys then transformed into an effective modality for performing gender (see Weiss 2010, 277). Consider Michel and Charlie's accounts:

> I needed to feel powerful so people left me alone. There was a time in my life, when I was the one that was scared and picked on, and I just reversed the tables. I hurt a lot of people [males]. I sought them out. I would never see them again and didn't know who they were, so it wasn't like they were going to fear me in the future. I guess I just got power from hurting [men]. (Michel)

> I became violent when I was ten. I fought all my life, but to defend, never to just hurt. It changed. People who had instilled fear in me [*pauses*] – I became a very good fighter and I started hurting people [males], and I hurt a lot of them. I think initially it wasn't with anger [*pauses*] – it was survival? It had nothing to do with reputation. It did later on in life. (Charlie)

For every man except James, fighting continued beyond the adolescent schoolyard to include bar brawls, beating and robbing men on the street, enforcing gang territories, and random violence without apparent cause. Before incarceration, most men expressed pride in being "the craziest," "the badest," "the meanest," and in demonstrating strength by "never showing tears," "never losing a fight," and "never surrendering," even under threat of greater violence against them. Fighting other men was a subjectifying power that was productive and relational. It created a hegemonic masculinity through the other person's subordination. In their stories, "A man that can't fight isn't a man" was a constant refrain (see Tomsen 2002). Beyond this deliberate performative feature, fighting was also a gender-made practice for handling emotional distress, anxiety, and pain. Private feelings of fear, helplessness, worthlessness, embarrassment, and shame often prompted aggressive and punitive responses that restored my participants' gender, rather than expressed it. Michel's comment is typical:

> I think I have shame-based anger. I didn't really call it that until we talked about it one afternoon in group. It made sense. It has to do with pride

– looking bad, looking foolish, and saving face – low self-esteem. But it kind of derives from all those areas. It's all really one big area called low self-esteem, but I act on it in an angry way – to restore face.

Rather than providing generic clues for risk-managing sex offenders, as evinced in treatment therapies, my participants' relations with women reveal a variety of conventional heterosexual attitudes about women. Other than Michel, James, and Cam, fourteen was the average age of first heterosexual intercourse. Harvey, Cam, Marvin, and Simpson were married when they committed stranger rape, and the rest of the men had consensual sexual opportunities with women at one time or another. Simpson, Fred, Bob, and Paul capitalized on their self-defined physical finesse with women, and drew on a "phallocentric framework" to affirm cultural ideals of hegemonic manhood (cf. hooks 1992, 94). At the time of their interviews, each man had a common-law partner or girlfriend. Paul speaks for this group when he claims that he was better at the "initial romance stuff." Each man had many casual, consensual female partners, and experienced volatile relationships characterized by male infidelity, jealousy, and anxiety over losing control of a woman to another man. As the only man in this foursome with children, Simpson rejected a provider masculinity role and refused to support any of his eight children or their four mothers.

Cam's boyhood lessons that "women were good for one thing" followed him into manhood. During his second marriage, he says, he "felt owned" by his wife and regularly sought out sex workers as substitutes. He even contemplated killing his wife for her money. Although Marvin dated women outside his marriage and visited sex workers, he admits he did not have overt control in his marital relationship. His wife worked full-time, managed their money, and refused to sexualize herself or "make herself look nice" for him. She exercised autonomy in the household, and Marvin felt he had to manoeuvre her into arguments and storm out of the home in feigned anger to avoid being questioned about his clandestine affairs. Marvin claimed that his dates were more about "showing affection" than having sex. He and his partner remained together for the sake of their son, whom Marvin cherishes. Charlie and Paddy dated women intermittently and both were direct in their disdain for them. Kerry admits that for him, heterosexuality shifted from boyhood fantasies of consensual sex to adult ones of sexual control. Brian and Harvey expressed their intense hatred for specific women, but as teenagers both were affectionate and responsible in their romantic partnerships. At his trial, Harvey's female and male friends submitted letters that portrayed him as a "gentleman" and "supporter of women's rights." Harvey idolizes his three sons and, unlike Simpson, assumed financial responsibility for his wife and sons' welfare. Michel and James desired girlfriends. Michel got close to and respected female staff while incarcerated, but otherwise he and Brian felt too insecure and intimidated to approach women. Bear stated that he viewed women as sexual objects, yet he also admired his common-law partner's intelligence and never tried to control her because "she was her own person." Long-term incarceration separated Bear from his two daughters from different common-law relationships. James is the only man who in his teens fits the stereotype of the rapist as a "bush-lurking," "inept," "social outcast" who "can't get a woman" (Stanko 2000, 151).

Conflicts and reconciliations marked many of my participants' romantic relationships. This is not especially unique and evinces a broad cultural pattern. Yet seven of my participants indicate that partner conflict set them on a course of action that ended with them raping an anonymous woman. The common denominator in these cases is that each man's partner acted unilaterally and subverted his sense of agency and control within the relationship. On one level, these admissions seem to support the thesis that links rape to male power and control. But at another level, many accounts also reveal the psychic pain and loss to men pursuant to a failed romantic relationship. While popular culture does not embrace the idea that men rather than women can be degraded by rejection (Bordo 1999), rejection devastated Paul's, Charlie's, Fred's, and Brian's lives, intensified their lived sense of powerlessness, and reaffirmed the hegemonic norm that men should not express emotional distress and weakness when failures occur. Overall, only James' life history confirms Messerschmidt's conclusions about why boys choose sexual practices rather than violence against females. Once my assaultive participants entered adulthood, each also committed sexual offences against women. All fourteen participants identified with a hegemonic masculine subjectivity materialized through biological maleness and gender-specific practices of coercion and domination. The life course my participants followed into adulthood suggests that Messerschmidt's "assaultive boys" may have eventually followed a similar pattern into sexual assault.

Although some of the men in my study were once enthusiastic students, none significantly valued education. The interplay between family and school that supported violence and aggression was also what induced them to abandon education and forego what Connell (1995, 81–3) calls the *patriarchal dividend*: better jobs, higher incomes, corporate authority, and other material resources that give men social power over women. Similarly, work in the paid labour force, a gendering norm that constitutes hegemonic masculinity by linking subjects to independence, citizenship, and the ability to support a family, was absent for many of the subjects in my study (Segal 2006; 1990, 186). Economic self-sufficiency and its absence both stabilized and destabilized a sense of masculine identity for Paul, Fred, Bear, Cam, Paddy, Harvey, James, and Kerry. Only Simpson refused the working-class masculine ideal of working for wages, although most men also supplemented their income through property and drug offences. Cam exemplifies his cohorts' general relationship to paid work:

> I've never had a problem being lazy. Work gave me a sense of worth and responsibility and taking care of my bills. I knew what I had to do and I done it. And it made me feel good because I had the funds to do it. To some, it might not be a lot of money, but to a guy who come from prison and didn't have a lot, this type of work was good. It didn't matter if you had a criminal background. If you don't have money, it's harder to survive. If you have a background, it's even harder because nobody wants to put you in a position where you can make honest money. It also comes with not having the education.

The men revelled in describing the pleasures of what they called "manly jobs" that personified their physical superiority to women and other men. Charlie conveys the near-transcendent quality of work that emphasized strength and brute force in contrast to the pain and hurt he experienced elsewhere:

> I became a workaholic. Work made me feel energetic. By the time I was sixteen I had been working at least two jobs steady. I was good at it – physical labour type jobs. Every time I've applied for a job, I've got it. I didn't apply for jobs that I thought I might not get – clerical type jobs. I was a bona fide manual labourer. I didn't think about the pains and hurts. I didn't think about what was going to happen after work. I put everything into it. And my problems were always away from work, never at. When I wasn't working, I didn't know what to do. I felt useless.

For many of the participants, labour was not a degrading or alienating activity. Instead, they appreciated and actively embraced it because of its physical quality. The physicality of rigorous manual jobs and the affirmation of traditional breadwinner status marked them as real men. In conditions of unemployment or underemployment, the men risked losing these signs of masculinity. At the times that Kerry, Bear, Paddy, Fred, and Harvey committed rape, they attributed some of their emotional turbulence to a bleak employment situation and the related absence of manhood.

Men's Pain: No One to Talk To, Building Walls, and Wearing Masks

A significant feature in all fourteen life histories is a father-son relationship without physical affection, intimacy, compassion, or counsel. Only Bob and Brian somewhat bonded with their fathers. Yet both men note that their fathers' lack of emotional resources and capacity to care stymied their emotional needs. In all accounts, the absence of traditional patriarchal fatherhood meant that no boy had someone to talk to when troubling circumstances arose in his life. Bob explains:

> I don't blame my parents, but family is where I learned to deal with my feelings. How my dad dealt with them? It's a cycle – my grandpa learned from his dad and on we go. It got to me. My dad could have easily broken it by being more emotional. My dad didn't come home, give me a big hug saying, "I missed you today." He never sat down when I came home from school and [said], "So, how are you feeling?" My dad played with me as a kid. He taught me how to skate, play hockey, hunt. But the emotional part didn't exist. When he had a bad day at work I never seen him and mom talk about *how* he's feeling, what happened at work. The emotional intimacy part of their relationship – I never seen. Now, it's my responsibility when I have children to be more intimate with them emotionally. I'm going to have family nights once a week.

Indeed, Brian insists that his father's failure to communicate intimacy was not only an individual shortcoming but a failure of culturally circulated gender ideals and gendered divisions of labour within the family:

> This stereotype that men are supposed to be tough and not show their emotions – they're in charge of the household and stuff like that – men ain't like that, they got emotions. Fathers taking their sons out for walks and doing things and, you know, giving them a hug and [*pauses*] I really admire that kind of father, eh? That's the way it should be – talking and loving and

reading stories and spending dinner together, going to a movie. I really love my dad even though there were no hugs or "I love you"s. My dad's not a communicator. I never had no one I could talk to about any of this crap. I know some day when I have kids I'm doing to do that. Communication's important. (Brian)

My participants' narratives, bolstered by group therapy, are replete with retrospective yearnings for adults to whom they wished they could have voiced their boyhood pain. Evans and Wallace (2008, 486), who explored masculinity narratives among young male prisoners, also find that most were deprived of "socially acceptable outlets for painful or troubling experiences." They conclude that "even one positive, loving respectful relationship with a man in a father figure role would have been enough for these boys to have developed a more balanced view of what being a man involves" (501). My interviews also reveal the injury related to another gender norm, namely, that real men do not cry or display emotion because they consider such actions feminine and feminizing (e.g., Garde 2003; Weiss 2010, 277). My subjects saw aversion to emotional display as the salient feature of being a man. Messerschmidt (2000) also reports that all his assaultive boys had non-nurturing fathers, but he does not discuss the emotional side of their engagement with hegemonic masculinity. This may be because gender barriers restricted male expression, or because his subjects lacked a vocabulary to express such sentiments. In any event, my participants learned to articulate a range of new emotions to accompany their behaviours. They had little difficulty expressing fear, loneliness, frustration, and confusion (see Evans and Wallace 2008; Pollack 2000; Haaken 1999). These emotions were evoked through physical punishment, sexual or verbal abuse, as well as through silence and alienation. Paul explains:

I wasn't beaten up or anything like that by my parents, but hearing other people talk, I sure as hell *felt* the same way. The fear I felt – was because of, not the *threat* of violence, but, you know, you get scared. Nothing would be said. That was the hard part – that was so hurtful. My mom didn't say a thing. Not a damn thing. I felt really helpless. I didn't know what to do to get my parents to love me.

It is easy to see how blatant and repeated incidents of sexual and physical assault on children are destructive. However, the most damaging assault on participants' boyhood sense of identity was their inability to obtain and cultivate compassion, love, and understanding from another person, and particularly from the persons legally responsible for their care and protection (see Haaken 1999). Fred puts it this way: "A person who was hurt as a child by his parents. What does that hurt? These are the most significant people in your life; they're your world and they are supposed to be there for you and when they're not, and when they do the things that my parents did to me, that hurts." Several men in my sample can identify the precise moment they engaged with their contradictory experiences of power (cf. Connell 1995), and when they consciously decided to stop crying. With the exception of anger, all the men learned to exercise public control over their private emotions. Anger represented a gender-appropriate way to manage their emotions rather than a loss of control over them. "Numbing," "stuffing," or "shutting down" was a coping strategy for salvaging a modicum of control over intolerable childhood events. Contrary to penal treatment program presumptions that link sexual offending to empathy defects, I heard many men voice tender feelings for their mothers, fathers, sisters, grandparents, and other family members. Rather than lacking empathy, many of my subjects developed boyhood survival tactics to seal off sympathetic responses. Bear recalls:

> When I have those feelings, this front would come up right away, like my wall [treatment staff] calls it. I would put up this front and try to be this tough person. But inside it's hurting. I'm crying – I want to cry, but there's that fear that dad put there that crying is wrong. I always felt that when he locked me up that feeling of shame, embarrassment, for crying. I felt I did something wrong because I cried. And that's where I go when I feel those feelings. I put up this wall or mask. There's a lot of fear there that I can't seem to express. I got addicted to hiding my feelings. It took me anywhere I wanted to go.

Cam adds:

> I was so good at it – building walls around me that you couldn't get through. That was what protected me so I didn't have to deal with them kinds of feelings and stuff. I can't show any kind of fear. I have to cover it up.

The gender norm that boys and men don't cry or show vulnerability contributes to what Kaufman (1994) and Kimmel (2005) call men's silence or their inability to communicate their inner turmoil to others.

All my participants expressed pain through practices of self that sequestered them from feminizing weakness and fear, steeled them against expressing sympathy or compassion for others, and welcomed unspoken suffering as a gender performative. Treatment programs certainly endorsed ideas about coming to terms with *wearing masks* and *building walls* to uncover a true inner self. But both of these phrases are more apt metaphors for performing gender and making masculinity. Masks and walls in this sense are productive, rather than repressive, practices that materialize and anchor a masculine identity around pain. Cam, Paddy, Simpson, Harvey, Charlie, Michel, Marvin, Kerry, and Brian learned to mobilize physical pain and injury as a deliberate gendering strategy. Both the endurance and infliction of corporal pain were techniques of self to muster a hegemonic masculinity at the level of the individual and in the eyes of others. Simpson personifies Kaufman's dialectic between men's power and pain and reveals how most of the men embraced bodily based pain to create gender. His account indicates that hegemonic masculinity is a composite of social gendering practices that produce and sustain male dominance, as well as a mode of domination at the level of the individual psyche. Simpson elaborates:

> I remember I stopped crying when I was about ten. Crying meant you were vulnerable. I took some very serious beatings because I wouldn't cry. I would never give *up*, whenever I was being beaten or whatever I've been *subjected* to. I *told* myself that I wouldn't. To be tough to me means a lot. To endure pain, that's what it means to me. I think that when the crying stopped? That stopped something inside of me too. I saw tears as surrendering to that person. Later on, when I fought, there seemed to be a need for the perpetrator to have you break, and to break meant crying. And when you cried, that meant they won. My entire life – I'd never give up. I took a lot of abuse and beating when I fought, 'cause I'd never give up. The more that that was inflicted, the stronger I became. Pain made me fierce. Pain made me indestructible, [*pauses*] feel indestructible.

In sum, while the interplay between home and school is fundamental to constructing violent adolescent masculinity, so too is the interplay between two culturally embedded gendering norms: real men fight, and real men show no weakness or tears. The deployment of both these practiced definitions of men's power speaks volumes as to how and why the men in my study learned to use physical violence and pain to stabilize a masculine identity in the face of perceived public challenges and psychical emotional chaos.

Men's Social Powerlessness

"Criminals ... think they have all the power in the world." (Lucie McClung, CSC Commissioner of Corrections 2001, cited in Stewart 2002)

The life histories in my study document the process of men's marginalization from positions of power in society. They personify yet another instance of what happens to masculinity in conditions that sever men from the socio-structural tools that give them social and economic power as opposed to physical or bodily based power. While male-to-male violence, consensual heterosexual sex, and property crimes sustained a hegemonic masculinity for many of my participants during adolescence (see Messerschmidt 2000, 2002, 2004), once they approached adulthood, they were confronted with a new measure of manhood – economic success – which most could not achieve. None of my participants could structurally access available forms of power to anchor themselves to a masculine identity and hegemonic manhood. Even the men with wives or partners could not obtain the material resources required to reproduce their own fathers' provider masculinity. Kerry's statement is worth recalling: "If I'm not a provider, I'm nothing as far as a man goes." There is little doubt that all my participants believed that men were supposed to exercise power. Yet they also recognized the disjuncture between their experiences of power and social expectations about men's power more generally. Each man was unable to actualize constructions of men's power through non-bodily based forms of masculinity. In Eldridge Cleaver's (cited in Segal 2006; 1990, 181) words, they were deprived of "developing a mental life" around the labour process. Fred exemplifies his cohort when he self-consciously tabulates his social powerlessness and notes its effect on his gender identity and gendering practices:

My job [delivering drywall] sucked. I couldn't see myself putting my body through this punishment for too many more years. I'm stupid. I left high school. I didn't believe in my ability to improve my employment situation. I'm a failure. I wished I wasn't an Indian. I hated my body. I had a car and was having car troubles, but couldn't afford the repairs so I put up with the embarrassment. I'm pretending I have it all together by dressing as though I was financially better off than I was. I am spending everything I earn on day-to-day costs of living. I'm dependent on others for financial support. My girlfriend won't take rent money from me because she likes her independence. I am denying my feelings of powerlessness. I am getting into fights with strangers when I drink. I am stuffing my sad feelings of shame and hopelessness. I'm having as much sex as possible with as many women as possible. I even started to make a list to keep track of all their names. Sex with women made me feel powerful. (Fred)

Diana Scully also found that her sample of rapists achieved minimal education, came from working-class backgrounds, and had sporadic employment patterns (see Hopkins and Koss 2005, 705). Her subjects identified with a "traditional masculinity" that "validates masculinity through strength and aggression and discourages emotional sensitivity and feelings of vulnerability and weakness." She contrasts this with what she calls the "modern male role" that validates masculinity "through economic achievement and power, which requires intelligence and control over emotions like anger" (Scully 1990, 82). While Scully recognizes the co-existence of different masculinities, she does not locate the men in a wider context of power relations. She does not examine whether her participants' identification with "traditional masculinity" versus "the modern male role" is really a free choice or a necessary accommodation to material circumstances and cultural opportunities. My findings indicate that none of my participants possessed the physical safety, financial security, or social capital to engage with a hegemonic masculinity based on intellectual and emotional rationality. To the contrary, the role of the body rather than the mind was crucial to the men in my sample as they struggled with structural constraints and learned about constructions of hegemonic masculinity based on biological maleness.

Rape as a Gendering Practice

Scully and other feminist and critical works on motivations to rape help to situate my own findings about rape, power, and control and to explore the contingency of male power, the difficulties of achieving a credible version of manhood, and the propensity to rape. I now explore the issues of revenge and rape, chivalry and rape, rape and feminized bodies, rape and access to unwilling women, rape fantasy and pornography, and rape and the abuse of emotions, and conclude that rape is a gendering practice for most rapists.

Revenge and Women's Vicarious Liability

In Scully's first category, rape is motivated by violence rather than sex. For her, "revenge rape" flows from an "upsetting event involving a significant woman ... typically related to a ... standard of sexual conduct that they required from their women" (Scully 1990, 138). Such rapists displace their revenge onto substitute women to get even with their wives or significant women. Scully states that this type of rape is authorized by a cultural belief that men have the right to "discipline and punish women" and hold them "collectively responsible and liable for [men's] problems" (140). However, Scully does not explore why this discipline takes the form of rape. Since men do not generally broadcast a rape, how does raping a substitute woman get even with the rapists' wives or girlfriends? If men believe that they have the right to punish and discipline women, why don't rapists punish the women they believe violate prevalent gender norms?

These questions aside, Scully's first contention that rape is about violence does resonate with many of my participants' accounts. Many of the rapes I heard about in this study stemmed from upsetting events that involved the general behaviour, rather than the sexual conduct, of significant women. Many men in my sample identified women as the agents responsible for their pain, and as human beings upon whom they could, in Nietzsche's (cited in Brown 1995, 68) words, vent their emotions "actually or in effigy ... to deaden pain by means of affect ... to drive it out of consciousness at least for the moment." They conveyed this intersubjective desire to displace their pain onto typically weaker others as "wanting somebody else to feel what I was feeling." This need to anaesthetize pain by means of affect, however, was more linked to challenges to their precarious sense of masculine identity than to a sexual double standard. It sometimes issued from psychical or bodily challenges to their investment in the discourse of men's domination and control over women, but more often came from emotions, such as fear, vulnerability, sorrow, and helplessness, which they saw as feminine and repelled through violence (see Kimmel 2005). Because Scully tends to isolate rape from a wider social context of gendering practices, she misses a prominent theme found in my interviews and field observations. Many of my participants, especially Charlie, Simpson, Paddy, Fred, and Michel, believed that they had the right to physically discipline and punish men as well as women. Some, such as Bear and Bob, transferred their anger against a man onto other men, which suggested that they saw men as well as women liable for revenge and violence. From a quantitative point of view, the men I studied hurt more men than women. For many, apart from stranger rape, violence against women was an idiosyncratic act and was not easily reduced to only misogyny, although that certainly existed (see Cameron and Frazer 1987, 166). By contrast, nearly all the men either fantasized about or engaged in physical aggression against men as a regular gendering ritual. Only Simpson and Cam disclosed any prior history of violence against women before they raped. No evidence exists in trial and pre-sentence testimony or interviews with past and present girlfriends and wives to implicate the men in other forms of physical violence against women.

Gender-Encoded Chivalry Scripts

Except for Simpson, who claims that he indiscriminately "beat the shit out of man or woman," none of the men espoused a right to physically discipline women. Instead, most remember hearing explicit cultural messages not to hit women. Of course, six of fourteen father figures regularly contradicted this teaching through their own physical violence against the boys' mothers. Nevertheless, most men grew up with an understanding of this cultural taboo. Their life stories reveal repeated instances where they consciously controlled an impulse to hit women in retaliation to physical or verbal attacks. With six rapes or attempted rapes, Paul says, "I know this sounds retarded, but you can't beat up a woman. You don't even *think* of it as the thing to do." The reason he offers is telling: men should not hit women, not because women are individuals with rights and feelings, but because women are weak. There is no social gender currency to be gained in doing so. As Alder and Polk observe about child homicide (1996, 408) and Jefferson notes about men who batter known women (2002, 70), such violence carries a different social meaning from hitting men. It is unmanly, and embodies "a (feminine) inability to control emotions and cowardice in attacking someone (usually) weaker than oneself" (71). Several men in my sample consciously refrained from hitting women during a rape. Bob captures this contradiction: hurting a woman affirms gendered social power hierarchies, but it also spoils the perpetrator's masculine identity. In his words: "Men are supposed to love women. Protect women. But I hurt them. That makes me different than men on the street. That makes me a coward. I'm a man and I victimized a woman. Why couldn't I have hurt a man?" Of course, Bob did hurt men, but his comment suggests that hurting women offends a cultural code of male chivalry, in which women and children are under male protection and provision and men can affirm their subjectivity by living out that script (cf. Strange 1992, 151). This culturally entrenched predator/protector dichotomy allows men to form a recognizable dominant masculine identity by linking their subject position to the male protector who safeguards women and children from male predators, and thereby solidifies the line drawn between ordinary men and deviant rapists (Cowburn and Dominelli 2001, 407).

Both gender-encoded chivalry scripts and male protector/predator discourses help explain why my subjects chose to attack female strangers rather than family or acquaintances who are, statistically speaking, the normal targets of male physical and sexual violence (Johnson 1996). Even in the midst of emotional crises with mothers or girlfriends, each man realized that he owed these women the gender prerogative of care and protection and that he had violated a code of conduct which he had tried to preserve in his everyday relationships. These encoded scripts and discourses also shed light on the often-voiced statement that rape was "out of character" for many of the men in my study, and help explain why they insist that: "I raped a woman, but I'm not a rapist." The conscious choice *not* to beat up a woman is, in effect, a gendering practice that recognizes and reiterates men's physical superiority and social power over women. Yet paradoxically, for many of my participants, the dual discourses of women's weakness and men's power created situations where they could not find legitimate practices for resolving interpersonal conflict with women. Charlie reveals how gender-encoded conventions thwarted his primary masculinizing practice and sense of agency:

> Adult women had more power than men in my eyes because you couldn't touch them. I got abused physically and sexually but I always took strength in the fact that I knew I could hit back one day. I thought, "I'm going to get bigger than you one of these days and then you're in trouble." But never with a woman or a girl that slapped me or degraded me in front of other people or made fun of me. Men can put up with embarrassment in front of other men. Not a problem. Get too cocky, I'll slap him in the mouth. But, put a woman in the room and embarrass me, and there's nothing I can do.

Indeed, my participants' insistence that women have more power than men is more than the cognitive distortion that penal governance regimes suggest it is. Harvey's fears about losing his "sense of being a man," for example, attest that gender identity is neither fixed nor embedded within a body but is accomplished in specific situations. His words convey his lived reality that psychic and bodily formations do not always overlap:

HARVEY: I still have problems expressing my emotions with women. It's fear. I fear what they can do.

Q: What can women do?

HARVEY: They can laugh. They can take all my sense of being a man away from me and make me less of a person. They can laugh. They can belittle. They can do anything. And I have to sit there [*pauses*] how do you [*pauses*] you can't yell at a woman – all these things come to my head. You can't get aggressive – it's not a man, it's a woman, so you have to be polite, and how do you be polite with anger, you know?

The experiences of losing signs of gender, of losing one's sense of being a man, and of being unable to practice gender in the company of women are reoccurring themes in almost all my life history interviews.

The Sexual Specificity of Rape:
Creating Feminized and Masculinized Bodies

Many of my participants conveyed the view that stranger rape is a gender-specific (although not appropriate) act of attacking a woman that produces subjectifying effects similar to beating up a man. Rather than a political practice for controlling women's sexuality, these men saw stranger rape as an individual strategy for *defeating* women's sexuality, which they saw as the locus of their power. Consider the following four observations:

Why do women wear tight skirts? It's not because they're comfortable. That's what I wanted beaten. When you attack that, you eliminate [women's] power – it's beaten, gone. (Charlie)

As for why I wanted to have power and control over women, I think I held the belief that women have the sexual power. I felt they had something I could never have. They can also make men feel bad about it, and after awhile, I suppose I did. (Michel)

What power do women have? They have the right to say "no." So, when you *take* that power, see, it's a *power* thing, since women have the right to say no, and the power and all *that*. You take that away, and that's the same thing, I think, as beating up a man. (Paul)

Men become disrespectful to women when they think [women] are using their power to disrespect them. Sexuality and attractiveness for a woman is power. Sexuality and violence are both forms of power. If you watch a super model walking down the runway, she exudes sexuality. She has the look, the clothes. She knows she has the look that everyone appreciates. And it *is* powerful. Sexuality equals power. If I'm trying to get power, I must be more powerful than the sexuality. (Fred)

These passages question Catharine MacKinnon's (1989, 172) claim that men view female sexuality as "a thing to be stolen, sold, bought, bartered, or exchanged by others," rather than as an attribute that women own or possess. To the contrary, many of my participants see women's subjecthood as a conscious sexual force that is independent and not derivative of male power, which is perhaps the reason why for them it must be "destroyed." These statements convey a preferred belief about male heterosexuality, namely that women are gatekeepers who control access to sex (Mooney-Somers and Ussher 2010, 360). To be sure, MacKinnon might reply that this standpoint is a cognitive distortion and insist that for these men women's power is object, not subject. Certainly, these narratives corroborate feminist arguments that link sexual assault to women's social inequality (e.g., Martin, Vieraitis, and Britto 2006; Whaley 2001). The rapists in my study understood that women have no form of social or physical power to attack other than their sexuality. But many saw their desire for control by defeating women's power as an individual strategy, rather than a core value of hegemonic male sexuality. Michel, Fred, Harvey, Charlie, and Paddy's life stories all refute the idea that rape happens top-down from men's social power. By their accounts, rape is a decentred, localized practice for negotiating power – whereby they create or recreate gender – by temporarily "getting the power back from women" that they exercise in everyday life. Although many of these men used the language of losing or returning their power, their experiences suggest that power is not seized, held, or lost, but "exists only when it is put into action" (Foucault 1982, 219).

My subjects' accounts of stranger rape suggest refinements to two general statements advanced by Scully. First, Scully identifies rape as a form of attack against the only source of power associated with women, namely, their bodies. But the power that the men in my study identified with women was not their bodies, but their discursive control over consent to sex. For many of these men, rape is a form of violence that targets dominant discursive constructions of women's power. Ironically, the turn of phrase coined by feminists that gives women *the right to say no* simultaneously singles out something tangible – a gender-specific form of agency – that men can then attempt to deny women. Moreover, the gender-affirming effects of rape are most obvious in men's accounts of male-on-male rape. As Charlie puts it, "Raping a man is trying to turn him into a woman. Raping a woman is because she is a woman." Indeed, after his uncles raped him, Bear says he knew that he was "weak – just like mom." Kerry, as he discusses his sense of gender following his own gang-rape, acknowledges that rape works through bodies to create gender regardless of so-called biological sex. The gender effects of rape occur as part of a pre-existing social structure that inscribes and reproduces the feminine as weak, passive, and possible to victimize and rape (Tithecott 1997, 155). Kerry reflects on how rape temporarily recreates masculine and feminine subjectivity (see Atmore 1999; Marcus 1992):

> [*With some sarcasm*] Oh, the men who assaulted me were real men. They were real tough men. Part of my mind thought that. Because it's the antithesis to what I thought about myself – which was that I wasn't a real man. I wasn't strong. I must be weak. It's the nature of the act that's unmanly. It's sort of like being branded. (Kerry)

Rather than attacking or destroying pre-existing feminine bodies, as Ann Cahill (2001, 133) claims rape does, I found that stranger rape creates feminized bodies. Rather than attempting to destroy their victims' personhood, my participants sought to re-create, dramatize, and stabilize a feminine subjecthood. Second, Scully (1990, 163) also refers to rape as the exercise of an always already existing male power. Douglas Pryor (1996, 267) suggests that explanations of sexual offending often presume that the perpetrator, typically gendered as a man, always has all the power. This, he says, is how they are able to rape and why they desire to do it. My participants display a different logic and pattern. For them, power is the intentional effect rather than the cause of rape, and for some of the men it is even a form of resistance to their own powerlessness. All my participants raped from a social position and psychical identity that was far removed from cultural expectations of men's social power and privilege. Rather than assume men's power, most of the men who planned to rape a woman decided to brandish a weapon rather than rely on their superior physical strength to overpower their victims.

Sexual Access to Unwilling Women

My own data suggest strong links between sex, sexuality, and rape. This confirms Scully's second motivation for rape, namely that it is about obtaining sexual access to unwilling women. While there is no doubt that stranger rape is always an act of violence from the victim's perspective and that each sexual assault perpetrated by my subjects involved sexual access to unwilling women, some of my subjects initially wanted to *take* sex rather than use it as a weapon to punish or degrade women. Cam, for example, portrays himself as a victim of his own sexual desire, deliberately excited by the woman whom he decided to rape after she rejected his sexual advances. In fact, contrary to the prevalent feminist idea that a woman's sexual appeal has little to do with whether she becomes a rape victim (e.g., Stanko 2000), I found that appearance was relevant to victim selection for many of my participants. Marvin and Michel targeted young, sexually attractive women, and Simpson and Paul chose women desirable enough to suggest they wanted consensual sex before they eventually committed rape. My participants attest to the sexual dimension of rape. They say they have no sexual interest in men and they connect rape, at some level, to sexual desire and identity. In Michel's words, "I don't like men – they don't turn me on." While participants in my study who had been raped by men fantasized about forms of extreme physical retaliation, rape was not a gender-appropriate revenge. I asked Bear:

Q: Did you even think of sexually assaulting a man? Men have hurt you more than women have.

BEAR: Ya. Ya. I've never thought about it that way. When I went through thinking about when [my uncles] sexually assaulted me, my thoughts were to hurt them, to do something to them that they will remember.

Q: A man would remember a sexual assault.

BEAR: I was thinking more or less of, ah, [*pauses*] crippling them, you know.

Q: Why not cripple a woman instead of rape her?

BEAR: You know, that thought would never cross my mind – to cripple a
woman ... to hurt a woman that way. I thought of [raping a woman as]
more like a taking without asking.

Like Scully, I found that some men saw their victims and women generally as sexually unattainable. For them, sexual gratification, rather
than violence against women, was the original objective. Scully links
this motivation for rape to "male entitlement" (1990, 144), but my participants implicate compulsory heterosexual normalcy in stranger rape
(Renold 2003, 2007). For example, Marvin, James, and Michel link their
sexual assaults to the distance they experience from the hegemonic
masculine ideal to perform penetrative sex with adult women. The reason they want to "take sex" stems from the desire for masculinity and
compulsory heterosexuality, rather than from masculinity and violence or masculinity and sexual aggressiveness. Rather than an extension of so-called male normative sexual behaviour (cf. MacKinnon
1989), rape for at least some men in my study was an attempt to create
a link with a heterosexual identity and to construct masculine normality through sex acts with women. Michel remarks: "I didn't feel like a
man. My own ideas about sex involved penetration. I judge *some* of my
worth as a man on what I *know* that I can do with sex and lovemaking.
And I know society does too. It's something you can never get away
from." He identifies the dominant norm of penetrative heterosexual
sex as a salient feature of being a man, but he also recognizes that this
norm is part of a wider heterosexual regime that he must enact in order
to qualify as a genuine man. This idea is echoed in Messerschmidt's
(2000, 48) study that found that adolescent sex offenders attributed
their serial attacks to the hegemonic belief that "to be male, you have
to be sexual with a female." Unlike Messerschmidt's sexual offenders,
however, Michel was capable of performing gender through alternative practices such as male-to-male fighting and crime. Still, Michel
acknowledges that he "had no power in the sexual aspect of his life,"
and says that he thought that rape would fortify his psychical, as opposed to public, identity as a man. Like most of his treatment group, he
formed the will to rape not from a position of men's power but from a
position in which he experienced depression and identity crisis and
contemplated a "miserable existence."

Many of my subjects recognized that they were powerless to do anything as men other than have sex with women and beat up men. They
saw the mutually constitutive relationship between heterosexual practice

and masculinity and understood the general idea that norms that support maleness produce and reproduce the effects of a masculine subject (see Mooney-Somers and Ussher 2010). Thus prior to raping women, many of my participants, including Simpson, Fred, Bob, Paddy, and Harvey, embodied hegemonic masculinity through heterosexual practices in which sex, control, consent, and coercion often coexisted. Many interviews revealed that compulsory heterosexuality and male sexual power were intersubjective. Several participants' female partners affirmed women's sexual subordination by collaborating in hegemonic gender-encoded scripts about men's aggressive sexuality, which Larombe found is also the staple of romance novels (2005). To some degree, women participated in hegemonic masculine beliefs and practices by actively re-inscribing gender difference and hierarchies (Lusher and Robbins 2007; MacKinnon 1989; Mooney-Somers and Ussher 2010). For example, Marvin sees his desire for non-vaginal sex as indicating homosexual rather than heterosexual subjecthood: "To me, it wasn't normal." His self-calculated deviance from the heterosexual norm propelled, in large part, his serial sexual assaults on women. He linked himself to men's power by adopting anonymous sexual coercion orchestrated to create gender through his victims' pacification, fear, and helplessness. While Marvin agrees that he could have found sexual release without stalking and attacking a stranger, he adds, but "not the same way. Not like this." Indeed, one of Marvin's victims validated his consternation about his sexual desires. She followed a conventional gendered rape script (cf. Marcus 1992), and was compliant until she realized that Marvin was interested only in her feet. According to her victim statement she then stood up, yelled, "What is this bullshit?" and ordered Marvin to leave, which ended the assault.

Paul, Fred, and Simpson's life stories illustrate how intentions can shift from sexuality and sexual access to revenge, punishment, and women's vicarious liability. Sex and sexual conquest was integral to their masculine identity and it was, in their view, their only cultural capital for exercising power in their social relationships with women. After an argument or break-up with their partners, each used sex with another woman to restabilize gender or tie himself to a masculine identity. For example, Paul suggests that he viewed his victims "like a substitute," and surmised, "maybe I can have *her* [in lieu of his girlfriend]." Rebuked by their girlfriends and partners and denied consensual sex by unknown women, these men had no gendering strategy. They resorted to extremely brutal sexual attacks characterized by utter disregard for whether or not their victims lived or died. Yet before these attacks, none of these men had thought or planned to rape and kill or nearly kill female strangers.

Rape Fantasy, Pornography, and the Rapist as a Masculinizing Subject-Position

Scully's third category of rape motives evinces a causal connection between pornography and rape (see Bourke 2007, 141–6; Russell 1998). Even though she did not directly question her participants about sexual fantasies or pornography, Scully says she was struck by the parallels among her subjects' accounts of rape, male rape fantasies reported by other researchers, and themes depicted in violent heterosexual-pornography, most notably men who control and dominate women through rape (Scully 1990, 149–51). She concludes that "the stimulation of sexual arousal within a violent context may result in a conditioning process in which violent acts become associated with sexual pleasure" (153). On the one hand, Scully persuasively debunks the excuses for rape prevalent during the 1970s and 1980s, particularly alcohol intoxication and discourses that suggested sickness or psychological infirmity. On the other hand, she offers up "deviant sexual fantasies" as a more contemporary cultural excuse for rape. Scully's focus on pornography foreshadows contemporary cognitive-behavioural presumptions about a causal relationship between rape fantasy and rape. Penal treatment experts, I learned in my study, view any sex offender who denies he has deviant sexual fantasies with scepticism. Some of my participants do bear out Scully's hypothesis that rapes are shaped by pornographic genres and many of their life stories reveal the wisdom of Sharon Marcus' (1992) claim that rape scripts pre-exists the rapists and rape victims. But links between stranger rape and pornography are difficult to untangle because representations of rape circulate independent of an individual's choice to view pornography or fantasize about rape. As Mooney-Somers and Ussher (2010, 360, 7) note, nearly all men admit some exposure to pornography and their fantasy scripts typically feature strangers or famous models and actresses. An anecdote by researcher Bart Delin illustrates the ubiquity of rape scripts. She attended a community symposium on sexual offending where men and women produced short plays on rape. One male actor voiced his distress when he discovered that he knew all too well how to perform the role of a rapist. According to Delin, society had taught him "very well" (1978, 96). She adds: "I'm not saying that all males are hopeless. I'm just saying that most men under certain conditions have these tendencies and don't know it. I think men are particularly armored against understanding this characteristic" (1978, 96). In this sense, the subject-position of the rapist is available to all males, including those who never consciously consider it, which evokes Brownmiller's declaration, echoed by Scully, that all men are potential rapists. It would seem that rapists cannot be reliably differentiated from non sex-offenders or men in the wider population (Cowburn 2005; Ellison and Munro 2009, 299). Indeed, Delin's scenario resonates with some of my participants' bewilderment with the role. Paul acknowledges that "a rapist wasn't something I planned to be." Marvin says, "I was the soccer parent picking up kids to take them to their game. We could be the person next door. And we were." Harvey reflects on his relationship to masculine normalcy:

> I was a nineteen-year-old kid, or, young man. I was a very normal guy – *very* normal in the surroundings where I was. I stood up for women. I supported women's issues. Female friends testified for me in court. I played football. I drank. I partied. I had girlfriends who were total nerds – extremely pro-social and went to church on Sunday. People would never suspect. It's actually in letters provided to the court – what a total gentleman I was around women. I have all sorts of letters from people in my hometown that said, at no time would anybody have believed that I could have done this crime. (Harvey)

Kerry historicizes the claim that rape is a plan in every man's head:

> I remember times in my life when it wasn't common knowledge. I remember not knowing what rape was and having to ask. I was fifteen. Today, I think you could ask any fifteen year old [*pauses*] what the mechanics are – what the rape script is. They could probably give you a bunch of them.

Some of my subjects' stories included pornography-based sexual fantasies, but it is difficult to sort out how much of this is attributable to the penal cognitive behavioural framework that pressures sex offenders to link rape fantasies to their actual sex assaults, or how much of it is attributed to actual fantasies before the rapes occurred. I accept the feminist-inspired thesis that there is nothing natural about the practices through which human sexual desires are channelled. Sexual desires are malleable and conditioned to respond to all types of stimuli with or without commercial sexual imagery. Yet at the same time, other participants in my sample dismissed any conscious associations between rape fantasies, including those in pornography, and the decision to rape. The question is: What did pornography and rape fantasies contribute to stranger rape?

First, at the most general level, pornography helped shape and construct desire in several participants. Commercial rape imagery gave them a visual representation for doing men's power by dominating anonymous women through specific, non-consensual sex acts. When Kerry, Brian, James, and Michel assaulted female victims, they tried to reproduce specific sexual scenarios from pornographic magazines or films. Indeed, some of their imagined rape scenarios were so embedded in their minds that when their victims disrupted their rape scripts, they had to improvise, often by inflicting unplanned physical force against their victims. My findings suggest that it is unlikely that women can prevent rape by disrupting the intended rape script, as Sharon Marcus (1992) suggests. Other men – Paddy, Harvey, and Bob – singled out their rape victims' passivity along with the own sense of control as eliciting sexual desire or sustaining sexual arousal. This type of narrative evinces an eroticization of power as manifested through overt control, a staple of pornography, where men are typically sexual agents and women are sexual objects. Harvey, Michel, Michael, Paddy, James, and Brian admit they are aroused by knowing they have power over a woman, but they also reveal that the actual act of rape or attempt rape is not usually sexually satisfying. The contrast between fantasy and reality suggests that some of the men in my study had eroticized the idea of total control over women, rather than force and violence against them.

Second, for some of the men, pornography was a primary gendering practice with women. Absent sexual and social relationships with real women, they typically knew women and women's sexuality through pornographic genres. As Michel remarks, "When I was twelve, I didn't think, 'There aren't many women who would like to have sex that way unless they were paid to do it.' I just think, 'That's what sex is all about.'" These images both gave the men subject-positions with which to identify and also constituted a masculine subjectivity for them. But there were reported paradoxes and ironies attributed to this subjectivity. Pornography, for example, enabled James, Brian, and Michel to partake psychically in the dominant masculine discourse and practice of controlling women's sexuality, but it also underscored their social distance from normal masculine heterosexual performances (see Segal 2006; 1990, 220–1).

Third, Brian, Bob, Kerry, and Michel deliberately conjured rape fantasies to cope with their loss of control over women and over their own sexual subjecthood. At a psychic level, pornography enabled some men to resurrect their social and sexual agency over women and "get their power back," even though that power and pleasure of agency was imaginary. While pornography helped some men connect their anger and frustrations with sexual thoughts and bodily desire, most of my subjects evinced a stronger association between physically violent acts and masculinity than between physically violent acts and sexual pleasure.

Finally, rape fantasies helped some men discipline their minds and bodies to the act of rape. For example, Brian, Bob, and Michel acknowledge that their boyhood sexuality focused almost exclusively on masturbating to images that eroticized male control and women's sexual subordination, passivity, and pain. Several of the men had mentally disputed or denied women's consent to sex before they encountered their actual rape victims. Some of the men who actively planned their rapes, such as Brian, Kerry, Marvin, and Michel, wrapped themselves in rape fantasies prior to offending and later reported that they felt unable to prevent themselves from crossing over the boundary between rape fantasy and reality. Nevertheless, most men in my study emphasized that fantasizing about rape and killing was qualitatively different from actually raping and killing. No man said that pornography caused them to rape or that without pornography they would not have raped. As Paul explains, "My sexual assaults were different from my fantasies because I knew it was wrong. I tried *not* to think about it." Nevertheless, Paul's abduction fantasies mirrored his actual abductions of women in broad daylight, except for the fact that his victims often disrupted his abduction script by refusing consensual sex. None of the men explained his sexual offending as a direct fall from fantasy to reality. Each man agreed, however, that no internal or external barriers prevented them from acting out against anonymous women. Thus the men regularly stated that the key difference between themselves and other men is that they acted on their fantasies or acted out in a sexually motivated way (Cowburn 2005).

"Feeling Rules": The Absence of the Rapist's Emotions

In answering why some men "act out," Scully (1990, 132) speculates that the "feeling rules" that govern sexual violence evoke emotional numbness or neutrality. She elaborates: "To understand the absence of [the rapist's] emotions, it is necessary to examine the perspective of these men towards women in general and their victims in particular"

(165). But I found that my participants displayed more emotional neutrality, less hesitation, and less guilt about hurting men than women. To focus on only sexualized forms of violence against women misses the common thread in many of these rapist narratives. Rapists are more likely to use gender-specific forms of aggressiveness as context-dependent performatives to create gender (see Alder and Polk 1996). I also found that the *feeling rules* that govern sexual violence were not really neutral. For some men, the decision to rape was catalyzed by anger and rage. But this anger, they say, stemmed from the threat to manhood posed by the emotional chaos in their lives. In Fred's words, the "anger alleviates the fear." Harvey and Paul, who defined themselves as angry prior to or during rape, did not characterize themselves as angry men. They reported that they felt hurt and helpless before they became angry. Others who self-defined as angry, like Bob, Charlie, and Michel, describe frustration and depression, not anger, as the dominant emotion that precipitated rape. Marvin, Bear, James, and Kerry did not portray their everyday selves or pre-offending emotional state as angry. For them, the dominant emotions prior to rape were pain, worthlessness, depression, embarrassment, fear, and despair – emotions that real men try to avoid admitting because of their association with weakness and womanhood rather than male power (Weiss 2010; Alder and Polk 1996, 406). My participants' stories do confirm Scully's findings that rapists display an utter lack of compassion and empathy for their victims during actual sexual assaults. They humiliate, brutalize, and kill. In Bear's words, "It's like my mind stopped listening. I could hear her, but there was no feeling there for that woman." Scully links the men's absence of emotions to an abstract gender-based disdain for women generally. But this is too simple and singular, and misses one of the most prominent themes found in my life history interviews, namely, that this absence of emotions in the rape act itself develops long before the men ever encounter their victims. It is shaped by boyhood desensitization to being hurt and hurting others. Each life history chronicles a process of emotional alienation from self and others before engaging in stranger rape.

Men's Agency: Choice, Risk, and Reward in Stranger Rape

> I had this little glimpse of choice. I had the choice of going to my left or my right. (Bear)

Each sex offender program participant must use the language of choice to explain their reasons for rape. Feminist theories of rape also presume that men choose to rape. While penal treatment models operate on the presumption that rape is an irrational choice and that the rapist has power but no control, feminist writers deny that the rapist is out of control and argue that he uses rape as a deliberate strategy to establish or maintain power and control. But these either/or dichotomies of ir-rationality/rationality, expressive/instrumental, and control/no con-trol are insufficient to understand the rapist as a subject. I found that stranger rapists fall along intersecting continuums of rationality and control, and range from Marvin's exhaustive monitoring of his victims' behavioural patterns to Simpson's or Charlie's spontaneous lethal rage. Seven men in my sample committed a total of fourteen unplanned sex-ual assaults that arose from the contingency of each situation. The other seven men planned to rape for minutes, hours, days, or weeks. Bear and Harvey's decisions to rape appear to emanate from a loss of control over their own pain, fear, and anger, and not from a loss of control over women. By contrast, Paddy, Bob, and James seized the occasion to rape, and recognized that their control over social situations gave them op-portunities. Michel, Kerry, and Brian deliberately created the opportu-nities to rape, but weapons rather than rape itself gave them control over women (see Segal 2006; 1990, 211). Finally, Paul and Fred's attacks on women included elements of no control whatsoever, which indi-cates elements of automatism in some rapes. Contrary to gendered findings that men's violence is always instrumental while women's is expressive (Campbell 1993, 56), I found that instrumental and emo-tional elements were inextricably linked in the act of rape.

The men's motives to kill further illustrates the scope and complexity of rationality and control. None of the participants in my study who killed their rape victims approximated Cameron and Frazer's (1987) definition of a sexual murder "where the killer was motivated by sadis-tic and sexual impulses – the lust to kill" (18). Five men chose to kill their victims to prevent them from reporting the sexual assaults. Brian and Bob planned in advance to kill, while Paddy and Cam killed as a calculated response after the act of rape. In these instances, the acts of killing were deliberate, separate events. Brian and James killed their second victims after they experienced a loss of control over their first victims. After he accidentally killed his first victim, Paddy attempted to kill his second victim because "it worked the first time," even though he had no intent to kill the first time. In four rapes, however, death or near-death was a reckless effect of ferocious physical force inflicted in tandem with rape. Fred, Paul, and Charlie displayed a loss of conscious control and even memory during their assaults. The moments of rational choice and the loci of active control are impossible to discern in their stories. For example, Fred's first rape and murder were so spontaneous that he has no rational basis for gauging whether or not he will rape and kill again. Fred embodied moments of control and no control in his actions when he provided a confidante with incriminating evidence about his crime and subsequent instructions to report him to the police if he suspected Fred of future rapes or killings. Instead of planning to rape, Fred created his own deterrent. He pre-planned his capture by turning control over to another party. If rape is a rational and deliberate choice these actions ought to have dissuaded Fred from committing more sexual assaults. They did not.

Together, these life history stories reveal ambiguity around the rhetoric of choice. Charlie puts it this way:

> Sex offenders are created by experiences, by choices. I see violent and sexual elements of the human being to be a part of every human being. Exposure to the proper circumstances develops very different concepts, I believe, and builds very different perceptions about what we have the right to take, what a woman is, what we are as human beings. We each have a point of choice in being a sex offender – it may be subconscious, okay? But, at what point does that choice begin?

These life stories emphasize both individual agency and its limits. On the one hand, none of the men are responsible for the social structure and discursive forces into which they were born and they certainly could not choose to not perform gender. On the other hand, they all chose to rape a woman. Nine raped or attempted to rape a second time and two others said that they would have re-offended if they had not been arrested. In one sense, these men personify Susan Brownmiller's statement that "man rape because they can," because they are biologically capable of doing so. When confronted with a paucity of masculinizing practices and the "terror of losing proper gender" (cf. Butler 1993b, 238), rape is a cultural strategy that men can choose to recoup agency and re-materialize a masculine subjectivity. The element of coercion and heterosexuality as identified by Catharine MacKinnon (1987, 1989) is also evident in many of my participants' stories, but not in the manner that she supposes. Hegemonic heterosexuality pressured men such as Paddy, James, Marvin, and Michel to perform sex acts with women, but also to conform to conventional culturally circulating scripts about men's sexual assertiveness (see Segal 2006/1990, 210–2). The pressures placed on Paddy to embody male sexuality and control his sex partner against his own desire for intimacy, for example, exemplify how men as well as women experience the negation of genuine agency under patriarchal constructions of compulsory heterosexuality.

Viewed through the lens of contemporary penal treatment regimes, once choice is instated the chooser can be held responsible and accountable for his decisions. In this model, men choose to rape because they are unaware that they have other choices and options for reacting to problematic situations (SOP instructional handout for developing the crime cycle 2001, 2). Accordingly, programmed sex offender prevention plans encourage offenders to identity the choices and options available to them to prevent re-offending. Some of the cognitive interventions include: (1) stop negative thinking and do a perception check; (2) log emotions, fantasies, and warning signs; (3) use positive self-talk and change negatives to positives; (4) plan leisure time, housing, and work; (5) avoid high-risk places, people, and things; and (6) ask for help and use support people (Course Material, Relapse Prevention Plan 2001). Of course, correctly identifying the problematic situation is the critical factor. If the cognitive behavioural presumptions underlying treatment have misinterpreted the problematic situation, then the cognitive solutions provided to sex offenders will be misplaced. Indeed, if we take performing gender as the problematic situation and explore men's agency as circumscribed by a wider social context, including social discourses about masculinity, gender norms, social class and race, material resources, and practical lived experience, then none of these men had gendering options when they chose to rape. Nor did penal treatment experts provide them with any viable gendering alternatives. To different degrees, each man in my sample comprehended this dilemma. Their stories dramatize an element missing from feminist accounts of stranger rape, namely the links between practices of rape and male power. Thus a fully gendered understanding of stranger rape – and consequent prevention strategies – must appreciate not only the mutually constitutive relationship between the subject of rape and hegemonic masculinities, but also the class and race character of gendering norms reliant on biological maleness or sexed bodies in the social construction of masculinities (Segal 2006; 1990, 240).

Finally, I want to qualify Scully's (1990, 155, 159) conclusion that rape occurs inside the normative boundaries of the culture and that men rape because they have learned that it is a "low-risk, high reward behaviour." Without doubt, rape-as-entertainment is standard cultural fare and a dominant feature of the pornography industry in contemporary Western cultures (see Russell 1998). Indeed, society's devaluation and objectification of women made it easier for some of my subjects to hurt and kill women. Cam, Simpson, and Bob stated that they could kill "without a thought." Prior to his arrest, Cam agreed to kill two men for undercover police officers. Paddy insisted that "he objectified *everybody*," and Michel, Kerry, Paul, and Bear killed or nearly killed men. These men generalized gender-specific practices of objectification to women and men. As Cameron and Frazer (1987) note, the subject-position of the murderer and the social practice of killing a human being, rather than killing a woman, are cultural measures of manhood and available subject-positions for constituting a masculine subjectivity. To be sure, Brian, Paddy, Cam, and Bob perceived stranger rape as a high-risk, socially reprehensible behaviour that lead them to kill their victims to avoid detection. None of these men contemplated killing a man to escape detection for serious physical assault; instead, they feared the social consequences of stranger rape. Many repeated a dominant discourse about rapists as "scum." They believed that they would be stigmatized, arrested, convicted, and imprisoned for raping a woman. Finally, men such as Kerry, Paul, and Bear, who each reoffended sexually after they served federal time for rape, belie rape as a high-reward behaviour. For them, heightened feelings of shame, self-worthlessness, and guilt characterized the aftermath of stranger rape. Bear explains:

I remember seeing her in court. I took a quick look and she was crying. There were people in the courtroom [*pauses, whispers*] she was humiliated. I've humiliated her. I've shamed her. I scarred her for life and I could never take it back. But, it was like, you did something? And boom, you just forgot it. Like, you knew it happened, but you never thought about it. It's just like when you are a kid. Like, when you seen mom beat? You forgot about it. You never brought it up. Somehow, that became a way of dealing with things. But it was still always there. It would make me feel shamed. It would make me feel worthless. At my dangerous offender hearing [1980], they decided I was capable of killing somebody. I remember them saying it. [*Pauses.*] I was too afraid to kill somebody. I just boxed myself in. Didn't express myself. Didn't say much to the psychologist. I knew it was a life sentence. I just sat there with my head down.

Of course, many participants savoured the immediate power effects of stranger rape: "Fantasy and reality meshed for a time and that was quite powerful" (Kerry); "there were times where I felt powerful" (Michel); and "I was thinking, this is what it feels like to be powerful" (Paddy) were typical refrains in their stories. Nevertheless, these effects were as temporary and contingent as the hegemonic masculine subjectivity they constituted. Otherwise, stranger rape was a low-reward act outside the zone of constructed masculine normality. Once detected and convicted, the stranger rapist was further marginalized from other men and relegated to the status of a non-citizen with a completely spoiled identity (cf. Adamoski, Chunn, and Menzies 2002).

Conclusion

My subjects' stories indicate that men don't decide to rape and kill independently of other factors. Men's relationships to forms of violence must be situated within a social context that understands the demands of gender norms and the material and cultural constraints for performing gender or making masculinity. All the men in my sample identified with contemporary Western ideals of hegemonic masculinity – compulsory heterosexuality, physical toughness, emotional stoicism, and white supremacy – which shaped and preserved their power over others and enabled and reinforced women's subordination. Lacking access to social power through economic, educational, occupational, and cultural channels, the participants in my study created gender through bodily centred performances and social interactions that materialized bodies as masculine and feminine (Butler 1993a, 1993b; Connell 1995; Kaufman 1994; Messerschmidt 2000, 2004; Segal 2006, 1990). Their accounts provide empirical support for James Messerschmidt and Lynn Segal's hypotheses, which link stranger rape to men who are most disenfranchised from the materially based economic, cultural, and social capital of society. Their life stories contradict the view that stranger rape is the manifestation of men's power. Their life experiences with violence, chronic neglect and abuse, and economic, cultural, and racialized marginalization indicate that their self-identity was determined more by feelings of powerlessness than of potency when they committed rape. Following Judith Butler's (1993a, 1993b) insight that gendered subjectification is a practice that must be constantly repeated by the subject rather than one that emanates from an always already gender-inscribed body, I found that there were contradictions between a desired subject-position and a psychic identity. The rapists in this study were invested in hegemonic masculinity, but did not always feel included in it. Their sense of masculinity was always provisional and their life stories reveal the separation of psychic subjectivity and bodily formation. Their thoughts, feelings, and acts associated with stranger rape are best understood as losing signs of gender; stranger rape was a subjectifying practice of power meant to recreate gender by fusing biological maleness with discursive attributes of hegemonic masculine subjects and identities such as sexual agency and domination, non-contestable authority and control, and physical power and aggression (Butler 1993b).

Michael Kaufman (1994) suggests that contemporary hegemonic masculinity correlates to exercising power over something. He invokes Foucault's notions of sovereign power as repressive, coercive, and constraining, and disciplinary power as normative and productive. Feminist scholars, such as Scully, Brownmiller, MacKinnon, Marcus, and Cahill, represent rape as both sovereign and disciplinary forms of power. As sovereign power, rape dominates, humiliates, and punishes women. But it also produces disciplinary effects and trains women about how to behave and dress, whom to associate with, and where and when they can be in public. Feminist researchers and writers have documented these effects of rape, including fear of rape against women in particular and fear of harm more generally (Cahill 2001; Stanko 2000). Neither sovereign nor disciplinary forms of power, however, fully capture the intentional power effects communicated by the rapists I studied. Kerry, for example, insisted that stranger rape cannot be understood as an attempt to gain control through a repressive and repressing sovereign power over somebody in the everyday world. He noted that stranger rape was primarily cerebral; it was going on in his head. Similarly, when Michel explained why he wanted to beat up men whom he knew he would never see again, he recognized that this form of power was not disciplinary training to teach others to fear him in the future. He does not say that he needed to *be* powerful, but rather "that he needed to *feel* powerful." Indeed, none of the rape victims in this study were women whom the participants knew or wanted to control in their actual everyday worlds. The participants primarily intended stranger rape as a private or psychic affirmation of masculine subjecthood, and not usually as a dramatization of power and control, although that did sometimes occur.

In addition to the sovereign and disciplinary elements of rape, my participants' stories convey rape as a subjectifying power that parallels Foucault's (1994a, 1994b) notion of "techniques of the self." I found that stranger rape was one practice, altogether horrific, that allowed individual bodies to effect by their own means a gendered subjectivity. Although practices of self evoke active subjects, they are not something that individuals invent by themselves. Instead, practices of the self as rape are "proposed, suggested and imposed" on men by their culture, society, and social groups (Foucault 1988, 11). These narratives of rapists indicate that stranger rape was at once an objectifying gendering practice for dominating others and a subjectifying technology of self for fashioning a dominant masculine subject and a feminized object of rape (Foucault 1994b, 225). Or to put it in Kaufman's (1994) words, stranger rape was a transitory and troubling resolution to men's contradictory experiences of power.

Given the connections between stranger rape and practices formative of hegemonic manhood, it seems relevant to ask: To what extent can hegemonic masculinity be re-formed and rehabilitated in coercive penal settings? Is prison able to reduce violence against women? If the embodiment of gender norms is a compulsory practice, then what material and discursive techniques exist in prisons for personifying and stabilizing gender norms and reforming masculinity? The next chapter draws on my participants' carceral histories in nine Canadian federal penitentiaries and their shared experiences with different treatment regimes to explore these questions and determine whether penal governance produces rehabilitation or reproduces the effects they seek to reform and restrain.

7 Breaking Out: Challenging Hegemonic Manhood in Prison

It seems from age six my life had been a preparation for prison. Violence was not a choice anymore. It was a reality. This was sort of the cream of violence. My life was to prepare me for what *this* was, and this was extreme, man. Brutality, I had endured it, but not to what this was. Back in the 1970s, there was no accountability whatsoever. You now have an environment where guys can semi-relax. Prisons are like chameleons. They are what they are, but they can portray something very different. But if you go into the belly of what it is, it's the same – just an amazing ability to camouflage. Prison's just changed its appearance. It has a clinical mask on now.

(Cam)

This [treatment] group is based on the healing circle. Telling someone – whew, it's like, "Wow, somebody's listening." It means somebody cares. You know, all your life you stuff it – it's hard for a Native guy to communicate and bring stuff out. This treatment program, I couldn't wait to come back. I came here, and I looked around the room and I thought, "These guys have the same kind of shit that I'm going through." I said, "Whew, I'm not alone. There's other guys who feel the same way." We all know what we've done – the pain that we fucking caused. We can never change that. And we all related how we felt about that. Facilitators can take university and learn all this stuff. Sure, they can write it down on paper in their own words, but they can never understand the reality. They haven't felt what we've done.

(Brian)

In 1969, the Canadian Committee on Corrections concluded that treatment programs are best suited to community, rather than custodial, penal settings. Forty years later, Canadian federal prisons authorities are re-asking the same old question about whether treatment writ large can work in prisons (e.g., Burdon and Gallagher 2002). The final chapter of this book explores penal governance. It looks at the contradictory experiences Cam and Brian describe in their comments introducing this chapter. These statements imply that penal authorities force prisoners to seek help and healing from the very practices of power and ruling that perpetuate, deepen, and multiply their oppression and injury. In Cam's words, "It's like having supper with a wolf. And you *know* it. You just know it." In contrast, the second passage likens penal treatment experiences to Aboriginal healing circles, but acknowledges that science can never understand the reality of rape because it cannot "feel" what rapists have done to their victims and to themselves. My analysis explores both issues. I ask: Is there a fundamental contradiction at the heart of penal policy? Is it possible for prisoners to apply the knowledge of treatments in prison environments? I do not say that penal regimes are purely oppressive social control measures that ignore the agency of the men they treat. Instead, I deploy Foucault's (1990) idea that techniques of modern power produce effects that variously subjugate, govern, and foster individual lives and provide for continuity and change.

At point of entry into Canada's federal prison system, penal staff measure each prisoner's life history and lifestyle against seven gender-specific "needs." The prevailing assumption is that unmet needs increase a prisoner's risk to reoffend (e.g., Andrews, Bonta, and Wormith 2006; Jackson 2002). While penal treatment experts view gender as increasingly relevant to understanding the programming needs of female convicts (e.g., Dell and Boe 2000; Hannah-Moffat 2006; Pollack and Brezine 2006), they often ignore the proven empirical relationship between masculinity and violence for male convicts (Seymour 2003, 48; Whitehead 2005). The Correctional Service of Canada's rehabilitative regime, for example, does not designate hegemonic masculinity as a high-risk, high-needs criminogenic factor. Indeed, the scope and character of prisoners' needs is defined in advance of their own experiences and accounts of their crimes (cf. Fraser 1989). The CSC advances taken-for-granted knowledge claims that all violent offenders, including sex offenders, need cognitive-behavioural retraining and that existing treatment programs alleviate the risk/needs associated with sexual and violent reoffending. Penal authorities do not examine the spectrum of prisoners' needs; they only consider those that are changeable and capable of lower recidivism (e.g., Andrews, Bonta, and Hoge 1990; Andrew, Bonta, and Wormith 2006). In conducting my research, however, it was apparent that rapists entered prisons and treatment programs with different and often unspoken and unmet needs. Unfortunately, many of these needs did not fit with criminogenic *needs* as embodied in CSC funded research, clinical risk assessments, and individual treatment plans.

I draw once more on "con texts" in this chapter to explore the extent to which prison settings and penal treatment programs challenge or reproduce men's power and men's pain. I follow then-sixteen-year-old Brian into a maximum-security prison to view how gender was accomplished in homosocial penal environments. His prison narrative illuminates the practices of gender and power, which I then explore further through other carceral histories in his cohort, in regard to controlling emotions, materializing bodies, reproducing gendered hierarchies of power through cognitive corrections, and reforming the self. Finally, I discuss ongoing points of resistance and contradiction in recreating and stabilizing masculine selves, reforming gender, and doing masculinity differently in prison sites.

Exercising Power over Emotions

Brian's early official progress report reads in part as follows:

> He suggested that I write him up for RPC [regional treatment centre], but considering the fact he has 24 years left in a 25-year sentence, it doesn't seem very likely that they would accept him. There is very little that can be done for this young man at this time. (cf. Brian's Progress Report 1984)

Four years later, Brian's assessment for penal treatment had not changed:

> There is little value in him to be included in a therapy program considering the length of his sentence. (cf. Brian's Progress Report 1988)

Brian remembers his feelings in the aftermath of these two reports. He tells me:

> Kevin, I'm angry. Maybe five or six times I was ready to deal with things ten years ago. But they kept turning me down for programs because of my time. You know, I was seven years into my bit – I didn't care. I was doing drugs, alcohol, and I was in the hole – we called it the Penthouse … anyway, I was in the hole and I got this letter – it was just a small letter. And a book on forgiveness … and – it was from my victim's mother, eh? [*Very softly.*] They forgave me. [*Pauses.*] Well, I couldn't understand it, and actually I

always had shame in jail for what I done, but I didn't express it. I covered it up with drugs – that's why I was in the hole, for making brew. And I looked at myself in the mirror and said, "Who are you?" I promised myself, "Whatever it takes, I'm changing myself." So, when I got out [of the hole], I went to my correctional officer and said, "I want to take programs." I didn't believe in spiritual stuff then, but I knew there was something spiritual about it. I wrote [my victim's parents] back and promised that I was going to change and we wrote for a few years [*pauses*] then the guilt came with me lying at the trial. I wanted to be honest with them. So I told the chaplain and he set up a place to meet. [*Pauses.*] And, I couldn't look them in the eye, but I said what I had to say – that came from my heart too. Everybody cried that day. Even the guards were crying. That was the toughest day of my life. I seen the power of forgiveness. It changed my whole life in prison. I still write them this day. It's hard to write them – especially at Christmas. We spoke a good hour or two. I spoke and they spoke. That was tough. They basically wanted to know "why." The thing for them was me taking responsibility. I told them I lied in court and all that. [*Pauses for one minute.*] That was tough – whew. [*Pauses.*] I told them about my abuse in prison, but I can't tell them about the priest or my first sexual abuse. Stuff like that? It did have an effect, but I don't want to make it look like I'm the victim. I got to move on. Forgiveness is powerful, 'cause, I seen my victim's family – what they done to me. I seen it in their faces. Once I seen that – whew – I had no right to hate nobody or judge nobody. You look at these people, and – I killed their daughter, and [*pauses*] it's hard. [*Pauses.*] I have to prove to these people that I'll do good. I know how life can be like. I've seen it through other people and I read books. The big deterrent for me – it's what I've done – it's right here in my soul. It's a personal thing with me. And then you see the family. And if that ain't going to change you, nothing will.

Seemingly unaware of the reasons for Brian's transformation since his last institutional infraction for "making brew," the next progress report observes: "He seems to have changed since then, and has become fully involved with his Correction Plan" (cf. Brian's Progress Summary Report 1995).

Brian commends the penal treatment program for helping him, but he attributes the primary catalysts of change to the opportunity for forgiveness afforded by the victim's family and to the new material practices he discovered that linked him to life-affirming representations based on his Aboriginality (see Jackson 2002, 103–10; Waldram 1996). He elaborates:

I didn't go to Native Brotherhood meetings in [the federal penitentiary] 'cause I felt different. Other guys called me an apple. It wasn't until I came to this province – that's where I learned it. And that's starting to feel good – who I really am. I'm Native. And I told myself, "It's not my fault that I lost my culture. It's not my fault I lost my identity, my language." I'm getting it back. So, once I got that into my heart, I felt good about who I am. I am a Native man. Even without a program, if I knew this culture stuff, I might have decided not to do no harm to nobody. But this program helped me look at things and feel things better.

Like Brian's pre-carceral life, prison was a site of unbearable events and contradictions regarding his subjectivity. Prison exacerbated his boyhood strategies for dealing with pain and fear, especially emotional closure and estrangement from self and others (Evans and Wallace 2008). In Brian's words, "even though I was a quiet man before, I really shut down" in prison. Prison engenders unspoken suffering as a gender performative that ties psychic and bodily formations together (Sabo, Kupers, and London 2001; Toch 1998). Brian calls them survival strategies. He adds, "We have all these survival techniques – these ways of keeping it in – 'cause you've got to be a man." Michel confirms the bodily expectations in total institutions:

In prison, a man has to learn that whatever makes you appear vulnerable is not acceptable. Necessary behaviour in jail is not expressing your feelings – being tough, or appearing tough. You have to do a stern face. If I come across as friendly and happy, then people are going to try to take advantage – and I can't afford to have that happen. I would like to be positive and be myself around everyone in this institution, but it will never happen. In here, I have to be very guarded, and to act once someone has acted upon me.

The range of emotions that Brian and Michel hold in check surface repeatedly in the participant life histories. They include pain, worthlessness, depression, confusion, shame, sadness, fear, and despair. These unexpressed emotions perpetuate the men's lived sense of powerlessness in society as teens and young adults and are reproduced in prison. More ominously, these emotions resonate with many descriptions of the feelings they associate with committing rape. Viewed from a clinical perspective, penal social relations add to and reproduce the men's crime cycles. This occurred suddenly to Harvey in an interview with me. He exclaimed, "the fact is, I am in my [crime] cycle. Since coming [to prison], I'm rarely not in my cycle." Prison, he observed, is a high-risk factor that men like him can neither avoid nor escape, which ironically is one of the key officially recommended treatment strategies for managing high-risk situations.

The comments and observations from the next five men display the deep tension between prison survival techniques and men's pain. They indicate that exercising public control over their private emotions by refusing prison's effects on them is a modality for anchoring masculine subjecthood that is not unlike their boyhood practices for survival more generally. In Kerry's words, "Our attitude becomes see how strong I am. This doesn't touch me." Bear explains further:

> With my [boyhood] sexual abuse, the fear came of somebody touching. I'd freeze. Get all confused. So, coming to jail, you never had that. You put up a wall. Putting up a tough image, just the way my dad wanted me to be. Not letting your guard down. Not showing fear to nobody. In prison, if you start showing your feelings, guys think you are a wimp – just like my dad did. People would think I was softening up. They'd walk all over you. So, when I came to prison, it's like I fit in. This is what dad wanted me to be. You didn't have to express any of it. Inside, I was afraid. Of a lot of things. Getting into a fight. Getting killed. Every day. I was afraid everyday. You become numb.

Paul confirms the prevalence of concerted numbness:

> Prison was a piece of cake 'cause I never expressed any emotions. Maybe that's why prison's always been so easy for me. If I was vulnerable and had all those feelings on my sleeve then, perhaps it would have been a different story. But it didn't happen that way. Prison was just like home.

Fred admits that expressing emotions is risky unless it is gender appropriate:

> Anger is the only emotion that *other* prisoners will allow you to express in prison. Or laughter. It's not *okay* to feel lonely, or sad, or depressed. Actually, depression is okay to a degree, unless it becomes chronic, then it's "get a rope you whiner."

Channelling emotions and pain into anger is more than an acceptable performative in prison, it is a prerequisite for survival. Brian's explains,

"You get angry for protection and you block it out because if it gets to you, you ain't never going to last." The ability to marshal and substitute anger for emotions that cannot be expressed safely within penal culture enhances both the probability of surviving in prison and the likelihood of being hurt or killed and hurting or killing others (see Rhodes 2004). Simpson puts it this way:

> I've had facilitators state that anger isn't healthy – it's almost an insult to me – I was a creation of anger. That's what I would use when I'd fight. It would protect me. I spent years unwilling to decrease any power that I had of hate and anger, 'cause I owed my life to that. It would be like betraying it after it had given me life. I seen what happened to guys in prison that cared and who were loved – they're hanging from their cells. They couldn't stand the pressure.

Each man in my sample understood the cognitive-behavioural directive to identify their anger and self-manage it by dealing with the emotions beneath it. Many, however, noted a fundamental contradiction in penal governance. On the one hand, prisoners use anger to vent and manage other emotions otherwise unacceptable in a prison environment (see Gadd and Farrall 2004, 144–5). On the other hand, penal treatment authorities want prisoners to forestall anger, and ask them to express emotions that are typically forsaken in prison culture. This therapeutic corrective discounts the deployment of anger and the importance of "not feeling" as penal *techniques of self* to stabilize penal subjecthood and preserve life (see Rhodes 2004, 55). Fred puts it poignantly:

> For now I must remain like a stone. I won't change in substance, but the pressures and stresses I continue to endure will determine how hard I become. It may be a defence mechanism that keeps me sane; it may just be a necessary and unavoidable adaptation; either way it is not easily understood by people who have not lived the prison experience for a significant length of time.

Giving individual prisoners the responsibility to manage their own anger also diminishes official state responsibility for the role that prisons and penal staff play in generating and reproducing angry convicts (see Rhodes 2004, 83). Charlie and Cam elaborate:

There was nowhere you could go in that joint without having a gun pointed at you. The walls [in that prison] breathe death. I can stand in that yard. I could point to spots where bodies have been. A lot of blood has been spilt in that vault. The walls in the hole [solitary confinement cells] were painted the colour of blood, man. I can't honestly say that it's that extreme today, but no one's ever taken accountability. They represent society. It reinforces how much of an enemy society is. You get guys coming out so angry. (Charlie)

See, the system is abuse too. It's being told when to think something, when you can't do something, when to eat, when to work. There's so many games that go on to belittle ya in order to break you down and let you know who's in authority. How do I deal with that kind of *shit*? And in the end, you have two choices – to lay down and sort of take everything that's given to ya, or harden up inside. But, again, that builds rage. That builds hate. That builds a lot of stuff that you're never going to get rid of. I don't want to harden up inside, because if I harden up inside, [*pauses*] if I don't have no respect for myself or value on my own life, I'm sure the hell not going to have value on somebody else's. (Cam)

Ironically, the treatment program's slogan that "nobody can make you feel anything that you don't want to" fits with the men's own gendering practices for limiting and controlling emotional displays inconsistent with their boyhood and manhood experiences. The recurring analogy between prison and home in their narratives is hardly surprising. These men have experienced high-risk emotions since childhood and have repressed them for years. Inciting them to risk-manage their feelings and discipline their bodies reiterates, in a new form, the hegemonic masculinizing themes of rationality and emotional control. It does not create or add much to honest emotional expression or genuine interpersonal communication. Indeed, the opposite may be true. According to Evans and Wallace (2008), the continued estrangement of male prisoners from public expressions of vulnerable emotions reproduces a "prison within a prison."

Materializing Bodies: Violence is Not a Choice Anymore

In prison, masculinity instils fear and intimidates other men. Michel states this clearly:

Brian's always got his head down and he's quiet – another inmate looking at him would think that he's either very dangerous or he's very passive. I'm very similar – I don't make a lot of eye contact, I don't talk to a lot of other guys – the general impression, which has been proven, is that I *appear* to be an easy target. I punched one guy out in [prison], I sprayed urine on a guy in [prison] and I'm suspected of punching out another guy [in a maximum security prison] and hitting him with a hammer. I did those behaviours as retaliation or to save face. You need those behaviours in jail.

To be sure, the men's earlier masculinizing practices at home and school centred on hand-to-hand combat with other men. Everyday penal reality, however, further valorizes aggressive physicality in materializing gendered identities and bodies (Cowburn 1998; Seymour 2003; Sim 1994; Sykes 1958) and restricts the practices to sustain former identities outside prison or build new ones for the future (Sabo, Kupers, and London 2001). Contrary to the critical masculinities view that a hegemonic position is always contestable, convicts typically do not have alternative cultural capital for linking themselves to different forms of men's power. Everyone in my sample corroborated the statement that in prison, a man gets power from fighting, not from having education or higher income (see Evans and Wallace 2008; Rhodes 2004). Indeed, their accounts emphasize that the ability to generate fear-based respect is a matter of life or death in prison. Men in prison cultivate intimations of dangerousness through bodily performatives intended to repel rather than celebrate violence. Paddy puts it this way:

I hate fighting. I always did [*pauses*] except in hockey. I work out on the fringes and stay in shape partially so no one messes with me. I want 'em thinking they don't want to tangle with me. Violence doesn't happen that often. It's just the threat of it. It's controlled violence, believe it or not. You can control it by allowing others to feel your own intimidation. Muscles, tattoos – those are very helpful tools in prison to keep people away. Although a lot of people aren't intimidated by that, enough are that you limit your defences. You need to show hints of aggression so that others believe the possibility is there.

Alternatives measures that validate masculinity through economic achievement and power or intelligence and control over emotions like anger have little currency in most prison environments (see Tomsen 2002). Efforts to resolve conflict through problem-solving strategies can label individuals as weak and demote them to "womanhood" status in the prison population (see Rhodes 2004). Fred warns of the illusionary nature of diction: "Words are nothing without a known history of actual violence to back them up. Words might almost be seen as a weakness. You know who's serious by their history, reputation, and way they carry themselves." The men's unanimous and constant refrain that *violence is not a choice* is not necessarily a cognitive distortion about power and control or a failure to internalize positive social values (see Fox 1999). Rather, the embodiment of gender norms in prison is always compulsory and always performed under duress of sanction. Harvey emphasizes this well with the observation that "a man who can't fight is not a man." He adds:

> Certain people carry a rep with them. If they're Hell's Angels they're pretty much left alone, right? But the majority of guys in jail, like myself, don't have this so-called rep. In the beginning I have to make my bones, and I *had* to – I actually had no choice about it. It was brought right to me. And that's the majority of the people – especially if you're young when you come in here.

Even prisoners who try to avoid violence must sometimes decide whether or not to take a stand. This requires physical retaliation against shows of disrespect, which ironically often decreases the likelihood of future violence in prison (see Hearn 1998; Rhodes 2004, 49, 55). To not take a stand connotes weakness and singles that prisoner out for future harassment, intimidation, and violence (see Bourke 2007, 347–9; Toch 1998). In their interviews, the men make it clear that choosing not to fight is tantamount to choosing serial victimhood. Charlie is adamant:

> I've been threatened and challenged in prison. You must retaliate. If you don't, you won't survive in jail. You will be beat. And you will end up dead. Guaranteed. It's harsh. If you fight – even if you get beat up – you're left alone after that. You don't have to worry about guys coming up and trying it. Especially if you are a lifer. You've got to deal with it *now*, or else they will come back and they will remember you. So, you're always in a catch-twenty-two. If you get into a fight – you get caught – boom, you got to do more time, or you're shipped to a max. But if you don't get in a fight, you might not live to do the rest of your time. And you're going to get confronted. There's not a fucking thing you can do about it. You're going to have to deal with guys that aren't programmed.

The likelihood of confrontation for sex offenders is high, especially when they move from protective custody into lower security areas with general populations of prisoners convicted for all types of crimes. The nature of a prisoner's conviction locates him on a gender hierarchy. This enables "solid cons" with convictions for acceptable crimes, such as robbery, drug offences, and murder, to mobilize a protector/predator masculinity against sex offenders (Cowburn and Dominelli 2001). Fred elaborates:

> It could be argued that a large part of the reason most prisoners look down upon sex offenders is because the idea of sexual offending violates their idea of what a man is. I had to fight to survive. I do whatever I can to maintain my sense of dignity, despite the dehumanizing aspects of prison itself and life in prison as a sex offender.

Rapists, in turn, participate in this penal gender order and direct contempt and violence at men convicted for sex acts with children. In some instances, sex offenders disclose their paperwork to other convicts to prove that they are rapists and not child molesters. In other instances, prisoners about to confront sex offenders post the latter's paperwork on prison bulletin boards to expose the specifics of sex offences to the rest of the population and to justify their acts of retribution. Indeed, some staff members are complicit in this practice of punishing convicts who violate the ideal masculine role of male protector. Michel recounts:

> When I went to the Regional Reception Centre they throw you all together in a sardine can. I refused to go out to the yard. It was a battle zone. The weight pit doesn't have a camera, and that's where most of the sex offenders got it – they'd get piped or beat up. The guards can visually see it, but they let it go on. They hate sex offenders. It's a general population jail, and most guards are as bad as inmates. One guard – he wanted me to get beat up. He tried to force me out to the yard one day. He said he was doing a search. I said, "You're just trying to set me up." He took me into a room and he said, "How does it feel to be a piece of shit rapist?" He came to my cell door and opened it. And I know he wants these guys to come in and beat me up. So, I shut my door. I sat at my desk and I had my little makeshift weapon ready. He came by and opened it again. [*Mocking voice.*] Poor me. I mean, I go and rape a woman and I feel like I'm victimized. This example is just to show you the mentality of the guards.

Prisoners cannot easily opt out of penal power relations, practices, or programs. The recipe for male-to-male violence in prison ignores the possibilities of alternative masculinities and materializes only dominated and subordinated bodies. Brian's story, mentioned at the beginning of this chapter, also indicates the penal authorities' inability to protect prisoners and unwillingness to comprehend their transition into institutional life (also, Bourke 2007, 340–3). Seen from the inside out, Brian's eventual violence against the prisoner who raped him for three years seems more like a life-preserving penal practice rather than a *prima facie* irrational act or thinking error (see Fox 1999). Kerry adds further clarification to this perspective: "I never turned down a challenge. Ever. And I'm talking challenge in the prison sense. And that can be a look. You learn to know that somebody's going to get you. And you don't wait to get hit first." Prisoner-to-prisoner violence is also a dividing practice that separates the penal world into gendered subject-positions (Connell 2000; Messerschmidt 2001). Charlie clarifies: "Victim and women all seem to be the same to me. In prison you don't want to look weak. Victims are women. Victims are weak. I have no problem *in group* saying that I was a victim. But, back in prison, you're setting yourself up to be victimized." The fusion of femininity with weakness and victimhood links passive bodies with femininity and fighting bodies with masculinity (cf. Marcus .1992). Even in homosocial environments, women's subordination and devaluation are seen as gendering currency that reaffirms men's power over the very idea of women (Sabo, Kupers, and London 2001). Thus prison becomes yet another site for recreating gendered hierarchies of power that privilege men and foster contempt for women by devaluing attributes ascribed as feminine (see Cowburn 1998; Toch 1998, 173). Michel sums it up clearly:

> I know it would be good if men behaved in a certain way – loving, caring, nurturing, affectionate, responsible for children. But men who do that are called pussy whipped. The biggest insult you can get in jail – other than words indicating that I wasn't stand-up or trustworthy – are words that indicate being feminine.

The men in my study demonstrate that their everyday social practices and knowledge shape their ideas about male-to-male violence in prison. By contrast, cognitive behavioural therapies endeavour to teach them that irrational thoughts and feelings trigger violent encounters and a prisoner's relationship to penal violence can be self-managed through cognitive corrections and better choices. This sets up problematic dilemmas for prisoners who embark on rehabilitation.

Christina's Thumb: Reproducing Gendered Hierarchies of Power through Cognitive Corrections

Although Correctional Service Canada is not thought of as every prisoner's friend, among the men I studied, CSC had a special role in prisoner's everyday cognition and mental health. Charlie explains:

> Over the years, I've watched CSC abuse prisoners in jail. No matter how smart you think you are, you will lose when it comes to battling [penal authorities]. If you're a convict, you're a liar. You cannot prove yourself right. The only answer to those concerns that staff gives me is *life's unfair. Deal with it*. And it finally clicked for me – it's the environment, it's the staff I have to work with and who I'm living with. There's not a damn thing I can do to change the scenario. I can only change how I view it. We have to learn that there's nothing that happens in jail that we don't cause ourselves. If you get beaten up, it's your own fault.

How did Charlie, and others for that matter, come to accept responsibility for what happened to them in prison? In order to answer this question, I will explore a sample of Fred's 312 "high-risk" thoughts and CSC-approved cognitive corrections taken directly from his relapse prevention plan. Since treatment staff reviewed and revised Fred's reflections several times, it is reasonable to assume that his discourse embodies CSC-endorsed responses across a range of penal relationships. One such staff member was Christina,[1] a clinical psychologist who worked one-on-one with Fred at one of CSC's regional treatment centres and provided extra-curricular therapy outside group sessions. In one of her cognitive retraining exercises, she got Fred to repeatedly grasp her thumb and squeeze it while he experienced his high-risk feelings until she said, "let it go Fred, let it go." Thus, one of Fred's approved correctives to manage his high-risk thinking was "to remember Christina's thumb." Below is a list that outlines Fred's high-risk thoughts around identity, communication, and authority, and CSC's therapeutic corrections to them.

Fred's first high-risk thought cluster, "this is not who I am," conveys his awareness that identity is performative and shaped by available penal scripts and norms for performing gender in jail. For penal staff,

High-Risk Thought	CSC-Approved Cognitive Correction
This is not who I am, but I can't let people see my fear or they will mistake it for weakness.	I can be myself, for it takes much strength and courage to allow others to see my fear and weakness. Use reality theory.
I have to make an example of that guy or others will challenge me as well.	I will be a positive example to others. By challenging myself to change and "let it go."
I could get killed in here.	God grant me the serenity.
If you don't control your environment, your environment controls you.	I will control my thinking and myself because this is all I can control. I will stop predicting the behaviour of others and will be more trusting.

however, the only alternative to male-on-male violence is abstinence and pacifism (Fox 1999). Even though Fred masculinizes his cognitive challenges by couching them in the gendered sub-text of "strength and courage," his corrective feminizes him and links him to public displays of weakness, vulnerability, and victimhood. Indeed, the new cognitive directives encourage *reality theory* as Fred's beacon for the future but this does not reflect his everyday penal life-world. To placate treatment staff and move forward in the program, Fred must discursively surrender his right to safety, self-protection, and self-determination in prison. These correctives of surrender, serenity, and thought control deny Fred's own agency and power and tie him to a rather helpless subject position in a violent environment.

Bodily based manhood is not the only form of masculinity that penal authorities view as high-risk. Fred's second cluster of risky thoughts and appropriate correctives makes it clear that prisoners who emulate the hegemonic (white, middle-class) Western man of rational thought are also vexatious to penal governance. Consequently, his cognitive emancipation, exemplified in the phrase "I would rather be happy and free than right and imprisoned," dissuades Fred from using democratic participatory practices, such as the legal system, to seek justice for himself and other prisoners. On the one hand, Fred is sent the message that he must abstain from male-on-male violence. On the other hand, penal authorities regard non-violent legal alternatives to resolving conflict and challenging the system of penal governance as equally problematic and illegitimate.

High-Risk Thought	CSC-Approved Cognitive Correction
I am going to use the prisoner grievance system to get my point across and fight for prisoners' rights.	I waste my time trying to prove my point. I would rather be happy than right. "Let it go."
The system is not fair; it is corrupt.	The system is only partially unfair/corrupt
I will bide my time and one day I will have the opportunity to expose penal authorities.	Legal action is appropriate only if my motive is pure.
I am going to use the law to fight the system on this issue.	I would rather be happy and free than right and imprisoned. "Let it go."

High-Risk Thought	CSC-Approved Cognitive Correction
I cannot let the guards catch me in a vulnerable position. They were after me.	The guards of yesteryear are all but gone, and I am safe from them now. "Let it go."
I can't believe how many staff assaulted prisoners and got away with it. How can they be employed by the government?	The guards who threatened me are mostly retired now. I will let go of my past experiences.
I can't believe the treachery and unfairness I see around me.	I am responsible for my actions and will let go of issues I am unable to change.
The system is not fair.	The system is mostly fair, and I can accept unfairness when I see it. "Remember Christina's thumb. Let it go."

Fred's treatment remedies reproduce gendered hierarchies of power among male prisoners and bolster the authority of penal governance, as shown in the third cluster of thoughts and correctives. The cognitive corrections invite Fred to turn a blind eye to abuses of state-sanctioned power in the prison. He is encouraged to take the view that violence in the form of the state is either absent or legitimate. These correctives endorse a life of unquestioned submission to rules and regulations, even if authorities are partially unfair and corrupt. Given Fred's Aboriginal status, it is difficult not to conclude that penal authorities produce a colonial subject within the context of a white settler-like environment. Dissuaded from pursuing political responsibility, Fred and his cohort must internalize their own powerlessness and weakness to survive the rehabilitative ideal of the penal order. Rather disturbingly, this psychic subject position in prison seems to recycle the very same social powerlessness that structured the choices to rape women in the first place.

Challenging Constraints on Identity and Gender: "I'm Not Alone," "I'm Breaking Out"

Brian's prison narrative at the start of this chapter indicates the importance of understanding needs from below, rather than from above as defined by psycho-medical, penal, or actuarial needs experts (cf. Fraser 1989). Along with many of his cohort, Brian must come to terms with the shame he carries for killing someone's daughter, which in his words makes him "a freaking animal," and the shame of his own victimhood, a "weak" "punk-ass kid." He needs to reconcile the shame of hurtful and alienating family relationships, which make him "dysfunctional" and "bitter." He needs to rebuild connections to family, friends, and communities. He needs to learn to communicate with people. He needs someone to listen to and understand him. He needs to know that he is not alone, that he is accepted, and that there is hope for the future. He needs to express his "anger towards the system" for intensifying his pain and failing to provide him with a "safe, secure, and humane environment." He needs to reconcile himself every day to an irreparable past and the unending "pain that [he] fucking caused." He says that whatever it takes, he needs to "change himself." With all this work to do, what convinces Brian, who has nearly two decades of carceral history, to say that "the program saved my life" and to endorse it to fellow convicts? Brian says that he "couldn't wait to come back" for a second treatment program. Clearly there were life-affirming moments in the penal treatment programs that he and others experienced as transformative (see Hudson 2005).

Brian Fay (as cited by Lather 1991, 60) observes that change is never an abstract exercise, and that coming to a radical new self-conception requires:

> An environment of trust, openness, and support in which one's own perceptions and feelings can be made properly conscious to oneself, in which one can think through one's experiences in terms of a radically new vocabulary which expresses a fundamentally different conceptualization of the world, in which one can see the particular and concrete ways that one

unwittingly collaborates in producing one's own misery, and in which one can gain the emotional strength to accept and act on one's new insights.

The men in my sample reported environments and experiences similar to those that Fay discusses. While penal governance eschewed the "personal is political" position adopted by feminist and other consciousness-raising groups, it did convince the men that their old techniques of self and gendering norms did not work and resulted in damaged people (see Evans and Wallace 2008). At a general level, the penal treatment group provided a supportive setting for men to contest and renegotiate some of the cultural constraints placed on their identity and self-expression. As Culhane and Taylor (2000, 129) note, penal treatment groups often mark "the only time in their lives where men are offered alternative explanations" of their deeds (see Hudson 2005). In Michel's opinion, the treatment group sessions provided "an opportunity to make sense of our lives." He adds, "Even clinical labels are better than being called a monster." Fred's experience with the treatment group also typifies the sense of relief associated with sharing experiences with other men who also committed dreadful acts. The group, he says, generated an oppositional discourse that helped the men refuse imposed identities and change themselves:

> The most significant thing I got out of group was seeing that I was not unique. You're sitting in a room with fifteen other guys and over time you start to see pieces of you in others and, in turn, you have pieces of them in you. You see that it's normal to feel this fucked up – it's a normal reaction to where I've been. You think, maybe some of this can be fixed. If I was the only one, then I'm a freak. I'm not normal. None of this takes us off the hook, but we can see that there's reasons – not excuses, but reasons. Before that the only reason is that I'm just a bad person – that's what the courts say. I'm a mistake. The courts and newspapers don't know what to think, so you're evil. (Fred)

Group treatment seems to incorporate marginalized population into middle-class self-help and self-esteem programs not typically available to low-income groups (e.g., Culhane and Taylor 2000). In effect, the men felt better about themselves. Their experiences together cultivated insight, self-confidence, and a will to change and continue to change. James elaborates:

> I came in with life-twenty-five in '83, and other than work – because we had to – I coped by stuffing my fat little face. And I wound up well over

220 pounds at five-foot-eight. It wasn't until 1995 when someone actually took an interest in me. This was another convict. He pushed me to get back into my education, care for myself, exercise. I had basically given up. I was prepared to stay in prison my whole life. I was barely Grade 7 on the academic tests. Started playing handball. Got my Grade 12. Lost fifty pounds. Started hearing good things about the treatment centre. I won't deny that a transfer to a better institution wasn't part of my initial motivation to do programs. But I also feel *better* about myself. I took this second program because I *wanted* to. I wanted to *keep* changing.

Most men in my sample identify the opportunity to talk "without fear of being ridiculed" as transformative. They see their former selves limited by a lack of vocabulary and an inability to explain personal problems and interact in social relationships. The treatment curriculum, they say, helped them develop an emotional vocabulary and narrative style with which to express their unarticulated relationships and "unformulated experiences and feelings" (Cain 1993, 90) and "re-interpret their life experiences" (Darville 1995, 255). Regular literate practices and exercises enabled each man to develop language skills and reflect on thoughts, attitudes, and memories that he previously could not put in words or communicate to others (see Duguid 2000). Fred notes the value of speech: "If you have a thought or an idea, you can't comprehend it or express it without words." Just as important as promoting new language skills, the treatment programs also afforded opportunities for the men to bond and socialize together. Bear remarks:

This program has helped me a lot. It's helped me to see myself – who I really am. Who I really was. And that wasn't who I wanted to be. Before, I was always the outsider looking in. For the first time in my life, I felt like I belonged in something – this group. Being able to sit there, and talk about my life, and not be pushed away. The feeling was something that I never had before. I had to come here to get help. Otherwise I would have been walking around like – a lost person. So this is good for me. I got to learn about myself. Now I'm aware of a lot of things that I wasn't.

Michel adds:

Most of the work I did had nothing to do with the group. It's just the fact that I'm in the group that I'm thinking about it – I'm looking at myself.

That's the difference. Something really profound would have had to happen without these programs. There's no way I was going to look at myself without a program – all four of them. Without programs, I wouldn't be sitting here talking to you. I wouldn't know how to. I'd be scared of you.

The men insisted, however, that it was not the penal treatment program's formal curriculum and teaching exercises that they valued most, but the forum in which they could finally speak without fear of judgement. They rethought their horrible acts and harmful displays of emotions. Because it was impossible to articulate their shame, hurt, and confusion without crying openly and displaying vulnerability, the forum endorsed expressions of emotions that were reconcilable with heterosexual manhood. This enabled them to experiment with a range of questions and answers that they had actively denied or refused since boyhood (O'Leary 1998, 29). The group sessions provided the men with opportunities to challenge their homophobia and misogyny and to learn and practise emotional reciprocity in the company of men. Harvey observes:

I remember [two male facilitators] from my first group. Well, we assumed that they were homos. I'm not condemning it or anything, but they were, like, feminine. Their emotions are right out on their sleeves. With a regular guy, I could say something, and, if he's offended, then it's aggressive right? And it's so much easier to deal with aggressiveness than to deal with a guy that's *hurt*. Or, you know, *offended*. You didn't *hear* those words. In my family you didn't hear those words. Well, my mom expressed stuff like that, but she's a woman, right? Men, you didn't hear that from. So, it was really awkward. The first step for me. They cracked me in group – prodding around some abuse issues. I just broke down. I turned into a puddle of mud. But it was that incident that started to change my opinion because I wasn't condemned by anyone in that group. And, if anything, I felt a lot of compassion. And I said to myself, "I need to be able to express my feelings like that." 'Cause I felt good. Well, not right off the hop. I was still questioning what people were thinking. The next week, any time anyone said anything to me, I was kinda making sure that it was still understood that I was still a man, *and* willing to do this thing. [*Pauses.*] It opened up that door a little bit more to how people perceive that – specifically men.

The treatment group's exploratory dynamics gave the men a mechanism to overcome what Walker and Kushner (1999) call emotional illiteracy. They were permitted to disengage from cultural and penal imperatives that surround hegemonic manhood and contemplate new ways to be men. They were praised for having the courage or strength to question and reject gender constraints placed on them since boyhood and to explore their role in their own contradictory experiences and expressions of power (see Evans and Wallace 2008; Pollack 2000) Fred calls the process "coming out or breaking out":

> The way our society imposes rigid roles on [men] causes problems because the individual is bigger than those constraints – he needs to feel more and express more but society and his family don't allow him to do that. They get that angst and tension, unrelenting tension, and it finally drives them over the edge. It drove me over the edge. This group allows us to express beyond those constraints and express outside what men are allowed to express. But it's a struggle because those roles and expectations are so well ingrained. It's almost like coming out, or breaking out.

Some men even challenged physical taboos. They simply touched or embraced other men outside the treatment group setting. Harvey called it liberating and took pleasure in telling me about it:

> When I first came in? I wouldn't in any way make an emotional connection with a man. The façade was there – the wall was up. Now, I grab guys. I wrestle around – and it's not wrestling in the *physical* sense, it's *contact*. I feel *good* when I'm in contact with people. And even if it's just a hand on the shoulder, I feel comfortable. Bear was a challenge for me. Because, the first time – like, man, he was cold. And I felt – I almost felt compelled to break him out of his shell. *Now*, I had to tell him the other day, "Bear, slow down."

Harvey did help Bear "break out of his shell," along with Brian. All three men gradually overcame their self-imposed alienation from human touch and their experiences as victims of physical and sexual violence. Brian and Bear elaborate:

> I carried [my sexual assaults] all through my prison. I tried to have relationships with women. You meet them through a friend. When I meet a woman, it was difficult – people touching you and stuff. You just want to be alone and do your time and try to survive. Even a man hugging me. You know, big Harvey in group here. He used to hug me and [*laughs*] I joke

with him, "you remind me of that priest and some other people." I joked, but I had to overcome those fears. (Brian)

For the years that I was in jail, when somebody touched me, I would break into a sweat, you know? And fear. Triggers would come and my mind would just race, you know, with fear. Now, I've turned it into a positive – this person wants to be acknowledged. (Bear)

The Transformative Power of Self-Expression

Whether or not confession is an effect of power, as Foucault says (1990), or delivers one from a power that silences and represses, there is no doubt that the men experienced talking about their lives as emancipatory. Recovery from boyhood abuse unfolded slowly over time, rather than through sudden revelations and disclosures. Eleven of the men waited until their second or third penal treatment group to reveal their experiences with physical, emotional, or sexual abuse. Simpson conveys the pain and relief in saying what he had not been able to say before:

The guys I've met in group are much like guys that I've met in jail, but the difference is we haven't had the opportunity to verbally express things. Over the months, I've been allowed to talk and express many things, but when I express the pain comes, like, so much [*pauses*] it hurts a lot [*pauses*] and it becomes unbearable and [*pauses*] like, for me to cry takes a lot. Like, I didn't think I could cry anymore. To go to there, I have to feel intense. It has to come back. And it has. But it comes out in anger. I start to feel angry about my victimization. And it just becomes too much, hey. This is the first time in adult life that – even my childhood – that I was able to express those feelings [*pauses*] crying [*pauses*] I'm ashamed of that I cried. When I cry in here, I stay in my cell for days.

For most of the men, the unexpected dividend of treatment was their ability to express their own emotional, sexual, and physical abuse and despair and discuss family and other relationship problems. That prison was the first safe space they had to express their own victimization is a recurring irony in many male and female convicts' life stories (Comack 1996). As Cam suggests:

I've been badly abused, probably twelve, fifteen years of my life. Outside of treatment, I've never mentioned it. Who's going to listen anyway? It makes you sound that much more fucked up. It's a real taboo area to talk about. I surely wasn't going to share all that with my wife. It would say that I was just some fucked in the ass punk kind of kid. Before? If I know you come from that kind of background, and you're a woman, I'm going to think you're a dirty little slut. You'll fuck anything. You got no morals, no beliefs, no self-respect or anything. What am I going to think of you if you are a man and telling me that? You know what I mean? And that's heavy shit to say. But that's what my beliefs would have been – that's how *I* feel, so that's how I'm going to judge you. So how am I going to walk into a group of men on the street and say, "Hi my name is so and so, and start talking about my experiences?" [*Laughs.*] I've *done* it now. Just in this program.

Despite the consternation about appearing vulnerable in the eyes of other men, no one was ever shunned or scorned for displaying weakness or disclosing victimhood in the group sessions I observed. Marvin explains:

I remember coming here in a van telling myself, "Well, I'll just try to slip through," you know, "I won't even bother trying to open up in group. Even if I just sit here for eight months I get credit for being here." But when I came here, some of the things that guys were saying I could relate so much to them, you know, "Wow, that happened to you as a kid?" I'm thinking, "Well, that happened to me." And no matter what you said in that group, nobody was laughing. You know? They were all able to relate.

These narratives indicate that bodily centred masculinizing practices around disclosing victimhood can be challenged. In an environment of trust and support, individuals can refuse to assume those norms and practices *and* find some relief in overcoming them, at least in the short term (see Evans and Wallace 2008; Kimmel and Kaufman 1994).

Rethinking and Redoing Family

To some extent, the penal treatment group was a site of local resistance to familial relations of power even though the program never criticized the dominant nuclear family form (Fraser 1989, 92–3). Treatment programs opened up hidden interpersonal dynamics to scrutiny and censure. The men de-privatized practices of violence in the family and exposed myriad points of conflict within the patriarchal family form (e.g., Boyd 1997). Fred acknowledges:

> Nothing is more powerful than keeping a secret. But it's also powerful to unburden yourself of secrets that you need to talk about. I knew my family was messed up and I knew it was wrong, but I refused to acknowledge it because to admit it is worse, so you keep it hush-hush and you don't talk about it with anyone. A family shares responsibility for its members. If one family member fucks up, the whole family is shunned. Just like a child reflects his parents, parents reflect the child. Having abnormal parents is shameful. Somehow it reflects on me.

The men in my study were relieved to discover that other men had endured hardships within their families. Sharing such experiences normalized so-called dysfunctional families and allowed the men to express their intense frustration and anger. Brian recounts:

> In my first program, we learned about our family environment and abuse. I was just ticked at my mother. And I told her, "We're going to have a trailer visit, just you and me." She apologized to me. We hugged each other. And she talked about her views, so I got a better perspective. I want to move on. We can start a relationship – it's perfect right now. We're communicating. I tell her I love her – that's big for me. She knows what she did. She didn't have a chance to talk to a therapist. That's the difference between me and her. I'm trying to help her talk about it. I don't want to hate her no more. I've had enough talk about my mom. It's hard though. A lot of anger.

Most of the men I observed and interviewed, however, wanted a second chance to "do family." They accepted idyllic constructions of family life and ignored discussions about whether the treatment program's vision of family carried any currency outside prison for politically and economically disenfranchised men like them. They were nostalgic about family, embittered about boyhood, and inspired to fix family relations. Two reoccurring topics in group discussions were the desire to reunite with family members and guilt over not being able to care for their aging parents. The lure and lore of dominant family ideology waxed strong for most of the men. Michel admits:

> I'd like to speak to my mom, either face-to-face or in a letter. She remembers me as a fat young punk with a bad attitude who liked to hurt people.

Basically, I killed a man, stabbed people, raped a woman – all these bad things. That's how she remembers me. There's no connection between me and her. Now that she's sober and has got some therapy – she might better understand what I have to tell her even though she was done with me long before that. She sent me into group homes. [*Pauses.*] The only connection we have is she's *my mom*. It must be a powerful connection 'cause I still want to talk to her, [*pauses*] for some reason.

The evolution of their own awareness also prompted some men to understand their families and try to overcome the past hurt their parents perpetrated on them. Marvin, along with Michel and Brian, cited earlier, describe the difficulty of reconciling with physically abusive mothers who bear cultural or actual responsibility and guilt for raising a sex offender. Marvin elaborates:

Today I can't get used to my mom touching me. See, before? *She* couldn't get used to it. It's so hard for me to sit there and my mom wants to hold my hand now. She holds my hand. She holds my arm. She wants to sit next to me. If I get up and go to the pop machine, I come back and sit across from her. She gets up and moves directly beside me! And it's all so overwhelming. It's not that I don't like it when she touches me, it's just that, when she *touches* me, I still remember.

However, the neoliberal strategy of penal treatment with its emphasis on individual responsibility and cognitive correction limits the nation-state responsibility for social problems. For example, Aboriginal men are given no resources with which to explore and understand the connections between colonialism and the pathology that affect their families and communities (Lane et al. 2002; Pollack 2007; Royal Commission on Aboriginal Peoples 1993). Listening to the Aboriginal men in my sample, it is clear the state only became an asset to them after they were imprisoned. At that point they comprehend that prison provides them with more resources, programs, and assistance compared to their family and community members. Rather distressingly, Bear and some of his cohort are "thankful for jail." He puts it as follows:

I worry about all my family. I told the facilitators that for my family to carry on, to listen to me talk about this, this, and this – they have nobody to support them, to listen to them, to talk to them because, they never express themselves – they haven't learned that. They're just going to stuff all these feelings. You have to practice expressing yourself. My family gets all screwed up and confused when they try to express. But, if you took a cup and put some booze in it and gave it to my sister, you know, "express yourself" – she will. But she will express herself in a very verbal, angry way: "I hate you. I don't like you. I don't like what you did to mom. I don't want to see you any more." That's how they know how to express themselves. That's how they bury their pain is through alcohol. She's totally ignored what happened to both of our sisters, because alcohol took both of my sisters. And she used alcohol to cover that up – her feelings, her thoughts, her hurt, you know? I guess I'm thankful to jail for that. I wished they knew what I know. I wished they believed in themselves too. "It's best that it stays buried" – that's what my sister says.

Individual Change, Community Reintegration, and the Recognition of New Identities

Apart from penal treatment programs, incarcerated sex offenders lack sites and practices for revisiting and revising media-shaped representations of them as "remorseless predators," "untreatable animals," or "gravely ill people who should be harnessed and dealt with on a medical basis for the rest of their lives" (Pool 2003, A5). Dominant discourses typically collapse all sex offenders into a type of person, which forecloses possibilities for self-change and restricts opportunities to have change socially validated. So penal treatment talk encourages the men to believe that changing their behaviour is a choice, yet public culture is often antagonistic towards viewing sex offenders as redeemable citizens (e.g., Petrunik and Deutschman 2007). Cam expresses this paradox well:

I know I'm not the same as I was, but society never knows that. And I have nobody [*pauses*] – it's hard to identify who I am because I have no one to recognize those changes. Who do I share that with? I'm all this new stuff that I feel inside, but, I don't have nobody to talk to in my life. Who am I changing for? Who knows if I change? I spend my life in a cell by myself. So, who am I? I'm feeling good now after the program, but how long will that last? You can't change by yourself. That's for sure. [The facilitator] did my paperwork. It's stunning. I can look at that and think, everybody else can trash me, I don't care. I've got this [*laughs*] you know! And it means *a lot*. Um, the biggest thing for me in this program was *he* recognized the changes I made. I really poured myself out and I was acknowledged for that [*laughs*], I got to be at my strongest point when I say goodbye to him. [*Embarrassed laugh.*]

If, as Judith Butler (1992) notes, identity is not self-identical but must be instituted again and again, then how did these men sustain their changed identities in the absence of social recognition? For some men, the program led to new subject-positions. Kerry used the family counselling program to re-perform gender within the marriage:

> My wife and I did this program together. We were going together at the time of my last offence. There's a script that Sara and I struggle against, and that is that the one inside is totally dependent on the person outside in the relationship. I want to feel like I'm contributing equally to the relationship because I love her and I cannot support her. For the rest of my life, Sara is going to earn more money than I do. I'm glad one of us has got a steady income. We're blessed. I do our investing. Sara doesn't like to read the stock markets every day. I've gotten us into designing Celtic jewellery. And in her school, I learn the names of all of her [students] and I want to know how they're doing. So that, by the end of the year, I feel like I really know the kids. So, yeah, I don't feel like a supplicant in our relationship, but that's taken ten years.

Other men with no family or sustaining relations such as Cam relied on treatment staff's official reports or parole board hearings to confirm self-change and build new identities. Bear, however, struggled unsuccessfully to link himself to a new subject-position and evoke positive self-change in the eyes of parole board members:

> When I expressed in my parole hearing [*pauses*] they didn't know what I was talking about. It scares me sometimes because [*pauses*] it's like there's two people. There's the person who's talking to you now. And there's that person over there, you know. I see that person [over there] as a sex offender. [CSC and the Parole Board] don't see that with me. They just see the past. They see the criminal. I can't be trusted. And society can't trust me. I'm a hazard to, like, when I read my file, I'm a hazard to others around me [*softly*] I'm not a hazard to anybody, you know. I'm trying to help myself, trying to change. I'm trying to recognize some things by doing programs. All they do is see this person over *there*, you know, not this person over *here* who's talking to you.

James used the program to connect to the community and to help take responsibility for his past deeds. One component of the treatment program included a group session with Colleen, a female survivor of childhood sexual abuse. This was a rare occasion for sex offenders to interact and exchange views with the public (see Petrunik 2002). James opted to test community reaction to his crime through a spontaneous restorative justice response to Colleen's presence (see Hopkins and Koss 2005). James viewed Colleen as symbolic of the community, and used her visit to make public his apology, take responsibility for the injury he inflicted, and express his remorse. Her receptiveness to his confession enabled James to transcend his identity as a "dirty, fucking scumbag." Colleen helped James anchor himself and imagine the possibility of community reintegration rather then alienation and isolation from society. He elaborates:

When the victim [Colleen] came to visit our group, this was the first time I was ever able to talk to a victim. I haven't heard a victim impact statement. I felt a need to talk to Colleen. I wanted *her* view of the impact that my crime would have on a survivor. She would be about the age of *my* victim's mother. I told her about what I did. [*Pauses.*] For me, it was like her opinion mattered more than all CSC combined. Hearing her say what you did was terrible, but that's not what you are now [*pauses*] when she said that, that made me feel so good – that I'm not the person I was and she doesn't consider me as that. [*Pauses.*] She thanked me for my courage, for being able to speak to her that way. This had been eating and eating away at me. This was the first time I ever disclosed it to anybody – well, it's in my files. I never discussed my mutilation of my victim in my previous programs. These guys in group didn't know. Colleen didn't reject me. And that gives *me* power to say, "*Yes*, I can do this, and some people will accept me after what I've done," as opposed to saying, "You're a dirty, fucking, scum bag." Some people will say that. But others won't. And I know that now. That is the *best* experience that this whole program has done. I realize this does not mean my victim's family is going to feel or think like Colleen. But saying to somebody else, "Yes, I am responsible for what I've done." To be able to say, "I'm sorry." That's what that meant to me. [*Pauses.*] No matter what else happens, no matter how much of this group I wind up forgetting, I will never be able to forget that moment. Colleen walked straight across the room to me. She shook my hand. [*Whispers.*] That was incredible.

More Gender Trouble: Practising Program Skills in Prison

According to Brian Fay (as cited by Lather 1991, 60), "Radical social change through rational enlightenment requires some mechanism for ensuring that those conditions necessary for such enlightenment will be established and maintained." Regional penal treatment programs represent a brief time in a long-term prisoner's carceral history. Invariably, each man is shipped back to a prison to serve out the remainder of his sentence and become the con again. Not surprisingly, a return to a site where manhood is associated with domination and gender hierarchies is not conducive to reinforcing desired change (see Evans and Wallace 2008). It often leads to the following type of official assessment decision:

> While at [Minimum Prison], Mr. [Prisoner] has failed to show that he has internalized the skills from the program. Mr. [Prisoner] must be able to demonstrate his internalization of the skills he's learned in the Intensive Sex Offender Program if he is to be considered manageable at minimum security. (Assessment for Decision, approving an emergency involuntary transfer to a medium security prison, 2003)

Paddy elaborates further:

> They want us to become different men, but the environment they put us in doesn't foster that. We've taken the belief system that men are supposed to be strong, dominant, don't cry, don't show their emotions to the extreme. As a whole, for whatever reason, our inhibition to violence is much less than other men. And then they put us together in an environment where violence is not a choice. How do you choose not to be a part of it?

Listening to and observing the men, it is apparent that it is impossible to develop a viable alternative to hegemonic masculinity in prison. While the men acknowledge the potential of the programs for "creating a new person" and for "becoming different men," they all insist that the subjecthood cultivated in treatment programs is irreconcilable with the lived reality of prisons (see Cowburn 1998, 246; Seymour 2003, 47). Charlie articulates the practical problems of living an alternative masculinity in prison:

> Actually, program skills can be dangerous in prison. If you really try to work on them? On the one hand, you're trying to be open and vulnerable

with other men, and, on the other hand, you better be prepared for violence ... you're setting yourself up to be victimized. And you will be.
Sometimes programs try to teach you to paint a target on your goddamn
chest. It ain't happening.

Similarly, Michel identifies the social barriers to performing gender differently in prison. He simultaneously bears and critiques hegemonic
masculinity where manhood is associated with the mastery of emotions, physical expressions of power, and isolation from other men. He
puts it this way:

You *can't* use program skills with the guards. [*Laughs.*] What am I supposed to do? "Please sir, could you move me to another cell. I'm feeling
uncomfortable with my cell mate." It's more, "Okay you fucking screw, get
me out of this cell or I'm going to freak out." You have to talk that way.
That's the reality. So, the guards almost teach you behaviours. You *have* to
act in a certain way to get what you want. You can't practice these new
behaviours if you're not placed in a good environment when the program's
over. Program skills sure don't help me in a max, and I wouldn't even want
to try. Maybe if you're in a medium security prison. But you have to change
everything – erase everything and recreate yourself ...

I wrote in my log once. And I thought about it for a long time before opening up about it in group, by saying that "I'm lonely." I felt so stupid – embarrassed, not stupid. I wasn't asking people to do anything about it. I had
to work myself up for a long time just to say I felt lonely 'cause it's almost
a self-pity feeling. If I went back to a max, there's not a chance in hell that
I'd tell anyone how I feel – I mean, that's standard. In prison, no one wants
to hear about your *feelings*. Guards don't want to hear about your *feelings*.
Other *convicts* don't want to hear about your feelings ...

Even now, if somebody makes me look bad or gives me a problem, I react
instantly – usually with violence. Or I'll call them on it – "Fuck you, let's
see what you got." Quite often I'll back down 'cause I'm just playing the
role, but I don't want to even get to that point. I'd rather just be able to
walk away, and handle it in such a way that I let them know that I'm no
pushover and I'm not going to put up with your shit forever. Basically,
leave me alone and let me do my thing and I'll let you do yours – otherwise
I'm going to mess you up. How do you say that without spewing anger or
hatred? That's what I got to learn how to do. I got to stick up for myself

verbally, not physically. When I attacked the guy in [a max], never once did I try to stick up for myself verbally. I just waited 'till the pressure was over and I just, assaulted him – with no warning or nothing. He didn't have a clue it was coming. He thought I was some idiot pushover – I've got to try other methods [*pauses*] somehow.

For many men in my sample even imagining new communication skills and expressing emotional literacy in the company of heterosexual men beyond prison walls was a difficult task. Bob speaks for many when he says:

Now, on the street, I'd have no problems with just meeting a woman and talking about how I'm feeling. With a man I would. It's easier with a woman than a man to start talking deep and emotional. Women are willing to do it. A man would be putting up his guard: "Where's this guy going? Is this guy gay or is he coming on to me?"

Despite positive program progress in penal settings, emotionality and intimacy still remain gendered in prison and still link men to subordinated forms of masculinity. Reminiscent of his cohorts' boyhood and rape narratives, Bob still sees women as willing agents upon whom men can privately displace their emotional angst.

Conclusion

This chapter investigated whether or not Canadian men's prisons in general and sex offender penal treatment programs in particular challenge or reproduce hegemonic forms of masculinity. I found that penal social relations cultivate an embodiment of manhood based on the ability to hurt other men and a misogynist discursive regime that impugns the feminine. Prison magnified the pre-carceral gendering practices of all men in my study. In a passage that bears repeating, Kerry encapsulates the embodiment of manhood in prison through silence:

It is the willingness to be violent, and shut down anything that I thought was sensitive or emotional because the only acceptable emotion was anger, actually, sort of a rage. Even anger wasn't acceptable because that was a loss of control. And even rage had to be somewhat controlled. That's what I put together. Don't show pity. Don't show concern. Don't show any of those kinds of things – 'cause that's a sign of weakness. Like, you should be able to see somebody get their brains bashed out literally in front of you.

Yet prisoners did not experience the penal treatment regime as solely oppressive. Each man I interviewed drew something from the programs to resolve some of his troubles, rekindle his connection to others, and discover his own inherent worth, dignity, and potential for growth. However, internalizing the lessons of personal change and maturity was irreconcilable with the lived reality of men's prisons. Program skills that emphasized alternatives to male violence, emotional reciprocity with men, and new attitudes and values against hegemonic masculinity created impossible conflicts for convicts who were forced to choose among diametrically opposed goals such as personal safety and survival, administrative compliance and freedom, and individual self-change and prison culture. In short, existing social and structural arrangements posed a formidable barrier to the implementation of personal change, and the men I interviewed knew it:

> The liberation of women that they've taken on has changed some men, right? Men *can* change. You can choose not to objectify. Very difficult as a teenager to go against the grain. But I'm forty years old. I've seen what my objectification does. (Paddy)

> To believe that you can go into a social structure and implement change? No, it's not going to happen. I can only change myself. (Charlie)

> The people who are doing time are, quote, "sex offenders." It's not "men." I have heard in my life – from men who will never see the inside of a jail and who will never be charged with a sex offence – the verbalizations of sex offenders. And I think any honest man will agree with me. And these verbalizations have effects. (Kerry)

Conclusion

It is useful to conclude this book by summarizing some of the major findings and discussing some of the major lessons learned from investigating the stranger rapist, recovering them as subjects of masculinity and perpetrators of violence, and examining their experiences as subjects of penal governance.

Investigating the Stranger Rapist

I have argued that the stranger rapist is the archetypical rapist that women fear most and that breeds reliance on traditional patriarchal institutions for protection. Therefore, it is important to investigate the stranger rapist; to examine what they actually do, think, and feel in their everyday world; and to explain how men produce and work on patriarchy, men's power, women's inequality, gender, and gender hierarchies in the context of rape. At psychic and social levels, the men in my study were each acutely aware of the contingency and contradictions of masculine subjecthood. For them, stranger rape was performative. It either materialized or was intended to materialize effects that linked male bodies to different elements of hegemonic masculinity. To paraphrase Judith Butler (1990), stranger rape endeavoured to create *bodies that matter* versus feminized or homo-sexualized bodies that were subordinated.

In saying that stranger rape materialized men's power, I do not dismiss feminist claims that rape is caused by men's power over women. But physical and sexual violence produced only fleeting moments of power in those I studied and bodily based violence as a gendering practice failed to eliminate pain and powerlessness among my sample of sex offenders. In examining behaviours through individual histories, it is clear that male sexual violence is not inevitable or inherent. None of the men in my study were predisposed to relate to their worlds through practices of control and power. Instead, structural and cultural forces often beyond a young boy's control shaped their aggressive conceptions of masculinity. They then learned to experience and understand their bodies as receptacles and finally as instruments of oppression and pain.

Clinicians might want to deploy life narratives to explore the interplay between masculinity and individual pathology – including domestic violence; severe physical, psychological, institutional, and sexual abuse; mental health issues; substance abuse; and more. I have touched on these issues and I know more must be done to unravel these complex matters to fully understand stranger rapists. However, I have tried to resist turning life stories into clinical cases. My goal was not to pathologize individuals, but to explore hegemonic masculinity and the unequal social and gender hierarchies that it sustains. In my view, these social relations constitute a set of practices that authorize stranger rape as a culturally available choice in our society, which simultaneously reaffirms men's sexual assertion as hegemonic while also distancing men who rape from the ideology of male chivalry and protection vis-à-vis women.

Recovering the Stranger Rapist-as-Subject

The stranger rapist's emotions, needs, motives, and lived realities are often hidden in many general explanatory frameworks that link rape to discourses about men's power and control, faulty thinking, and sexual violence. The men in my study do not fit the populist representation of stranger rapists as irrational, remorseless predators, the feminist-informed understanding of rapists as every man, or the penal treatment view of rapists as cognitively impaired subjects. To the contrary, I found that rapists were active agents who used biological maleness and gender-specific forms of violence to materialize and stabilize a coherent masculine self in a world where bodily based practices provided them with credible incarnations of manhood. This is not to say that middle-class men do not experience the contradictions of being a man or are any less likely to rape. While I did not interview middle-class men, I imagine that they would handle the pains and perplexities of being a man differently than racialized or working-class men. The former, for example, have access to non-bodily based gendering resources such as economic and cultural capital. Their access to the "patriarchal dividend" gives them more social power over most women and men, and ties them in different ways to subjects of masculine power and to rape and rape victims. Simply put, the connections of male bodies to power take different forms across different races, classes, genders, and cultures, and may not be reduced to either individual causes or simple singular patterns. Each man in my study exhibited extreme male-to-male fighting and ultimately female stranger rape. Their boyhood experiences of abuse and failure, which they found inexpressible, led them to deploy bodily based physicality as a practice for restoring signs of gender rather than use it as an extension of already-existing power and control. Physical and sexual violence enabled each man to reconcile, at least temporarily, the lived contradiction between culturally circulating images of masculine power in regards to women and men, and their own lived experiences of pain and powerlessness across settings that included family, heterosexual relationships, school, community, workplace, and prison.

The Return of the Medical Model of Rape?

The original political objectives of the anti-rape movement were to accentuate the normalcy and ubiquity of rape and to transform the structural circumstances supportive of rape, especially women's inequality. Towards this end, feminists debunked medicalized vocabularies of motive for rape that centred on psychologically abnormal men who were unable or unwilling to control their behaviour. Diana Scully (1990, 167) warns her readers to "understand the power of those who define knowledge and be ever vigilant, because just as one ideology of denial begins its demise, another comes along." More recently, Laureen Snider (2006, 338) cautioned that "going silent means that the only voices governments and correctional authorities hear are vindictive and fear-obsessed." Unfortunately, feminists have not always heeded this good advice, especially when it comes to vocabularies of rape motives. As noted, contemporary penal treatment experts have deformed feminist ideas that men choose to commit rape into neoliberal strategies for individualizing and giving responsibility to convicted sex offenders. Clinicians have reinvented a new disease model of rape where sex offenders not only lack control over their actions, but also suffer from cognitive distortions that structure gendering practices. Moreover, claims by feminist and other critical writers that the overrepresentation of incarcerated racialized and working-class men reflects discriminatory policing and legal biases have been interpreted by penal treatment experts to mean that all types of convicted sexual offenders are equal and that considering the role of inequality in social, economic, political, and penal responses to rape is not necessary. No one, of course, denies that stranger rape and sexual assault extend beyond convicted sex offenders. In 2008, 21,483 incidents of sexual assault were reported to Canadian police, a figure that does not include sexual violations against children (Wallace 2009). Considering the figure of unreported sexual offences, this data suggests that there are tens of thousands of sexual offenders whom penal psychologists would label as cognitively deficient and trapped in crime cycles. But does the alleviation of sexual assault lie in convincing thousands of men to build crime cycles to monitor their high-risk thinking and triggers? Does imagining the problem of sexual violence against women in terms of cultural monikers such as untreatable monsters and remorseless predators contribute to the safety of women and children? I think not.

Lessons Learned from the Subject of Stranger Rape

This book listens to men convicted of stranger rapes and documents their life stories. I cannot, of course, expect fourteen men to provide all or even most of the answers as to why men rape, but their stories have implications for reducing sexual violence against women. Most men, for example, were able to identify moments of salvation before life events and circumstances narrowed their gendering options and overdetermined a violent life course. While the tragic effects of their choices can never be undone for their victims or for them, there may be some interventions that could prevent potential rapists from deploying gender practices that lead to such dire consequences for women. There are several sites for intervention. First is the patriarchal family form long noted by feminists. Second are the contradictions between men's power and pain, violence, and the absence of non-coercive early interventions for boys in trouble. Third is prison, which ignores viable alternatives to bodilybased masculinity and men's social powerlessness in marginalized populations.

Hegemonic Masculinity and Patriarchal Families

These life stories reveal how hegemonic masculinity jeopardizes the physical safety of women, children, and men. All the men in my study and their families were injured by patriarchal family relations. While some researchers report that male violence is lower in cultures that permit men to acknowledge fear (Kimmel 2005), the subjects in my study learned to suppress their emotions and express pain through bodily based violence that ultimately hurt anonymous others. The fact that many participants began to smother their emotions by the age of ten underscores the importance of providing young boys with emotional literacy early in life. This might take the form of rituals of affirmation in schools and at sports or community events. For example, during a graduation ceremony from a prison program Simpson received an award for bravery and courage because of frank and emotional disclosures during treatment group talk.

Each man in my study also expressed a desire for alternative father figures and nurturing mothers in whom they could confide their angst without fear of real or imagined insults to their psychical sense of masculinity. Each man praised the male treatment facilitators for demonstrating empathy and compassion which was both envied and desired. Consensus existed that emotional conduits, especially their own fathers' active involvement in primary childcare, may have changed the course of their lives. In their view, it would have tempered dominant notions of patriarchal manhood. However, my subjects' boyhood relationship to violence within their families was varied. Many had physically violent fathers and others had physically violent mothers. Many also witnessed inter-parental violence. The common thread in each case was traditional gendered divisions of familial labour and hierarchies of power (Messerschmidt 2004, 2006). The problem to be addressed most forcefully is not domestic violence per se, but rather the make-up of the hegemonic nuclear family form itself, which permits private violence against weaker family members, creates contrasting definitions of femininity and valorizes men's power over women and children as normative.

Hegemonic Masculinity and Women's Inequality

The patriarchal family form and women's structurally and culturally enforced subordination were troubling social matters for both the men and their victims in my study. If the hegemonic masculine project is about maintaining women's inequality, then feminist black-letter legal challenges to it need to question dominant heterosexual family practices, reform familial power relations, and redefine femininity and womanhood from materially disempowered subject positions to empowered ones (Connell 2009). Feminists should never abandon law as a site of struggle for protecting women from violence. They should mobilize law to strengthen women's economic, legal, and cultural choices, provide alternatives to the compulsory heterosexual family, and contest impressions of motherhood and womanhood as weak, potential sites of victimhood, and dependent on men for a feminized identity.

Hegemonic Masculinity and Treatment Programs

Penal sex offender treatment programs promote change at the level of the individual and ignore the masculine culture of violence in society. The men in my study engaged in male-to-male violence years before they raped adult strangers. State agencies, in the form of public schools, foster care facilities, welfare units, child protection services, police agencies, and youth detention centres, missed numerous opportunities to provide care, guidance, therapy, and assistance during boyhood rather than simply administering treatment and punishment after the fact of violence in adulthood. These life stories suggest that treatment programs in penal contexts can help working-class and racialized men with histories of sexual abuse and neglect, but they also suggest that help should have been available before men committed rape or rape and murder.

Moreover, treatment regimes in prison should not prevent convicted sex offenders from making links between their lives and wider social and cultural contexts. This means developing group discussions and assignments that examine the effects of gender, race, and class-based power imbalances on reproducing a social order that connects convicts to cycles of social and psychical despair that have devastating consequences for others. There is a profound paradox at the core of penal governance. On the one hand, treatment experts condemn power and control as social practices for men. On the other hand, they downplay the unprincipled practices of power and control by some of their own penal agents, and emphasize individual responsibility and self-management, which deflects attention from the cultural and practical complexities of men's lives and reifies the same masculine value system that the program is intended to transform. Efforts to change men must also account for the economic, social, and cultural realities of their lives. Viable alternatives to prevailing models of manhood, in turn, must reconcile social structures and social circumstances with new and positive forms of male embodiment, masculine psyche, and racial identity.

The men in my study did not usually think of themselves as psychologically different from normal men who shared similar class and race positions, except to identify their acute physical and sexual violence and neglect as problematic. Their designation as sex offenders ignores the fact that other men were the primary target of violence for nearly all of them. Only later in life did the men add sexual assault to their bodily based practices and rituals of violence. Unfortunately, the absence of historical and biographical contexts precludes treatment regimes from exploring the crucial links between race- and class-based experiences and sexual violence against women, and between sexual offending and extensive carceral sentences for non-sexual crimes within gendered and gendering male prisons. Consequently, intra-male violence should be revisited and highlighted as a site for treatment intervention and, for that matter, as a site of study for understanding sexual violence against women. For example, Michel, who has thirteen assault convictions against men, has still not learned to cope with bodily based manhood and relationships with men:

> The first time I even heard the word empathy was when I came [to treatment groups]. I don't know if I learned it or if it just came out of me naturally, somewhere. But today my fantasies and thoughts of friends on the outside are almost always with women. [*Pauses.*] I still have violent tendencies towards men. I don't like men. I hate living with men. I generally don't like men. I'd rather just crawl up in a little *hole* for the rest of my life and avoid all the men that I know that I'm going to meet down the road – which isn't good – I guess I got to change that attitude, but I just generally don't like men. I don't like men and never will.

Men's Social Powerlessness and Gendered Hierarchies of Power

These life stories emphasize that gendering practices are responses to socio-structural circumstances. Feminist writers grapple with the problem of praxis and many suggest that improving women's socio-economic status relative to men may help ameliorate rape victimization (e.g., Martin, Vieratis, and Britto 2006; MacKinnon 1981, 1983; Brownmiller 1991; Marcus 1992). I think that this is true. But my data also suggest that if men's powerlessness and pain are implicated in stranger rape, then feminist and critical scholarship must address the social inequality associated with working class, racialized, and disenfranchised men as well as women. Rather than lobbying for more state coercion and control, which invariably targets more and more poor, young, and racialized men, feminist thought and praxis should expand its scope to include men victimized by violence, racism, sexual assault, and poverty. This approach prioritizes the materiality of class- and race-based oppression (e.g., Hennessey 1992; Snider 2006) and argues for alliances and net-works with grassroots organizations that struggle against structural barriers that sustain all sex/gender hierarchies. Rather than reforming criminal law and punishing more men for sexual offences, this study suggests that there is a need to improve the material, social, and cultural opportunities of marginalized male citizens, increase their access to law, status, and income, and decrease their resort to violence. If men's lived experiences of structural and social powerlessness over-determine the use of bodily based physicality as a masculinizing practice, then why would more punishment work as a strategy to protect women and children? The fact that all participants in my study learned to mobilize subjective experiences of pain and punishment as ways of performing gender should temper the popular and political calls to further amplify sex offenders' suffering and cultural ostracizing (e.g., Lippke 2003; Pratt et al. 2005). Indeed, when hurting others including women is an antidote for men's pain, then the complicity of penal authorities in giving men sole responsibility for their actions by silencing their victimization and adding to their pain through punishment is misplaced and potentially counterproductive to preventing future victimization.

Following years of activism and advocacy by Aboriginal women and feminists, penal policy makers acknowledge that gender and social context are relevant to understanding the needs of female convicts who suffer from sexual and physical abuse and poverty (e.g., Dell and Boe 2000; Hannah-Moffat 2006). However, this is not the case for male prisoners, let alone sex offenders (Seymour 2003, 48; Whitehead 2005). While some research notes the benefits of rehabilitative programs for sex offenders on women and children (Evans and Wallace 2008; O'Leary 1998, 29), no one seems to know how to provide masculinizing alternatives to male prisoners. Indeed, the trend over the past two decades has been for prison administrators to limit penal subjects' access to forms of social and intellectual capital. At the time of writing, the rehabilitation and training arm of Canadian penitentiaries was CORCAN Industries, a partnership between CSC and private sector industries (Delaney 2010). CORCAN generates profits for CSC, but it almost always trains prisoners in obsolete factory-style assembly work that is steadily being outsourced as piecemeal labour (Delaney 2010). This is not the kind of work training that leads to stable futures or enhances different forms of masculinity for prisoners. Canadian and American penal authorities, for example, have eliminated opportunities for free post-secondary college and university education (Duguid 2000; Page 2004), reduced grants that fund legal challenges and defend human rights (Belbot 2004), restricted access to recreation, entertainment, and diversion programs (Lippke 2003), and imposed limitations on prisoners' purchase and use of personal computers. The penal trend is towards forced idleness and warehousing of convicts; the CSC spends less than 4 per cent of its $1.8 billion budget on education and rehabilitation programs (Delaney 2010). Even traditional vocational training that provides prisoners with opportunities to link themselves to a working-class provider type of masculinity has been supplanted by cognitive-behavioural training. Canadian penitentiaries once provided male prisoners with the means to learn a trade in welding, plumbing, bricklaying, automechanics, and stone masonry, but do not do so anymore. Recently, CSC announced its plan to eliminate agribusiness operations at its six minimum-security prison farms. Farm closures, they say, will enable prisoners to learn more marketable skills associated with CORCAN's "furniture-making" assembly approach to work and working (Delaney 2010). In light of my research findings that show the connection between abject employment prospects and the decision to rape, a policy priority for CSC should be to reintroduce and fund post-secondary education along with genuine marketable forms of vocational training to all male prisoners, including those who have been convicted of violent crimes.

Finally, these life stories suggest that feminist and critical writers and activists should include men in their research agendas by developing the same contextually sensitive approach they use to understand women in order to illuminate how choices are made, and to understand that they are not always made in circumstances of one's choosing (cf. Comack 1996). This might include studies that emphasize the role of family dynamics and peer groups in the formation of rapists; the intersubjective character of rape and its power effects and resistances on men and women; the different class dynamics, gendering relationships, and forms of masculinity associated with stranger rape committed by the powerful; and the different cultural processes, gendering relationships, and forms of racialization associated with the making of rapists and the determination of rape victims.

I end this book with a short epilogue: a continuation of Bear's life story. After reading so many grim and gruesome accounts of violence, shame, and guilt, and after considering the paradoxes of penal governance as they relate to sex offenders and individuals' responsibility for their own actions, I leave you with a compelling story of how change can happen in spite of long-term incarceration. By giving Bear the last words, I want to underscore that prisoners' life stories also reveal the possibility of life-affirming practices. These narratives need not index futility. They may countenance the resolutions to past deeds and the reconciliations of past relationships with hope for the future in a reoccurring world of pain and fear.

Epilogue

The previous chapter began with a description of Brian's solitary struggle to endure, survive, and prevail over the effects of prison on his soul. I end this book with thoughts from Bear's journey towards peacemaking. I maintain that positive changes that transpire in prison and prisoners occur mostly in spite of prison. Most of the men, including Brian and Bear, were encouraged to recreate themselves while behind prison walls. Their stories, however, also question the character of penal governance with its technical assessments, medical diagnoses, psychological programs, risk management techniques, and increased punishments. The men in my study had to set aside claims to their own injury and injustice as conditions for their betterment. Prison, they say, deepened their pain and powerlessness and reiterated and reinforced the very same hegemonic masculinity that facilitated rape. Despite years and years of imprisonment for Brian, Bear, and others, their will to change, repent, forgive, love, and survive – rather than be broken by penal power – evinces a positive quality of spirit. They continue to try to experience themselves as connected to others and find an inherent goodness in human nature despite the horrors of their actions and the violence of their lives. Nowhere is this better illustrated then in Bear's quiet walk along what he calls the "Red Road" to redemption.

Bear's Story Continues

In prison, nobody knows you. They saw you, but they never knew the person. I never expressed my thoughts to anybody. Every time I went to some kind of social or powwow, I would sit in the corner. I was invisible. Just sit there with bitterness in my face. It's amazing – the turnaround?

That it happened. I'm thankful to my daughter Glenda for that. When I was in Prince Albert [Prison], I would always think about how my daughter was. How she looked. What kind of person she was. I would wonder if she would like me. If she would call me "dad." Then it would end: "No she wouldn't like me because I'm a sex offender." In 1994, I was working in the metal shop in Prince Albert. And somebody kept telling me about this guy that was a rat. And every day I would really hate this guy. And so I went in the metal shop. I started making this shank. I was working on it for four days. And this guy I was working with took it to the big sheer, chopped it all up. And he said, "Listen, someday you'll get out, but do you think that guy's worth what you were going to do to him?" And it was a week later. Somebody said, "You have a call." I dialled the number. It was my daughter Glenda. I was just in awe and didn't know what to say. I hadn't seen her for twenty-five years when she was six months old. She told me how she found out that I was her dad. She asked what have I been doing in jail. I said, "Oh, just feeling lost, getting lost in drugs, and getting drunk – hiding you know."

After that I went into my cell and thought about all the things I wanted to be. I looked at why I'm here. I'm not going nowhere. I'm just being warehoused. I'm not caring for myself. And I said to myself, "I don't want my daughter to see me like this. I don't want her to know me as this person." So I started working on myself. Going to school, programs. I think to meet her and my grandkids, that was the best thing that ever happened to me. I have five. I use her to inspire me to get to the next level. I've really found it hard to talk to her because she was sexually abused when she was thirteen. It was her stepdad. I was uncomfortable because I was a sex offender too. I was afraid to say the wrong thing to her. I told her, "Talk to somebody." I told her, "Don't do something stupid. Talk to your mom – express yourself."

I remember in 1995, when I was leaving PA [Prince Albert], that was the first time I ever got hugged in – man, [*pauses*] years. This friend of mine pulled me into his arms. And I wasn't expecting it. That fear just shot through my mind – the fear of somebody touching from my sexual abuse. There's always something that will remind me of it, like guys here joke around about homo sex. It makes me really uncomfortable because of what happened. And I get all confused about whether I'm like that or not. I get all angry to shut it off. Sometimes, I'm laying on my back [sleeping] and I'm laying there and I see this image of my uncle coming down. And as he gets closer, he pins me, you know, and I can't move and I can't yell. I can't open my eyes. I can't do nothing. This happened in PA. And I woke up screaming. Guys come over and asked me, "Why are you yelling?" I told them I was having a nightmare. It happened last year. I was just laying there – I didn't even see him coming. And [*pauses*] my eyes – I was already sweating. I sat on the bed. It was, like, about three in the morning, and I turned on the light and sat there. I was scared to go back to sleep. I never talk about it. I never really express it – what it really does to me. It happened here a couple of times after we talked. I was just, like, my sheets were soaking. I had to go do my laundry, wash my sheets and my blanket 'cause it was just soaked. I get scared. I get distant from people when that happens. I put up a front like everything is okay. Today, when somebody wants to give me something, I can't. Someone giving me something – that's what led off to my sexual abuse. I think they want, you know. The feeling, that fear all comes back to me. It was okay for me to give, but when somebody offers me something, I could never take it.

And when I got here, I had to go down and see the Elder. And I seen this big, big man. Weighed about 290 pounds. He says, "Hi, my name is Bernie," and he pulled me in, and man! This guy just grabbed me and hugged me and I just freeze. And he said, "you better get used to that. You're going to be getting a lot of that." And I'm just sweating. After a while, the hugs started coming naturally. People coming up to me and calling me a brother. I started thinking, this is the kind of man my grandpa was – this friendly, caring, positive person, always accepting somebody. That's the man I want to be. Like, today, I'll be sitting playing a game, and somebody will always come up to me and they have to *touch* me. For some reason, they have to touch me. Before? I would just freeze. Now, I've turned it into a positive – this person wants to be acknowledged. Last night, Harvey comes over, and he's like this [*holds his arms for a hug*]. He said, "I want attention. I want a hug." He puts his arms around me. He hugged me like, for thirty seconds!

I'm still two people – the person that hides and the person that's honest and open. It's still a struggle not to go back to that person that holds stuff in. I've been doing that all my life. I'm much more aware of myself – my thinking, my feelings, why I'm feeling negative. I've got to be aware of that and somehow express what I'm feeling – talk about my sexual abuse, talk about my childhood.

There's a link between my childhood and my victims. Remember, I had that little glimpse? I knew it was wrong. But the stronger urge of seeing what happens as a child – having no respect for that person's feelings, never thinking about her feelings. Not even seeing that person as a person. And my sexual abuse played a part in it. I didn't go to [my uncle's gang] until after it happened. Then, boom, I had no second thoughts. That was my way of numbing what I was feeling. And I got addicted to hiding what I was feeling. It carried me wherever I wanted to go.

Maybe one day I'll see myself as a victim. Right now, I'm starting to think about the person I hurt – the main victim. I've been too much into myself, and saying, "poor me." Now, I'm trying to be aware of the next person's feelings. Coming to programs, I started putting a body and face to that person. That hurt. It's like putting my mom's body and person there. It's in writing actually that I have no sympathy for my mom. I was hurt by that actually. [*Pauses.*] I told them I left my mom because I couldn't stand seeing her in pain. It's not because I didn't have any sympathy. They try to compare my mom and my victim – that I have no empathy for my victim, and I have no empathy for my mom, so I did this. It hurt me. I guess I have to express it better. I couldn't help my mother. I couldn't support her. In this program, I wrote a letter to my mom expressing how much I missed her, and I'm sorry that I wasn't there for her, and that I loved her.

I felt hurt when somebody told me one time, "If your mom had loved you so much she would never have put you in that position." That really hurt. 'Cause mom was afraid. Mom was helpless. That was the only way for her to try to protect herself. And I go through fears and stuff watching a violent, violent show, you know? Before, I just boom. Like a switch – you shut it off, don't even acknowledge it. [Now] somebody beating up someone's mom. I go through all that. All the feelings that I used to go through. I can still see myself crying, hanging on to mom, me and mom both crying. She's taking off my clothes – I got blood all over myself – and I can hear her justifying, "Daddy is just drunk. He'll be okay when he's sober." That's what she was always telling me. We would both be afraid. And, you know, we would fall asleep together. Wake up – mom's got a fat lip or a black eye.

Today I care about [my sister] Rose. I never cared about her before. And I care about my brother too, which I never done before. I phone him and I tell him, "I love you bro." I worry about all my family. I told the facilitators that for my family to carry on, to listen to me talk about this, this, and this – they have nobody to support them, to listen to them, to talk to them because, they never express themselves – they haven't learned that. They're just going to stuff all these feelings. You have to practise expressing yourself. My family gets all screwed up and confused when they try to express. But, if you took a cup and put some booze in it and gave it to my sister, you know, "express yourself" – she will. But she will express herself in a very verbal, angry way: "I hate you. I don't like you. I don't like what you did to mom. I don't want to see you any more." That's how they know how to express themselves. That's how they bury their pain is through alcohol. I wish it wasn't. I want to be able to talk to her, but I can't. All I can do is write letters. It's up to her to change. I'm not going to preach. I'm just going to try to make her see something that I wish she could see and grasp on to. She's totally ignored what happened to both of our sisters, because, alcohol took both of my sisters. Alcohol killed my sisters. And she used alcohol to cover that up – her feelings, her thoughts, her hurt, you know? I guess I'm thankful to jail for that. I wish they knew what I know. I wished they believed in themselves. "It's best that it stays buried" – that's what my sister says.

My dad died last year. They asked me if I wanted to go see him before he died. That was the first time I hugged him. I was expecting him to push me away. I used to say that I would never hurt for dad when he died – that I hate him. But I didn't hate him. I hated his behaviour – what he did to mom. But I didn't hate that person. I wanted his love. I wanted to know if he really did care for me. I think he did. He just didn't know how to do it because he probably had a dysfunctional life. It seems like I'm making excuses for him, but that's the only way I can look at it. I'm not going to go with this regret, and that regret, but accept that he was in my life for a while.

When he did accept me, two weeks before he died, it was like this door just opened for me. I didn't want to hate him no more. I felt that acceptance, and, man, I've always looked for that with him. I knew how it would feel when I got it, and it felt like *wow* – it was like the day was just clear. I'm looking out onto this ocean. I'm just smiling. And man, I was on a high all through the journey back. I knew I was going back to prison, but I didn't let that get me down. I thought, "I got dad. Dad accepted me. [*Whispers.*] Dad [*pauses*] loves me." I had all these thoughts going through my head in the car going back to prison. I wanted to look after him now and spend time with him. I wanted to help him, sit there, talk to him, listen to him, you know? And then he passed away. I felt really hurt that [CSC] wouldn't let me go to his burial. They said I hadn't earned the right. I didn't get to say goodbye. It's kinda hard because these people are trying to teach you about showing respect for others. [*Pauses.*] I'm trying really hard to think something good about dad – what he done for me. [*Pauses.*] You know he had my dog killed? [*Pauses.*] I couldn't come up with anything but that he provided for the family. Dad was a good worker.

The Elder said dad hung on to say goodbye, and for me to be happy. I hurt for two weeks. It took a lot of energy to hold back the tears. Finally, one night I just closed my door. I put my head in the pillow, and I started crying. I would say, about a week later, I started using that as how my victim felt. I started using that pain, that confusion, that hurt, that anger, the frustration, the hate and – she probably felt worse than this. They probably felt worse than I did. How did *they* get rid of it? I could never imagine. I said to myself, "I killed that person's spirit," because I know it killed mine for a while. That's the worst thing you can do to a person. Nobody deserves that. And then I started feeling bad because, I've done it. I can't excuse what I've done. It will always be a part of my life until the day I die …

I came here for me. Not for anybody else. I came here to search within myself for why I was this person, and to work on myself. I used to think I was going crazy, you know? I used to think that [*exhales*] I was unloveable. I was this worthless person, you know. And this program has made me see that I'm not this worthless person. The program has given me something to look forward to with myself. Making drums, being nice to people, I figured I'd never do it. I have lots to learn. I still have a lot of hurt, a lot of anger, and a long way to go.

Actually, it wasn't until I came here that I really started thinking about it – this was just three months ago. I was down in the Sweat Lodge. I started thinking, "this is my culture – this is what feeds my spirit. This is what I need. This is what I believe in strongly." When I'm feeling down, I sing a spiritual song. I go down there to think, and all the problems I have just boom – they're lifted off. And then I start praying to the great grand-mothers and grandfathers and four sacred directions, and the Creator. Thanking him for the life that I have today – you know:

Bear pauses for a moment and then softly chants his thanks:

For the fresh water, for my mind, so I can think of the good things in life. I thank him for my eyes, so I can see the good things in life. I thank him for my ears, so I can hear the good things in life. I thank him for my voice, so I can talk the good things in life. I thank him for my arms and fingers so I can touch the good things in life. I thank him for my health, my body, my legs, so I may walk the Red Road. And I thank him for the four legged, for the ones that slither and crawl, the ones that don't see, the ones that sacri-fice their lives for us so that we may have nourishment. I thank him for my daughters, my common-law, their friendship, and yours, guys, the friends I have today. And for helping make me aware of my negatives, my posi-tives, and somebody else.

APPENDIX Participants' Age, Race, Employment and Marital Status, and Prison History

Name	Age	Race*	Job at Index Offence(s)	All Adult Convictions for Violence-Related Offences. Current Offences Underlined	Highest Grade	Sentence***	Years Served in Current Sentence	vs. Total Years for All Convictions	Marital+ at Index Offence
Brian	32	A	paper route	1st Murder	9	Life 25	16	16	B/U
Harvey	23	W	unemployed cement finisher	Sexual Assault/weapon Assault w/weapon**	8	5 yr 6 mo	4	4	B/U
Marvin	44	R	mill worker	Sexual Assaults, Sexual Assault/weapon, Robbery	12	DO	8	8	C/L
Cam	36	W	auto/pawn	Bank Robbery, Murder	8	Life 25	6	>15	M
Charlie	32	W	manual labourer	Robbery/violence** Sexual Assault, Sexual Assault, Murder	7	Life 14	7	>12	B/U
Kerry	51	W	hospital orderly	Armed Robbery** Murder** Rape, Indecent Assault, Kidnapping Sexual Assault/weapon	9	DO	9	>30	G/F
Simp.	34	A	never employed	Weapons, Agg. Sexual Assault, Manslaughter	7	15 yr	7	>8	C/L
James	35	W	never employed	Indecent Assault, Murder	8	Life 25	16	>18	S
Paul	38	A	stable hand /welder	Rape, Kidnapping, Assault/bodily harm, Unlawful Confinement, Attempt Murder	7	Life 7	10	>17	B/U

APPENDIX (continued)

Name	Age	Race*	Job at Index Offence(s)	All Adult Convictions for Violence-Related Offences. Current Offences Underlined	Highest Grade	Sentence***	Years Served in Current Sentence vs. Total Years for All Convictions		Marital+ at Index Offence
Paddy	39	W	unemployed labourer/ logger	Murder, Attempt Murder, Rape, Gross Indecency	11	Life 25	16	16	S
Bob	23	W	unemployed car lot boy	Robbery** Murder	9	Life 10	6	6	B/U
Michel	26	W	unemployed (in prison)	Manslaughter** Sexual Assault/ weapon	7	17 yr 9 mo	6	>9	S
Fred	40	A	p/t drywall delivery	Murder, Attempt Murder	11	Life 15	18	18	G/F
Bear	42	A	unemployed	Robbery, Rape, Rape	6	DO	16	>20	C/L

*   A=Aboriginal, W=White, R=Racialized Non-Aboriginal

**   Male victim

***   Life 25, Life 15: In any life sentence Canada's judges must designate the minimum number of years to be served before parole eligibility

        DO=Dangerous Offender (indeterminate sentence)

\+   Marital Status at Current Offence: M=Married, C/L= Common Law, G/F= Steady Girlfriend, S=Single, B/U= Recent Relationship Break-Up

Notes

Foreword

1 Personal communication, memories of Kevin Bonnycastle by her friend and neighbour Alison MacNeil, and from Mira MacNeil, neighbour and friend, 7 June 2011.
2 See for example Bonnycastle and Villebrun 2011.
3 See for example Bonnycastle 2009.
4 See for example Bonnycastle 2000. See also Bonnycastle and Rigakos 1998.
5 Personal communication, Catherine Shields to Lawrence Buhagiar, 20 June 2011.
6 Personal communication, Lawrence Buhagiar to John McMullan, 20 June 2011.
7 Personal communication, Lawrence Buhagiar to John McMullan, 20 June 2011.

1. The Subject of Stranger Rape and Stranger Rapists

1 "The support of the Correctional Service of Canada is gratefully acknowledged, however, the reported findings and their interpretation do not necessarily reflect the official policy of the Correctional Service of Canada."
2 By *relative stranger*, I mean a woman relatively or completely unknown to the perpetrator prior to his index offence. The perpetrator had insignificant social or verbal contact with the woman, although he may have known her by sight or hearsay. Relative stranger contrasts with acquaintances, casual acquaintances, or family members whom the perpetrator knows as social subjects.
3 While the idea originates in (or perhaps, was merely appropriated by) clinical practices, most people today "get to know someone" by exchanging memories of "growing up." In this manner, we try to convey to others how and why we became who we are. When tethered to institutions of social

control and conditions of freedom, however, this practice becomes oppressive to the extent that the storyteller's narrative and the listener's interpretation are restricted and over-determined by the "true" discourse and theory decreed by contemporary psycho-medical penal experts.

4 I use the word "con text" to denote the original words, grammar, and intonation of my participants in contrast to a paraphrase of their words and my own commentary.

2. The Sexual Offender: Every Man, Other Men, and Monsters

1 Sherene Razack is one exception, although she re-constructs men's reality through reading the transcripts of a murder trial. She links the killing of an Aboriginal woman by two middle-class white male university athletes to white masculine privilege, constructions of heterosexual masculinity, and dehumanizing discourses of Aboriginal women as "licentious squaws" (2002, 135).

2 One exception Mardorossian overlooks is Ann Cahill's *Rethinking Rape* (2001).

3 Subjectification is Michel Foucault's term. It conveys "the making" of subjects (see Foucault 1980, 117). Subjectification is the processes or practices of power, such as cultural and legal categories, that bind human beings to subject-positions and constructed identities that help render people into individuals. Foucault defines subjectification as "subject to someone else by control or dependence," or "tied to [one's] own identity by a conscience or self-knowledge" (1983, 212). Therefore, gendered subjectification refers to social practices that tie us to feminine and masculine identities.

3. Of Mountain Goats and Rabbits: The Penal Context

1 I gave each participant a pseudonym or nickname that represents a supportive person or element from their past or present but does not reveal their identity.

2 A PPG or penile plethysmograph is a technology that purports to scientifically measure relative sexual arousal to a range of visual and auditory sexual stimuli from consensual to non-consensual sex and across different age and gender categories.

4. Beautiful Baby Boys: Gender Relationships

1 In addition to reproducing extended passages spoken by my participants, I incorporate many of the men's own words and phrases into my own com-

mentary. I use double quotation marks to denote that those words are the actual words used by that participant.

2 I use the term Aboriginal to refer to every man who identified himself as "Native."

3 I gave all people in the participants' narratives pseudonyms to preserve their anonymity.

4 I have omitted Marvin's race/ethnicity to preserve his anonymity.

5 According to Marvin's files, at the time of trial, his father was convicted for the historical sexual abuse of his biological sister, Marvin's aunt, which occurred over a ten-year span that included Marvin's birth year. Marvin recalls that his mother sometimes referred to this particular aunt as "your mother." This aunt also bought Marvin a car on his sixteenth birthday. He wonders today if he is the offspring of his father's sexual abuse of his sister, and subsequently bore the wrath of his mother's humiliation and his father's shame.

6 Women's objectification and reduction to body parts is not always culturally produced. Women's legs and feet became the object of Marvin's erotic interest during his adolescence, almost by accident, after his family moved into a business district. He continued to spend time alone in his basement bedroom, watching the world through a window. Business-attired women walked by regularly, but from his ground-level basement, Marvin could only see and fantasize about their legs and high-heeled shoes. In Marvin's case, the objectification of women's body parts is an artefact of his location in time and space.

7 I designate the American state penitentiary where Kerry served time as Arkansas to help protect Kerry's anonymity.

8 Simpson's father has agreed to participate in Simpson's Shame Feast after his son's release from prison. The traditional Aboriginal ceremony will involve Simpson, along with his family, apologizing to his victim's family and her entire community during a public gathering.

9 To protect James' anonymity, I have substituted Poland for his adoptive parents' actual Eastern European country of origin.

5. Good Human Beings Doing Horrible Things: Stranger Rape as a Gendering Practice

1 According to the police report in Brian's file, his victim's mother heard her daughter scream once. She immediately hung up the phone and called the police. Seven years later, she and her husband sent Brian a letter in prison telling him that they forgave him.

2 Details of Marvin's arrest and conviction are omitted.

3 Richard von Krafft-Ebing put forth this still-unchallenged observation in *Psychopathia sexualis* (1885). He wrote: "The presumption of a murder out of lust is always given when injuries of the genitals are found, the character and extent of which are such as could not be explained by merely a brutal attempt at coitus; and still more, when the body had been opened, or part (intestines, genitals) torn out and are wanting."

4 One of Scully's research subjects admits that he routinely stole to get money. He recounts threatening a potential female robbery victim by brandishing a knife. She was pregnant, and told him that "she would do anything if he didn't harm her." He says: "I wasn't thinking about sex. But when she said she would do anything not to get hurt … I thought, 'why not.'"

7. Breaking Out: Challenging Hegemonic Manhood in Prison

1 "Christina" is a pseudonym for a clinical psychologist affiliated with the Intensive Sex Offender Treatment program.

Bibliography

Abracen, J., D. Mailloux, R. Serin, C. Cousineau, P. Malcolm, and J. Looman. 2004. "A Model for the Assessment of Static and Dynamic Factors in Sex Offenders." *Journal of Sex Research* 41 (4): 321–28.

Adamoski, R., D. Chunn, and R. Menzies. 2002. "Rethinking the Citizen in Canadian Social History." In *Contesting Canadian Citizenship*, edited by R. Adamoski, D. Chunn, and R. Menzies, 12–41. Peterborough: Broadview Press.

Adler, C., and K. Polk. 1996. "Masculinity and Child Homicide." *British Journal of Criminology* 36 (3): 396–411.

Anderson, I., and K. Doherty. 2008. *Accounting for Rape: Psychology, Feminism, and Discourse Analysis in the Study of Sexual Violence*. New York: Routledge.

Andrews, D.A., J. Bonta, and J.S. Wormith. 2006. "The Recent Past and Near Future of Risk and/or Need Assessment." *Crime Delinquency* 52 (1): 7–27.

Andrews, D.A., J. Bonta, and R.D. Hoge. 1990. "Classification for Effective Rehabilitation: Rediscovering Psychology." *Criminal Justice and Behaviour* 17: 19–52.

Archambault, J. 1938. *Royal Commission Report on Penal Reform in Canada*. Ottawa: Queen's Printer.

Ashe, M., and N. Cahn. 1994. "Child Abuse: A Problem for Feminist Theory." In *The Public Nature of Private Violence: The Discovery of Domestic Child Abuse*, edited by M. Albertson Fineman and R. Mykitiuk, 166–95. Routledge: New York.

Atmore, C. 1999. "Victims, Backlash, and Radical Feminist Theory." In *New Versions of Victims: Feminists Struggle with the Concept*, edited by S. Lamb, 183–211. New York: New York University Press.

Auburn, T., and S. Lea. 2003. "Doing Cognitive Distortions: A Discursive
    Psychology Analysis of Sex Offender Treatment Talk." *British Journal
    of Social Psychology* 32 (2): 281–98.

Bar On, Bat-Ami. 1993. "Marginality and Epistemic Privilege." In *Feminist
    Epistemologies*, edited by L. Alcoff and E. Potter, 83–100. New York:
    Routledge.

Barrett, K., and W. George. 2004. *Race, Culture, Psychology, and Law*. Thousand
    Oaks: Sage Publications.

Belbot, B. 2004. "Report on the Prison Litigation Reform Act: What Have
    the Courts Decided So Far?" *The Prison Journal* 84 (3): 290–316.

Bennice, J.A., and P.A. Resick. 2003. "Marital Rape: History, Research,
    and Practice." *Trauma, Violence & Abuse* 4: 228–46.

Blanchette, K. 1996. *Sex Offender Assessment, Treatment and Recidivism:
    A Literature Review*. Research Division: Correctional Services Canada.

Boe, R., L. Motiuk, and M. Nafekh. 2004. *An Examination of the Average Length
    of Prison Sentence for Adult Men in Canada: 1994 to 2002*. Research Branch,
    Correctional Service of Canada.

Bonnycastle, Kevin. 2000. "Rape Uncodified: Reconsidering Bill C-49
    Amendments to Canadian Sexual Assault Laws." In *Law as a Gendering
    Practice*, edited by D. Chunn and D. Lacombe, 60–78. Don Mills: Oxford
    University Press.

– 2009. "Not the Usual Suspects: The Obfuscation of Political Economy and
    Race in CSI." In *The CSI Effect: Television, Crime and Governance*, edited by
    M. Byers and V.M. Johnson. Toronto: Lexington Books.

– 2011. "Injecting Risk into Prison Sentences: A Quantitative Analysis of a
    Prison-Driven Survey to Measure HCV/HIV Seroprevalence, Risk
    Practices, and Viral Testing at One Canadian Male Federal Prison."
    The Prison Journal 9 (3): 325–46.

Bonnycastle, Kevin, and G. Rigakos, eds. 1998. *Unsettling Truths: Battered
    Women, Policy, Politics, and Contemporary Research in Canada*. Vancouver:
    Collective Press.

Bonta, J. 2002. "Official Risk Assessment Guidelines for Selection and Use."
    Criminal Justice and Behaviour 29 (4): 355–79.

Bordo, S. 1999. *The Male Body: A New Look at Men in Public and Private*. New
    York: Farrar, Strauss, and Giroux.

Bosworth, M. 2007. "Creating the Responsible Prisoner: Federal Admissions
    and Orientation Package." *Punishment and Society* 9 (1): 67–85.

Bourke, J. 2007. *Rape: Sex Violence History*. Berkley: Counterpoint.

Boyd, S.B. 1997. "Challenging the Public/Private Divide: An Overview."
    In *Challenging the Public/Private Divide: Feminism, Law, and Public Policy*,
    edited by S.B. Boyd, 3–33. Toronto: University of Toronto Press.

Boyle, C. 1984. *Sexual Assault*. Toronto: Carswell.

Brennan, S., and A. Taylor-Butts. 2008. *Sexual Assault in Canada 2004*. Ottawa: Canadian Centre for Justice Statistics Profile Series (Catalogue No. 85F0033M-No 19).

Brown, W. 1995. *States of Injury: Power and Freedom in Late Modernity*. Princeton: Princeton University Press.

Brownmiller, S. 1975. *Against Our Will: Men, Women and Rape*. New York: Simon and Schuster.

– 1991. *Against Our Will: Men, Women and Rape*. Updated edition. London: Penguin Books.

Burdon, W., and C. Gallagher. 2002. "Coercion and Sex Offenders: Controlling Sex Offending Behaviour through Incapacitation and Treatment." *Criminal Justice and Behaviour* 29 (1): 87–109.

Butler, J. 1990. *Gender Trouble: Feminism and the Subversion of Identity*. New York: Routledge.

– 1992. *Gender Trouble: Feminism and the Subversion of Identity*. Updated edition. New York: Routledge.

– 1993a. "Imitation and Gender Subordination." In *Lesbian and Gay Reader*, edited by H. Abelove, M.A. Barale, and D. Halperin, 307–20. New York: Routledge.

– 1993b. *Bodies That Matter: On the Discursive Limits of "Sex."* New York: Routledge.

Cahill, A.J. 2001. *Rethinking Rape*. Ithaca: Cornell University Press.

Cain, M. 1993. "Realism, Feminism, Methodology, and Law." *International Journal of the Sociology of Law* 14 (3/4): 255–67.

Cameron, D., and E. Frazer. 1987. *The Lust to Kill: A Feminist Investigation of Sexual Murder*. Oxford: Polity Press.

Campbell, A. 1993. *Men, Women, and Aggression*. New York: Basic Books.

Caputi, J. 1987. *The Age of Sex Crime*. Bowling Green, Ohio: Bowling Green State University.

Carbado, D., and M. Gulati. 2003. "The Law and Economics of Critical Race Theory." *Yale Law Journal* 112: 1757.

Carrington, K., and P. Watson 1996. Policing Sexual Violence: Feminism, Criminal Justice, and Governmentality." *International Journal of Sociology* 24: 253–72.

Chamallas, M. 2005. "Lucky: The Sequel." *Indiana Law Journal* 80.

Chan, H., and K. Heide. 2009. "Sexual Homicide: A Synthesis of the Literature." *Trauma, Violence, and Abuse* 10 (1): 31–54.

Chunn, D. 2004. Written comments to author, January 2004.

Chunn, D., and D. Lacombe. 2000. *Law as a Gendering Practice*. Don Mills: Oxford University Press.

Clark, L., and D. Lewis. 1977. *Rape: The Price of Coercive Sexuality*. Toronto: Women's Press.

Cohen, J.M. 1994. "Private Violence and Public Obligation." In *The Public Nature of Private Violence: The Discovery of Domestic Abuse*, edited by M. Fineman and R. Mykitiuk, 349–81. New York: Routledge.

Comack, E. 1996. *Women in Trouble: Connecting Women's Law Violations to Their Histories of Abuse*. Halifax: Fernwood Publishing.

Comack, E., and G. Balfour. 2004. *The Power to Criminalize: Violence, Inequality and the Law*. Halifax: Fernwood Publishing.

Connell, R. 1987. *Gender and Power: Society, the Person, and Sexual Politics*. Stanford: Stanford University Press.

– 1995. *Masculinities*. Berkley: University of California Press.

– 2000. *The Men and the Boys*. Sydney: Allen & Unwin.

– 2002. "On Hegemonic Masculinity and Violence." *Theoretical Criminology* 6 (1): 89–99.

Connell, R., and J. Messerschmidt. 2005. "Hegemonic Masculinity: Rethinking the Concept." *Gender and Society* 19 (6): 829–59.

Corkel, J.D. 2003. "Embedded Surveillance and the Gendering of Punishment." *Journal of Contemporary Ethnography* 32: 41–76.

Correctional Service of Canada. 2006. *The Changing Federal Offender Population: Profiles and Forecasts* 2006. Ottawa: Research Branch CSC.

Cowburn, M. 1998. "A Man's World: Gender Issues in Working with Male Sex Offenders in Prison." *The Howard Journal* 37 (3): 234–51.

– 2005. "Hegemony and Discourse: Reconstruing the Male Sex Offender and Sexual Coercion by Men." *Sexualities, Evolution, and Gender* 7 (3): 215–31.

Cowburn, M., and L. Dominelli. 2001. "Masking Hegemonic Masculinity: Reconstructing the Paedophile as a Dangerous Stranger." *British Journal of Social Work* 3 (1): 399–414.

Crenshaw, K. 1994. "Mapping the Margins: Intersectionality, Identity Politics, and Violence Against Women of Color." In *The Public Nature of Private Violence: The Discovery of Domestic Abuse*, edited by M. Fineman and R. Mykitiuk, 93–118. New York: Routledge.

Crooks, C., G. Goodall, R. Hughes, P. Jaffe, and L. Baker. 2007. "Engaging Men and Boys in Preventing Violence Against Women: Applying a Cognitive-Behavioural Model." *Violence Against Women* 13: 217–39.

Culhane, D., and R. Taylor. 2000. "Theory and Practice: Clinical Law and Aboriginal People." In *Law as a Gendering Practice*, edited by D. Chunn and D. Lacombe, 120–37. Don Mills: Oxford University Press.

Curran, D.J., and C. Renzetti. 2004. *Theories of Crime*. Needham Heights: Allyn & Bacon.

Currie, D. 1998. "The Criminalization of Violence Against Women: Feminist Demands and Patriarchal Accommodations." In *Unsettling Truths: Battered Women, Policy, Politics, and Contemporary Research in Canada*, edited by K. Bonnycastle and G. Rigakos, 41–51. Vancouver: Collective Press.

Curthoys, J. 1997. *Feminist Amnesia: The Wake of Women's Liberation*. New York: Routledge.

Darville, R. 1995. "Literacy, Experience, Power." In *Knowledge, Experience, and Ruling Relations: Studies in the Social Organization of Knowledge*, edited by M. Campbell and A. Manicom, 249–61. Toronto: University of Toronto Press.

Davis, Angela. 1981. *Women, Race, and Class*. New York: Random House.

de Carvalho Figueiredo, D. 2001. "Victims and Villains: Gender Representations, Surveillance and Punishment in the Judicial Discourse on Rape." *International Journal of Speech Language and the Law* 8 (1): 163–65.

Deer, S. 2004. "Towards an Indigenous Jurisprudence of Rape." *Kansas Journal of Law and Public Policy* 14: 121–43.

Delaney, J. 2010. "Prison Farms Close As Get Tough Crime Initiative Moves Ahead." *Epoch Times*, 26 August 2010.

Delin, B. 1978. *The Sex Offender*. Boston: Beacon Press.

Dell, C.A., and R. Boe. 2000. *An Examination of Aboriginal and Caucasian Women Offender Risk and Needs Factors*. Ottawa: CSC Research Branch.

Dubinsky, K. 1993. *Improper Advances: Rape and Heterosexual Conflict in Ontario, 1880–1929*. Chicago: University of Chicago Press.

Duguid, S. 2000. *Can Prison Work? The Prisoner as Object and Subject in Modern Corrections*. Toronto: University of Toronto Press.

Ellerby, L.A., and P. MacPherson. 2002. *Exploring the Profiles of Aboriginal Sex Offenders: Contrasting Aboriginal and Non-Aboriginal Sexual Offenders to Determine Unique Client Characteristics and Potential Implications for Sex Offender Assessment and Treatment Strategies*. Forensic Behavioural Management Clinic, Native Clan Organization, Ottawa: CSC Research Branch.

Ellison, L., and V. Munro. 2009. "Of 'Normal Sex' and 'Real Rape:' Exploring the Use of Social Sexual Scripts in (Mock) Jury Deliberation." *Social and Legal Studies* 18: 291–312.

Estrich, S. 1987. *Real Rape*. Cambridge: Harvard University Press.

Evans, T., and P. Wallace. 2008. "A Prison within a Prison? The Masculinity Narratives of Male Prisoners." *Men and Masculinities* 10 (4): 484–507.

Fauteux, G. 1956. *Report of a Committee to Inquire into the Principles and Procedures Followed in the Remission Service of the Department of Justice*. Ottawa: Queen's Printer.

Ferro, C., J. Cermele, and A. Saltsman. 2008. "Current Perceptions of Marital Rape: Some Good and Not So Good News." *Journal of Interpersonal Violence* 23 (6): 764–79.

Finch, E., and V. Munro. 2007. "The Demon Drink and the Demonized Woman: Socio-sexual Stereotypes and Perceived Attitudes in Rape Trials Involving Intoxicants." *Social and Legal Studies* 16: 591–614.

Foucault, M. 1972. *The Archaeology of Knowledge*. New York: Pantheon.

– 1979. *Discipline and Punish*. London: Peregrine Books.

– 1980. "Truth and Power." In *Power/Knowledge: Selected Interviews and Other Writings, 1972–1977*, edited by Colin Gordon. New York: Pantheon.

– 1982. "The Subject and Power." In *Michel Foucault: Beyond Structuralism and Hermeneutics*. Afterword, edited by H.L. Dreyfus and P. Rabinow, 208–26. New York: Pantheon.

– 1988. "The Ethic of Care for the Self as a Practice of Freedom." In *The Final Foucault*, edited by J. Breneau and D. Rasmussen. Cambridge: MIT Press.

– 1990. *The History of Sexuality: An Introduction, Volume 1*. New York: Vintage Books.

– 1994a. "Technologies of the Self." In *Ethics, Subjectivity and Truth: The Essential Works of Foucault, 1954–1984*, vol. 1, edited by P. Rabinow, 23–37. New York: The New Press.

– 1994b. "The Ethics of the Concern of the Self as a Practice of Freedom." In *Ethics, Subjectivity and Truth: The Essential Works of Foucault, 1954–1984*, vol. 1, edited by P. Rabinow, 281–301. New York: The New Press.

Fox, K. 1999. "Changing Violent Minds: Discursive Correction and Resistance in the Cognitive Treatment of Violent Offenders in Prison." *Social Problems* 46 (1): 88–103.

Fraink, R., J. Seefell, S. Cepress, and J. Vandello. 2008. "Prevalence and Effects of Rape Myths in Print: The Kobe Bryant Case." *Violence Against Women* 14: 287–309.

Fraser, N. 1989. *Unruly Practices: Power, Discourse and Gender in Contemporary Social Theory*. Minneapolis: University of Minnesota Press.

– 1997. *Justice Interruptus: Critical Reflections on the "Postsocialist" Condition*. New York: Routledge.

Fudge, J. 1989. "The Effects of Entrenching a Bill of Rights upon Political Discourse: Feminist Demands and Sexual Violence in Canada." *International Journal of the Sociology of Law* 17: 445–63.

Gadd, D., and S. Farrall. 2004. "Criminal Careers, Desistance and Subjectivity: Interpreting Men's Narratives of Change." *Theoretical Criminology* 8 (2): 123–56.

Garde, J. 2003. "Masculinity and Madness." *Counselling and Psychotherapy Research* 3: 6–16.

Garland, D. 1990. *Punishment and Modern Society: A Study in Social Theory.* Chicago: University of Chicago Press.

– 2001. *The Culture of Control: Crime and Social Order in Contemporary Society.* Chicago: University of Chicago Press.

Gavey, N. 2004. *Just Sex? The Cultural Scaffolding of Rape.* New York: Routlege.

Gendreau, P. 1996. "Offender Rehabilitation: What We Know and What Needs to Be Done." *Criminal Justice and Behavior* 23 (1): 144–61.

Gottfredson, S.D., and L.J. Moriarty. 2006. "Statistical Risk Assessment: Old Problems and New Applications." *Crime & Delinquency* 52 (1): 178–200.

Greer, C. 2003. *Sex Crime and the Media: Sexual Offending and the Press in a Divided Society.* Cullompton: Willan Publishing.

Griffiths, C.T., and A.J. Cunningham. 2000. *Canadian Corrections.* Scarborough: Nelson Thomson Learning.

Grosz, E. 1994. *Volatile Bodies – Toward a Corporeal Feminism.* St Leonards: Allen & Unwin.

Haaken, J. 1999. "Heretical Texts: The Courage to Heal and the Incest Survivor Movement." In *New Versions of Victims: Feminists Struggle with the Concept,* edited by S. Lamb, 13–41. New York: New York University Press.

Hacking, I. 1986. "Making Up People." In *Reconstructing Individualism: Autonomy, Individuality, and the Self in Western Thought,* edited by T. Heller, M. Sisna, and D. Wellbery, 222–36. Stanford: Stanford University Press.

– 1995. *Rewriting the Soul.* Princeton: Princeton University Press.

Hannah-Moffat, K. 2006. "Empowering Risk: The Nature of Gender-Responsive Strategies." In *Criminalizing Women,* edited by G. Balfour and E. Comack, 250–66. Halifax: Fernwood Publishing.

Hanson, K., and M. Bussiere. 1998. "Predicting Relapse: A Meta-Analysis of Sex Offender Recidivism Studies." *Journal of Consulting and Clinical Psychology* 66 (2): 348–62.

Hearn, J. 1998. *The Violence of Men.* London: Sage.

Hennessy, R. 1992. *Materialist Feminism and the Politics of Discourse (Thinking Gender).* New York: Routledge.

Hood, R., S. Shute, M. Feilzer, and A. Wilcox. 2002. "Sex Offenders Emerging from Long Term Imprisonment: A Study of the Long Term Reconviction Rates and of Parole Board Members' Judgement of their Risk." *British Journal of Criminology* 42 (2): 371–94.

hooks, bell. 1992. *Black Looks: Race and Representations*. Boston: South End Press.

Hopkins, C.Q. and M.P. Koss. 2005. "Incorporating Feminist Theory and Insights into a Restorative Justice Response to Sex Offenses." *Violence Against Women* 11 (5): 693–723.

Hudson, K. 2005. *Offending Identities: Sex Offenders' Perspectives on Their Treatment and Management*. Cullompton: Willan Publishing.

Jackson, M. 2002. *Justice Behind the Walls: Human Rights in Canadian Prisons*. Vancouver: Douglas and McIntyre.

Jackson, W. 1939. "Constitutional Law: Validity of Sex Offender Acts." *Michigan Law Review* 37 (4): 613–25.

Jaggar, A.M. 1983. *Feminist Politics and Human Nature*. Totowa, New Jersey: Rowman and Allanheld.

Janus, E. 2000. "Civil Commitment as Social Control: Managing the Risk of Sexual Violence." In *Dangerous Offenders: Punishment and Social Order*, edited by M. Brown and J. Pratt, 71–90. New York: Routledge.

Jeffries, S. 2006. "Interview with Catharine MacKinnon." *The Guardian*, April 12.

Jefferson, T. 2002. Subordinating Hegemonic Masculinity." *Theoretical Criminology* 6 (1): 63–88.

Jhappan, R. 1996. "Post-Modern Race and Gender Essentialism or a Post-Mortem of Scholarship." *Studies in Political Economy* 51: 15–63.

Johnson, H. 1996. *Dangerous Domains: Violence Against Women in Canada*. Scarborough: Nelson.

Kane, S. 1998. *AIDS Alibis: Sex, Drugs, and Crime in America*. Philadelphia: Temple University Press.

Karpman, B. 1954. *The Sexual Offender and His Offenses: Etiology, Pathology, Psychodynamics and Treatment*. Washington, DC: Julian Press Inc.

Kaufman, M. 1994. "Men, Feminism, and Men's Contradictory Experiences of Power." In *Theorizing Masculinities*, edited by H. Brod and M. Kaufman, 142–63. New York: Sage.

Kimmel, M. 1994. "Masculinity as Homophobia." In *Theorizing Masculinities*, edited by H. Brod and M. Kaufman, 142–63. New York: Sage

– 2005. *The Gender of Desire: Essays on Male Sexuality*. Binghamton: SUNY Press.

Kimmel, M., J. Hearns, and R.W. Connell, eds. 2005. *The Handbook of Studies on Men and Masculinities*. Thousand Oaks: Sage.

Kimmel, M., and M. Kaufman. 1994. "Weekend Warriors: The New Men's Movement." *In Theorizing Masculinities*, edited by H. Brod and M. Kaufman, 259–88. Thousand Oaks: Sage.

Kirby, S., and K. McKeena. 1989. *Experiences, Research, Social Change: Methods from the Margins*. Toronto: Garamond Press.

Lacombe, D. 2008. "Consumed with Sex: The Treatment of Sex Offenders in Risk Society." *British Journal of Criminology* 48 (1): 55–74.

Lamb, S. 1999. "Constructing the Victim: Popular Images and Lasting Labels." In *Versions of Victims: Feminists Struggle with the Concept*, edited by S. Lamb, 108–38. New York: New York University Press.

Lane, P., M. Bopp, J. Bopp, and J. Norris. 2002. *Mapping the Healing Journey: The Final Report of a First Nation Research Project on Healing in Canadian Aboriginal Communities* (Cat. no. JS42-105/2002E). Ottawa: Solicitor-General Canada.

Larombe, W. 2005. *Compelling Engagements: Feminism, Rape Law, and Romance Fiction*. Sydney: The Federation Press.

Lather, P. 1991. *Getting Smart: Feminist Research and Pedagogy with/in the Postmodern*. New York: Routledge.

Lawrence, B. 2002. "Rewriting Histories of the Land: Colonization and Indigenous Resistance in Eastern Canada." In *Race, Space and the Law: Unmapping a White Settler Society*, edited by S. Razack, 21–46. Toronto: Between the Lines.

Lea, S., and T. Auburn. 2001. "The Social Construction of Rape in the Talk of a Convicted Rapist." *Feminism & Psychology* 11 (1): 11–33.

Lee, W. 2006. "On the (Im)materiality of Violence: Subjects, Bodies, and the Experiences of Pain." *Feminist Theory* 6: 277–95.

Levan, A. 1996. "Violence against Women." In *Women and Canadian Public Policy*, edited by J. Brodie, 319–54. Toronto: Harcourt Brace.

Levinson, D. 2002. *Encyclopedia of Crime and Punishment*. Thousand Oaks: Sage.

Liddle, M. 1989. "Feminist Contradictions to an Understanding of Violence against Women: Three Steps Forward, Two Steps Back." *Canadian Review of Sociology and Anthropology* 26 (5): 759–75.

Lippke, R. 2003. "Prisoner Access to Recreation, Entertainment and Diversion." *Punishment and Society* 5 (1): 33–52.

Los, M. 1994. "Feminism and Rape Law Reform." In *Feminist Perspectives in Criminology*, edited by L. Gelsthorpe and A. Morris, 160–72. Philadelphia: Open University Press.

Lusher, D., and G. Robins. 2007. "Hegemonic and Other Masculinities in Local Social Contexts." *Men and Masculinities* 8: 44–63.

MacKinnon, C. 1981. "Introduction, Sexual Harassment: A Symposium Issue." *Capital University Law Review* 1: i.

– 1983. "Feminism, Marxism, Method, and the State: Toward Feminist Jurisprudence." *Signs* 8 (4): 635–58.

- 1987. *Feminism Unmodified: Discourses on Life and Law*. Cambridge: Harvard University Press.
- 1989. *Towards a Feminist Theory of the State*. Cambridge: Harvard University Press.

Mandel, N., M. Bittner, R. Webb, B. Collins, and P. Jarcho. 1965. "The Sex Offender in Minnesota." *The Journal of Sex Research* 1 (3): 239–48.

Marcus, S. 1992. "Fighting Bodies, Fighting Words: A Theory and Politics of Rape Prevention." In *Feminists Theorize the Political*, edited by J. Butler and J. Scott, 385–403. New York: Routledge.

Mardorossian, C.M. 2002. "Towards a New Feminist Theory of Rape." *Signs* 27 (3): 743–75.

Marecek, J. 1999. "Trauma Talk in Feminist Clinical Practice." In *New Versions of Victims: Feminists Struggle with the Concept*, edited by S. Lamb, 158–82. New York: New York University Press.

Marshall, W.L. 1996a. "Assessment, Treatment, and Theorizing about Sex Offenders: Developments During the Past Twenty Years and Future Directions." *Criminal Justice and Behaviour* 23 (1): 162–99.

- 1996b. "The Sexual Offender: Monster, Victim, or Everyman?" *Sexual Abuse: A Journal of Research and Treatment* 8: 317–35.

Marshall, W.L., L. Marshall, G. Serian, and Y. Fernandez. 2006. *Treating Sex Offenders: An Integrated Approach*. Brunner–Routledge.

Martin, K., L. Vieraitis, and S. Britto. 2006. "Gender Equality and Women's Absolute Status." *Violence Against Women* 12 (4): 321–39.

Mason, P., and J. Monckton–Smith. 2008. "Conflation, Collocation, and Confusion: British Press Coverage of the Sexual Murder of Women." *Journalism* 9 (6): 691–710.

Matthews, N. 1994. *The Feminist Anti-Rape Movement and the State*. London and New York: Routledge.

McCallum, D. 1997. "Mental Health, Criminality, and the Human Sciences." In *Foucault, Health, and Medicine*, edited by A. Peterson and R. Bunton, 53–73. New York: Routledge.

McIvor, S.D., and T.A. Nahanee. 1998. "Aboriginal Women: Invisible Victims of Violence." In *Unsettling Truths: Battered Women, Policy, Politics, and Contemporary Research in Canada*, edited by K. Bonnycastle and G. Rigakos, 63–70. Vancouver: Collective Press.

Messerschmidt, J. 1986. *Capitalism, Patriarchy and Crime: Towards a Socialist Feminist Criminology*. Totowa: Rowman and Littlefield.

- 1993. *Masculinities and Crime: Critique and Reconceptualization of Theory*. Lantham: Rowman and Littlefield.

– 1997. *Crime as Structured Action: Gender, Race and Crime in the Making*. Thousand Oaks: Sage.

– 2000. *Nine Lives: Adolescent Masculinities, the Body and Violence*. Boulder: Westview Press.

– 2001. "Masculinities, Crime, and Prison." In *Prison Masculinities*, edited by D. Sabo, T.A. Kupers, and W. London. Philadelphia: Temple University Press.

– 2002. "On Gang Girls, Gender and a Structured Action Theory." *Theoretical Criminology* 6 (40): 461–75.

– 2004. *Flesh and Blood: Adolescent Gender Diversity and Violence*. Lanham: Rowman and Littlefield.

– 2006. "The Forgotten Victims of World War II: Masculinities and Rape in Berlin, 1945." *Violence Against Women* 12 (7): 706–12.

Mills, C.W. 1940. "Situated Actions and Vocabularies of Motives." *American Sociological Review* 5 (December): 904–13.

Mooney-Somers, J., and J.M. Ussher. 2010. "Sex as Commodity: Single and Partnered Men's Subjectification as Heterosexual Men." *Men and Masculinities* 12 (30): 353–73.

Moore, D., and K. Hannah-Moffat. 2004. "The Liberal Veil: Revisiting Canadian Penality." In *The New Punitiveness: Trends, Theories, Perspectives*, edited by J. Pratt, D. Brown, M. Brown, S. Hallsworth, and W. Morrison, 85–100. London: Willan Publishing.

Moorti, S. 2002. *Color of Rape: Gender and Race in Television's Public Sphere*. New York: University of New York Press.

Motiuk, L., and B. Vuong. 2005. *Homicide, Sex, Robbery, and Drug Offenders in Federal Corrections: An End of 2004 Review*. Ottawa: Research Branch CSC.

Mullaney, J. 2007. "Telling It Like a Man: Masculinities and Battering Men's Accounts of Their Violence." *Men and Masculinities* 10 (2): 222–47.

Newburn, T., and E.A. Stanko, eds. 1994. *Just Boys Doing Business? Men, Masculinities, and Crime*. London: Routledge.

O'Leary, P. 1998. "Liberation from Self-Blame: Working with Men Who Have Experienced Child Sexual Abuse." *Dulwich Centre Journal* 4: 24–40.

O'Malley, P. 2006. "Governing Through the Democratic Minimization of Harms." In *Institutionalizing Restorative Justice*, edited by I. Aertsen, T. Daems, and L. Roberts, 225–40. London: Willan Publishing.

– 2008. "Experiments in Risk and Criminal Justice." *Theoretical Criminology* 12 (4): 451–69.

Page, J. 2004. "Eliminating the Enemy: The Impact of Denying Prisoners' Access to Higher Education in Clinton's America." *Punishment and Society* 6 (4): 357–78.

Pardue, A., and B. Arrigo. 2008. "Power, Anger, and Sadistic Rapists: Toward a Differentiated Model of Offender Personalities." *International Journal of Offender Therapy and Comparative Criminology* 52 (4): 378–400.

Paul, D. 2006. *We Were Not the Savages: Collision between European and Native American Civilizations*. Halifax: Fernwood Publishing.

Petrunik, M. 2002. "Managing Unacceptable Risk: Sex Offenders, Community Response, and Social Policy in the United States and Canada." *International Journal of Offender Therapy and Comparative Criminology* 46: 483–511.

Petrunik, M., and L. Deutschman. 2007. "The Exclusion-Inclusion Spectrum in State and Community Responses to Sex Offenders in Anglo-European and European Jurisdictions." *International Journal of Offender Therapy and Comparative Criminology* 20 (10): 1–21.

Petrunik, M., and R. Weisman. 2005. "Constructing Joseph Fredricks: Competing Narratives of a Child Sex Murderer." *International Journal of Law and Psychiatry* 28: 75–96.

Pollack, S. 2007. "'I'm Just Not Good in Relationships': Victimization Discourse and the Gendered Regulation of Criminalized Women." *Feminist Criminology* 2 (2): 158–74.

Pollack, S., and K. Brezine. 2006. "Negotiating Contradictions: Sexual Abuse Counselling with Imprisonment Women." *Women and Therapy* 29 (3/4): 117–33.

Pollack, W. 2000. *Real Boys' Voices*. New York: Random House.

Pool, G. 2003. "'Gutter Decisions' More Troubling." *Abbotsford and Mission News Saturday*, August 30, p. A5.

Pratt, J. 2000. "Sex Crime and the New Punitiveness." *Behavioral Sciences and the Law* 18: 135–51.

Pratt, J., D. Brown, M. Brown, S. Hallsworth, and W. Morrison, eds. 2005. *The New Punitiveness: Trends, Theories and Perspectives*. Devon: Willian Publishing.

Pryor, D. 1996. *Unspeakable Acts: Why Men Sexually Abuse Children*. New York: York University Press.

Ratner, R.S. 1984. "Inside the Liberal Boot: The Criminological Enterprise in Canada." *Studies in Political Economy* 13: 145–64.

Razack, S. 2002. *Race, Space and the Law: Unmapping a White Settler Society*. Toronto: Between the Lines.

Renold, E. 2003. "If You Don't Kiss Men, You're Dumped: Boys, Boyfriends, and Heterosexualized Masculinities in Primary School." *Education Review* 55 (2): 179–94.

– 2007. "Primary School Studs: Deconstructing Young Boys' Heterosexual Masculinities." *Men and Masculinities* 9 (3): 275–97.

Rhodes, L. 2004. *Total Confinement: Madness and Reason in the Maximum Security Prison*. Berkeley: University of California Press.

Roberts, J.V., and M. Grossman. 1993. "Sexual Homicide in Canada: A Descriptive Analysis." *Sexual Abuse: American Journal of Research and Treatment* 6 (1): 5–25.

Rose, N. 1996. "Governing 'Advanced' Liberal Democracies." In *Foucault and Political Reason: Liberalism, Neo-liberalism and Rationalities of Government*, edited by A. Barry, T. Osborne, and N. Rose, 37–64. London: UCL Press.

Royal Commission on Aboriginal Peoples. 1993. *Aboriginal People and the Justice System*. Ottawa: Minister of Supply and Services.

Rumney, P. 1999. "When Rape Isn't Rape: Court of Appeal Sentencing Practices in Cases of Marital and Relationship Rape." *Oxford Journal of Legal Studies* 19: 243–69.

– 2003. "Cases Progress at a Price: The Construction of Non-Stranger-Rape in the Millberry Sentencing Guidelines." *Modern Law Review* 66 (6): 870–84.

Russell, D. 1982. *Rape in Marriage*. New York: Macmillan.

– 1984. *Sexual Exploitation: Rape, Child Sexual Abuse, and Workplace Harassment*. Beverly Hills: Sage.

– 1998. *Dangerous Relationships: Pornography, Misogyny, and Rape*. London: Sage.

Sabo, D., T.A. Kupers, and W. London, eds. 2001. *Prison Masculinity*. Philadelphia: Temple University Press.

Sarachild, K. 1978. *Feminist Revolution*. New York: Random House.

Schultz, P.D. 2004. *Not Monsters: Analyzing the Stories of Child Molesters*. Lanham: Rowman and Littlefield.

Schwendinger, J., and H. Schwendinger. 1981. "Rape, Sexual Inequality, and Levels of Violence." *Crime and Social Justice* 16: 3–31.

– 1982. "Rape, the Law and Private Property." *Crime and Delinquency* 28 (2): 271–91.

Scott, J. 1986. "Gender: A Useful Category of Historical Analysis." *American Historical Review* 91 (1): 1053–75.

Scully, D. 1990. *Understanding Sexual Violence: A Study of Convicted Rapists*. Boston: Unwin Hyman.

Segal, L. 1990. *Slow Motion: Changing Masculinities, Changing Men*. New Brunswick: Rutgers University Press.

– 2006. *Slow Motion: Changing Masculinities, Changing Men*, 3rd ed. Basingstoke: Palgrave Macmillan.

Seymour, K. 2003. "Imprisoning Masculinity." *Sexuality and Culture* 7 (4): 27–55.

Sim, J. 1994. "Tougher than the Rest? Men in Prison." In *Just Boys Doing Business? Men, Masculinities, and Crime*, edited by T. Newburn and E.A. Stanko, 100–17. London: Routledge.

Simon, J. 1998. "Managing the Monstrous: Sex Offenders and the New Penology." *Psychology, Public Policy, and Law* 4 (1/2): 452–67.

– 2007. *Governing Through Crime: How the War on Crime Transformed American Democracy and Created a Culture of Fear*. New York: Oxford University Press.

Smart, C. 1995. *Law, Crime, and Sexuality: Essays in Feminism*. London: Sage.

Snider, L. 1998. "Struggles for Social Justice: Criminalization and Alternatives." In *Unsettling Truths: Battered Women, Policy, Politics, and Contemporary Research in Canada*, edited by K. Bonnycastle and G. Rigakos, 145–54. Vancouver: Collective Press.

– 2006. "Making Change in Neo–Liberal Times." In *Criminalizing Women*, edited by E. Comack and G. Balfour, 323–42. Halifax: Fernwood Publishing.

Sokoloff, N.J., B.R. Price, and J. Flavin. 2004. "The Criminal Law and Women." In *The Criminal Justice System and Women: Offenders, Prisoners, Victims, and Workers*, edited by N.J. Sokoloff and B.R. Price, 11–29. New York: McGraw Hill.

Stanko, E. 2000. "Naturalizing Danger." In *Dangerous Offenders: Punishment and Social Order*, edited by M. Brown and J. Pratt, 147–63. New York: Routledge.

Staples, R. 1982. *Black Masculinity*. San Francisco: Black Scholars Press.

Statistics Canada. 1999. "Sex Offenders (Cat. no. 85-002-XIE)." *Juristat Canadian Centre for Justice Statistics* 19 (3): 1–16.

– 2004. *Canadian Crime Statistics 2003* (Cat. no. 85–205-XIE). Ottawa: Minister of Industry.

Stein, G. 1935. *Lectures in America*. New York: Random House.

Stermac, L.E., J.A. Dumont, and V. Kelemba. 1995. "Comparison of Sexual Assault by Stranger and Known Assailants in an Urban Population of Women." *Canadian Medical Association Journal* 153 (8): 1089–94.

Stewart, B. 2001. "Special Report: 'Not a Country Club.' Interview with Lucie McClung." *Maclean's*, April 9.

Strange, C. 1992. "Wounded Women and Dead Men: Chivalry and the Trials of Clara Ford and Carrie Davies." In *Gender Conflict: New Essays in Women's History*, edited by F. Iacovetta and M. Valverde, 149–88. Toronto: University of Toronto Press.

Sykes, G.M. 1958. *The Society of Captives: A Study of a Maximum Security Prison*. Princeton: Princeton University Press.

Tager, D., G. Good, and J.B. Morrison. 2007. "Our Bodies, Ourselves Revisited: Male Body Image and Psychological Well-Being." *International Journal of Men's Health* 5 (3): 228–37.

Tatar, M. 1995. *Lustmord: Sexual Murder in Weimar Germany*. Princeton: Princeton University Press.

Taylor, I. 1983. "Some Reflections on Homicide and Violence in Canada." In *Crime, Capitalism, and Community: Three Essays in Socialist Criminology*, edited by Ian Taylor, 83–113. Toronto: Butterworth.

Tithecott, R. 1997. *Of Men and Monsters: Jeffrey Dahmer and the Construction of the Serial Killer*. Madison: University of Wisconsin Press.

Toch, H. 1998. "Hypermasculinity and Prison Violence." In *Masculinities and Violence*, edited by L.H. Bowker. Thousand Oaks: Sage.

Tomsen, S. 2002. "Hatred, Murder and Male Honor: Anti-homosexual Homicides in New South Wales, 1980–2000." *Research and Public Policy Series*, 43. Australian Institute of Criminology: Canberra, Australia.

Vancouver Rape Relief and Women's Shelter. 2008. *Statistics*. Vancouver: Vancouver Rape Relief and Women's Shelter.

Vogelman, L. 1990. *The Sexual Face of Violence: Rapists on Rape*. Johannesburg: Ravan Press.

Waldram, J. 1997. *The Way of the Pipe: Aboriginal Spirituality and Symbolic Healing in Canadian Prisons*. Toronto: Broadview.

Walker, B., and K. Kushner. 1999. "The Building Site: An Educational Approach to Masculine Identity." *Journal of Youth Studies* 2 (1): 45–58.

Walker, G. 1995. "Violence and the Relations of Ruling: Lessons from the Battered Women's Movement." In *Knowledge, Experience, and Ruling Relations: Studies in the Social Organization of Knowledge*, edited by M. Campbell and A. Manicom, 65–79. Toronto: University of Toronto Press.

Wallace, M. 2009. "Police-Reported Crime Statistics in Canada, 2008" (Cat. No. 85-002-X). *Juristat* 29 (3): 1–37. Ottawa: Minster of Industry.

Walmsley, C. 2005. *Protecting Aboriginal Children*. Vancouver: UBC Press.

Ward, T., D. Polaschek, and A. Beecher. 2005. *Theories of Sexual Offending*. University of Leicester: Wiley Press.

Websdale, N., and M. Chesney-Lind. 1998. "Doing Violence to Women." In *Masculinities and Violence*, edited by L.H. Bowker, 55–82. Thousand Oaks: Sage Publications.

Webster, C., and S. Hucker. 2007. *Violence Risk: Assessment and Management*. University of Leicester: Wiley Press.

Weiss, K.G. 2010. "Male Sexual Victimization: Exploring Men's Experiences of Rape and Sexual Assault." *Men and Masculinities* 12 (3): 275–98.

Whaley, R.B. 2001. "The Paradoxical Relationship between Gender Inequality and Rape." *Gender and Society* 15 (4): 531–55.

Whitehead, A. 2005. "Man to Man Violence: How Masculinity May Work as a Dynamic Risk Factor." *Howard Journal of Criminal Justice* 44 (4): 411–22.

Wilcox, P., C. Jordan, and A. Pritchard. 2003. "Fear of Acquaintance versus Stranger-Rape as a Master Status: Towards Refinement of the Shadow of Sexual Assault." *Violence and Victims* 21 (3): 355–70.

Wriggins, J. 2004. "Rape, Racism, and the Law." In *The Criminal Justice System and Women: Offenders, Prisoners, Victims, and Workers*, edited by N.J. Sokoloff and B.R. Price, 335–42. New York: McGraw Hill.

Wyatt, G.E. 1992. "The Sociocultural Context of African and White American Women's Rape." *Journal of Social Issues* 48: 77–91.

Cases Cited

R. v. Chase, [1987] 2 S.C.R. 293.

Leach v. Warden of Fenbrook Institution, 2004 FC 1570.

Index

Aboriginal experience: collective responsibility, 174, 297n8; colonial legacy, 103, 260, 269; life-affirming practices, 249–50; sex-offender interviewees' experience, 55, 208–9; terminology, 297n2; women sexual assault victims, 23. *See also* race; and *under* life stories of sex-offender interviewees, Bear, Brian, Fred, Paul, Simpson

abuse as children: Bear's story, 146, 198, 211, 287–92; Brian's story, 73–7; Cam's story, 87–91; Charlie's story, 92–5; disclosed in group treatment, 266–8; Harvey's story, 77–82; Marvin's story, 82–4, 297n5; Michel's story, 130–1; non-participant survivor at group session, 272; Paul's story, 114–15; Simpson's story, 101–5

abuse in prison: physical, 210, 246; sexual, 96, 97–9, 171 (*see also under* life stories of sex-offender interviewees, Kerry)

acquaintance rape, 6–7, 20

African American men, 7, 27, 32–3

age of sex-offender interviewees, 56, 293–4

Alder, C., 226

alternatives: constructions of masculinity, 33, 37, 40, 145, 257, 282; to current practices, 280–6; to everyman rapist, 36; to heterosexual family, 282; in penal treatment groups, 258–61, 262–6; prison not providing, 241, 254–5, 259, 273–6, 280, 284; sex-offenders lack of, 9, 28, 281

Amir, Menachem, 20

Atmore, Chris, 42

autobiography in sex-offender program. *See under* life stories

automatism, 239–40

biology and essentialism: biological maleness, 33; critical masculinities genre, 40; rape as biological, 23, 25, 45; various embodiments, 35

Bourke, J., 16

Brownmiller, Susan, 24–5, 235, 240, 244

bullying. *See under* education